COLUMBIA UNIVERSITY STUDIES IN ENGLISH
AND COMPARATIVE LITERATURE

# THE RELATIONS OF SHIRLEY'S PLAYS
# TO THE ELIZABETHAN DRAMA

# THE RELATIONS OF SHIRLEY'S PLAYS TO THE ELIZABETHAN DRAMA

BY

ROBERT STANLEY FORSYTHE, Ph.D.

Sometime University Scholar and University Fellow
in English, Columbia University

Benjamin Blom

First published by Columbia University Press, 1914
Reissued by Benjamin Blom, Inc., 1965
Library of Congress Catalog Card No. 65–19615

*Printed in U.S.A. by*
NOBLE OFFSET PRINTERS, INC.
NEW YORK 3, N. Y.

TO
MY MOTHER
AND TO
THE MEMORY
OF
MY FATHER

*This Monograph has been approved by the Department of English and Comparative Literature in Columbia University as a contribution to knowledge worthy of publication.*

A. H. THORNDIKE,
*Executive Officer.*

# PREFACE

The treatment of Shirley's dramas with regard to their sources—chiefly those in the works of the Elizabethan dramatists—is the task which I have attempted to accomplish in The Relations of Shirley's Plays to the Elizabethan Drama. I have dealt with the sources of Shirley's plays in a manner radically differing from that of other similar pieces of research in modern English literature. The influence of the component parts of a literary form upon a modern writer has never before received anything like adequate consideration. I have aimed in the following pages to show that Shirley's true sources were, in perhaps the majority of cases, not single plays, incidents, or characters, but the aggregate, the sum total, of the similar plays, incidents, or characters, of earlier and contemporary playwrights. In other words, I have emphasized particularly the influence upon the plays of Shirley of the stock or conventional elements in Elizabethan dramatic literature. By reason of his chronological position and his unquestionable habit of studying the works of the other Elizabethans, Shirley is one of the best possible subjects for such an essay in historical dramatic criticism, but the method may be applied, I believe, with at least some degree of success to the works of many other modern authors.

Aside from whatever light this book may throw upon the sources of Shirley's plays, it may be used to fill, partially, at least, another need. The lists of stock incidents, situations, devices, and characters in Chap. IV (as well as those elsewhere) represent the first attempt at classifying and grouping the various conventionalized elements of the Elizabethan drama. Although they have been collected solely because of their relationship to, and possible influence upon, Shirley's plays, the lists may be used as indexes to the occurrence of such elements. These lists are not complete. I have had access to not more than five hundred and twenty Elizabethan plays, in the first place; secondly, I have curtailed certain lists because of the more or less obvious nature of the devices therein grouped; and lastly, through oversight some instances of the occurrence of elements perhaps have been omitted. I have read for the purposes of this study only the more important of the plays written before 1580, as the influence of the earliest Elizabethan plays upon the latest, such as those of Shirley, is practically negligible. The masque, being as it is, an illegitimate dramatic type, has received but little attention in the present book, since I have endeavored to confine myself primarily to the treatment of the drama proper.

It seems advisable to point out that the present book infringes only very slightly upon the territory of Professor A. H. Nason's excellent study, James Shirley, Dramatist. Professor Nason's book of which the first chapters give the fullest and most careful account of Shirley's life now in existence is devoted chiefly to the æsthetic criticism of the plays, and to the development of Shirley's art as therein displayed. I have, on the other hand, passed over Shirley's life, almost altogether and have occupied myself almost exclusively with the discussion of his sources. The two books are to a considerable degree supplementary, each to the other.

Much of the content of my study would, I believe, be of value in the preparation of a new edition of Shirley's plays. As it stands, the greater part of the last six chapters of

my dissertation is, as a result of the extreme condensation
necessary, practically in the form of notes upon passages
in the various plays. It is my hope in the future to prepare, or to have a hand in preparing, an edition of Shirley's
dramatic works which will be more accurate and more
scholarly than that of Gifford and Dyce.

I have based my study upon the Gifford-Dyce edition.
The early quartos and duodecimos of Shirley's plays are
generally so scarce as to preclude their use by many scholars; and as my treatment of the plays has had to do chiefly
with the action and but little with the text itself, I have
thought it best to use and to refer to the more accessible
(though unsatisfactory) collected edition. I wish to call
attention to the fact that in my citations of acts and scenes
I have referred to the numbers at their beginnings, and
not to those at the tops of the respective pages which are
often incorrect.

To Professor A. H. Thorndike of Columbia University,
under whose supervision this book was prepared as a dissertation for the doctor's degree in Columbia University,
I am most deeply indebted. Professor Thorndike has encouraged me in every way during the progress of my study,
and has assisted me, not only in the general plan and arrangement of my book, but with many valuable suggestions
as to the content. He has been so kind, also, as to read
and criticize the manuscript of the book, and to read the
proofs.

I am indebted to Professors Matthews and Wright of
Columbia University, who have read my manuscript, for
many valuable suggestions as to form and material.
Professor A. H. Nason of New York University has been
so kind as to allow me to read the proofs of James Shirley,
Dramatist, and to refer to his book wherever necessary.
I wish to express my appreciation of the constant courtesy

and coöperation of the officials of the Columbia University Library, particularly of those of the loan department.   To the Library of the University of Pennsylvania, I am indebted for the use of the Duke of Newcastle's plays, and to the Library of Yale University and the New York Public Library for the use of certain books.

R. S. F.

September, 1914.

# CONTENTS

# SHIRLEY'S PLAYS AND THE ELIZABETHAN DRAMA

## CHAPTER I

### THE ENGLISH STAGE, 1620–42

Preliminary to the detailed discussion of Shirley's plays which takes up the greater part of this book, it is perhaps advisable to point out the ways in which the later Elizabethans gained a knowledge of the plays of their predecessors and contemporaries, to describe very briefly the dramatic situation about the year 1625, and to sum up concisely the works of Shirley's immediate contemporaries. A few words concerning the theaters and their frequenters seem also not out of place.

### A. The Acted and Printed Plays

Since the greater part of the subsequent discussion of Shirley's plays is devoted to a consideration of their sources and analogues, a little space may be profitably devoted to the ways in which the dramatic writers of that period grew familiar with the plays of their predecessors and contemporaries. First, undoubtedly they witnessed the presentation of many plays. In those days, although every year saw the production of a number of new plays, yet many old plays either held the stage, or were revived, with or without alterations. For instance, between 1618 and 1625, Twelfth Night and The Winter's Tale were played twice each at court and Henry IV, Part I, The Alchemist, Volpone, Greene's Tu Quoque, and Cupid's Revenge, once each (Fleay, Stage, pp. 257–58). After 1625 these old plays

1

were acted at court: Richard III, The Taming of the
Shrew, Cymbeline, The Winter's Tale, Julius Cæsar
(Shakespeare's or May's?), The Woman's Prize, The Loyal
Subject, The Faithful Shepherdess, The Knight of the
Burning Pestle, The Elder Brother, The Bloody Brother,
Cupid's Revenge, A Wife for a Month, Wit without
Money, Philaster, The Scornful Lady, Epicœne, Bussy
D'Ambois, Hymen's Holiday, The Jew of Malta (Fleay,
Stage, pp. 315 ff., 424). From this list (a very incom-
plete one certainly) we may judge reasonably of the size of
the repertory of the Elizabethan theatrical company and
be justified in concluding from this and from other evi-
dence that many plays were acted over, year after year.[1]

Then, too, the printed play is important. Not only had
the plays of Ben Jonson and of Shakespeare appeared in
folio, the one in 1616, the other in 1623, but many of them
existed in quarto editions. Many of the plays of other
dramatists were extant in the latter form. In the Epistle
Dedicatory to Histriomastix in 1633, Prynne says there
were "above forty thousand playbooks printed within
these two years," and quotes the stationers as authority.
Of course, what is meant is that forty thousand *copies* were
printed, perhaps fifteen hundred or two thousand to an
edition, so that in reality we have about ten or twelve
plays printed for each of Prynne's two years. But at any
rate, whatever the number is, we must reckon with the
printed playbook in considering the literary relations of
the later Elizabethan dramatists with one another and with
their predecessors.

In the case of the unpublished plays, playwrights had access to MS. copies in the possession either of the players or
of other persons. Then furthermore, it is probable that

[1] See, for instance, the records of court performances in Murray,
Eng. Dram. Cos., I (particularly of the King's Men, 173 ff.).

writers, critics (or "wits"), and managers discussed among themselves the drama of the past, and thereby circulated a knowledge of particular incidents and characters, which might have been utilized in the plays of their own day.

Certainly there were comparatively few, if any, plays acted after the real beginning of the Elizabethan drama which Ford or Shirley, for example, could not have gained a knowledge of, either from their presentation, their published or MS. form, or from oral accounts.

## B.  THE DRAMATISTS

At the beginning of the year 1625 (as well as for years after) John Fletcher was undoubtedly the most influential figure among English dramatic writers.  His importance is attested to not only by the most flattering notices, contemporary and posthumous, but by the unmistakable traces of a greater or less degree of conscious imitation of his methods in the plays of nearly every dramatist of the time. Fletcher's prolificity and the fact that so many of his plays are extant combine further to show his popularity and, consequently, his influence.  Of some ninety-seven plays, extant and non-extant, produced between 1620 and 1625, twenty-three are Fletcher's, either solely or in part.[2] Some of these were, no doubt, reworkings of old plays, a fact which does not lessen the importance of the poet's productivity in estimating his influence.  If we add to them the contribution of Massinger amounting to eight plays (besides eleven with Fletcher which are included in his twenty-three) and that of Middleton and his collaborators—six plays—we have a total of thirty-seven plays in five years, all written plainly more or less under the dominant dramatic influence of the day.  The fact that between 1621 and 1624 nine of Fletcher's plays were presented at

2 From Schelling's play-list, Eliz. Dram., II, 538 ff.

court, one of them three times and two twice each, further emphasizes his position as the chief dramatist of England during the last years of his life.

The fifty-odd plays in which Fletcher had a hand fall into the classes of tragedy, tragicomedy, and comedy of manners or, better, of intrigue. Each of these has certain characteristics which differentiate it from the corresponding types of an earlier date. For instance, The Maid's Tragedy is essentially different from King Lear, Philaster from The Malcontent, or Measure for Measure, and The Wild Goose Chase from Twelfth Night.

The tragedies and tragicomedies of Fletcher and his collaborators differ mainly in the happy ending, and in the preponderance of surprises in the tragicomedies, due often to the element of diverted tragedy. "Their main plots, largely invented, are ingenious and complicated. They deal with royal or noble persons, with heroic actions, and are placed in foreign localities. The conquests, usurpations and passions that ruin kingdoms are their themes. . . . Usually contrasting a story of gross sensual passion with one of idyllic love, they introduce a great variety of incidents, and aim at constant but varied excitement. . . . The tragic, idyllic, and sensational material is skilfully constructed into a number of theatrically telling situations, which lead by a series of surprises to very effective climaxes or catastrophes. All signs of the epic methods of construction found in the early drama have disappeared; there is usually a chance until the last moment for either a happy or an unhappy ending, and in every case the *dénouement* or catastrophe is elaborately prepared for and complicated. The *dramatis personæ* belong to impossible and romantic situations rather than to life, and are usually of certain types.[3] . . . The plays depend for interest not

[3] The sentimental or violent hero, the faithful friend or blunt

on their observation or revelation of human nature, or the development of character, but on the variety of situations, the clever construction of which holds the interest through one suspense to another up to the unravelling at the very end, and on the naturalness, felicity and vigor of the poetry" (Thorndike, The Maid's Tragedy and Philaster, Belles Lettres Series, Introduction, pp. xix–xx). The speech is hardly ever bombastic; often it approaches the language of every day life in diction and general style.

The comedies, which are likewise laid frequently in unfamiliar countries, have generally at least a touch of romanticism about them. They are lively and vivacious, and thus make up in wit and cleverness for what they want in decency. Unmorality, rather than immorality, is present. Usually two contrasting plots are found, one more or less sentimental, the other frankly comic. The clever scamp and the witty young lady are often characters.

Although Massinger's work before 1625 had been principally in collaboration with Fletcher, he had undoubtedly produced enough plays unaided to have made himself some reputation. He was a steady, serious workman, careful and painstaking. In spite of the fact that his share in the Fletcherian dramas seems to have made little difference in their tone, his unaided work reveals a strong moralizing tendency. His themes are often repulsive and horrible, but, unlike Fletcher, he seems to have discerned the difference between right and wrong, and to have attempted to illustrate the distinction. In setting, theme, incident, and characters (save in his comedies of English life) his plays resemble Fletcher's. Furthermore, unlike Fletcher, Massinger often alludes to contemporary politics or religion. He is capable of characterization, but his plays soldier, the sentimental heroine (often disguised as a page), the evil woman, the lustful tyrant, the poltroon (usually comic).

are heavy and move slowly. He is fond of declamation and soliloquizing. His heroes and heroines often are less really sophisticated than Fletcher's. Their innocence makes no such appeal to the pruriency of the audience as often Fletcher's supposedly "innocent" characters do. In his two great realistic comedies, The City Madam and A New Way to Pay Old Debts, Massinger broke away from the influence of Fletcher and combined his own genuine earnestness and power with a photographic reproduction of manners like that of Middleton. The humoristic touch of Jonson is almost altogether absent in them, although his satiric earnestness is closely imitated. For a sober presentation of London and provincial life without flippancy or caricature, they have few real rivals in Elizabethan dramatic literature. Massinger's low comedy is generally contemptible; obscenity is palmed off as humor.

In 1625 Ben Jonson was a power more on account of what he had done than on account of what he was doing. Nine years had elapsed since the production of his last play. During this period he had been occupied in masque-making, and in general literary work, the fruits of which had perished with his library (in 1623). His place as a critic, and the recollection of his earlier comedies, and tragedies also, force consideration of him as an influential figure at this time.

Jonson's tragedies, however, need no particular notice here. The exuberant romanticism of Beaumont and Fletcher's tragic drama had swept away nearly all tendency toward imitating the cold correctness of Sejanus and Catiline. Even May and Goffe, the only dramatists of any repute who follow at a distance classical models, introduce into their fables elements of romantic horror. With Jonson's comedies, however, it is another thing. Although Fletcherian or Shakespearian romance creeps into a num-

ber of the realistic comedies of the early twenties, there
are many vestiges of Jonsonian influence.

Not only was Jonson possessed of a powerful personality
which might well impress the dramatists of the time, but
his comedies have qualities which mark them for imitation.
His striking ability to draw types embodying contemporary
fads or vices and to unfold such characters through a succession of incidents accounts for much of the respect in
which his comic drama was held. His humoristic characters are pretty frequently imitated and are often inserted
in plays which otherwise show no Jonsonian influence.
His careful construction and his conscious moral purpose
(to link two not necessarily compatible characteristics)
are factors in his influence. Jonson's learning and his
high opinion of the art of dramatic composition must also
be reckoned with. Yet in spite of the personal and literary
qualities which inspired respect and admiration in his contemporaries, it is a fact that after 1620 the thoroughgoing
and consistent imitation of Jonson by a first class playwright is uncommon. His most genuine follower is Brome,
who is by no means more than third-rate.

The influence of the dead Shakespeare was like that
of the living Jonson. Perhaps more of his plays than of
Jonson's held the stage. Nevertheless, although we often
find characters, episodes, incidents, passages and lines obviously drawn from the plays of Shakespeare (all of which
were in print by 1623) the fact remains that his closest
follower in 1625 was Massinger, and in Massinger's plays
the predominant influence was that of Fletcher. Indeed,
if we take the plays of Fletcher as criteria of the demands
of the playgoer of 1625 we find that Shakespearian tragedy
and comedy do not meet those demands in such a way as
to justify careful imitation.

Middleton's career as a dramatist was practically ended

in 1625, but his lively comedies and his sometimes powerful tragicomedies and tragedies deserve mention. His
earlier plays are rather loose and stringy, but with time
his technique improved until he arrived at the constructive
excellence of the main plot of The Changeling. Middleton's early plays (even his first romantic efforts before
1600) are gross, even frankly immoral. Their appeal was
to the coarser side of the audience. Naturally, therefore,
when we find him turning from satirical comedy and realistic comedy of manners to romance of the Fletcherian sort
(in which, it must be remembered, William Rowley collaborated), we expect him to revel in lust and horrors, and
we are not disappointed. The Witch, however, suggests
Tourneur rather than Fletcher, yet its surprising ending
seems a conscious (but inartistic) imitation of the methods
of that author. Sentiment and idealization are absent in
Middleton's later plays. However, honor is a theme, courts
are the loci of plays, and rape, incest, murder, revenge, las-
civious sovereigns, wicked women and Machiavellian villains of the old school all appear in the dramas of the
Middleton and Rowley group.

Like Jonson, Webster had practically retired from writing for the stage, but it is not to be expected that such
plays as The White Devil and The Duchess of Malfi would
be without their imitators in an age when the sensational
was sought for on every hand for dramatic presentation.
It is evident, however, that Webster recognized the too
tangible and fundamentally physical nature of many of his
earlier horrors, and substituted for them the sheer loath-
someness of his Devil's Law-case, with its rivalry of mother
and daughter and its generally repulsive atmosphere. In
this play, too, the Fletcherian tragicomedy betrays its influence in the various surprises and the happy ending.
The Devil's Law-case, however, may be considered a sort of

experiment, since in A Cure for a Cuckold we have a subplot reminiscent of his early comedies with Dekker although joined to a Fletcherian tragicomic main plot, and
since in Appius and Virginia, we have a tragedy which
deals with a classical theme in a restrained and elevated
manner. But though scattered traces of Webster's influence are to be found here and there, his grim saturnine
humor and slowness of movement seem to have deterred
the dramatist of 1625 generally from any particular imitation of his plays.

The playwrights briefly discussed in the foregoing pages,
then, were the writers most to be reckoned with as influential when Shirley came to London about the year 1625.
But besides them we have a few figures who deserve mention. Among these is Chapman, whose tragedies on French
history are recalled by the Sir John Van Olden Barnavelt
of Fletcher and Massinger. An unacted Roman history
play, Cæsar and Pompey, and a few passages in Shirley's
Ball are his only contributions to the drama after 1620
(Chabot was composed earlier; see Chap. X). Dekker had
also practically retired from the stage. Between 1620 and
1625 he seems to have had a hand in only five plays, a
small number for a period of five years, when one remem-
bers that he had been concerned in sixteen plays in the
year 1598 alone. It is worth noting that in his Match
Me in London (perhaps a reworking in 1623 of an earlier
play) he dips into serious romantic comedy among the
characters in which are a lecherous king, a virtuous
wife, and a jealous but loyal husband. Heywood, too,
appears to have been comparatively inactive during
the same period in spite of the vast number of plays
he claimed to have had a finger in. Not until in the
thirties does he seem to have attempted seriously the new
romantic drama, and then with no particular success, in

A Maidenhead Well Lost. There he seems unable to get
very far away from his old methods. Davenport, who was
concerned in some seven plays between 1620 and 1625, is
interesting in that in two of the seven he revived the chronicle play.

Before entering upon the discussion of Shirley's immediate contemporaries, we must halt a moment to consider a
powerful foreign influence which first became evident about
the middle of the reign of James I. Spanish literature was
in full flower about 1620. True, Cervantes was dead, but
he had left behind him a wonderfully rich literary legacy.
Lope de Vega was producing with almost lightning rapidity
play after play of remarkable quality, and certain of his
contemporaries, notably Tirso de Molina, and Guillen de
Castro were not unworthy rivals. Hence, it is not strange,
if we consider the emphasis of Spanish drama upon situation, that the popular English playwrights, either directly
or through translations, drew upon this great store of
material. Among the number who utilized Spanish sources
are Beaumont and Fletcher, Massinger, Middleton and
Rowley.[4] According to Schelling, seventeen of the fifty-
two Fletcherian plays show traces of Spanish origin (Eliz.
Dram., II, 215). Of these most are dated after 1618. The
chief sources drawn on by the English writers are Don
Quixote and the Novelas Exemplares, perhaps because they
existed in English and French versions. Here in Spanish
contemporary literature we find complicated, improbable
plots, intrigues, love and honor, duels, noble heroes and
disguised ladies, with many other of the elements characteristic of the English literature of the time. The influ-

---

[4] Later Shirley drew upon the Spanish for six plays, according to
Stiefel (Romanische Forschungen, V, 196, note). Boyle quotes
Stiefel as saying that more than half of Shirley's plots are from
the Spanish (Englische Studien, XVIII, 295).

ence of Spain seems to have been mainly one of plot, not of spirit, for there seems very little effort to bring over the essentially Spanish elements. As Ward says, the Spanish drama was too national to be transplanted (Hist. Eng. Dram. Lit., III, 267–68; cf. Hume, Spanish Influence on English Literature, p. 265 ff.).

The five years between 1620 and 1625 are not unlike the period between 1590 and 1600 in one respect. In both we find a new group of dramatists coming to the front in England, and succeeding to the places left vacant by the death or retirement of the playwrights of preceding years. As in the earlier period the places of Marlowe, Greene, Peele, and Kyd were filled by Jonson, Chapman, Middleton, Marston, Heywood, and Dekker, so in the later James Shirley, Ford, Brome, Glapthorne, Goffe, and May took the places of Fletcher, Webster, and the others who had practically ceased to write for the stage. As Shakespeare passes on from the days of Marlowe through to those of Fletcher, so Massinger remains active down nearly to the closing of the theaters. Then too Davenant and Carlell make their appearance as dramatists in 1626 and 1629, respectively.

During the years from 1625 to 1642 which were dominated by the younger dramatists and Massinger, the influence of Fletcher was paramount, as has been noted. True it is that Jonson had a devoted follower in these years— Brome—but even he broke over into Fletcherian tragicomedy as in his aptly named Lovesick Court, and into comedy of intrigue as in The Novella, while even in his comedies of London life evidences of the influence of Fletcher's comedy of intrigue are visible. Other writers, still less prominent, such as Marmion and Nabbes, followed Jonson more or less, while Cartwright and Mayne each tried his hand at a realistic comedy in Jonson's vein. Suckling seems to have

been—and at a distance—Shakespeare's only real imitator.
No thorough-going and consistent Shakespearian, however,
would have composed the tragicomic fifth act for Aglaura.
Davenant began, it would seem, with an attempt at the
old tragedy of blood in Albovine, in imitation perhaps of
Webster, or Tourneur, but he soon went over to the
Fletcherian camp, in which he remained with lapses into
Jonsonian humoristic comedy in his Wits and News
from Plymouth. The occasional tragedies on classical
themes with more or less imitation of classical structure,
such as those of May, Nabbes, and Richards, ought at
least to be noted as indicative perhaps of a tendency
toward classicism, or a recollection of Jonson's two tragedies.

Two points in regard· to the drama of 1625–42 deserve
mention since they throw some light upon theatrical conditions between those two years. The first is the increase
in the number of authors of rank or birth. Among these
dabblers in the drama are the Earl (afterwards Duke) of
Newcastle, Sir John Suckling, Sir William Berkeley, Sir
William Lower, Sir John Denham, Carlell, Lovelace, Habington, Marmion, and the Killigrews. The famous preacher
and University Orator, Cartwright, as well as the clergy-
men Goffe, Mayne, and Meade, and the Cambridge scholar,
Randolph, must not be forgotten in this connection.
Among the chief professional dramatists of this period,
however, only Massinger seems to have been of gentle birth.
Ford and Shirley sprang from the middle classes, while
Jonson was the stepson of an artizan, and Brome had been
once a servant. But the emergence of the amateur, or
professional, dramatist of birth testifies to a changed feeling towards the stage. This feeling had been changed by
two main causes: the taking up of professional play-writing
by men of family such as Beaumont, and Fletcher, and the

seriousness with which the chief critical force of the time—Jonson—regarded his vocation.

In the second place, the attitude of the playwright towards the citizen had changed by 1625. After that date (and indeed for years before it) we find no plays exploiting city life, such as The Four Prentices of London or The Shoemaker's Holiday. There is hardly a play of the type of Eastward Ho, after Massinger's City Madam. On the contrary, we find the citizen usually appearing as a butt, often merely an appurtenance to an unchaste wife, or a person to be gulled. Nowhere does he appear save in comedy. In Shirley's plays, which may be taken as fairly indicative of the fashionable drama of the time, we find in eight comedies laid in London only three characters who have any expressed connection with city life and with business. Of these two are usurers, and the other (Old Barnacle in The Gamester) is the mouthpiece for a satirical attack upon his class. Shirley's untitled characters belong to the gentry or else have no visible means of support. Almost invariably we find city life and the citizen satirized, or placed in an unfavorable light. When this is not the case, we have mere copies of the Jonsonian or Middletonian realistic comedy with their situations and characters reproduced. Evidently the appeal of the dramatists was not to the citizen but to the gentleman and to the rabble. This significant change in the nature of the later Elizabethan drama should be noted in connection with the last section of this chapter.[5]

Among the immediate contemporaries of Shirley, Ford stands first. He is imitative in a general sense and original in a special sense. While carrying on the traditions

[5] For an interesting and full discussion of the attacks upon city manners in general, see Thompson, The Controversy between the Puritans and the Stage, p. 195 ff.

of the sensational tragedy of Fletcher, he borrows too from the earlier tragedy of horror. He imitates Fletcher's romantic tone. His scenes are laid in remote lands. Love and lust, crime and revenge are his themes. But he is not content with the old plots. He takes the central theme of A King and No King, eliminates the element of surprise which had made Fletcher's play a tragicomedy, embellishes it with the romantic lusciousness of Romeo and Juliet, and the result is 'Tis Pity She's a Whore. That play evidences that Ford's art is entirely divorced from morality. In the case of The Fancies, however, he seems to have forgotten his art, and at the same time to have constructed a comedy whose chief claim to distinction is its remarkable appeal to pruriency. Ford creates a problem which he studies and analyzes during a play, without any regard for the inculcation of a lesson by its solution. In his remarkable chronicle-history, Perkin Warbeck, the reader is as much in the dark at the end of the play as at the beginning as to whether the hero was considered an impostor by the poet. Finally in any consideration of Ford's dramas, his remarkable poetic powers must be noticed. In this respect, at his best he is unequalled by either Shirley or Massinger.

Davenant, as has been said, began by heaping horror on horror, in the manner of the older tragedy. However, he soon reverted to the Fletcherian type of tragicomedy with its stereotyped elements of divine right, jealousy, love and honor, lecherous sovereigns, intriguing favorites, noble heroes, and devoted heroines. His audacious choice of subjects suggests not only a recollection of Fletcher, but the influences of the contemporary Ford. Quick changes of front, an overcrowding of incidents, rant for passion,— these are the chief characteristics of Davenant.

Carlell seems to have been popular in his day. Still his connection with the court may have been instrumental in the frequent production of his plays before the King and Queen (see Fleay, Stage, pp. 317, 349, 424). Fletcher seems his master, although in The Fool Would Be a Favorite, the influence of Jonson is perceptible. His tragicomedies, which are laid in the usual Never-Never Land of romance, were well adapted for a favorable reception in their day. The customary trials of lovers, love and honor conflicts, surprises, and disguises occur. His plays, like Davenant's, suffer from too great an accumulation of incident. His style is over-ornate, and his verse bad.

Glapthorne's dalliance with unnatural situations, as in The Lady Mother, and his use of horrors and intrigue, as in Albertus Wallenstein, betray his affinity with Fletcher, and perhaps, with Ford. Some passages betray an apparent influence of Shirley. Glapthorne is more of a poet than Carlell, but he is addicted to verbiage and over-luxuriance.

Brome has already been mentioned as a disciple of Jonson's who occasionally experimented with Fletcherian tragicomedy and comedy. His comedies are often amusing, but they have little originality. His characters are the conventional gulls, country-gentlemen, and citizens of ordinary Elizabethan realistic comedy. As a playwright, Brome is very skilful; as a poet he is contemptible. The chief intrinsic value of his comedies is because of the light they throw on the London of Charles I. Among the other minor dramatists of the last decade of the Elizabethan period we find, as imitators of Fletcher, although generally with certain experiments in Jonsonian or Middletonian realism or pseudo-realism: Cartwright, Thomas Killigrew, Henry Killigrew, Suckling (notwithstanding his regard for Shakespeare), Mayne, Rawlins, and Tatham. But among these men, Fletcher (or Shakespeare or Jonson for that matter) is cruelly maltreated. His pet situations, incidents, devices, and characters are recognizable, but they survive as the merest formal copies which lack almost without exception that plausibility which we generally find in his plays.   In other words, the drama in the decade before the closing of the theaters had throttled itself by its own conventions.   Only men of exceptional talent, such as Ford, Shirley, and Massinger were able to rise far above the general level of mediocre imitativeness; of these, the first on account of his courageous yet perhaps misdirected striving for originality, the last two because of their cleverness in the recombination of old elements.

The revival of the pastoral under the influence of Queen Henrietta Maria should not be passed over in silence, especially since Shirley has left us a dramatization of part of Sidney's Arcadia.   About 1630, the Aminta of Tasso, the Pastor Fido of Guarini, and the Filli di Sciro of Bonarelli were translated.   The Faithful Shepherdess was revived. Besides Shirley, Randolph, Heywood, Rutter, Cowley, Goffe, and Glapthorne ventured into the pastoral field, and they were by no means the only writers who dealt with the affairs of Arcadia during the reign of Charles I (Schelling, Eliz. Dram., II, 139 ff.).   It is a matter of record (as a cause and effect of the popularity of the pastoral) that the Queen herself took part in the performance of Montague's Shepherd's Paradise in 1633.

### C.   THE THEATERS AND COMPANIES

By the year 1625 theatrical conditions had become fixed. Although we are unable to trace the history of the minor playhouses very satisfactorily, there is nothing like the confusion of companies and theaters of fifteen or twenty years earlier. Now certain companies occupied certain theaters exclusively. Probably few changes of house took place and few reorganizations.

Between 1620 and 1625, six theaters existed in London. These were the Globe and the Blackfriars, at which the King's Men played; the Curtain used by the Prince's Men until 1623; the Red Bull, at which the Revels Company acted in 1622 and 1623, and the Prince's Men after the latter date; the Fortune used by the Palsgrave's Men until its destruction by fire in 1621, and then after its being rebuilt in the following year until 1625; and the Cockpit, or Phœnix, at which the Lady Elizabeth's Men acted. All these theaters, with the exception of the disused Curtain, were occupied up to the closing of the playhouses in 1642 (Fleay, Stage, p. 368). In 1629 a new private house, which was sometimes called the Whitefriars, was opened in Salisbury Court, and here the King's Revels Company played until 1636 (save during the occupancy of the house in 1632–33 by the Prince's [Charles II's] Men). Of these theaters the Blackfriars, the Cockpit, and the Salisbury Court were "private houses," and the Globe, Fortune, Red Bull, and the deserted Curtain were "public" theaters (*ibid.*, p. 368).

At the death of James I, the King's Men were continued under that designation and under the patronage of King Charles. The Lady Elizabeth's Men became at the same time the Queen's Men. In 1632, Prince Charles was made the patron of the Palsgrave's Company, which acted at Salisbury Court (1632–33) and at the Fortune (1633–36). The company which opened the house in Salisbury Court in 1629 was taken under the King's protection as the King's Revels. Besides these, a company without a patron played now at the Red Bull and now at the Fortune (Fleay, Stage, pp. 312–13). Up to about 1637 the principal dramatic companies were the King's Men who played at the Blackfriars and the Globe; the Queen's Men at the Cockpit; and the Prince's Company. During the period between 1625 and 1642, the changes in company and theater are, as usual, obscure; but it seems that in 1637 the best actors of the Queen's Men and the King's Revels Company joined and thenceforward played under the former title at Salisbury Court. A new company, called "Beeston's Boys," or the King's and Queen's Young Players, was formed in the same year and established at the Cockpit where they remained until the closing of the theaters.

The common idea that there was necessarily any constant connection between a dramatist and any particular company is disproved by Fleay's own lists (Stage, pp. 305 ff., 340 ff., 362–63).[6] It is true that Fletcher, for ten or fifteen years before his death, wrote exclusively for the King's Men, and that Massinger from 1625 to the time of his retirement or death seems to have composed exclusively for the same company. Probably these dramatists had annual, or "continuing," contracts with the King's Company during the years in which they seem to have composed exclusively for it. Possibly some of the later dramatists had similar contracts. However, between 1614 and 1625, Massinger's plays were produced by the King's Men, the Lady Elizabeth's Men, and the Revels Company. Dekker's plays during the same period were acted by the Lady Elizabeth's Men, and Prince Charles' (Charles I) Company. Ford, who had collaborated with Dekker on some of the plays just referred to, had one drama acted at the Fortune by the Palsgrave's Men. Middleton seems to have written for the King's Men, the Prince's Men, and the Lady Elizabeth's.

    [6] For a refutation of Fleay's theories regarding the authors and the companies at an earlier period, see Thorndike, The Influence of Beaumont and Fletcher on Shakespeare, p. 11 ff. Professor Thorndike's arguments in favor of the free literary market apply as well in the post-Fletcherian period as the Fletcherian.

After 1625, the relations of the dramatists and the companies continued, in general, as before. The plays of Brome were produced by the King's Men, the Queen's Men and the King's and Queen's Company. Those of Glapthorne were acted by the King's Men, the King's Revels Company, and the King's and Queen's Company, and those of Nabbes by the Queen's Men, the Prince's Men and the King's and Queen's Company. Marmion seems to have written for both of the two last named companies. Shirley, himself, began with a play for the Lady Elizabeth's Men, and then wrote apparently two or three plays for the successors of that company (the Queen's Men) after which his Brothers was brought out in 1626 by the King's Men. With the exception of Love in a Maze, acted by the King's Revels Company in 1632, his other plays up to his departure for Ireland were produced by the Queen's Men. At his return he appears to have hesitated between the reorganized Queen's Men and the King's Men. Perhaps influenced by the fact that Massinger had died a year or two earlier, thus removing the chief dramatist of that company, he cast his lot with the King's Men.

The truth seems to be that the average dramatist wrote for a single company as long as it was to his interest to do so, and that the leaving of one company for another by a playwright, of which Fleay and some other critics make so much, is merely evidence that the author could sell a play for more money to one company than to another. Therefore, it is hazardous, not to say productive of serious error, to base any conclusions upon the presumption that an author (save Fletcher and Massinger as stated, and possibly Shirley just before the closing of the theaters) was permanently retained to write for any single company.[7]

[7] Note the preceding discussion in connection with The Politician, and The Brothers, Chaps. VI. and VII, respectively.

## D.  THE AUDIENCE

Very necessary in the discussion of a popular drama, such as that of Elizabethan England, is the consideration of the audience whose collective criticism was the chief factor in determining the character of the plays which were written for it.

At the accession of Charles I, England was divided both politically and religiously.  On one hand, headed by the King and including most of the nobility and those who depended upon the court, were the upholders of absolutism, episcopacy, and more or less license of manners.  Opposed to them were ranged the Puritan party, composed of many country gentlemen and the bulk of the trading classes, which advocated a limited monarchy, ecclesiastical reformation, and sobriety of life.

These two parties which dated from a much earlier period came into especial prominence first after the accession of James I.  The absolute cleavage between them was hastened and contributed to by the King's obstinate adherence to the theory of the divine right of kings and bishops, by his unpopular foreign and domestic policies, and by his submission to unworthy favorites.  To these, as lesser causes of this well-nigh fatal division, may be added the personal unpopularity of the King as a foreigner and as a weak and undignified figure, the extreme corruption in the public offices, and the licentiousness and extravagance that reigned at court, to the last of which the King himself gave great encouragement.

For the first of these two great parties the dramatist wrote.  Like Stephens' Common Player ''he was never a Puritan'' (Essays and Characters, Bk. II, Character 4). Indeed May (who had personal grounds for his action) seems to have been the only dramatist who supported the

Parliament in the later Civil War. Newcastle, Davenant, Shirley, Lovelace, and Lacy, to name only a few, bore arms for the King in that contest. The theaters had been under the patronage of the royal family since the accession of James I, and they seem to have been filled chiefly by members of the court-party. When his plays were printed the dramatist dedicated them, not to a butcher, a mercer, or a Puritan of birth, but to a courtly gentleman, at least, if not to a peer. If an author were fortunate, his plays were presented at court; after the accession of Charles I, the Queen attended performances at the private theaters. James I seems to have been interested more in controversial literature than in the drama, although somewhat of a poet himself and an admirer of splendid shows, while Queen Anne appears to have been attracted by the pageantry of the masque, more than by the less sumptuously presented play. On the other hand, both Charles I and his Queen patronized the fine arts with intelligence and taste.

From the preceding pages it is evident that the courtiers and those favorably affected towards the court were the principal patrons of the theater. It was they who set the fashions in plays. At the same time it must be remembered that the public playhouses were still frequented by the lowest orders. Indeed, the theaters seem to have been supported by the two extremes of society.

For the "groundlings," primarily, was intended the low comedy (almost always in prose) with its almost inevitable broadness and frequent obscenity and immorality, which is found in the majority of Elizabethan plays. The part of the audience that sat upon the stage or in the more expensive seats was the class for which the most studied and literary portion of a play (the poetical main plot) was composed. However, there were certainly many persons of high station and birth who, together with the common

herd, enjoyed ribaldry, and at the same time, doubtless, in
the pit were some individuals of education and taste, such
as poor students from the universities, or struggling
authors. No more then than now did rank, wealth, and
fashion indicate the absence of vulgarity and ignorance.

Now it is a truism to say that in the capital of a kingdom
ruled by such a king with such a court, a literary type,
governed, as is the drama, in material and presentation by
the demands of its audience (and an audience composed of
persons, high and low, whose fundamental differences are
rank and cultivation, not morals) will reflect the tastes
of that audience. Here then we have the explanation of
the Fletcherian play and its popularity. Thrilling tragedies and tragicomedies with their presentation of abnormal
situations, amusing comedies with their vivacity and frequent realism, and all three forms devoid of any real
earnestness, the dramas of Beaumont and Fletcher are the
natural dramatic food for such a period as that described
above. The general merit of the plays (for those that are
not great are always entertaining) enabled them to maintain their popularity through the reign of Charles I, when
society was outwardly more decent than in the preceding
or the succeeding reign, far on into the moral reaction of
the eighteenth century.

During the seventeen years between the death of James I
and the outbreak of the Civil War, social conditions changed
little. Vices were practiced privately which had been practiced in public at the less strict and less outwardly decent
court of James I. The line of demarcation between playgoer and Puritan became more pronounced as the King,
who had inherited his father's theories, endeavored to force
them upon his people. Still do we find on one side the
court, many of the great lords, and lesser nobility, and the
rabble, and on the other the majority of the country gen-

tlemen and the citizens (see Clarendon, Hist. I, 349, on the disaffection of the city of London in 1640). It is evident that plays were written, *not* for the mercantile classes, but for their political and religious adversaries, the members of the court and high church party. Therefore, during the literary lifetime of Shirley, the demands of the audience upon the dramatist were practically the same as during the activity of Fletcher. Furthermore, the high quality of Fletcher's plays contributed, as noted above, to the frequent imitation of them during the reign of Charles I.

## BIBLIOGRAPHICAL NOTE

The chief authorities on which this chapter is based are: Thorndike, Tragedy, The Influence of Beaumont and Fletcher on Shakespere, and his lectures on the Elizabethan drama delivered at Columbia University, 1908-09; Ward, Hist. Eng. Dram. Lit., II, III; Schelling, Eliz. Dram.; Fleay, Stage; Murray, Eng. Dram. Cos. (Fleay's statements have been checked by Murray's book); Traill, Social England, IV; Clarendon, Hist., I, II; Gardiner, Hist.; Green, Short Hist.

# CHAPTER II

## BIOGRAPHY; STAGE HISTORY; CHRONOLOGY

### A. BIOGRAPHY

James Shirley was born probably on the thirteenth of September, 1596, in or near the Parish of St. Mary Woolchurch, which has since been incorporated in that of St. Mary Woolnoth, Walbrook. It has been conjectured that he was descended from the Shirleys of Sussex or Warwickshire; but Sir A. W. Ward (D. N. B., LII, 126) denies this and states that he was not of gentle blood. The fact remains that he is designated on the titlepages of his plays as "James Shirley, gent." Fleay conjectures that James Shirley was the son of Henry Shirley, the dramatist, and says that Corydon (J. Shirley) as the son of Midas (H. Shirley) in Heywood's Love's Mistress goes to prove this relationship (Anglia, VIII, 414). There is no ground, apparently, for any such belief.[1] There is no mention of a relationship in the dramatist's dedication of Love in a Maze to the wife of Sir Robert Shirley, bart. On October 4, 1608, the young Shirley was admitted to Merchant Taylor's School. Here in 1612 he is mentioned in the records as monitor.

In the same year he was enrolled at St. John's College, Oxford. His intention was to enter the Church, but from this he was dissuaded for the time being by his patron and

[1] See Nason, James Shirley, Chap. I, for the probable ancestry of Shirley.

24

friend, Dr. William Laud, then Master of St. John's, the reason for Laud's objections to his taking orders being that Shirley had a mole or some similar mark upon his left cheek. Possibly as a result of this interference with his plans for his future, Shirley left Oxford before taking a degree and entered Cambridge as a member of Catharine Hall. Here he seems to have proceeded Bachelor of Arts before 1618, judging from the MS. copy of the titlepage of his non-extant Echo. Soon after 1619 he seems to have proceeded Master of Arts. The anonymous Compendious History of the English Stage (p. 29) says, "After the death of Beaumont, it has been said, Fletcher was assisted in his plots by Shirley; but there appears little foundation for this assertion." Certainly while a mere boy at Oxford Shirley did not collaborate with the chief dramatist of the time, so this "assertion" may be dismissed with less consideration than the anonymous historian just quoted gave it.

Upon leaving Cambridge, Shirley entered the Church and held a living in or near St. Albans, Hertfordshire. In January, 1621, he became head-master of St. Albans Grammar School. Having been converted to Catholicism, he gave up this position July 1, 1624. It has been conjectured that he was "negligent and unworthy" (Victoria History of the County of Hertfordshire, II, 63), but there is no proof of this. On the other hand, the fact that he was in comfortable circumstances when his will was made a short time before his death, after twenty years of school-teaching, goes to show that he was at least not unsuccessful as a pedagogue. The judgment of the historian above quoted may be suspected justly, for he gives (ibid.) the date of Shirley's first play as February 4, 1625–26. Mathias Shirley, the dramatist's son, was christened at St. Giles', Cripplegate, February 26, 1624. The poet seems therefore in that year, before his formal relinquishment of his position at St. Albans, to have sent his wife to London. Shirley himself appears to have established himself in Gray's Inn, where he "set up for a playmaker."

Schipper surmises that Shirley took up the study of law, basing this conjecture upon the poet's residence in Gray's Inn, his familiarity with legal procedure as shown in Chabot, III, 2, V, 2, and his connection with the Inn as indicated on the titlepage of The Triumph of Peace (James Shirley, p. 9). This is not at all an untenable theory. Indeed, it seems quite probable that Shirley at least pretended to take up the legal profession, while, in reality, working as a dramatist. We find, for instance, in addition to the above examples of the dramatist's familiarity with the law, further evidence of a considerable knowledge of its terminology and methods in Love Tricks, III, 5 (the Country Magistrate's Speech), The Traitor, III, 1, and in Honoria and Mammon, which contains much legal verbiage. Other references to the law occur in the prologues to Love Tricks, The Example, The Imposture, The Sisters, among Shirley's own plays, while the prologues supplied by him for No Wit to a Woman's, "Another of Master Fletcher's plays there" (i.e. Ireland) and The General (VI, 492, 493, 495, respectively) also contain more or less elaborate comparisons based upon the practice of law.

Love Tricks, Shirley's first play, was licensed February 10, 1624-5 for the Lady Elizabeth's Men (shortly to become the Queen's) at the Cockpit (or Phœnix) theater. For this company, he wrote almost exclusively until 1636, the date of his departure for Ireland. The only exceptions were: The Brothers, first acted by the King's Men at Blackfriars in 1626; Love in a Maze, produced by the King's Revels Company at Salisbury Court in 1632; and The Arcadia, perhaps privately played about 1630.

In 1635 John Ogilby, as Master of the Revels in Ireland,

established a play-house in Dublin, the Earl of Strafford being then Lord Deputy. During the period of his deputyship, Strafford seems to have maintained an almost regal court at Dublin (see Howell, Familiar Letters, I, 341 ff., II, 420). In 1636, after the London theaters were closed on account of the plague, Shirley went to Ireland, where with the probable exception of a short visit to England in 1637 (see Nissen, James Shirley, p. 17 ff., and the dedication to The Royal Master), he remained for about four years, returning apparently in the early part of 1640 (dedication to The Coronation). The Earl of Kildare, to whom The Royal Master was dedicated, seems to have been a patron of Shirley's, as well as the Earl of Strafford himself, to whose son Shirley dedicated The Court Secret many years later. At least four of Shirley's plays were produced in Ireland, if not more.[2]

After the reopening of the theaters in London in 1637, Shirley's plays were presented by the King's Men at Blackfriars. Up to the closing of the theaters in 1642, this company produced all of his plays save The Politician and The Gentleman of Venice. At the breaking out of the Civil War, the dramatist entered the royal service under the Earl, afterwards Duke, of Newcastle to whom he had dedicated The Traitor in 1635, and whom, according to Wood,[3] he had aided in the composition of his own plays (see Chap. X, Captain Underwit, The Variety, etc.). In 1644, Newcastle retired to the Continent, and Shirley seems to have been thrown partly on his own resources. He pub-

---

[2] For a full discussion of Shirley's residence in Ireland, see Nason, James Shirley, Chap. IV, and Nissen, James Shirley, p. 17 ff.

[3] Wood's exact words are: "Our author Shirley did also much assist his generous patron William Duke of Newcastle in the composure of certain plays which the Duke afterwards published" (Ath. Oxon, III, 737).

lished his Poems in 1646, and in 1647, aided in the collection of the plays of Beaumont and Fletcher for their publication in the folio edition of that year, to which he furnished a preface.   He lived under the protection of Thomas Stanley, the poet and philosopher, to whom The Brothers is dedicated.   Between 1644 and 1649 Shirley seems to have returned to his early profession, and to have kept a school in Whitefriars.   Various of his own plays, masques and entertainments were printed during this period.   Also he produced some elementary school-books, Via ad Latinam Linguam Complanata, etc.

After the Restoration Shirley continued at his occupation of keeping a school, instead of returning to the stage (his resolve not to do the latter is expressed in the preface to Honoria and Mammon in 1659).   He was not, therefore, as Mr. Kingsley seems to assert in Plays and Puritans, p. 13, a court poet of Charles II.   It is said by Wood that he aided Ogilby in his translations of Homer and Vergil at this time, and in a scurrilous poem called The Session of the Poets, it was hinted that the Honorable Edward Howard's plays were partly composed by Shirley.   Certainly, as to the latter, there is no internal evidence of Shirley's hand in Howard's plays.   In 1666, during the Great Fire, the venerable poet, now in his seventieth year, was driven with his wife Frances "from their habitation near to Fleet Street, into the parish of St. Giles's in The Fields in Middlesex, where being in a manner overcome with affrightments, disconsolations, and other miseries, occasion'd by that fire and their losses, they both died within the compass of a natural day: whereupon their bodies were buried in one grave in the yard belonging to the said Church of St. Giles's on the 29th of October" (Wood, Ath. Oxon., III, 740).   And so died James Shirley, the last of that wonderful succession of dramatic artists and poets to whom

the greatest period in the literature of our race owes chiefly
her preëminence.

One of his sons was butler of Furnival's Inn in Wood's
time. The poet's will mentions three surviving sons and
two daughters, one a widow; one married daughter had
pre-deceased him (see Nason, James Shirley, Chap. V, and
cf. Dyce, Some Account, Ward, D. N. B.). In his Roscius
Anglicanus, p. 2, Downes mentions a Mr. Sherly as entering Killigrew's Company after they had begun to play in
Drury Lane in 1663; but neither in Roscius nor in Genest's
Stage does there seem to be any further mention of this
Sherly. It may be that he died soon after or quit the
stage. Whether he was any relation to the poet is, of
course, unknown, but that he was a son is by no means
impossible.

Shirley seems to have been a favorite of Queen Henrietta
Maria, perhaps, like Massinger, on account of his religion.
He appears also to have been in the good graces of King
Charles, since he was commissioned to write The Gamester
on a plot of the King's. A further indication of Shirley's standing may be found in the fact that it was he who
composed the "libretto" for the magnificent Masque of
Peace (the most elaborate ever produced in England)
which his brethren of the Inns of Court presented in reply
to Histriomastix.

From his works Shirley appears to have been a man of
upright principles, with well-defined ideas of right and
wrong. Indeed, his constant conversions of his wicked
characters are in some cases inartistic, and after a time,
certainly monotonous. In no play does wickedness go unpunished if persisted in. Lady Bornwell in The Lady of
Pleasure and Lady Huntlove in Captain Underwit come
nearest to being exceptions to this general rule. It may be
said that a man who, in spite of attempts at dissuasion,

enters the Church of England, and shortly after quits his profession and enters the Church of Rome, at a time when no possible advantage could accrue from his conversion, but on the other hand, many inconveniences, shows a degree of thoughtfulness and conscientiousness which could not help manifesting itself in his writings. In the dedication to The Maid's Revenge (1639) Shirley describes himself as having never been a flatterer and of having been thought, as a result, not to have attained preferment as he might otherwise have done. As to the precise meaning of this passage, of course, we are in ignorance. Certain it is that his dedications, while complimentary, do not seem fulsome and are not nauseating to the modern reader because of their gross flattery. The various references to English politics found in some of his plays show the author, in spite of his court affiliations and his religion, not to have been blind to the abuses of the time. It is well-known, of course, that his satiric pen came close to getting him into trouble in regard to The Ball (see under that play). We find among his patrons and friends the King and Queen, Archbishop Laud, the Earls of Kildare, Strafford, and Newcastle, the Countess of Ormond, Jonson, May, Ford, Habington, Randolph, Massinger, Stanley, Sherburne, Richard, and Alexander Brome, and these are only the most prominent. Shirley seems, also, to have been a sort of master to Glapthorne; and there appears to have been some borrowing by each from the other. The Earl of Newcastle's literary connections with Shirley have already been mentioned. Langbaine (Dramatic Poets, p. 476) quotes Choice Drollery, p. 6, thus,

> "Shirley (the morning child) the Muses bred,
> And sent him born with bays upon his head."

Anthony Wood, writing less than thirty years after his

death calls him, "the most noted dramatic poet of his time" (Ath. Oxon., III, 737).

However, he seems to have formed no school—he was not original enough—but rather to be a link between Elizabethan and Restoration comedy as well as one of the last eminent representatives of poetic stage tragedy and tragicomedy in the English drama.

## B. Stage History

Shirley's fame, like that of most of the Elizabethans, declined rapidly after the Restoration, although certain of his plays were acted apparently in their original form for several years. Langbaine, who died in 1692 at the age of thirty-six, mentions having seen The Court Secret, and The Chances (Love in à Maze) at the King's House; and The Grateful Servant and The School of Compliments (Love Tricks) at the Duke's House (Dramatic Poets, p. 475). This was perhaps about 1675. Pepys saw The Court Secret as a new play August 18, 1664; Love in a Maze five times between May 22, 1662, and April 28, 1668; The Grateful Servant, February 20, 1668–69; and Love Tricks, August 5, 1667, and January 7, 1667–68. In addition to these he records having witnessed three performances of The Cardinal, two of The General (which is not Shirley's), one of Hyde Park, two of Love's Cruelty, four of The Traitor, and four of The Country Captain. Downes (Roscius Anglicanus, p. 8) includes The Opportunity, The Example, The Cardinal, and The Traitor in a list of Killigrew's Theater Royal plays, to which he adds (p. 15) Love in a Maze.

Malone published a list of plays acted immediately after the Restoration from a MS. of Sir Henry Herbert's. Here we find recorded performances of The Traitor, Love's Cruelty, The Opportunity, The Wedding, The Country

Captain (Captain Underwit), The Little Thief (The Night-walker), Love in a Maze, The Brothers, and The Cardinal, between November 6, 1660, and July 23, 1662 (Shakespeare Variorum, III, 273 ff.). Herbert, according to Malone (*ibid.*), lists The Traitor, Love's Cruelty, and The Wedding among the stock plays of the company which later played at the Theatre Royal.

Downes says (p. 27) that after the Great Fire when Davenant's Company opened in Lincoln's Inn Fields, they revived The Grateful Servant, The Witty Fair One, and The School of Compliments. Genest adds The Nightwalker to this list of plays of Shirley's which still kept the stage (see Stage, I, 349, and note 339–352). Thirteen, then, of Shirley's plays were certainly played after the Restoration, besides two in which he was not the sole author, and one which is attributed to him on very inadequate grounds.

Two of Shirley's plays seem to have been known abroad before his death. The Opportunity was acted by English comedians at Dresden in June, 1660; and The Traitor was played also by an English company at Dresden during the carnival in 1661. The identification of the latter play is a trifle doubtful, however, according to Dessoff (Studien zur vergleichenden Litteraturgeschichte, I, 421 ff.).

The process of alteration and revision which will concern us during the remainder of this portion of the chapter,[4] seems to have begun before Shirley's death. A droll called Jenkin of Wales was founded on Love Tricks, played about 1647 (Halliwell's reprint, titlepage), and published in The Wits, in 1672 (Halliwell, Dict. O. E. Plays, p. 132). The Rival Sisters of Gould, played at Drury Lane in 1696 (Genest, II, 73–74), seems based on the same source as The

---

[4] The various plays will be considered in the order in which they will be treated in the later portion of the book—approximately chronologically in the types in which they fall.

Maid's Revenge, not on that play.  Alonzo's speeches (III, p. 24) seem stolen, however, from Orlando Furioso's, Love Tricks, III, 5 (pp. 47–48).

The Traitor was revived with alterations at the Theatre Royal (Drury Lane) in 1692, as by Anthony Rivers.  The "alterations, amendments and additions" with which the play was published are very few, and consist, indeed, chiefly of omissions.  As a matter of fact, it appears that the text of the tragedy was probably printed from the prompter's book of the original play.  This version was repeated in 1703 and 1704 (Genest, II, 295, 316).  In 1718, further alterations were made by C. Bullock, and The Traitor was produced at Lincoln's Inn Fields, October 11, 1718 (*ibid.*, II, 648).  On February 10, 1819, Shiel brought out at Covent Garden a version of The Traitor, entitled Evadne, or the Statue.  This alteration was acted thirty times.  In New York, Evadne was played as late as December 13, 1881 (Brown, Hist. N. Y. Stage, III, 30).  There is more dramatic unity in Shiel's play than in Shirley's (Genest, VIII, 699 ff.).  Almeyda, Queen of Granada, by Miss Lee, produced at Drury Lane, April 20, 1796, is based avowedly to some extent on The Cardinal (see Miss Lee's Advertisement).  The catastrophes come about in the same manner, and Almeyda follows the general plot of The Cardinal.  This tragedy was acted five times (*ibid.*, VII, 238 ff.).

Alphonso, King of Naples, a play by Powell, produced at Drury Lane in 1691, borrows some names and eight characters from The Young Admiral.  In the first three acts Powell follows Shirley's language and plot rather closely.  The parts of the Sicilians are omitted, various characters are combined and others added, while the action is made tragic (cf. *ibid.*, II, 10–11).  The Bird in a Cage, with Money Works Wonders as a second title, was revived at Covent Garden as Quick's benefit, April 24, 1786.  The alterations were slight (*ibid.*, VI, 399–400). An apparent borrowing of Philenzo's device for entering the ladies' prison is found by Genest (VII, 554–5) in The Cabinet, an opera by Thomas Dibdin, first played at Covent Garden, February 9, 1802. Dibdin claimed to have got the idea from an old ballad called The Golden Bull, and discredited the other sources offered. In The Cabinet, Constantia escapes from her father's castle, and thereby from an unwelcome suitor, in a cabinet. This is the only resemblance to Shirley's play, and it is a rather slight one. However, in a song in II, 2, occurs the line: "The bird that sings from yonder cage" (referring to the cabinet). This opera was very successful, being presented thirty times, and holding the stage for many years. In New York it was acted last, December 30, 1840 (Ireland, Records N. Y. Stage, II, 343–44). According to Halliwell (Dict. O. E. Plays, p. 200), The Opportunity was turned into a droll and published in The Wits, 1672, as A Prince in Conceit. The Sisters was altered by an anonymous author, and first presented at Lincoln's Inn Fields as Like to Like, or a Match Well Made Up, on November 28, 1723. It is said to have been acted twenty years earlier (Genest, III, 142 ff.). The Fancied Queen, "a moderate opera in one long act," brought out in the summer of 1733, was founded on the same play of Shirley's (*ibid.*, III, 395).

The characters of the fat and lean suitors, Lodam and Rawbone, in The Wedding, have been used on at least two occasions. Howard's All Mistaken, or the Mad Couple, produced at the Theatre Royal, December 28, 1667, and Molloy's farce called The Half-Pay Officers, which was brought out at Lincoln's Inn Fields, January 11, 1720, borrow these personages from Shirley. The latter has also taken over Rawbone's man Camelion and renamed him Jasper (which is Haver's assumed name in The Wedding). Henry

Ward's farce, The Widow's Wish, or an Equipage of Lovers, is based on The Half-Pay Officers (*ibid.*, IV, 116; III, 35 ff.; X, 172). The Witty Fair One is the source of Hamilton's Doting Lovers, or the Libertine Tamed, which was brought out at Lincoln's Inn Fields, June 23, 1714. The characters and a large part of the dialogue are drawn from Shirley (*ibid.*, II, 569–70). Oulton's musical farce, Frightened to Death, produced at Drury Lane, February 27, 1817 (*ibid.*, VIII, 589), seems based upon the portion of The Witty Fair One, which deals with Penelope's plot for Fowler's reformation. In both productions a libertine who fills an assignation at night is reformed by his mistress' pretending he is dead. Certain details correspond as the attentions to the maids, the mock epitaph, the preparations for the funeral, and the pretended invisibility of the profligate after his death. Oulton claimed to have based his farce upon The Haunted Castle, a "juvenile production" presented in Dublin. It was acted seventeen times. It was last played in New York, November 8, 1838 (Brown, Hist. N. Y. Stage, I, 248). Langbaine (Dramatic Poets, p. 477) says that a scene (IV, 1) in Dryden's Secret Love, or the Maiden Queen, in which Melissa examines her daughters, Olinda and Sabina, as to their love for Celadon, is drawn from Love in a Maze (I, 2). The resemblance, however, is not a particularly striking one. Powell's Very Good Wife, presented in 1693 at the Theatre Royal, is partly taken from Hyde Park, with extensive indebtednesses also to The Court Beggar and The City Wit of Brome. Powell has used the names of Bonavent, Venture and Carol. In II, 1, III, 1, and IV, [2], Powell has drawn upon II, 4, and V, 1, of Shirley's comedy (cf. Genest, II, 50). The same comedy of Shirley's is used by Mrs. Cooper in The Rival Widows, or the Fair Libertine, which came out February 22, 1735, at Covent Garden, and was acted six times. She borrows from the dialogue between Fairfield and Carol in II, 4 (*ibid.*, III, 461–62).

The Gamester, notwithstanding Kingsley's opinion of it (Plays and Puritans, p. 54 ff.), has been the most utilized of Shirley's plays. According to Downes (Roscius, p. 48), The Gamester was the first play presented in Vanbrugh's theater in the Haymarket in 1705 (see Genest, II, 329), but it is likely that this was not Shirley's Gamester but Mrs. Centlivre's. On November 1, 1711, Charles Johnson's Wife's Relief, or the Husband's Cure, was produced at Drury Lane. This is an alteration of The Gamester, with some changes of characters and plot and with most of the dialogue re-written (*ibid.*, II, 490 ff.). Johnson discards all of Shirley's names save Hazard, which he gives to a subordinate character. Old Barnacle and Sir Richard Hurry are combined as Sir Tristram Cash. There is some reorganization and rearrangement of scenes with one added incident. The play is in prose. This comedy was acted repeatedly up to 1782, in which year it was acted twice at benefit performances and on another occasion (*ibid.*, VI, 226). Garrick first presented a revision of The Gamester under the title of The Gamesters at Drury Lane, December 22, 1757. Notwithstanding his assertion in the Advertisement, Garrick used Johnson's version, as well as Shirley's original play. A comparison of the three proves this point. Shirley's names were retained. The entire plot of Beaumont, Delamore, etc., was eliminated, as well as certain portions of the main plot. Garrick has made some additions, consisting of scenes as well as passages, all of which are in prose, while he preserves Shirley's speeches in verse. Certain changes in arrangement were also made. On the whole, this version of The Gamesters is nearer the original play than is Johnson's. It was acted six times (*ibid.*, IV, 512 ff.). This version of Shirley's comedy which was very popular for some years was, apparently, acted last as Bannister's benefit at Drury Lane, April 28, 1806 (*ibid.*, VII, 708). Poole made yet a third alteration of The Gamester, condensing it into three acts. This version was produced at Covent Garden, March 13, 1827, and was acted eleven times (*ibid.*, IX, 388–89). It was also acted in the following season.

Genest (VII, 304–5) suggests that Holman's comic opera Abroad and at Home, presented at Covent Garden, November 19, 1796, is in part based on The Example. In both pieces a man's debts are paid by a person in order that they may fight a duel—which does not take place in Holman's opera. There is also a lady of Lady Plot's stamp in the person of Lady Flourish. The indebtedness, however, is a rather dubious one. This piece was played as late as 1822. The Lady of Pleasure seems to have been drawn on first by Mrs. Behn in The Lucky Chance, or an Alderman's Bargain; II, 1, III, 2, IV, 1, are certainly based upon IV, 1 and V, 1, of Shirley's play. Taverner's Artful Husband, played first at Lincoln's Inn Fields, February 11, 1717, is taken from The Lady of Pleasure. Taverner borrows Bornwell's cure of his wife's extravagance, and makes use of Shirley's Decoy, who, however, in The Artful Husband does not practise upon the character corresponding to Lady Bornwell (*ibid.*, II, 609 ff.). This play was produced as late as 1746, when it was acted as Mrs. Woffington's benefit at Drury Lane, March 3 (*ibid.*, IV, 203; see also 205). The Artful Husband was in its turn altered by the elder Macready and produced as The Bank Note, or Lessons for Ladies, at Covent Garden, on the occasion of Johnstone's benefit, May 1, 1795. This version seems to have been very popular for the time being (*ibid.*, VII, 214, 216, 261). It was acted in New York, June 2, 1797 (Ireland, Records N. Y. Stage, I, 147).

Charles Johnson's Masquerade, played at Drury Lane, January 16, 1718, is also based upon The Lady of Pleasure. The indebtedness is mentioned in the epilogue (Genest, II, 640–41). Trick for Trick, or The Admiral's Daughter, a farce, produced at Covent Garden, July 2, 1812, as outlined (*ibid.*, VIII, 297–98), seems based upon The Constant Maid, both the sham physician and the misunderstanding of III, 2, of Shirley's play being used, as well as the name "Heartwell."

The story of The Arcadia of Sidney was dramatized by M'Namara Morgan and played first at Covent Garden, January 20 or 22, 1754, with Barry as Pyrocles. It was acted also in Dublin the following year. This play does not seem to owe anything to Shirley, but occasioned a reprint of his old drama (Genest, IV, 395–96). The Nightwalker was acted for the first time in six years September 18, 1705, at Drury Lane, after which we hear nothing more of it (*ibid.*, II, 335). Love's Pilgrimage, according to Genest (VI, 447–48), was the source for a scene of The Stage Coach, a farce first acted, as altered from Farquhar, at Quick's benefit at Covent Garden, April 16, 1787. As Edwin played the part of a hostler, probably part of III, 1, of the old play was used. According to Langbaine (Dramatic Poets, p. 213), The Noble Gentleman was revived by D'Urfey as The Fool's Preferment, or the Three Dukes of Dunstable. This adaptation was produced in 1688 (Ward, Hist. Eng., Dram. Lit., II, 739, note; see also Langbaine, Dramatic Poets, pp. 180–81). J. Sheridan Knowles adapted The Noble Gentleman under the title of The Duke of London, but his version seems never to have been acted and was printed first in 1874 (Hasberg, James Sheridan Knowles' Leben, pp. 25–26). Double Falsehood was acted as late as May 23, 1793 (at Bath), (Genest, VII, 117). The Mountaineers of George Colman the Younger which was produced at the Haymarket, August 3, 1793, was not, as Genest seems to intimate (*ibid.*, VII, 139), based upon Double Falsehood, but upon the story of Cardenio in Don Quixote. This is evident from the fact that the escape of the Christian prisoners from Granada with the Moorish princess which forms a part of the plot of Colman's play, is founded upon the captive's story, Don Quixote, Part I, Bk. IV, Chaps. XII, XIII, XIV (Smollett's translation). For many years The Mountaineers held the stage with fairly regular performances. In New York it was played last in March, 1865 (Brown, Hist. N. Y. Stage, II, 211).[5]

However, while certain of his plays still held the stage in a more or less altered form, and while others were plundered for farces and operas, as has been shown above, the fame of Shirley had become almost negligible. Phillips in his Theatrum Poetarum (p. 80), which is dedicated to Shirley's friends, Thomas Stanley and Edward Sherburn, and which was published in 1675, quotes "some" as placing Shirley "little inferior to Fletcher himself," and calls him "a just pretender to more than the meanest place" among the dramatic poets. The Glories of our Birth and State was published in folio as a broadside in black-letter about 1680, with seven additional stanzas under the title, The Vanity of Vainglory (Brit. Mus. Cat., CXI, 43). During the latter part of the seventeenth century Shirley is praised only by Gerard Langbaine, the first scholarly critic of the English drama. The introduction of Shirley in The Session of the Poets (Poems on Affairs of State, I, 208), is not complimentary. Dryden's contemptuous allusions to Shirley in Mac Flecknoe doubtless had much to do with the comparative oblivion in which

[5] There seems no foundation for Dibdin's assertion that Foote used Shirley as a source, Hist. Stage, IV, 38.

the old dramatist's works rested until the nineteenth century. Oldham in A Satire (Works, p. 417), makes Spenser couple Shirley and Silvester as mouldering in Duck Lane shops. Gildon in his Lives and Characters of the English Dramatic Poets, p. 131, wonders at Langbaine's praise of Shirley and decries the latter in comparison with Dryden. Robert Gould in a satire called The Playhouse, compares Shirley with D'Urfey (from the latter of whom Gould had previously filched a plot; earlier he had supplied Gould with a prologue and an epilogue for a play). Short notices of Shirley occur in Dodsley's Select Collection of Old Plays (1744), and in Chetwood's little volume with the same title (1751). Dibdin in his so-called History of the Stage (IV, 38 ff.) (c. 1800), in writing of Shirley (apparently from no acquaintance whatever with that author's works) says, in speaking of The Traitor (p. 40), that "tragedy was not his forte," and that The Cardinal "creates but little interest," and is "but a dull thing" (p. 45). However, he says that Mrs. Behn, Bullock, and Foote have taken materials from him and that "even Dryden has given no mean account of him" (p. 38). The first genuine appreciation of Shirley after Langbaine's is to be found in Dr. Farmer's Essay on the Learning of Shakespeare, p. 38, where it is said: "his [Shirley's] imagination is sometimes fine to an extraordinary degree." The Biographia Dramatica, I, 668, quotes the author of An Heroic Address in Verse to the Rev. Richard Watson, as calling for an edition of Shirley. Lamb in his Specimens from the Dramatic Poets makes extracts from Love Tricks, The Maid's Revenge, The Brothers, The Traitor, Love in a Maze, The Example, The Gentleman of Venice, The Lady of Pleasure, and The Politician. He ranks Shirley among the great Elizabethans. The actress Miss E. W. Macauley, who wrote some virulent pamphlets in the neighborhood of 1820, appears to have used Shirley's plays in her "Tales of the Drama, founded on the tragedies of Shakespeare, Massinger, Shirley, and others." However, since 1833, when Shirley's works became accessible to the general reader in the long delayed and characteristically unscholarly edition by Gifford which Dyce finally completed, that dramatist has approached more closely the prominence among the Elizabethan playwrights to which his talents entitled him.

## C.  Chronology

There is certainly no dramatist of importance in the Elizabethan period whose plays can be dated as exactly as Shirley's by external evidence; and if we add internal evidence, there are very few plays indeed which can not be placed within a year or two. Following is a list of Shirley's works, dramatic and non-dramatic, including those sometimes assigned to him, in their probable order of production, with the dates of licensing for the stage in the case of the plays, of registration at Stationers' Hall, and of the first printed edition.[6]

\* 1. A Yorkshire Tragedy; 1605; 1608 (not Shirley's).

\* 2. The Faithful Friends; 1614? (Thorndike, The In-

---

1 In the case of plays, the first date, that of licensing for acting, is based, when not otherwise specified, upon Malone, Shakespeare Variorum, III, 231 ff. The second date (for non-dramatic works the first), which is that of licensing for the press, is drawn from Arber's Transcript of the Stationers' Registers. The third date, that of the printed book, is based on Greg's List of English Plays. . . . Printed before 1700, and the titlepages of the volumes.

In the list above, the plays and other works, which have been assigned to Shirley, but in which he seems certainly to have had no part, are indicated by an \*.

fluence of Beaumont and Fletcher on Shakspere, p. 92);
1812.

3. Echo and Narcissus, the Two Unfortunate Lovers;
for Francis Constable, January 4, 1617–18; 1618.

* 4. The Laws of Candy; 1619 (Thorndike, The Influence of Beaumont and Fletcher on Shakspere, p. 93); 1647.

5. Love Tricks, or The School of Compliments; February
10, 1624–5; for Master Constable as The School of Compliment, February 25, 1630–31; 1631.

* 6. The Nice Valor; revived 1625 (Fleay, Biog. Chron.,
I, 196); 1647.

7. St. Albans; not licensed (?); for William Cooke, February 14, 1639–40; not printed (?); non-extant (see Chap.
VI).

* 8. The Noble Gentleman; February 3, 1625–26; 1647.

9. The Maid's Revenge, February 9, 1625–26; for William Cooke, April 12, 1639; 1639.

10. The Wedding; not licensed under that name?
Fleay, Biog. Chron., II, 236, dates it in May, 1626. Not
entered in the Stationers' Register, yet it was assigned by
John Grove to William Leake, September 25, 1637, and the
earliest extant edition is dated 1629.

11. The Brothers; November 4, 1626; 1652.

* 12. Dick of Devonshire, conjectured by Fleay (Anglia,
VIII, 406, etc.), to be the play licensed as The Brothers.
Not Shirley's (see Chap. X); printed from the MS. in
1883.

13. The Witty Fair One; October 3, 1628; for William
Cooke, January 15, 1632–33; 1633.

14. The Grateful Servant; November 31, 1629, as The
Faithful Servant; for John Grove, February 26, 1629–30,
as The Grateful Servant; 1630.

* 15. Phillis of Scyros; dated by Shelling, Eliz. Dram.,

II, 565, about 1630; printed 1655; not Shirley's (see Chap. X).

16. The Arcadia; perhaps privately presented, 1630 (see Chap. VIII); for John Williams and Francis Egglesfeild, November 29, 1639; 1640.

17. A Contention for Honor and Riches; not licensed; for William Cooke, November 9, 1632, as A Dialogue of Honor and Riches; 1633.

18. The Traitor; May 4, 1631; for William Cooke, November 3, 1634; 1635.

19 (A). The Duke; probably the same as The Humorous Courtier, and The Conceited Duke (?); licensed May 17, 1631.

19 (B). The Humorous Courtier; for license see above; for William Cooke, July 29, 1639; 1640.

20. Love's Cruelty; November 14, 1631; for Master Crooke and William Cooke, April 25, 1639, and for John Williams and Francis Egglesfeild, November 29, 1639, with the note, "Love's Cruelty is entered before to Master Crooke"; 1640.

21. The Changes, or Love in a Maze; January 10, 1631–32; for William Cooke, February 9, 1631–32; 1632.

22. Hyde Park; April 20, 1632; for Andrew Crooke and William Cooke, April 13, 1637; 1637.

23. The Ball; November 16, 1632; for Master Crooke and William Cooke, October 24, 1638, as by Shirley; 1639.

24 (A). The Beauties; probably the same as The Bird in a Cage; licensed January 21, 1632–33.

24 (B) The Bird in a Cage; for license see above; for William Cooke, March 19, 1632–33; 1633.

25. The Nightwalker; dated by Thorndike (Influence of Beaumont and Fletcher, p. 92) in 1612; revised after the publication of Histriomastix, 1632–33; May 11, 1633; for

Master Crooke and William Cooke, April 25, 1639, as The
Nightwalters; 1640.

26. The Young Admiral; July 3, 1633; for Andrew
Crooke and William Cooke, April 13, 1637; 1637.

27. The Gamester; November 11, 1633; for Andrew
Crooke and William Cooke, November 15, 1637; 1637.

28. The Triumph of Peace; presented February 3, 1633–
34; for William Cooke, January 24, 1633–34, as "The
Maske of the. four inns of Court with the Sceane as it is to
be presented before his Majesty at Whitehall the third of
ffebruary next"; 1633–34.

* 29. The Lover's Progress; revived May 7, 1634 (Fleay,
Biog. Chron., I, 219) ; 1647.

30. The Example; June 24, 1634; for Andrew Crooke
and William Cooke, October 18, 1637; 1637.

31. The Opportunity; November 29, 1634; for Master
Crooke and William Cooke, April 25, 1639; 1640.

32. The Coronation; February 6, 1634–35; for Master
Crooke and William Cooke, April 25, 1639; 1640.

33. Chabot, Admiral of France; April 29, 1635; for Master Crooke and William Cooke, October 24, 1638, as Phillip
Chabbott Admirall of Ffrance, and as by Shirley; 1639.

* 34. Love's Pilgrimage; revived September 16, 1635
(Weber, Works of Beaumont and Fletcher, XIII, 295) ;
1647.

35. The Lady of Pleasure; October 15, 1635; for Andrew
Crooke and William Cooke, April 13, 1637; 1637.

36. The Duke's Mistress; January 18, 1635–36; for
Master Crooke and William Cooke, March 13, 1637–38;
1638.

37 (A). Look to the Lady; for date, etc., see Chap. X;
for John Williams and Francis Egglesfeild, March 11,
1639–40; possibly the same as

37 (B). The Country Captain; printed as the Duke of

Newcastle's in 1649, and as Shirley's in 1883, under the title of Captain Underwit (see Chap. X).

38. The Royal Master; probably Shirley's first dramatic production in Ireland (Schipper, James Shirley, p. 191), and to be dated 1636-37 (Nissen, James Shirley, pp. 17-18; Nason, James Shirley, Chap. IV); licensed in England, April 23, 1638; for Master Crooke, John Crooke, and Richard Searger, March 13, 1637-38; 1638.

39. The Doubtful Heir; produced in Ireland as Rosania, or Love's Victory, probably after Shirley's return from England in 1637, and certainly after Aglaura and Claricilla (see the Dublin prologue); licensed in England as Rosania, June 1, 1640; 1652.

* 40. No Wit, No Help like a Woman's; 1613; revised by Shirley (?) 1638; 1657.

* 41. The General; played in Ireland in 1638 (a conjecture of Schelling's, Eliz. Dram., II, 568). Non-extant if Shirley's; a play was printed under this title in 1853 (see Chap. X).

42. The Variety; 1638 (?); 1649; in collaboration (?) with the Duke of Newcastle (if so it should be dated earlier).

43. St. Patrick for Ireland; produced in Ireland about 1639 (see Chap. VII); for Master Whitaker, April 28, 1640; 1640.

44. The Constant Maid; played in Ireland between 1636 and 1640; for Master Whitaker, April 28, 1640; 1640.

45. The Gentleman of Venice; October 30, 1639; 1655 (possibly first played in Ireland).

46. The Triumph of Beauty; presented privately about 1640 (Fleay, Biog. Chron., II, 244); 1646.

47. The Imposture; November 10, 1640; 1652.

48. The Politician; licensed as The Politic Father (see Chap. VI), May 26, 1641; 1655.

49. The Cardinal; November 25, 1641; 1652.

50. The Sisters; April 26, 1642; 1652.

51. The Court Secret; acted first after the Restoration (see Pepys, Diary, IV, 206); 1653.

52. Poems, &c.; 1646.

53. The Comedies and Tragedies of Beaumont and Fletcher; 1647; preface by Shirley.

\* 54. Wit's Labyrinth; 1648; not Shirley's ("J. S.").

55. Via ad Latinam Linguam Complanata; 1649.

\* 56. The Prince of Prigg's Revels; 1651; not Shirley's ("J. S.").

57. Cupid and Death; privately presented March 26, 1653; 1653.

58. The Rudiments of Grammar; 1656.

\* 59. Εισαγωγη sive Introductorium Anglo-Latino-Graecum; 1656.

60. Honoria and Mammon; composed earlier (?); 1659.

61. The Contention of Ajax and Ulysses for the Armor of Achilles; privately presented about 1658 (?); 1659.

62. Manductio; 1660.

\* 63. Andromana; after 1642 (?); not Shirley's.

64. The Humorous Lovers; after the Restoration (?); 1677; in collaboration with the Duke of Newcastle (?); (if so, an earlier date is necessary).

65. The Vanity of Vainglory; The Glories of our Birth and State with additional stanzas; 1680 (?).

\* 66. True Impartial History and Wars of the Kingdom of Ireland; second ed., 1692; dedication signed "J. S."

\* 67. Double Falsehood; published from the MS. with alterations by Theobald, 1728; authorship a problem.

## BIBLIOGRAPHICAL NOTE

The part of the foregoing chapter which deals with Shirley's biography has been drawn from Wood's Athenæ Oxonienses, III,

737 ff.; Dyce's Account of Shirley and his Writings, prefixed
to Gifford's edition of Shirley's works; Ward's Hist. Eng. Dram.
Lit., III, 89 ff., and his notice of Shirley in D. N. B., LII, 126
ff.; Schipper's James Shirley, Fleay's Annals of the Careers
of James and Henry Shirley, Anglia, VIII, 405 ff. (1885), Biog.
Chron., II, 233 ff. The best account of Shirley's life is that in
Nason's James Shirley, Chaps. I-V, inclusive, which is now in
proofs (March, 1914).

# CHAPTER III

## THE GENERAL CHARACTERISTICS OF SHIRLEY'S PLAYS

In the words of the author of the excellent article upon the Gifford-Dyce edition of Shirley in The Quarterly Review, XLIX, 14:

"When Shirley came on the stage, he might seem to succeed to a mine, of which the wealth had been completely exhausted—a land, of which every nook and corner had been explored and cultivated to its utmost height of productiveness. Every source from which dramatic invention had drawn its materials might seem dried up. The history of every country had been dramatized—every distinguished personage in ancient or modern times had appeared on the stage—even the novelists of Italy were well nigh run to their dregs; human nature itself might almost appear to have been worked out—every shade and modification of character had been variously combined, every incident placed in every possible light."

Not only were the sources for plays exhausted, but by reason of that very exhaustion, in part, the drama had become conventionalized "when Shirley came on the stage." The dramatic types which were to dominate the English stage until the closing of the theaters, and which were to exert a strong influence upon the drama of the Restoration, had been firmly established. The tragedies, tragicomedies, and comedies of Fletcher and his school were to define the plays of 1625–42. The influence of Jonson,

48

Shakespeare, and other playwrights still persisted, but in a less distinct form, or in minor writers, and in the case of Jonson, often intermingled with romantic elements from Fletcher.

Because of this very conventionalization of its elements, both in comedy and the more serious forms, and because of its subject-matter and treatment, the drama had drawn appreciably away from life and genuine realism. It had begun to receive its inspiration chiefly from earlier plays and from established convention rather than from the realism of observation or imagination. The drama was semi-literary, and therefore often dealt with life at second-hand. Two courses were open to the dramatist of this period: to carry on the established traditions or to seek out new material. Ford did the latter; almost all other dramatists did the former. As a result, we find Ford almost as far from real life as Carlell. One pictures the darkest and rarest emotions of the human heart (which earlier dramatists had never dared to portray); the other gives us wildly romantic plays "full of loue & the tryalls of louers." [1]

There is no unanimity among scholars as to what dramatist exerted the greater influence upon Shirley. Professor Thorndike considers that of Fletcher to be the strongest, as do Nissen (James Shirley, p. 2), Prölss (Das neuere Drama der Engländer, p. 210), Koeppel (Shakespeare's Wirkung, pp. 54–55). Ward intimates the same (Hist. Eng. Dram. Lit., III, 94), as does Neilson (Cam. Hist. Eng. Lit., VI, 223). On the other hand, Schipper (James Shirley, p. 345) and Schelling (Eliz. Dram., II, 323) consider Shirley either more a follower of Shake-

---

[1] From a quaint MS. critical note by "Frances Wolverton" in Mead's Combat of Love and Friendship, Columbia University Library copy.

speare or Jonson, or else more original than do other scholars generally.  Prölss (as cited above) sees a strong influence of Webster and Ford upon Shirley's dramas.  He is
not far wrong in regard to certain plays, but there are no
grounds for such a sweeping statement.

While it cannot be denied that to a certain extent Shirley follows Shakespeare and Jonson, still it seems that
Fletcher, whose name was so often linked with that of Shirley in comparisons in their own century, was his real master.  That this is the case, a study of the subject-matter
and methods of treating it of the two dramatists will show.
They handle the same situation in the same settings with
the same characters too frequently to permit the forming
of any other opinion.

It should not be supposed that Shirley followed Fletcher
blindly; such is not the case.  Not infrequently does he
introduce original variations upon the Fletcherian incident; but he exhibits the influence as well of Shakespeare,
Jonson, and others of the more important dramatists.
Sometimes, too, he draws upon such obscure writers as
Sharpham and Machin.  Furthermore, he seems occasionally beyond doubt to have invented certain of his incidents.
In any event, however, the sum of Shirley's borrowings
from single plays is insignificant when compared with his
general indebtedness to the great mass of extant dramatic
material.  *Most often his source is not a single play but the
various groups of plays which employ in common with his
dramas certain situations, incidents, devices, and characters.*

The plot of each of Shirley's plays—even to some degree those of The Arcadia and of The Opportunity—represents a combination of materials from various sources.
As is shown in Chap. V, Shirley had no scruples about
revising the plots which he borrowed.  He not only changed

their catastrophes to suit himself, but introduced new episodes, new incidents, new devices, new characters and new
characterizations.  These are new only in the sense that
they are the playwright's addition, for in fact they often
have many parallels in earlier plays.  With scarcely an
exception the incidents added by Shirley tend further to
complicate the plot.  The new characters fall in love and
thus create new entanglements, and so on.  Only in The
Young Admiral do we find Shirley cutting down his original without introducing new complications in place of
the expunged incidents.  It is true that he substitutes comic
scenes for the unused passages, but they are very simple
in structure, and do not add anything to the main plot.
When there is no discoverable specific main source for the
plot of a play of Shirley's, we are justified in asserting that
he follows the same course, whether his original be merely
unknown or whether the plot be of his own invention.  The
same process of combining anew old and conventionalized elements with perhaps slight variations or reversals
of the characters concerned runs through all his plays from
Love Tricks to The Court Secret.  Let any play of Shirley's, save The Arcadia, be compared with fifty earlier
dramas, and the poet will be judged an arrant plagiarist.
Let, however, the Shirleian play be considered in its relations to the entire earlier Elizabethan drama, and its author will be seen in his true light as a conformer to things
as they were whose originality lies not in his material, but
in his use of it, and as a writer who preferred morality (in
the Caroline sense) and some degree of probability to originality and novelty.

Before proceeding to a detailed consideration of the situations, incidents, devices and characters in Shirley's plays,
there are some general characteristics which should be

discussed. They serve either to relate the plays as wholes
with the body of the Elizabethan drama, or to differentiate
them from it.

Eighteen of Shirley's plays, not including Chabot, have
scenes laid at court either in entirety or in part. This
number includes all the tragedies save The Maid's Revenge, all eight tragicomedies, and all the romantic comedies except The Brothers, and The Sisters, in the latter
of which a prince in disguise and a mock-court occur. The
nearest approach in the realistic comedies to a court setting
is the sham-court of The Constant Maid. However, pure
realistic comedy is never laid at court, and save in chronicle plays sovereigns seldom take part in genuinely comic
scenes.

The characters in the plays which deal with life at court
are appropriate to the setting. Sovereigns, courtiers and
court-ladies are among the chief figures. Personages of
rank or of distinctly good birth figure in all the plays
except The Wedding. The characters in that play, it must
be noted, are by no means of the lowest orders.

Shirley usually shows no especial regard for the
"divinity that doth hedge a King." Sciarrha in The
Traitor, III, 2, makes his preparations for putting the Duke
to death in spite of Amidea's recalling to him that person's rank. The attempted assassinations of The Politician, The Duke's Mistress, and The Imposture fail
because of genuine loyalty on the part of a conspirator,
not because of any trepidation engendered by the prospec-
tive victim's rank. Vittori in The Young Admiral, who
is loyal at heart, is independent. The Court Secret is
Fletcherian in the great respect shown by Manuel for
Prince Carlos' person, but even Manuel fights the Prince
of Portugal in the course of the play without any compunctions. There is very little approach in Manuel or any

other character of Shirley's to the abject loyalty of Amintor, The Maid's Tragedy, III, 1, of Valerio, A Wife for a Month, III, 3, or of Lucio, The Cruel Brother, V, 1.

What is practically a single plot is met with in several of Shirley's plays. The Maid's Revenge, The Politician, The Cardinal, The Royal Master, The Court Secret, The Humorous Courtier, and The Coronation have in reality only one action. In a number of the other plays the secondary plot is so closely interwoven with the main action and the characters of both are so closely connected that they are very nearly entitled to membership in the same group. The broadly comic scenes in Shirley are generally so very much subordinated to the more serious plot that often they need hardly be considered as forming a separate action. Frequently they are extremely episodic, as in The Bird in a Cage, and sometimes, as in The Court Secret, the characters figuring in them take an important part in the main action as well. We find but one comic scene in The Maid's Revenge, The Traitor, and The Politician. There is one entirely comic scene and a humorous dialogue in another scene in Love's Cruelty. Only a portion of one scene in The Cardinal is devoted to comedy. The Coronation is nearly devoid of any low comedy. This comparative lack of a farcical sub-plot tends to unify the play, of course, and, generally speaking, a well unified plot is a characteristic of Shirley's.

As Ward says, Shirley "displayed in tragic as well as comic actions a curious presentiment of the modern theatrical principle that everything depends on the success of one great scene (*la scène à faire*)" (D. N. B., LII, 128). In evidence we may cite The Traitor, III, 3, Love's Cruelty, IV, 1, The Grateful Servant, IV, 2, The Example, III, 1.

The love element is sometimes very much subordinated in Shirley's plays, as in The Politician. In The Humorous

Courtier it is pretended love which is set to the front while genuine love is kept in the background. Rivalry in love is a prominent motive in most of the tragicomedies and some of the romantic and realistic comedies. Generally, in the first two classes the rivals are a prince or princess, and a mere gentleman or lady. The Young Admiral, The Duke's Mistress, The Court Secret, and The Opportunity are concerned with the love of a prince and a gentleman for the same lady. The last-named play also shows a princess and a lady as rivals for the hand of a private gentleman. In The Royal Master, and The Imposture we have a prince and a favorite as suitors to a princess. Two princely brothers are rivals for a lady's hand in St. Patrick for Ireland. Apparent or real disparity of birth used as an obstacle to love is found in The Royal Master, The Imposture, The Gentleman of Venice, The Bird in a Cage, and The Coronation. Disparity of fortune figures as a hindrance to love in several realistic comedies, as in The Wedding, The Witty Fair One, and Love in a Maze.

True love and lust are contrasted in The Traitor, Love's Cruelty, The Duke's Mistress, St. Patrick for Ireland, The Grateful Servant, The Arcadia, The Witty Fair One, Hyde Park, The Gamester, and The Example. In several of these, however, the contrast is not carried through the play or is perhaps more a contrast of character than of action, as in The Traitor. In The Example a contrast is furnished by the conversion of a rake in the middle of the play. St. Patrick for Ireland, The Witty Fair One, and The Gamester are the most Fletcherian in their presentation of the contrast.

Heroic love, the sort of love which to possess its object will go to any extreme of violent or unusual action, is most nearly approached in The Young Admiral, The Court Secret, and The Coronation. As a modification of heroic

love the renunciatory type of love as treated in the following chapter should be noted.   Closely connected with heroic
love are the conflicts of love and honor, love and friendship, and love and ambition.   These conflicts are not very
much emphasized by Shirley; he has frequently the opportunity for them, but generally does not utilize them.   Love
and honor enter into The Maid's Revenge, and The Young
Admiral, love and friendship into Love's Cruelty, and love
and ambition into The Opportunity, and The Coronation.

Inconstancy in love is not uncommon in Shirley's plays.
We have not only the lover who forsakes his mistress and
then returns to her to be forgiven and to be reconciled,
but also the corresponding female figure—the fickle mistress,—and the errant husband or wife.   The lovers who
leave one mistress temporarily for another or who hesitate
between two ladies but who return to their old loves or
definitely choose one lady are Cesario in The Young Admiral, the Duke in The Royal Master, Carlo in The Court
Secret, Alberto and Don Carlos (the latter of whom is
finally unsuccessful as is Aurelio in The Opportunity) in
The Brothers, the Duke in The Grateful Servant (a variation, as is Contarini in The Sisters), Arcadius in The Coronation, Thornay, Gerard, and Yongrave in Love in a Maze.
To their number Ferdinand in The Doubtful Heir may be
added, as far as his actions go; at heart he is faithful to
Rosania, even though he marries Olivia.

The fickle mistress is exemplified in Selina in Love
Tricks, Olivia in The Doubtful Heir, Maria in The Court
Secret, Estefania in The Brothers, the Duchess and Cornelia in The Opportunity, Sophia in The Coronation, Chrysolina in Love in a Maze, and Julietta in Hyde Park.   Possibly Berinthia's being won away from Velasco by Antonio
in The Maid's Revenge should be mentioned in this group,
but Shirley does not emphasize her previous regard for

Velasco. Certain of the characters above noted fall in this category as mistresses who merely transfer their love from one character to another. Selina, Maria, Estefania, Chrysolina, and Julietta are of this description.

The husband whose love for his wife is weakened for the time being by the charms of another lady is found in the persons of the King in The Politician, the Duke in The Duke's Mistress, Basilius in The Arcadia, Contarini in The Humorous Courtier, and Wilding in The Gamester. To these might be added the Duke in The Traitor (whose wife, a child of thirteen is mentioned *ibid.*, IV, 2) and Lodwick in The Grateful Servant whose infidelity is due to no particular lady. The Duke of Florence in the former play, it should be noted, is not finally reconciled with his wife.

The inconstant wife who finally returns to her husband is used four times by Shirley in uncollaborated plays, as Gynecia in The Arcadia, Mrs. Bonavent in Hyde Park, Lady Plot in The Example, and Lady Bornwell in The Lady of Pleasure. Lady Huntlove in the collaborated (?) Captain Underwit is a character of the same description. Mrs. Bonavent hardly belongs in this class since she remarries under the impression that her husband is dead. Clariana in Love's Cruelty, it must be remembered, is not won back by her husband.

Here then we have at least sixteen of Shirley's independent plays, to say nothing of one other in which he probably had a hand, which deal with errant affections that at last fix themselves upon the object to which they first were directed or that shift merely from one character to another. Not only do we have one case of this amorous instability in a single play, but even sometimes two or three, as in The Opportunity, The Coronation, or Love in a Maze.

Kingsley in Plays and Puritans has much to say concerning Shirley's immorality, which he asserts to be extreme. However, Kingsley has considered Shirley's plays apart from their own times and apart from the body of Elizabethan drama. In spite of his evident desire to make out a strong case against the Anglican priest turned papist and dramatist, Kingsley has actually missed the two really doubtfully moral plays—The Example and The Lady of Pleasure (Captain Underwit had not yet been connected with Shirley).

As a matter of fact, virtue is generally triumphant in Shirley's plays. When it is not, guilty and innocent fall together. Dramatic truth is sacrificed to the author's desire to reconcile his characters with virtue, as in the conversion of the Duke in The Duke's Mistress. In that play and in The Politician we find the wicked characters all receiving their just deserts while the virtuous live happily forever after. It is certainly true that assaults upon innocence play a large part in Shirley's plays; but it is true also that only in The Lady of Pleasure (if by any extreme of courtesy Lady Bornwell may be called innocent) does a woman yield to her desires without paying the penalty. Even she seems to suffer from her conscience. Lady Plot in The Example is ready to yield were she attacked, but she has at least a little excuse for her actions in Sir Solitary's mania. Lady Huntlove in Captain Underwit is another character of the same general sort. Clariana in Love's Cruelty and Marpisa in The Politician, who are both adulteresses, die after torturing mental struggles, one at the hands of her former paramour, the other by self-administered poison. Juliana in The Imposture, whose life has not been spotless, is sentenced to finish her days in a nunnery.

It cannot be denied that in some plays Shirley, like nearly every other Elizabethan dramatist, shows a certain moral

obtuseness or callousness.  Lodwick in The Grateful Servant, Contarini in The Humorous Courtier, and Cornari in
The Gentleman of Venice escape entirely too easily in every
way the consequences of their variations upon the situation of The Curious Impertinent.  Likewise, the horrible
effrontery of Wilding in The Gamester, who would have
his wife procure her kinswoman for him, certainly is not
adequately punished.  But in these four cases we must
remember that the characters mentioned believe themselves
cuckolds for a time and suffer accordingly.  Doubtless their
mental perturbation was made much more vivid on the stage
than it is in cold type to us.  Lady Bornwell suffers as a result of her transgression, but there seems no especial re-
gret on the parts of Lady Plot and Lady Huntlove for
their projected infidelity.

Shirley's habit of converting his wicked or licentious
characters (in tragicomedy and comedy) during the course
of a play has been mentioned before.  His young profligates do not (with the exception of Luys in The Brothers)
play various amusing but unexemplary pranks through a
comedy and make their final exits unsubdued and fortunate
besides.  His Fowlers and Lodwicks, unlike Fletcher's
Monsieur Thomases and Pinacs, finally are repentant.  Unconvincing as some of the conversions are, being purely
sops to the dramatist's conscience,[2] they are there in the
plays and the fact of Shirley's use of them forces their
consideration in any discussion of the dramatist's morality.

We find little grossness for its own sake in Shirley's
plays.  True, the discovery of Clariana and Hippolito in
bed in Love's Cruelty, IV, 1, is a strong situation even for
the Elizabethan stage, but it is not merely dragged in as
being *risqué*.  On the other hand, it heightens very much

[2] Malipiero, The Gentleman of Venice, V, 2, 4, Contarini, The
Humorous Courtier, V, 3.

the effect of Bellamente's surprise of the guilty couple, and thus serves an important theatrical purpose. In Love Tricks, II, 2, III, 1, old Rufaldo gloats over the charms of his youthful bride. If we compare these two passages with Mrs. Behn's Lucky Chance, I, 3, we can see what possibilities lay there, and can readily appreciate the discretion and decency of Shirley. Only in The Gentleman of Venice is a prostitute a character, and only in The Lady of Pleasure is a bawd introduced. Juliana in The Imposture has merely gone astray, and the Nurse in The Constant Maid is not a professional procuress. In none of the comedies (or any of the other plays) do we find even an approach to the utter vileness of thought and language of such a play as, for instance, The Parson's Wedding. Indeed in spite of occasional lapses (which are to be found in the plays of every Elizabethan dramatist) it cannot be said that Shirley was by any means consistently immoral in conception or gross in language.

Even in The Traitor or Love's Cruelty we find no such almost totally unrelieved atmosphere of lust and horror as we encounter in The Revenger's Tragedy, King Lear, The White Devil, Thierry and Theodoret, The Unnatural Combat, Women Beware Women, Albovine, and 'Tis Pity She's a Whore. The Traitor has the nobility of Cosmo (which is, however, a trifle dulled by his prudence), as a relief, and Love's Cruelty has a comparatively bright spot in the Duke's penitence and his proposed match with Eubella. The Cardinal, which is more consistently gloomy than any of the other tragedies, has lust merely as an incident, not as a motive.

For a writer who was evidently conversant with much of the earlier drama, and who wrote at a time when sensation of some sort was nearly the prime necessity in a play, Shirley has kept singularly clear of that element, as far as theatrical devices go.  We have indeed the old horror of kissing a corpse by mistake for a living woman in The Traitor.  Lorenzo's stabbing the Duke's picture in the same play is a bit of uncalled-for clap-trap.  Death by poison with its more or less gruesome accompaniments is introduced in The Maid's Revenge, The Politician, The Cardinal, and St. Patrick for Ireland.  Assassinations take place on the stage in The Maid's Revenge,[3] The Traitor, Love's Cruelty, and The Cardinal, and are attempted in The Politician, and The Imposture.  Duels are found in The Maid's Revenge,[4] The Cardinal, and The Court Secret. Deaths by violence are represented also in The Duke's Mistress, and St. Patrick for Ireland.  Murder in a masque occurs only in The Cardinal, although masques are introduced in The Maid's Revenge, and The Traitor.

Illicit relationships exist only in Love's Cruelty, The Politician, and The Lady of Pleasure, and in the last two plays they are not especially emphasized.  A sister in love with a brother is found in The Court Secret and The Coronation.  The same situation is made use of in The Opportunity.  In the first two plays the relationship is discovered or the love is transferred before the matter has gone too far, and in the last-named the relationship is not an actual one, but feigned.

Revenge, as a motive, plays an important part in The Maid's Revenge, The Traitor, Love's Cruelty, The Politician, and The Cardinal, and enters into The Duke's Mistress, and St. Patrick for Ireland.  The Cardinal, indeed, is strongly reminiscent of such plays as Hoffman, or Hamlet, for we have Columbo's revenge upon Alvarez, the revenge of Hernando and Rosaura upon Columbo and the Cardinal,

---

[3] A sister slays her brother while he sleeps.

[4] Two ladies, each of whom loves the other's brother, witness those same brothers engage in a duel which is fatal to one combatant.

and the revenge of the last upon them.  Single revenges
are found in the other plays mentioned above.

The family feud which is at the bottom of the action of
The Bloody Brother, and Thierry and Theodoret, for instance, is utilized by Shirley only in The Maid's Revenge,
The Gentleman of Venice, The Court Secret, and The Coronation.  In the last two plays it is the result of the
ignorance of the true identity of certain of the characters
involved.  Only in The Maid's Revenge does the feud assume anything like the proportions and the seriousness of
those in some earlier plays, and there, as well as in The
Gentleman of Venice, it is not laid at court.

Shirley possesses the fondness for surprises of the average dramatist of his time.  Usually, they are well handled.
Very seldom does he manage a sudden change in relationship as badly as the shift of Selina's affections from Rufaldo to Infortunio in Love Tricks.  After her passion for
the former has been emphasized, as it is, it is inadequate
in the extreme to introduce her without warning as having
fled from her father's house to avoid her impending marriage with Rufaldo.  Some of Shirley's other plays into
which surprise enters are The Traitor, Love's Cruelty,
The Politician, The Cardinal, The Duke's Mistress, St.
Patrick for Ireland, The Doubtful Heir, The Gentleman of
Venice, The Imposture, The Court Secret, The Brothers,
The Grateful Servant, The Bird in a Cage, The Coronation,
The Sisters, The Wedding, Hyde Park, The Gamester, The
Example, The Constant Maid.  The sudden changes in
some of these plays, like the conversion of Fitzavarice in
The Example, are more or less mechanical.  Nearly always
they are short cuts to the happy ending of the play (as
such devices often are).  Thus the discovery of Giovanni's
real parentage in The Gentleman of Venice removes the
only obstacle to his marriage with Bellaura.  Occasionally

the surprise is used with excellent effect and with considerable originality, as in Julietta's breaking her engagement to Trier because of the test to which he has subjected her (Hyde Park).[5]   Other circumstances of a novel nature (although not unparalleled) are the return of the Duke to the pursuit of Amidea in The Traitor, and the manner of the Cardinal's death in The Cardinal.  Most frequently resurrections, repentances, and the explanation of actions as trials of one quality or another are Shirley's favorite means of injecting the unexpected into a play.

Shirley was fond of introducing deliberate contrasts of character; and sometimes he has done it very effectively. Berinthia and Catalina in the first four acts of The Maid's Revenge illustrate very well this practice of the dramatist's. Often the contrast is almost too obvious to be really striking.  Thus the Duke and Cosmo in The Traitor, or Marpisa and Albina in The Politician, are too nearly the exact opposites of each other.  As further examples of this Fletcherian device we may cite Eubella and Clariana, Sebastian and Bovaldo in Love's Cruelty, Domitilla and Theodosia in The Royal Master, Rosania and Olivia in The Doubtful Heir, Conan and Corybreus in St. Patrick for Ireland, Giovanni and Thomazo in The Gentleman of Venice, Manuel and Carlo in The Court Secret, the Duke and Lodwick, or Foscari and Lodwick in The Grateful Servant, Ursini and Aurelio in The Opportunity, Polidora and Sophia, Seleucus and Arcadius in The Coronation, Angelina and Paulina in The Sisters, Aimwell and Fowler in The Witty Fair One, Yongrave and Thornay in Love in a Maze, Beaumont and Wilding in The Gamester, Lady Peregrine and Lady Plot in The Example, and Celestina and Lady Bornwell in The Lady of Pleasure.

[5] There is a somewhat remote analogue in The Humorous Lieutenant, IV, 8 (see under Hyde Park, V, 2).

The discussion of the leading motives of Shirley's plays might be continued indefinitely. It seems wisest, however, to halt at this point, after dwelling on some of their most striking characteristics, negative as well as positive, and to proceed in the following chapter to the consideration of the chief dramatic conventions which are met with in the plays.

# CHAPTER IV

## THE STOCK INCIDENTS, CHARACTERS, ETC., OF SHIRLEY'S PLAYS

In the preceding chapter, various leading motives and situations of Shirley's plays have been discussed. Certain of the points of contact between them and the Fletcherian group have been pointed out, such as the courtly setting, the preference for scenes from high life, the lack of definite connection of character and action with the life of the city, the use of surprises, and so on. In the present chapter many of the less important details of the plays will be considered with a view to showing their frequent use by Shirley himself and their true sources,—not in single plays but in many. In other words, the conventionalized elements which occur most frequently will be catalogued with their analogues in a roughly chronological order.[1]

[1] It should be explained that in the lists of Shirley's plays given in the present chapter and in the later ones the various tragedies, tragicomedies, etc., are grouped together and arranged in chronological order. The plays which, with or without reason, have been assigned to Shirley at one time or another, are also throughout the book arranged in chronological order. In the various lists of analogues, etc., the plays of each author are grouped together in approximately the order of production. Anonymous plays are inserted in their proper places among the various groups. For the dates of Beaumont and Fletcher's dramas, Thorndike, The Influence of Beaumont and Fletcher on Shakespeare, pp. 92-93, is the authority, while for the dates of the plays of the other dramatists, save Shirley, Schelling's List of Plays, Eliz. Dram., II, 538 ff. is the basis. The respective years of production which accompany

## A. STOCK INCIDENTS, ETC.

1. Women offer or confess their affection in word or act to the men whom they love without any advances or solicitation on the part of the latter in Shirley's Doubtful Heir, II, 4, The Arcadia, II, 1, The Coronation, I, 1, II, 3, III, 2, Love in a Maze, IV, 3. Cf. also The Example, II, 1, The Lady of Pleasure, III, 3, IV, 1, and note Hyde Park, V, 1, The Laws of Candy, III, 3, Captain Underwit, V, 1.

Cf. Sir Clyomon and Sir Clamydes, p. 511, The Arraignment of Paris, III, 2, Dido, Queen of Carthage, III, 4, IV, 2, The Birth of Merlin, III, 6, A Shoemaker a Gentleman, II, 3, A New Wonder: A Woman Never Vexed, II, 1, The Silver Age, I, 1, The Four Prentices of London, p. 77, The Fair Maid of the Exchange, pp. 31–32, 66, The Trial of Chivalry, I, 3, Jack Drum's Entertainment, IV, The Insatiate Countess, II, III, Every Woman in her Humor, II, 1, The Lovesick King, II, Northward Ho, IV, 1, The White Devil, V, 1, The Duchess of Malfi, I, 1, V, 2, A Cure for a Cuckold, IV, 2, The Isle of Gulls, II, 3, The Revenger's Tragedy, I, 2, All's Well that Ends Well, II, 3, Othello, I, 3 (reported), The Queen's Arcadia, V, 1, Monsieur Thomas, III, 1, Philaster, I, 2, Cupid's Revenge, I, 3, III, 2, The Captain, V, 4, The Honest Man's Fortune, IV, 1, V, 3, The Custom of the Country, III, 3, The Double Marriage, II, 3, The Sea Voyage, IV, 2, The Spanish Curate, V, 1, The Maid in the Mill, I, 3, The Fair Maid of the Inn, IV, 1, Bartholomew Fair, V, 2, The Hector of Germany, V, 4 (reported), More Dissemblers besides Women, IV, 2, The Partial Law, II, 1, The Maid of Honor, IV, 4, The Renegado, II, 4, The

certain plays are meant to call attention to the fact that they are contemporary with Shirley's dramas. All listed pieces after 1625 are not so distinguished, however.

Roman Actor, IV, 2, The Picture, III, 5, The Deserving
Favorite, III, 1, The Fool Would Be a Favorite, III, V
(1638), Love's Sacrifice, I, 1, 2, II, 4, Covent Garden, I,
6, Hannibal and Scipio, I, 2, Love Crowns the End, p. 15,
The Swisser, V, 3, The Costly Whore, IV, 3, The Ladies'
Privilege, IV, The Shepherds' Holiday, II, 5.

2. Pretended love is disclosed to men or to masquerading
women in The Doubtful Heir, IV, 2, The Lady of Pleasure, IV, 3, and The Constant Maid, I, 1.

Cf.   The Spanish Gipsy, IV, 1, Albovine, III, 1, Believe
as You List, IV, 2, The Court Beggar, II, 1, Tottenham
Court, IV, 3, A Challenge for Beauty, IV, 1.   Cf. Deloney's Jack of Newberry, Chap. I.

3. The making of love by one person on behalf of another is found in several of Shirley's plays.   A lover may
appoint a friend to address his mistress for him, or a lady
may deputize a person to advance her cause with the object
of her affections.   Occasionally, the love-agent acts on his
own initiative.   Courtship by proxy occurs in Love's
Cruelty, II, 2, IV, 2, The Royal Master, II, 1, The Arcadia,
II, 1, The Sisters, III, 2, Love in a Maze, III, 2, The
Example, I, 1.   Note also The Traitor, II, 1, The Arcadia,
1, 2, The Faithful Friends, II, 2, and see Section 5 following for a variation upon the incident.

Cf.   Fair Em, III, 1, James IV, II, 1, Edward III, II,
1, The Trial of Chivalry, I, 3, Every Woman in her Hu·
mor, II, 1, Englishmen for my Money, I, 1, Henry VI,
Part I, V, 3, The Merry Wives of Windsor, II, 2 (pre-
tended), As You Like It, III, 5, Much Ado about Nothing,
II, 1 (reported), The Death of Robert, Earl of Hunting-
ton, V, 1, Satiromastix, p. 219, The Fawn, I, 2, The Fair
Maid of the West, Part II, V, 1, A Challenge for Beauty,
IV, 1 (1635), The Lovesick King, II, Monsieur D'Olive,
III, 1, The Queen's Arcadia, II, 2, The Turk, I, 2 (pre-

tended), A Wife for a Month, I, 1, All's Lost by Lust, II, 1, Appius and Virginia, II, 1, The Lovesick Court, II, 1, Love's Sacrifice, I, 1, The Ordinary, III, 3 (1634), The Parson's Wedding, II, 2 (1635), The Combat of Love and Friendship, II, 2 (1636).

4. The renunciation by a lover of his mistress or vice-versa, accomplished or attempted, is found in The Traitor, I, 1, II, 2, IV, 2, The Doubtful Heir, III, 1, IV, 1, The Court Secret, III, 3, V, 2, The Grateful Servant, IV, 2, Love in a Maze, II, 2, The Gamester, IV, 2, The Constant Maid, IV, 2, Honoria and Mammon, V, 2. Cf. The Cardinal, II, 3. Renunciatory love which has as its aim the profit or advancement of its object is not unlike ''heroic love,'' but it does not involve the fate of dynasties or kingdoms, and is heroic in that it involves a violent struggle between selfishness and magnanimity in the lover's heart.

Cf. Campaspe, V, 4, Captain Thomas Stukeley, p. 161, Soliman and Perseda, IV, 1, Fair Em, I, 1, Friar Bacon and Friar Bungay, p. 166, The Two Gentlemen of Verona, V, 4, Edward IV, Part II, p. 130, The Fair Maid of the Exchange, p. 64, Every Woman in her Humor, III, 1, Monsieur Thomas, II, 5, The Mad Lover, V, 4, The Double Marriage, III, 3, The Maid of Honor, V, 2, The Bashful Lover, V, 2, The Lovesick Court, II, 1, Davenant's Siege, V, The Deserving Favorite, I, 1, The Fool Would Be a Favorite, IV (1638), Randolph's Amyntas, IV, 9, The Queen of Arragon, V, 1 (1640). For a pretended renunciation, see The Downfall of Robert, Earl of Huntington, I, 3.

5. Closely related to the subjects of the two preceding sections is the acting as a love-agent or messenger between two persons by a rival of one or the other. It may be, however, that the agent's love-affairs are only indirectly affected by his (or her) acting as a proxy. For examples, see The Grateful Servant, II, 2, The Sisters, III, 2, Love

in a Maze, II, 1, The Laws of Candy, III, 3, Phillis of
Scyros, II, 3.  Note here and in the analogues following
how this character overlaps the renunciatory lover.

Cf.  Friar Bacon and Friar Bungay, p. 165 (reported),
The Two Gentlemen of Verona, IV, 4, Twelfth Night, I,
4, The Fair Maid of the West, Part II, V, 1, Hymen's
Triumph, II, 4 (reported), The Sea Voyage, IV, 2, The
Maid of Honor, III, 3, The Partial Law, I, 3, The Ladies'
Privilege, I (1635).  Note also Montemayor's Diana, Bk.
II (the story of Felismena).

6. A pretense of love shown by one person for another
with the intention of deceiving, perhaps, not only the character towards whom the affection is simulated, but also
some eavesdropper, or a personage already on the stage, is
found in The Maid's Revenge, II, 2, The Cardinal, I, 2,
The Brothers, II, 1, The Arcadia, I, 2, II, 1, The Witty
Fair One, IV, 2, Love in a Maze, III, 1, V, 1.

Cf.  Endymion, II, 1, Mother Bombie, II, 3, The Jew
of Malta, II, 2, The Taming of the Shrew, II, 1, Wit at
Several Weapons, III, 1, IV, 2, The Roaring Girl, I, 1,
II, 2, Women Beware Women (Isabella for the Ward),
More Dissemblers besides Women, II, 1, III, 2, A Fine
Companion, III, 5, The Fool Would Be a Favorite, I (1638)
(a lady, surprised with her lover, pretends to repulse him,
thus reversing the incident).

7. The comic situation of a man making love in all
seriousness to another man who is disguised as a woman,
or whom he mistakes for a woman, is utilized in Love
Tricks, IV, 1, V, 1, 3, The Arcadia, II, 1, etc., Love in a
Maze, III, 1, etc., The Noble Gentleman, IV, 3, 5, The
Nightwalker, II, 2.  In Love Tricks and Love in a Maze,
a gull marries the supposed woman.

Cf.  The Wars of Cyrus, II, George-a-Greene, p. 268,
The Merry Wives of Windsor, V, 5, The Two Angry Women

of Abington, IV, 3, Englishmen for My Money, V, 2, What You Will, V, 1, The Wise Woman of Hogsdon, III, 1, V, 4 (a girl disguised as a boy and redisguised as a girl), The Isle of Gulls, II, 3, etc., Epicœne, II, 3, etc., The New Inn, V, 1 (an apparent boy disguised as a girl who proves indeed to be a girl), Amends for Ladies, V, 2, Monsieur Thomas, V, 3, ·The Loyal Subject, III, 3, The Humorous Lieutenant, IV, 4, 6, V, 2 (effects of a love-potion), The City Wit, V, The Hollander, V, 1 (1633).

8. The lady who falls in love with another lady who is disguised as a man (a reversal of the situation treated in Section 7) figures in The Sisters, IV, 4, and No Wit, No Help Like a Woman's, V, 1. In the Doubtful Heir, III, 1, IV, 2, Olivia pretends love for Rosania who is disguised as a page.

Cf. Gallathea, II, 1, III, 1, etc., James IV, V, 1, 5, As You Like It, III, 5, Twelfth Night, I, 5, III, 1, A Christian Turned Turk, p. 239 (reported), Hymen's Triumph, I, 4, The Widow, III, etc., The Lover's Melancholy, I, 3, II, 1, III, 2, Love's Riddle, II, 1 (1635), A Mad Couple Well Matched, II, 1 (1636), The Antiquary, IV, 1 (1635). A woman pretends love for a woman in a masculine disguise in Anything for a Quiet Life, III, 1.

9. Attempts at seduction which are indignantly resisted by the woman, often with one or more set speeches in praise of chastity, were popular with Shirley, as noted in a preceding chapter. Defenses of chastity resulting from the advances of male characters occur in The Traitor, III, 3, Love's Cruelty, II, 2, IV, 2, The Politician, I, 1, The Cardinal, V, 3 (preliminary to an attempted rape), The Young Admiral, IV, 3, The Duke's Mistress, III, 3, IV, 1, V, 1, St. Patrick for Ireland, II, 1, The Grateful Servant, V, 1, Hyde Park, V, 1, The Lady of Pleasure, V, 1, The Faithful Friends, II, 2, IV, 4. In The Royal Master, V, 2, is a

pretended attempt at seduction and in The Gamester, I, 1, III, 1, is a pretense by a lady of yielding to the solicitations of a man. Cf. The Wedding, V, 2.

Cf. The Wars of Cyrus, II, James IV, II, 1, Henry VI, Part III, III, 2, Measure for Measure, II, 4, Pericles, IV, 6, Cymbeline, I, 6, Edward III, II, 1, 2, George-a-Greene, p. 257, Lust's Dominion, III, 2, V, 3, Grim, the Collier of Croydon, IV, 1, The Death of Robert, Earl of Huntington, V, 1, The Case is Altered, V, 3, Volpone, III, 6, Catiline, II, 1, The Mayor of Queenborough, III, 2, A Fair Quarrel, III, 2, A Game at Chess, II, 1, The Weakest Goeth to the Wall, I, 3, The Blind Beggar of Bednal Green, IV, 2, Law Tricks, III, 2, How a Man May Choose a Good Wife from a Bad, p. 39, The Wise Woman of Hogsdon, I, 2, The Honest Whore, Part II, IV, 1, The Witch of Edmonton, I, 1, Match Me in London, II, The Atheist's Tragedy, IV, 3, The Revenger's Tragedy, II, 1, Westward Ho, II, 2, Appius and Virginia, II, 1, Amends for Ladies, IV, 1, V, 1, The Triumph of Honor, Sc. 2, The Coxcomb, III, 3, Valentinian, I, 1 (reported), 2, II, 6, The Loyal Subject, IV, 3, The Knight of Malta, I, 1 (reported), III, 4, The Humorous Lieutenant, IV, 1, 5, The Custom of the Country, III, 5, The Little French Lawyer, III, 3, V, 1, The Maid in the Mill, III, 3, The Fair Maid of the Inn, III, 1, A Wife for a Month, I, 1, Rule a Wife and Have a Wife, V, 5, The Second Maiden's Tragedy, I, 2, The Poor Man's Comfort, II, IV, The Hector of Germany, IV, 5, V, 3, All's Lost by Lust, II, 1, The Heir, IV, The Duke of Milan, II, 1, The Parliament of Love, II, 3, Believe as You List, V, 2 (reported), The Bashful Lover, III, 3, The City Nightcap, I, 1, IV, 1, Love's Sacrifice, II, 1, 3, The Fancies Chaste and Noble, III, 3, The Lady's Trial, II, 4 (1638), The Swisser, III, 3 (1631), Holland's Leaguer, III, 4 (1632), A Fine Companion, II, 1 (1633), The Jealous Lovers, III,

10 (1632), Albertus Wallenstein, I, 3, III, 3 (1634–38),
Osmond, the Great Turk, II (1638), The Distresses, I, 1
(1639?), The Queen of Arragon, IV, 1 (1640), The Distracted State, II, 1 (1641).

Pretended defenses of virtue occur in The Second
Maiden's Tragedy, V, 1, and The City Nightcap, II, 1.
Pretenses of yielding to the solicitations of a man are found
in All's Well that Ends Well, IV, 2, Measure for Measure,
IV, 1 (reported), The Little French Lawyer, V, 1.

10. More or less wicked characters, usually men of a
loose manner of living, announce their penitence for their
past misdeeds and their intention of reforming in Love's
Cruelty, II, 2, IV, 2, The Duke's Mistress, V, 4, The Gentleman of Venice, V, 2, 4, The Grateful Servant, V, 1, 2,
The Arcadia, IV, 3, The Witty Fair One, V, 3, Hyde Park,
V, 1, The Gamester, V, 2, The Example, III, 1, The Lady
of Pleasure, V, 1, Honoria and Mammon, V, 2, A Yorkshire Tragedy, Scs. 4, 10, Love's Pilgrimage, IV, 3, Chabot,
V, 2, Captain Underwit, V, 4. A penitence which is only
temporary occurs in The Traitor, III, 3, and pretended
conversions in The Cardinal, V, 3, and The Imposture,
II, 1.

Cf. Damon and Pythias, p. 98, A Looking-glass for
London, James IV, V, 6, The Wars of Cyrus, II, III, Edward I, p. 409 ff., Look About You, Sc. 33, The Two Gentlemen of Verona, V, 4, Richard II, V, 3, Henry IV, Part
II, V, 2, As You Like It, V, 4, Measure for Measure, V, 1,
Pericles, IV, 5, 6, Cymbeline, V, 5, The Winter's Tale, V,
1, 3, Edward IV, Part II, p. 165, The Iron Age, Part II,
III, 1, The Fair Maid of the West, Part II, III, 1, A
Woman Killed with Kindness, I, 3, IV, 6, The Wise Woman
of Hogsdon, V, 4, The Case is Altered, V, 4, Every Man
out of his Humor, III, 2, The Staple of News, V, 2, How
a Man May Choose a Good Wife from a Bad, p. 74, A

Warning for Fair Women, II (p. 325 ff.), The Downfall of
Robert, Earl of Huntington, V, 1, The Death of Robert,
Earl of Huntington, I, 3, III, 4, V, 1, 2, The Malcontent,
IV, 5, Eastward Ho, V, 1, The Thracian Wonder, III, 2,
The Revenger's Tragedy, IV, 4, The London Prodigal, V, 1,
The Old Law, V, 1, The Honest Whore, Part I, II, 1, V, 2,
Westward Ho, IV, 2, The Witch of Edmonton, I, 1, V, 2,
Match Me in London, V, The Gentleman Usher, V, 1, A
Mad World, My Masters, IV, 4, A Chaste Maid in Cheap-
side, V, 1, A Trick to Catch the Old One, V, 2, The Witch,
IV, 2, V, 3, The Widow, III, 2, The Spanish Gipsy, I, 3,
Women Beware Women, V, 1, Amends for Ladies, V, 1,
The Triumph of Honor, Sc. 4, The Coxcomb, V, 2, The
Maid's Tragedy, IV, 1, The Captain, V, 1 (reported), The
Honest Man's Fortune, IV, 2, The Bloody Brother, V, 1,
The Queen of Corinth, IV, 4, V, 4, The Loyal Subject, IV,
3, V, 7, The Knight of Malta, III, 4, The Humorous Lieu-
tenant, IV, 5, The Custom of the Country, III, 5, The Little
French Lawyer, V, 1, The Pilgrim, IV, 2, The Prophetess,
IV, 2, V, 3, The Spanish Curate, V, 2 (sic; 3 in reality),
A Wife for a Month, V, 3, Rule a Wife and Have a Wife,
V, 3, 5, The Miseries of Enforced Marriage, V, The Hog
hath Lost his Pearl, I, 1, The Second Maiden's Tragedy,
II, 1, The Duchess of Malfi, IV, 2, A Match at Midnight,
V, 1, The Fatal Dowry, IV, 4, The City Madam, V, 3, The
Duke of Milan, III, 3, The Maid of Honor, V, 2, The Par-
liament of Love, V, 1, The Renegado, IV, 1, The Picture,
IV, 4, Believe as You List, V, 2 (reported), The Guardian,
III, 6, A Very Woman, III, 3, The Bashful Lover, IV, 2,
The Bloody Banquet, IV, 3, The Old Couple, IV, V, Love's
Sacrifice, II, 4, V, 2, The Lady's Trial, V, 1 (1638), The
Swisser, IV, 2 (1631), Holland's Leaguer, III, 4 (1632),
Albertus Wallenstein, I, 3, III, 3 (1634–38), The Lady
Mother, V, 2 (1635), The Hollander, V, 1, (1635), The

Costly Whore, V, 1 (1633), News from Plymouth, V, The
Fair Favorite, V, 1, The Queen, V, The Conspiracy, IV, 1,
V, 1, Messallina, II, 1 (1637), The Noble Stranger, V
(1638).

A temporary penitence occurs in Edward III, II, 2, but
a second conversion takes place (II, 2); see also The False
One, IV, 3. For pretended repentances, see The Insatiate
Countess, III, The Double Marriage, I, 2, A Wife for a
Month, IV, 1, The Late Lancashire Witches, IV, 1.

11. In The Maid's Revenge, V, 3, and St. Patrick for
Ireland, III, 1, characters die from poisoning in agonies
which are expressed through their exclamations and outcries (in the latter play the character is revived by a
miracle).

Cf. Henry VI, Part II, III, 2, 3 (not directly represented), King John, V, 7, The Jew of Malta, V, 1, The
Massacre at Paris, I, 3, The Brazen Age, p. 248 ff., The
Revenger's Tragedy, III, 4, Lingua, V, 15, The Devil's
Charter, IV, 3, V, 4, Thierry and Theodoret, V, 2, Valentinian, V, 1, 2, A Wife for a Month, IV, 4 (the character
finally recovers), The White Devil, V, 3, The Duke of
Milan, V, 2, 'Tis Pity She's a Whore, IV, 1, Love's Sacrifice, V, 3, The Distracted State, IV, 1 (1641). Cf. the pretended sufferings from poisoning in Alphonsus, Emperor
of Germany, IV, 2, and note Otho and the burning crown,
Hoffman, I.

12. Comparatively peaceful deaths from poison are
found in The Politician, V, 2, and The Cardinal, V, 3.
There is, at least, little or no direct indication of pain in
the lines of the dying character.

Cf. Romeo and Juliet, V, 3, Hamlet, V, 2, King Lear,
V, 3, The Death of Robert, Earl of Huntington, I, 3, V, 1,
Bonduca, IV, 4, Valentinian, V, 8, The Duchess of Malfi,
V, 2, The Bloody Banquet, V, 1, Women Beware Women,

V, 1, The Lost Lady, V, 1 (1637?) (supposedly poisoned).

13. What is considered poison or as producing death but which proves really to be a sleeping-draught is employed in The Arcadia, IV, 3, and The Bird in a Cage, V, 1.

Cf. Romeo and Juliet, V, 3, Cymbeline, IV, 2, How a Man May Choose a Good Wife from a Bad, p. 59, Satiromastix, p. 255, Match Me in London, III, The Fair Maid of Bristow, IV, 3, The Fleire, V, The Puritan, IV, 3, The Turk, II, 1, The Knight of the Burning Pestle, IV, 4, The Triumph of Love, Sc. 8, The Knight of Malta, IV, 2, A Chaste Maid in Cheapside, V, 4, The Lovesick Court, V, 3, The Swisser, V, 3 (1631), The Costly Whore, V, 1, The Shepherds' Holiday, V, 2 (1634), Cartwright's Siege, V, 4 (1637). Some additions are made to this list by Adams, Introduction to The Turk, p. xx.

14. For the sake usually of providing an appropriate setting for a serious and romantic or sentimental action Shirley has laid the following scenes in prisons: The Doubtful Heir, II, 3, V, 2, The Court Secret, II, 4, V, 2, The Arcadia, V, 1, The Example, IV, 3 (an undersheriff's house), The Gamester, IV, 2, Honoria and Mammon, V, 2. The Court Secret, V, 1, as well as The Arcadia, V, 1, is more or less comic. Also Dick of Devonshire, III, 2, IV, 2, is laid in a prison.

Cf. Sir Clyomon and Sir Clamydes, p. 507, Tamburlaine, Part II, I, 2, Edward II, V, 5, Lust's Dominion, V, 4, 5, Henry VI, Part I, II, 5, Part III, IV, 6, V, 6, King John, IV, 1, Richard III, I, 4, Richard II, V, 5, Much Ado about Nothing, IV, 2, Twelfth Night, IV, 2, Measure for Measure, II, 3, III, 1, IV, 2, 3, Cymbeline, V, 4, The Winter's Tale, II, 2, Sir Thomas More, IV, 4, V, 3, The Wounds of Civil War, III, 2, Thomas, Lord Cromwell, V, 5, Antonio's Revenge, V, 2, Sir Thomas Wyat, pp. 36, 56 ff., The Honest Whore, Part II, V, 2, The Atheist's Tragedy.

III, 3, The Revenger's Tragedy, III, 2, 3, A Woman Killed
with Kindness, IV, 2, If You Know Not Me, You Know
Nobody, Part I, p. 210 ff., The Puritan, I, 4, etc., The
Travails of the Three English Brothers, p. 75, Humor out
of Breath, IV, 3, Byron's Tragedy, V, 1, The Dumb Knight,
V, 1, Greene's Tu Quoque, p. 563, The Fleire, V, Philaster,
V, 2, A King and No King, IV, 2, V, 2, The Two Noble
Kinsmen, II, 1, Sir John Van Olden Barnavelt, III, 4, 6,
The Double Marriage, II, 3, The Island Princess, II, 1,
The Devil is an Ass, V, 4, The Maid of Honor, IV, 3, The
Bondman, V, 2, The Renegado, IV, 3, V, 1, 6, 7, Believe as
You List, IV, 2, A Very Woman, V, 5, Appius and Vir-
ginia, V, 3, The City Nightcap, V, 1, The Martyred Soldier,
II, 3, III, 2, 3, A New Wonder: A Woman Never Vexed,
IV, 1, V, 1, The Queen's Exchange, V, 1, The Queen and
Concubine, II, 6, The Costly Whore, IV, 3, The Ladies'
Privilege, III, The Royal Slave, I, 1, The Goblins, III, 3,
IV, 2, V, 4, Brennoralt, I, 4, II, 1 (1639), The Sad One,
I, 1 (1640), Trapolin Supposed a Prince, III, 1, IV, 2,
V, 2, 5.

15. The test or trial of various qualities such as love
or chastity is found in The Traitor, II, 1, The Court Secret,
II, 1, The Brothers, V, 3, The Humorous Courtier, The Bird
in a Cage, IV, 2, Love in a Maze, III, 3, Hyde Park, V, 2,
The Gamester, II, 1, V, 2, The Example, IV, 1, The Lady
of Pleasure, IV, 3, The Constant Maid, III, 4, IV, 2,
Honoria and Mammon, I, 2, II, 2, The Faithful Friends,
II, 2, IV, 4, The Ball, IV, 3, Chabot, II, 2 (reported).
Shirley's trials usually consist of the broaching of some
proposition to a character in order to see how he receives
it, and thereby to estimate his, or her, love, virtue, etc.
The test may introduce additional complications into the
plot and also furnish a surprise, as in The Brothers, or
supply a comic scene or two, as in The Example (where it

is not far from the pretended test).   The entire Humorous
Courtier is a test of general uprightness.

Cf.   Campaspe, V, 4, The Woman in the Moon, II, 1,
etc., The Old Wives' Tale, p. 458, Captain Thomas Stuke-
ley, p. 244, Friar Bacon and Friar Bungay, p. 177, Look
About You, Sc. 10, The Iron Age, Part II, I, 1, The Royal
King and Loyal Subject, I, 1, etc., Love's Mistress, I, 1,
etc. (1634), A Challenge for Beauty, III, 1, V, 1 (1635),
The Taming of the Shrew, V, 2, All's Well that Ends
Well, IV, 3, Hamlet, III, 2, King Lear, I, 1, Macbeth,
IV, 3, Timon of Athens, How a Man May Choose a Good
Wife from a Bad, p. 24, An Humorous Day's Mirth, pp.
27, 30, The Widow's Tears, IV, V, The Downfall of Robert,
Earl of Huntington, II, 1, The Virtuous Octavia, III, 1,
The Old Law, V, 1, Satiromastix, p. 255, Match Me in
London, III, V, Blurt, Master-Constable, V, 3, Michaelmas
Term, V, The Roaring Girl, IV, 2, A Fair Quarrel, II, 1,
The Widow, III, 2, V, 1, The Revenger's Tragedy, II, 1,
IV, 4, The London Prodigal, I, etc., The Dutch Courtesan,
V, 1, Westward Ho, II, 3, The White Devil, V, 6, A Cure
for a Cuckold, I, 2, Law Tricks, I, 2, The Travails of
Three English Brothers, p. 74, The Dumb Knight, II, 1,
Greene's Tu Quoque, p. 570, The Woman Hater, V, 5,
Thierry and Theodoret, II, 2, The Knight of the Burning
Pestle, III, 1, The Maid's Tragedy, II, 1, The Honest
Man's Fortune, I, 3, The Loyal Subject, III, 6, The Knight
of Malta, III, 4, The Custom of the Country, I, 1, Women
Pleased, V, 2, The Spanish Curate, V, 2 (sic; 3 in reality),
The Second Maiden's Tragedy, I, 2, The City Madam, V, 3,
The Duke of Milan, I, 3, The Emperor of the East, III, 4
(a test in name), The City Nightcap, I, 1, III, 1, The Just
Italian, V, 1, The Deserving Favorite, II, 1, V, 1, Osmond,
the Great Turk, I (1638), The Noble Soldier, II, 2, III, 3
(1631), A New Wonder: A Woman Never Vexed, IV, 1,

The Jealous Lovers, II, 10, III, 10, IV, 8, Covent Garden,
V, 3 (1632), Tottenham Court, IV, 3 (1633), Microcosmus,
V (1634), The Queen, IV, The Novella, IV, 1 (1632), The
Costly Whore, V, 1, The Hollander, V, 1, The Ladies'
Privilege, V (1635), The Lady Mother, III, 1 (1635), The
Combat of Love and Friendship, II, 4, V, 4 (1636), The
Lost Lady, IV, 1 (1637), Messallina, I, 1, III, 1 (1637),
The Amorous War, V, 7, 8 (1639), Imperiale, III, 2. See
also under The Humorous Courtier. In Cymbeline, I, 4, a
trial of virtue is set under way which is later complicated
with a pretended test (see Sect. 16).

16. Sometimes a character admits that what has passed
for a test has not been one in reality, and perhaps more
frequently the excuse offered for performing some action
is that it has been a test or trial of some quality.[2]  These
pretended tests occur in The Traitor, III, 3, The Court
Secret, I, 1, III, 3, The Arcadia, IV, 3, The Gamester, V, 2,
The Example, III, 1, The Ball, III, 4, No Wit, No Help
Like a Woman's, V, 1.

Cf.  Captain Thomas Stukeley, p. 231, Lust's Dominion,
I, 1, V, 3, Every Man in his Humor, III, 2, Sir Giles
Goosecap, III, 1, Measure for Measure, III, 1, Cymbeline,
I, 6, Henry VIII, V, 3, Fortune by Land and Sea, III, 4
(sic; 2 in reality), Your Five Gallants, II, 1, The Widow,
I, 2, Law Tricks, III, 2, V, The Second Maiden's Tragedy,
I, 1, Valentinian, II, 6, The Island Princess, IV, 2, The
Picture, IV, 3, The Deserving Favorite, IV, 1, The New
Academy, V, 1.

17. Trials in courts of various sorts figure in The Doubtful Heir, II, 4, The Arcadia, V, 2, The Wedding, V, 2,
The Gamester, V, 2, The Constant Maid, V, 3, The Laws

[2] The distinction between the real and pretended test is a very fine
one. This should be borne in mind in connection with this convention.

of Candy, I, 2, Dick of Devonshire, II, 5, IV, 3, V, 1, The
Lovers' Progress, V, 3, Chabot, III, 2, V, 2, The Variety,
V, 1.   The trials, which are generally utilized for the de-
livery of one or more set speeches, range from courts in
which the judge is a sovereign, as in The Doubtful Heir,
down to hearings before a justice of the peace, as in The
Wedding.   In several of the plays mentioned above, complications are disentangled during the progress of the trial.
For the mock trial, see under The Traitor, III, 1.

Cf.   Gammer Gurton's Needle, V, 2, The Arraignment
of Paris, IV, 1, The Spanish Tragedy, III, 6, Soliman and
Perseda, V, 2, The Comedy of Errors, I, 1, Henry VI, Part
II, I, 3, II, 3, Richard II, I, 1, The Merchant of Venice,
IV, 1, Much Ado About Nothing, IV, 2, Measure for Meas-
ure, II, 1, V, 1, Othello, I, 3, Timon of Athens, III, 5,
Coriolanus, III, 3, The Winter's Tale, III, 3, Henry VIII,
II, 4, A Warning for Fair Women, II (p. 315), The Iron
Age, Part I, V, 1, If You Know Not Me, You Know No-
body, Part II, p. 205 ff., The Royal King and Loyal Subject,
V, 1, Every Man in his Humor, V, 1, Sejanus, III, 1, Vol-
pone, IV, 2, V, 6, 8, Catiline, V, 6, The Old Law, V, 1, If
This be Not a Good Play, the Devil Is in It, p. 314 ff., How
a Man May Choose a Good Wife from a Bad, p. 78, Sir John
Oldcastle, V, 10, The Weakest Goeth to the Wall, V, 3,
Antonio's Revenge, IV, 2, 3, The Fawn, V, Eastward Ho,
IV, 1, The Insatiate Countess, IV, Sir Thomas Wyat, p.
51 ff., The White Devil, III, 1, The Devil's Law-case, IV, 2,
Appius and Virginia, IV, 1, The Atheist's Tragedy, V, 2,
The Revenger's Tragedy, I, 2, The Fair Maid of Bristow,
V, 1, The Phœnix, III, 1, Michaelmas Term, V, 3, Byron's
Tragedy, V, 1, Philotas, IV, 2, The Fleire, V, The Woman
Hater, V, 1, Love's Cure, V, 3, Philaster, V, 2, 3, The Cox-
comb, V, 3, The Beggar's Bush, III, 3 (comic), The Bloody
Brother, III, 2, The Queen of Corinth, V, 4, The Knight of

Malta, V, 2, Sir John Van Olden Barnavelt, III, 4, 6, IV, 5,
V, 1, Women Pleased, II, 5, The Spanish Curate, III, 3, The
Fair Maid of the Inn, III, 2, Ram Alley, V, 1, The Poor
Man's Comfort, III, V, The Fatal Dowry, I, 2, The Un-
natural Combat, I, 1, The Bondman, V, 3, The Renegado,
IV, 2, The Parliament of Love, V, 1, The Roman Actor,
I, 3, The Great Duke of Florence, V, 3, Believe as You List,
II, 2, The City Nightcap, II, 1, III, 1, The Queen's Ex-
change, V, 1, The Queen and Concubine, I, 9 (reported),
II, 1, The Antipodes, III, 6, 7 (1638), The Ladies' Privi-
lege, IV, The Lady Mother, V, 2, The Goblins, V, 5, Tra-
polin Supposed a Prince, I, 2, Imperiale, III, 6.

18. Masques or entertainments are presented more or
less elaborately in Love Tricks, V, 3, The Maid's Revenge,
IV, 3, The Traitor, III, 2, The Cardinal, III, 2, The Ar-
cadia, I, 3, The Coronation, IV, 3, Love in a Maze, V, 5,
Hyde Park, V, 2, The Constant Maid, IV, 3, The Faithful
Friends, IV, 3, The Nice Valor, II, 1, The Ball, V, 1, No
Wit, No Help like a Woman's, IV, 2. Some elements of
the antimasque are found in The Grateful Servant, IV, 4.

Cf. The Spanish Tragedy, I, 3, Doctor Faustus, II, 2
(the seven deadly sins), Love's Labor's Lost, V, 2, A Mid-
summer Night's Dream, V, 1, Timon of Athens, I, 2, The
Winter's Tale, IV, 4, The Tempest, IV, 1, Henry VIII, I, 4,
The Golden Age, II, 1, An Humorous Day's Mirth,
p. 43, May-Day, V, 1, The Widow's Tears, III, 2, The
Gentleman Usher, I, 1, II, 1, Every Woman in her
Humor, V, 1, The Death of Robert, Earl of Huntington,
II, 2, Satiromastix, p. 253, The Whore of Babylon, p.
204, The Sun's Darling, II, 1, V, 1, The Wonder
of a Kingdom, IV, 1, Blurt, Master-Constable, II, 2, Your
Five Gallants, V, 2, The Changeling, IV, 3, Antonio
and Mellida, V, Antonio's Revenge, V, 5, The Malcontent,
V, 3, The Dutch Courtesan, IV, 1, Sophronisba, I, 1, The

Insatiate Countess, II, Histriomastix, III, 1, Cynthia's Revels, V, 3, The Revenger's Tragedy, V, 3, The Maid's Tragedy, I, 2, The Two Noble Kinsmen, I, 1, Valentinian, V, 8, The False One, III, 4, Women Pleased, V, 3, The Prophetess, V, 3, A Woman is a Weathercock, V, 2, The Duchess of Malfi, IV, 2, The Hector of Germany, V, 5, The City Madam, V, 3, The Picture, II, 2, The City Night-cap, IV, 1, Fuimus Troes, III, 7, 'Tis Pity She's a Whore, IV, 1, Love's Sacrifice, III, 4, The Lover's Melancholy, III, 3, The Broken Heart, V, 2 (revels), Perkin Warbeck, III, 2, The Fancies Chaste and Noble, V, 3 (1635), The Costly Whore, II, 2, The Lady Mother, V, 2, Hannibal and Scipio, II, 5 (a sort of entertainment), The Floating Island, III, 4, The Royal Slave, V, 5, Cartwright's Siege, V, 8, Alphonsus, Emperor of Germany, III, 1, Messallina, V, 1 (1637), The Obstinate Lady, IV, 3 (1638–39), Trapolin Supposed a Prince, II, 2, Osmond, the Great Turk, II (1638) (indicated by a stage direction), Imperiale, IV, 4, The Amorous War, III, 2 (1639).

To the above may be added the following masques in which Cupid is a character (see under The Coronation, IV, 3): The Fawn, V, Byron's Tragedy, I, 1, Women Beware Women, V, 1, More Dissemblers besides Women, I, 3, The Maid in the Mill, II, 2, A Wife for a Month, II, 6, The Courageous Turk, I, 4, 5, The Court Beggar, V, 2, The Antipodes, V, 11. Cupid also figures in the masques in Cynthia's Revels, and Timon of Athens.

19. A not uncommon incident in Shirley's comedies is the wit-combat between a young woman and the suitor whom she secretly favors, but whom she perversely delights in tormenting. The wit-combat is closely related to ''jeering'' (see Section 20), into which it sometimes degenerates, as in Hyde Park. The only distinctions that can be drawn, and they are not infallible, are the facts that the partici-

pants in the wit-combat meet on equal ground socially and mentally, and that furthermore the lady generally capitulates to her suitor and adversary at the end of the play. Also, the wit-combat often extends over several scenes, and even sometimes monopolizes one of the plots of a play.[3] Shirley has matches of this sort in The Witty Fair One, Hyde Park, The Gamester, The Example, and The Lady of Pleasure. See also The Ball, and Captain Underwit.

Cf. Love's Labor's Lost, As You Like It, Much Ado About Nothing, The Fair Maid of the Exchange, A Challenge for Beauty (1635), Law Tricks, Humor out of Breath, The Woman's Prize, Monsieur Thomas, The Scornful Lady, The Captain, Wit Without Money, The Little French Lawyer, The Wild Goose Chase, Amends for Ladies, The Miseries of Enforced Marriage, All's Lost by Lust, A Cure for a Cuckold, The New Inn, The Lady Mother, A Mad Couple Well Matched, The Combat of Love and Friendship (1636), The Lost Lady (1637?), The Queen of Arragon (1640).

20. "Jeering" is understood in this section as referring to a quarrel between two persons, usually of opposite sexes, in the course of which one character applies to the other a series of grotesque or scurrilous terms. Sometimes both the parties to the conversation (for there are but two, usually) malign each other equally. When a lady takes part in such a scene she is usually the victor. As has been mentioned in Section 19, the wit-combat sometimes overlaps this grotesque and often brutal raillery. Shirley introduces passages of the sort described above in The Duke's Mistress, III, 2, IV, 1, V, 3, The Bird in a Cage, II, 1, III, 1, The Sisters, I, 2, II, 2, The Witty Fair One, IV, 4, Love in a Maze, IV, 2, Hyde Park, II, 4, III, 2, V, 1,

[3] Hence, it does not seem worth while to give references to act and scene.

The Lady of Pleasure, III, 2.   See also The Ball, I, 2, II, 3, III, 4, No Wit, No Help like a Woman's, IV, 2 (the masque), Captain Underwit, IV, 3, The Variety, III, 1, IV, 1.

Cf. Lust's Dominion, V, 5, Richard III, I, 3, Henry IV, Part I, II, 4, Part II, II, 4, Much Ado about Nothing, I, 1, II, 1, Troilus and Cressida, II, 1, 3, III, 3, V, 1, King Lear, II, 2, Timon of Athens, I, 1, II, 2, IV, 3, Coriolanus, II, 1, The Iron Age, Part I, V, 1, The Fair Maid of the Exchange, p. 73, Jack Drum's Entertainment, IV, The Dutch Courtesan, IV, 1, Cynthia's Revels, IV, 1, Epicœne, III, 2, The Staple of News, II, 1, IV, 1, V, 2, Law Tricks, II, The Woman's Prize, IV, 3, Wit at Several Weapons, III, 1, IV, 2, The Woman Hater, II, 1, III, 1, Philaster, II, 2, The Scornful Lady, I, 1, III, 2, IV, 1, V, 1, The Captain, II, 2, III, 3, The Honest Man's Fortune, V, 3, Wit Without Money, IV, 4, 5, The Mad Lover, I, 1, The Humorous Lieutenant, IV, 5, The Little French Lawyer, III, 3, The Spanish Curate, V, 1, The Elder Brother, III, 5, IV, 4, A Trick to Catch the Old One, III, 4, The City Madam, II, 2, The Fatal Dowry, III, 1, The Duke of Milan, II, 1, The Renegado, III, 1, The Parliament of Love, II, 2, The Just Italian, III, 1, News from Plymouth, IV, V, The Queen, I, II, A Fine Companion, II, 4, The Ordinary, I, 2, The Lady Errant, I, 2, II, 2 (1635), The Royal Slave, II, 4 (1636), Wit in a Constable, II, 1, IV, 1 (1639), The City Match, II, 3 (1639).   The preceding list is not complete; only the more striking examples have been noted.

21. The description of a character, not as an individual, but as a member of a class, occurs in a number of Shirley's plays. Sometimes the descriptions are long; sometimes they are no more than a line in length. Irrespective of length, however, such passages—which generally are used to exhibit the author's wit—are based originally on the

popular character books of the early seventeenth century. Often the strong influence of this literary type is shown in the intrusion of the general type characteristics into what seems an attempt at a deliberately individual description of a personage. Shirley has utilized the methods of the character-books to a greater or less extent in Love Tricks, III, 5, The Politician, I, 1, The Sisters, IV, 2, The Wedding, I, 1, The Witty Fair One, I, 2, The Gamester, III, 3, The Example, I, 1, The Lady of Pleasure, I, 1, II, 2, III, 2, Honoria and Mammon, II, 2, Cupid and Death, pp. 349–50. See also The Faithful Friends, II, 2, The Nice Valor, I, 1, Dick of Devonshire, V, 1, Captain Underwit, I, 1, The Variety, I, 1, II, 1.

Cf. Nobody and Somebody, p. 288, Every Woman in her Humor, III, 1, Cynthia's Revels, II, 1, III, 2, Epicœne, I, 1, The Alchemist, I, 1, The New Inn, I, 1, IV, 2, The Magnetic Lady, I, 1, Twelfth Night, I, 3, May-Day, II, 1, All Fools, V, 1, Sir Giles Goosecap, I, 1, What You Will, III, 1, The Dutch Courtesan, I, 2, The Honest Whore, Part I, II, 1, Part II, I, 2, The Fleire, I, The Woman's Prize, II, 2 (Moroso), The Woman Hater, I, 3, II, 1, The Scornful Lady, I, 1, Wit without Money, II, 2, The Turk, II, 3, Ram Alley, IV, 1, The White Devil, III, 1, The Duchess of Malfi, I, 1, Appius and Virginia, III, 2, Love's Mistress, I, 1, A Challenge for Beauty, II, 1, All's Lost by Lust, II, 1, V, 3, The Parliament of Bees, Anything for a Quiet Life, I, 1, The City Wit, II, 3, The Northern Lass, IV, 1, The Sparagus Garden, III, 4 (1635), The Muse's Looking-glass, Covent Garden, V, 6 (1632), Holland's Leaguer, I, 1, II, 1, 5 (1632), The Parson's Wedding, I, 1 (1635), Argalus and Parthenia, II, 1, News from Plymouth, II, 1 (1635), Lady Alimony, II, 2 (1635), Cartwright's Siege, II, 2. See Adams' note, The Turk, p. 85.

22. Burlesque verses or bad verses used for comic effect

are introduced in Love Tricks, III, 5, IV, 1, The Humorous
Courtier, II, 2, IV, 1, The Bird in a Cage, IV, 2, The Witty
Fair One, III, 2, Love in a Maze, II, 2. Note Captain
Underwit, III, 2. These vary from what are apparently
parodies on the style of particular writers or schools of
writers to mere nonsensical poems composed by foolish
characters.

Cf. Endymion, IV, 2, Love's Labour's Lost, III, 1,
IV, 2, V, 2, A Midsummer Night's Dream, II, 1, V, 1,
As You Like It, III, 2, 3, Edward III, II, 1, Locrine, I, 2,
II, 3, Every Man in his Humor, I, 4, IV, 1, V, 1, Cynthia's
Revels, IV, 1, The Poetaster, III, 1, V, 1, Epicœne, II, 2,
Antonio's Revenge, III, 4, The Gentleman Usher, I, 1, A
Woman is a Weathercock, III, 3, The Spanish Gipsy, II, 1,
The Lover's Melancholy, III, 1, Love's Sacrifice, II, 1, 3,
The Seven Champions of Christendom, V.

23. In many early plays, particularly in tragedies of
revenge, as a sort of preparation, perhaps, for a serious
scene, characters were either discovered with books in their
hands or entered with them. Shirley has used this device
seriously on one occasion—The Doubtful Heir, V, 2.
Twice, however, his clowns appear with books and one of
them introduces the volume into his foolery. These burlesques occur in The Royal Master, II, 2, and St. Patrick
for Ireland, II, 1. See Honoria and Mammon, III, 1, for
a semi-comic use of books. Note The Lovers' Progress,
IV, 2 (serious), and The Variety, I, 1 (comic).

For the serious use of this device, cf. The Spanish
Tragedy, III, 13, Nobody and Somebody, p. 300, Titus
Andronicus, IV, 1, Henry VI, Part III, III, 1, Richard III,
III, 7, Hamlet, II, 2, Antony and Cleopatra, IV, 1 (a let-
ter), Edward IV, Part II, p. 162, Antonio's Revenge, II, 3,
A Shoemaker a Gentleman, III, 1, Every Man out of his
Humor, I, 1, Histriomastix, I, 1, Bussy D'Ambois, II, 1,

Cæsar and Pompey, IV, 1, V, 1, The Honest Whore, Part
II, I, 1, The Virgin-Martyr, II, 1, Law Tricks, I, 1, 2, The
Devil's Charter, IV, 1, V, 6, The Second Maiden's Tragedy,
IV, 4, The Duchess of Malfi, V, 5, A Cure for a Cuckold,
1, 2 (a letter), The Double Marriage, IV, 3, V, 2, The
False One, IV, 3, The Bloody Banquet, I, 4, III, 2, The
Maid of Honor, IV, 3, The Renegado, IV, 1, The Picture,
IV, 2, A Very Woman, IV, 2, The Bashful Lover, III, 1,
A Game at Chess, II, 1, The Raging Turk, V, 9, The
Courageous Turk, I, 5 (in a sort of masque), The Captives,
III, 1 (a letter), The City Nightcap, I, 1, Albovine, III, 1,
The Lovesick Court, II, 1 (a letter), May's Cleopatra,
III, 'Tis Pity She's a Whore, II, 2, The Lover's Melancholy,
II, 1, The Deserving Favorite, III, 1 (a letter), The
Queen, II (a letter), The Swisser, I, 2, Microcosmus, V,
The Floating Island, V, 8, The Royal Slave, I, 2 (1636),
Messallina, I, 1, II, 1 (1637).

For comic uses of the book, cf. Mother Bombie, I, 3, The
Birth of Merlin, III, 4, The Pilgrimage to Parnassus, II,
IV, The Return from Parnassus, Part II, I, 1, II, 3,
Monsieur Thomas, II, 3, The Humorous Lieutenant, IV, 5,
The Dumb Knight, III, 1, Greene's Tu Quoque, p. 543,
More Dissemblers besides Women, I, 2, The Antipodes, I, 6
(1638).

24. The ordinary supernatural elements of the Elizabethan drama are, with one exception, never used seriously
by Shirley. Ghosts are introduced only once—in St. Patrick for Ireland, IV, 2—and there they are not only coun-
terfeits but are used in a comic way. In The Nightwalker,
II, 1, 2, 4, III, 2, what are thought to be apparitions or
supernatural beings are really living personages. A more
or less comic ghost occurs in The Lovers' Progress, III, 5;
in IV, 2, he reappears, but seriously. Sharkino in The
Maid's Revenge, III, 2, Flavia in The Young Admiral,

IV, 1, Belinda in The Grateful Servant, IV, 4, 5, Bonamico in The Bird in a Cage, II, 1, the Banditti in The Sisters, III, 1, Caperwit in Love in a Maze, V, 5, Decoy in The Lady of Pleasure, IV, 1, are characters who pretend to occult knowledge. They are all masqueraders with the exception of Sharkino who is a fraud pure and simple. In each of these plays the fortune-teller, witch, demon, or conjurer takes part in comic scenes. The spirits, miracles, etc., in St. Patrick for Ireland, with the exception of the characters noted, are seriously used, however (for analogues, see under that play).

For false supernatural elements or for a comic use of them, cf. Gammer Gurton's Needle, II, 1, The Supposes, I, 2, The Old Wives' Tale, p. 455 ff., The Comedy of Errors, IV, 4, Henry VI, Part II, I, 2, 4, Antony and Cleopatra, I, 2, Mother Bombie, George-a-Greene, p. 261, Look About You, Scs. 25, 27, The Blind Beggar of Alexandria, pp. 1, 4, The Wise Woman of Hogsdon, II, 1, etc., The Puritan, IV, 2, The Woman Hater, III, 3, Thierry and Theodoret, III, 2, The Chances, V, 3, The Bloody Brother, IV, 2, The Mad Lover, V, 4, The Humorous Lieutenant, IV, 3, 4, The Custom of the Country, V, 2, Women Pleased, IV, 2, 4, The Fair Maid of the Inn, IV, 2, Rule a Wife and Have a Wife, V, 5, The Alchemist, Volpone, II, 1, The Spanish Gipsy, III, 2, A Game at Chess, III, 2, IV, 1, Albumazar, The City Madam, II, 2, The Fool Would Be a Favorite, IV, The Noble Stranger, IV. Jonson in Drummond's Conversations (Section XIII) is quoted as relating to the latter how he disguised himself as an astrologer and cozened a lady.

25. Cases of imaginary cuckoldom are introduced by Shirley in The Gentleman of Venice, V, 2, The Grateful Servant, V, 1, The Humorous Courtier, V, 1, The Gamester, IV, 1, etc., The Example, III, 1. Note also The Faith-

ful Friends, III, 3, Dick of Devonshire, III, 2. In each of these plays, save the last two mentioned, the husband, who has done, nevertheless, what he could to further the fancied illicit relations, suspects his wife of adultery, and suffers accordingly. In all he is convinced of the groundlessness of his suspicions and is reconciled with his wife.

For analogous *cocus imaginaires*, cf. An Humorous Day's Mirth, p. 38, Every Man in His Humor, II, 1, etc., Volpone, II, 3, The Devil is an Ass, V, 5, The Two Angry Women of Abington, V, 1, Grim, the Collier of Croydon, IV, 1, The Merry Wives of Windsor, II, 2, etc., Othello, III, 3, etc., Cymbeline, II, 4, The Winter's Tale, I, 2, etc., The Phœnix, I, 2, II, 2, A Mad World, My Masters, I, 2, The Family of Love, III, 3, The Witch, III, 2, Westward Ho, I, 1, V, 3, Northward Ho, I, 1, V, 1, The Fawn, II, 1, The Insatiate Countess, III, The Dumb Knight, III, 1, V, 1, Amends for Ladies, II, 2, The Honest Man's Fortune, I, 2, The Knight of Malta, III, 2, The Spanish Curate, V, 2, The City Nightcap, I, 1, Albovine, IV, 1, The Cruel Brother, IV, 1, The Platonic Lovers, V, 1, Love's Sacrifice, IV, 1, The Broken Heart, II, 2, The Fancies Chaste and Noble, III, 3, The New Academy, V, 2, The Sparagus Garden, IV, 10, A Mad Couple Well Matched, IV, 4, The English Moor, IV, 5, The Antipodes, V, 1, The Emperor of the East, IV, 5, The Guardian, III, 6, The Queen, III, The Hollander I, 1.

26. Drinking scenes (i.e., scenes laid in a tavern or a private house in which at least one character becomes intoxicated or visibly affected by his potations) occur in Love's Cruelty, III, 1, The Politician, III, 3, The Royal Master, II, 2, The Gentleman of Venice, III, 4, The Imposture, V, 1, The Gamester, II, 2, Captain Underwit, IV, 1. Note The Faithful Friends, I, 2, The Nightwalker, II, 1, The Variety, IV, 1.

Cf. David and Bethsabe, p. 469, The Jew of Malta,

IV, 5, The Iron Age, Part I, I, 1, Fortune by Land and
Sea, I, 1, Henry IV, Part I, II, 4, III, 3, Part II, II, 4, V, 3,
Twelfth Night, II, 3, Othello, II, 3, Antony and Cleopatra,
II, 7, The Tempest, II, 2, III, 2, Every Man out of his
Humor, V, 4, Eastward Ho, III, 2, Bartholomew Fair,
IV, 3, The New Inn, III, 1, IV, 1, 2, The Gentleman Usher,
II, 1, The Coxcomb, I, 5, The Scornful Lady, II, 2, The
Captain, IV, 2, The Beggars' Bush, II, 3, Amends for
Ladies, III, 4, A Chaste Maid in Cheapside, III, 2, Albo-
vine, II, 1, Covent Garden, IV, 2 (1632), The Queen, III,
A Very Woman, III, 5, The Conspiracy, IV, 1 (1634), The
Hollander, IV, 1 (1635), The Lady Mother, II, 1 (1635),
Wit in a Constable, V, 1 (1639), The Royal Slave, III, 1
(1636), The Princess, IV, 4 (1637). Note also Rule a
Wife and Have a Wife, V, 5.

27. Deliberate or unintentional ambiguity of speech
which leads a character to a misinterpretation of the meaning of the remarks addressed to him plays an important
part in certain of Shirley's dramas.  Ambiguous statements which mislead those to whom they are directed
occur in The Cardinal, II, 1, The Court Secret, III, 2, The
Humorous Courtier, I, 1, IV, 2, The Coronation, IV, 2,
V, 2, Love in a Maze, IV, 2.

Cf.  The Jew of Malta, II, 2, Edward II, V, 5, The Two
Gentlemen of Verona, II, 1, Romeo and Juliet, III, 5,
Othello, IV, 1, The Golden Age, II, 1, Edward IV, Part I,
p. 64, A Challenge for Beauty, II, 1, An Humorous Day's
Mirth, p. 30, Every Man in his Humor, II, 1, The Two
Angry Women of Abington, I, 1, The Revenger's Trag-
edy, III, 3, The Insatiate Countess, II, A Mad World,
My Masters, I, 2, III, 2, The White Devil, I, 2, The City
Nightcap, I, 1, Love's Sacrifice, II, 3, The Antipodes, V, 2.

28. Very closely connected with the subject of Section 27
is the variety of double meaning which serves as a hint

to some one to act on. These are supposed to be understood only by the characters to whom they are addressed. The hint is liable often to overlap the deliberate ambiguity. The difference between the two, such as it is, lies in the intention of the speaker. The hint is purposed to be understood correctly by at least one person, while the ambiguous statement is to be misunderstood by all. Hints occur in The Imposture, II, 3, The Opportunity, III, 3, IV, 1, The Witty Fair One, I, 3.

Cf. Sapho and Phao, III, 4, The Birth of Merlin, II, 3, The Iron Age, Part I, I, 1, The Fair Maid of the Exchange, pp. 31–32, A Shoemaker a Gentleman, II, 3, Much Ado about Nothing, II, 3, Twelfth Night, II, 2, Julius Cæsar, III, 2, The Fawn, III, IV, May-Day, II, 1, The Isle of Gulls, II, 4, 5, The Family of Love, I, 2, The Widow, I, 2, The Dumb Knight, IV, 1, A Christian Turned Turk, p. 216, Wit without Money, IV, 4, V, 3, The Island Princess, V, 4, The Broken Heart, IV, 1.

29. The coming to life (or resurrection) of a person who has been thought dead is frequently employed by Shirley. Often this incident—or device, for it is nothing more—is used as a solution to the plot, as in The Wedding, V, 2. Sometimes, the "death" and subsequent revival is a trick, as in The Bird in a Cage, V, 1. Generally, however, it is the result of a false report, as in The Coronation, III, 2, V, 3. Nearly always it is more or less of a surprise to the audience. This incident is employed also in Love Tricks, V, 2, 3, The Politician, IV, 6, V, 2, The Duke's Mistress, V, 4, The Doubtful Heir, I, 1, V, 4, St. Patrick for Ireland, III, 1, V, 1, The Court Secret, V, 1, The Brothers, V, 3, The Grateful Servant, I, 2, II, 1, V, 2, The Arcadia, V, 2, The Sisters, V, 1, Hyde Park, IV, 3, V, 2, The Gamester, V, 2 (reported), The Constant Maid, V, 3, Honoria and Mammon, IV, 3. Note also The Faithful Friends, V, 2,

Dick of Devonshire, V, 1, Phillis of Scyros, IV, 4, The Nightwalker, II, 4, The Lovers' Progress, V, 2, No Wit, No Help like a Woman's, I, 3.

Cf. James IV, V, 6, Alphonsus, King of Arragon, II, The Jew of Malta, V, 1, King John, IV, 2, Romeo and Juliet, V, 3, Henry IV, Part I, V, 4, Much Ado about Nothing, V, 4, Twelfth Night, V, 1, All's Well that Ends Well, V, 3, Measure for Measure, V, 1, Hamlet, IV, 7, Othello, V, 2, Antony and Cleopatra, IV, 14, Pericles, III, 2, V, 1, 3, Cymbeline, IV, 2, V, 5, The Winter's Tale, V, 2 (reported), 3, The Tempest, V, 1, The Iron Age, Part II, V, 1, The Fair Maid of the West, Part I, V, 2, A Challenge for Beauty, V, 1 (1635), The Wisdom of Doctor Dodypoll, IV, 4, The Trial of Chivalry, IV, 1, V, 2, Hoffman, II, How a Man May Choose a Good Wife from a Bad, p. 59 ff., Every Woman in her Humor, IV, 1, The Case is Altered, V, 4, Volpone, V, 8, The Staple of News, IV, 1, The New Inn, V, 1, The Sad Shepherd, The Weakest Goeth to the Wall, V, 3, Jack Drum's Entertainment, II, V, Antonio and Mellida, V, What You Will, V, 1, The Malcontent, IV, 5, V, 3, The Dutch Courtesan, V, 1, The Maid's Metamorphosis, V, The Fair Maid of Bristow, IV, 3, Satiromastix, p. 255, The Old Law, V, 2, The Honest Whore, Part I, IV, 4, Westward Ho, V, 2, If This Be not a Good Play, the Devil Is in It, p. 345, Match Me in London, III, V, Grim, The Collier of Croydon, V, 1, The Atheist's Tragedy, III, 1, Michaelmas Term, V, 1, A Chaste Maid in Cheapside, V, 4, The Witch, V, 1, 3, The Spanish Gipsy, V, 3, Anything for a Quiet Life, V, 2, The Widow's Tears, V, 1, The London Prodigal, V, 1, The Puritan, IV, 3, The Blind Beggar of Bednal Green, III, 2 (sic; 3, in reality), Law Tricks, IV, [1], V, [1], Humor out of Breath, III, 4, The Fleire, V, A Woman is a Weathercock, V, 2, The Woman's Prize, V, 4, Thierry and Theodoret, V, 2, Monsieur Thomas,

V, 10, The Knight of the Burning Pestle, IV, 4, The Triumph of Death, Sc. 4, The Triumph of Love, Sc. 8, The Faithful Shepherdess, III, 1, V, 5, The Coxcomb, V, 3, The Scornful Lady, III, 1, The Captain, IV, 3, The Honest Man's Fortune, IV, 2, The Mad Lover, V, 4, The Knight of Malta, IV, 2, The Humorous Lieutenant, IV, 8, The Custom of the Country, V, 5, The Maid in the Mill, V, 2, The Fair Maid of the Inn, V, 1, 3, A Wife for a Month, V, 3, Hymen's Triumph, IV, 4, The Turk, II, 1, IV, 1, The Hog hath Lost his Pearl, IV, Albumazar, IV, Sicelides, V, 5 (reported), The Old Couple, V, The Heir, V, A Cure for a Cuckold, IV, 2, The Devil's Law-case, IV, 2, V, 6, Revenge for Honor, V, 1, The Lady Mother, V, 2 (1635), The City Nightcap, V, 1, The Parliament of Love, V, 1, Believe as You List, I, 2, The Emperor of the East, V, 3, The Guardian, V, 4, 'Tis Pity She's a Whore, V, 6, The Just Italian, V, 1, Love and Honor, V, 1 (1634), The Fair Favorite, V, 1 (1638), The Distresses, V, 1 (1639?), The Deserving Favorite, V, 1, The Fool Would Be a Favorite, IV, V (1638), The Partial Law, V, 4, The Swisser, III, 2, V, 3, Love Crowns the End, p. 26 (1632), The Jealous Lovers, IV, 4, The Costly Whore, V, 1, The Shepherds' Holiday, V, 2 (1634), The Conspiracy, V, 1 (reported), The Floating Island, V, 8 (1636), The Lost Lady, V, 1 (1637?), The Prisoners, V, 3 (1637), The Princess, V, 8 (1637–38), The Obstinate Lady, IV, 1, 4 (1638–39), Imperiale, IV, 4.

30. Shirley employs eavesdropping more frequently than does any other Elizabethan dramatist. Conspiracies are overheard, as in The Maid's Revenge, III, 1; deceptions are discovered, as *ibid.*, II, 2; love-affairs are straightened out, as in The Example, V, 3; misunderstandings arise, as in The Constant Maid, II, 3; and the device is used in a dozen other ways. Other instances of eavesdropping occur in Love Tricks, I, 1, III, 2, The Maid's Revenge, II, 5, V, 2,

The Traitor, III, 3, The Politician, I, 1, II, 1, The Cardinal, V, 3, The Royal Master, V, 1, The Doubtful Heir, III, 1, St. Patrick for Ireland, II, 1, IV, 1, V, 1, The Imposture, IV, 3, V, 2, The Court Secret, II, 2, The Grateful Servant, I, 1, II, 1, III, 1, V, 1, The Opportunity, II, 3, V, 2, The Sisters, II, 2, The Wedding, IV, 3, The Witty Fair One, II, 2, Love in a Maze, I, 1, IV, 2, The Gamester, I, 1, IV, 2, The Example, I, 1, The Lady of Pleasure, III, 2, The Constant Maid, II, 1, The Contention of Ajax and Ulysses, Sc. 2, Honoria and Mammon, III, 1, IV, 3, V, 1, 2. Thus, in twenty-two dramatic pieces certainly his, Shirley has employed eavesdropping forty-one times. Note also The Faithful Friends, II, 2, IV, 4, The Nice Valor, II, 1, The Noble Gentleman, III, 4, Phillis of Scyros, V, 4, The Ball, I, 2, II, 3, V, 1, The Lovers' Progress, III, 3, V, 3 (reported), Captain Underwit, V, 1, No Wit, No Help like a Woman's, III, 1, V, 1, Double Falsehood, II, 1.

Although the overheard conversation frequently is an important constituent of a dramatic plot, it is essentially a minor incident. Hence, it seems more judicious to summarize the results of the investigation of this stock device than to cite the two hundred or more analogues that exist.

Udall uses eavesdropping on 2 occasions; Gascoigne, 3; Edwardes, 2; Lyly, 2; Marlowe, 3; Peele, 1; Greene, 4; Kyd, 5; Shakespeare, 50; the Shakespeare Apocrypha, 7; Heywood, 10; Dekker, 8; Munday, 2; Chettle, 1; Jonson, 17; Haughton, 2; Porter, 2; Chapman, 14; Brewer, 1; Marston, 6; Middleton, 17; Tourneur, 1; Day, 5; Webster, 6; Yarington, 1; Daniel, 7; Sharpham, 1; Machin, 2; Field, 4; Beaumont and Fletcher, 49; Mason, 3; Wilkins, 1; Barry, 3; W. Rowley, 1; Cooke, 1; Tomkins, 1; Massinger, 31; Daborne, 2; Wentworth Smith, 2; Davenport, 3; P. Fletcher, 4; T. D., 3; May, 6; Goffe, 2; Fisher, 1; Glapthorne, 2; Davenant, 7; Ford, 10; Brome, 1; Randolph, 4; Carlell, 4; Wilson, 4; Tatham, 1; Marmion, 1; Cartwright, 3; Rutter, 2; T. Killigrew, 2; Strode, 1; Cokain, 2; Sharpe, 1; Richards, 2; Freeman, 1; Quarles, 1.  Twenty instances are to be found in some 13 anonymous plays also.

31. Shirley has surpassed every other Elizabethan in the common practice of introducing the titles of his plays into their text, usually toward the close of the piece.  Sometimes, too, he uses the title in the prologue or epilogue, and when it is a phrase descriptive of a leading character he often tags the name of that personage with it in the *dramatis personæ*. That the occurrence of the title in the body of the play is not accidental is shown by the fact that often it is capitalized or distinguished in some other way from the context.  This labelling of the respective plays is found in Love Tricks, V, 2, 3, epilogue, The Maid's Revenge, V, 3, The Traitor, I, 2, etc., The Politician, *dramatis personæ*, I, 1, IV, 5, V, 2, The Cardinal, prologue, etc., The Young Admiral, *dramatis personæ*, The Duke's Mistress, *dramatis personæ*, The Royal Master, IV, 2, V, 2, epilogue, The Doubtful Heir, prologue, The Gentleman of Venice, *dramatis personæ*, I, 1, The Imposture, III, 3, The Court Secret, V, 1, The Grateful Servant, V, 3, The Humorous Courtier, *dramatis personæ*, The Bird in a Cage, IV, 2 (the play within the play), V, 1, The Opportunity, IV, 1, V, 1, The Coronation, prologue, V, 3, epilogue, The Wedding, V, 2, The Gamester, *dramatis personæ*, The Example, prologue, III, 1, V, 3, epilogue.  Note The Nice Valor, IV, 1, epilogue, The Noble Gentleman, *dramatis personæ*, Dick of Devonshire, II, 4, etc., The Nightwalker, V, 2.  In twenty plays, then, Shirley uses the play-title in the body of the piece at least once.

As in the preceding section the results of the investigation of this practice will be summarized, not given in full.

Stevenson has 1 play in which the title is used in the text; Gascoigne, 1; Lyly, 1; Marlowe, 1; Peele, 2; Greene, 1; Nash, 1; Shakespeare, 3; the Shakespeare Apocrypha, 3; Heywood, 6; Dekker, 6; Jonson, 14; Haughton, 1; Chapman, 1; Brewer, 1; Marston, 8; Middleton, 10; Tourneur, 1; Day, 3; Webster, 2; Beaumont and Fletcher, 21; W. Rowley, 1; Cooke, 1; Massinger, 7; Davenport, 1; May, 2; Glapthorne, 2; Davenant, 2; Ford, 5; Randolph, 1; Carlell, 1; S. Rowley, 1; Nabbes, 2; Marmion, 2; Cartwright, 1; H. Killigrew, 1; Strode, 1; Cokain, 2; Sharpe, 1. To these may be added seven anonymous plays which belong to the general group.[4]

## B.   STOCK CHARACTERS

Many of Shirley's characters stand in the same relationship to the earlier drama as the incidents, etc., which have been discussed in the preceding pages of this chapter. They are familiar figures, but their familiarity is due, not so much to a resemblance to any particular character in an earlier play, as to a dozen or to a score or more of personages in as many plays. Therefore, as with the stock incident, analogues to Shirley's stock characters are given in order to emphasize that writer's dependence upon the work of his predecessors and contemporaries taken *en masse*.

32. The woman disguised as a man or boy is introduced in the persons of Selina in Love Tricks, Castabella in The Maid's Revenge, Rosania in The Doubtful Heir, Florelia in The Imposture, Leonora in The Grateful Servant, Pulcheria in The Sisters, Lucibel in The Wedding. In the

---

[4] It should be observed that the names of localities such as Hyde Park, or of persons, as King Lear, when occurring as play-titles, have not been considered with regard to their appearances in the text.

plays conjecturally or only partially Shirley's we have the disguises of Lelia in The Faithful Friends, the Mistress to the Mad Lord in The Nice Valor, Alathe in The Night-walker, Theodosia and Leocadia in Love's Pilgrimage, Mrs. Lowwater in No Wit, No Help like a Woman's, and Vio-lante in Double Falsehood. In all the plays mentioned above, those doubtfully Shirley's as well as those certainly his, all the disguises are for sentimental or pathetic effect, save those in The Imposture, The Nightwalker, and No Wit, No Help like a Woman's. A little foolery occurs as the result of the masquerading of the girls in Love's Pil-grimage, but it is purely incidental. Generally speaking, however, the girl as a page is a serious character in all the plays connected with Shirley's name, in which she figures.

Cf. Neronis in Sir Clyomon and Sir Clamydes, Phillida and Gallathea in Gallathea, Alexandra in The Wars of Cyrus, Dorothea in James IV, Julia in The Two Gentlemen of Verona, Portia, Jessica, and Nerissa in The Merchant of Venice, Rosalind in As You Like It, Viola in Twelfth Night, Imogen in Cymbeline, Perseda in Soliman and Perseda, the French Lady in The Four Prentices of Lon-don, the Second Luce in The Wise Woman of Hogsdon, Bess in The Fair Maid of the West, Part I, the Maid in A Challenge for Beauty, Laurentia in Englishmen for My Money, Mellida in Antonio and Mellida, Eurymine in The Maid's Metamorphosis, Franceschina and Theagine in May-Day, Charlotte in The Revenge of Bussy D'Ambois, Anabel in The Fair Maid of Bristow, Bellafronte and Infe-lice in The Honest Whore, Part I, Winnifrede in The Witch of Edmonton, Gelaia in Cynthia's Revels, Laetitia in The New Inn, Mariana in The Dumb Knight, Nan and Susan in The Fleire, Constantia in Ram Alley, Lady Ruin-ous in Wit at Several Weapons, Euphrasia in Philaster, Aspatia in The Maid's Tragedy, Urania in Cupid's Revenge, Clara in Love's Cure, Alinda and Juletta in The Pilgrim, Aminta in The Maid in the Mill, Maria in The Hog hath Lost his Pearl, Moll Cutpurse and Honor in Amends for Ladies, Silvia in Hymen's Triumph, Alizea in A Christian Turned Turk, Moll and Mary in The Roaring Girl, Martia in The Widow, Mrs. Cressingham in Anything for a Quiet Life, the "Page" and Amelia in More Dissemblers besides Women, Eugenia in The Duke of Milan, Maria in The Bashful Lover, Leucothoë in The Heir, Florabella and Lucina in The Partial Law, Eroclea in The Lover's Melancholy, Clarinda in The Deserving Favorite, Evrina in The Swisser (reported IV, 1) (1631), Martha in The Hollander (1635), Parthenia in Argalus and Parthenia, Machessa and Philaenis in The Lady Errant (1635), Lysimella in The Prisoners (1637), Cleanthe and Rosinda in The Obstinate Lady (1638–39), Claramante in The Distresses (1639?).

See also Howell's Familiar Letters, I, 317, II, 654, for accounts of ladies who assumed masculine disguises, the one to follow her sweetheart, the other her brother.

33. The subtle, courtly villain whose machinations form usually a considerable part of the action is personified by Shirley in the following: Lorenzo in The Traitor, Gotharus in The Politician, the Cardinal in The Cardinal, Leontio and Valerio in The Duke's Mistress, Montalto in The Royal Master, Flaviano in The Imposture, Roderigo in The Court Secret, Cassander in The Coronation. Note also Rufinus in The Faithful Friends, Gonzalo in The Laws of Candy, the Chancellor in Chabot. The intrigues of these characters, who are either near relatives or favorites of their respective sovereigns, usually have as motives love or ambition, sometimes both.

Cf. Carisophus in Damon and Pythias, Lorenzo and Viluppo in The Spanish Tragedy, Lorenzo in The First

Part of Jeronymo, Ateukin in James IV, Eleazar in Lust's
Dominion, Aaron in Titus Andronicus, Richard of Glou-
cester in Henry VI, Parts II, III, and Richard III, Angelo
in Measure for Measure, Edmund and Cornwall in King
Lear, Iago in Othello, Synon and Cethus in The Iron Age,
Part II, Stroza in A Maidenhead Well Lost, Prince John,
Warman, the Prior, and Sir Doncaster in The Downfall,
and The Death of Robert Earl of Huntington, Mendoza in
The Malcontent, Proditor in The Phœnix, Guardiano in
Women Beware Women, Horatio in Law Tricks, the Duke
of Epire in The Dumb Knight, Medice in The Gentleman
Usher, Muleasses in The Turk, Cæsar Borgia and Pope
Alexander in The Devil's Charter, Timantus in Cupid's
Revenge, Hempskirke in The Beggar's Bush, La Torch in
The Bloody Brother, Ronvere in The Double Marriage,
Septimius in The False One, the Governor in The Island
Princess, Aper in The Prophetess, Oswell in The Poor
Man's Comfort, Francisco in The Duke of Milan, Montre-
ville in The Unnatural Combat, Flaminius in Believe as
You List, Isaac and Cherseogles in The Raging Turk,
Philocres in The Partial Law, Hermegild in Albovine, Ga-
leotto in The Unfortunate Lovers, Stratocles in The Love-
sick Court, Iacomo in The Deserving Favorite, D'Avolos
in Love's Sacrifice, Lorenzo and Alexander in Alphonsus,
Emperor of Germany, Callidus in The Noble Stranger
(1638), Machville in The Rebellion.

Pairs of villains working together as do Leontio and
Valerio are found in the persons of Ganelon and Didier in
The Distracted Emperor, Bourbon and Roderick in The
Trial of Chivalry, Hoffman and Lorrique in Hoffman, Don
John and Borachio in Much Ado about Nothing, Borgias
and Eunuchus in The Turk, Theanor and Crates in The
Queen of Corinth, Mountferrat and Rocca in The Knight
of Malta, Mazeres and Roxano in The Bloody Banquet.

(For dignitaries of the church as villains, see under The Cardinal).

34. Sometimes the Machiavellian villain is not connected with a court, and his plots have nothing to do directly with politics. Velasco in The Maid's Revenge is Shirley's only representative of this type (note also Leon in The Lovers' Progress). He is, moreover, rather a tool or accomplice, like Valerio in The Duke's Mistress, than an originator of wickedness. Henrico in Dick of Devonshire (which is probably not Shirley's) is a good example of the class. The villain in private life is usually actuated by revenge, love, avarice, or ambition. His "Machiavellianism" does not concern itself with courts or affairs of state but with events of private life.

Cf. Barabas in The Jew of Malta (who is not a courtier), Merry and Falleria in Two Tragedies in One, D'Amville in The Atheist's Tragedy, Colax in The Queen's Arcadia, Lavall in The Triumph of Death, Luke Frugal in The City Madam, De Flores in The Changeling (who is the needy retainer of a great house, but whose machinations are confined to private life).

35. The thoroughly wicked unscrupulous woman is depicted by Shirley in Catalina in The Maid's Revenge, Clariana in Love's Cruelty, Marpisa in The Politician. Note also Clarinda in The Lovers' Progress, and Andromana in Andromana. All these characters are murderesses, and three are adulteresses. All are deliberate and cold-blooded criminals.

Cf. Guenevera in The Misfortunes of Arthur, Tamora in Titus Andronicus, Lady Macbeth in Macbeth, Goneril and Regan in King Lear, Cleopatra in Antony and Cleopatra, the Queen in Cymbeline, Dionyza in Pericles, Alice in Arden of Feversham, Artesia in The Birth of Merlin, Clytemnestra in The Iron Age, Part II, Elinor in The

Downfall of Robert, Earl of Huntington, the Duchess in
The Revenger's Tragedy, Florence in The Fair Maid of
Bristow, Timoclea in The Turk, Megra in Philaster,
Evadne in The Maid's Tragedy, Bacha in Cupid's Revenge,
Lelia in The Captain, Brunhalt in Thierry and Theodoret,
Zanthe in The Knight of Malta, Hippolyta in The Custom
of the Country, Violante in The Spanish Curate, the Coun-
tess in The Insatiate Countess, Lucretia in The Devil's
Charter, Vittoria in The White Devil, Beaumelle in The
Fatal Dowry, Beatrice in The Changeling, Livia and Bianca
in Women Beware Women, Rhodolinda in Albovine, Fior-
munda in Love's Sacrifice, the Queen in The Noble Soldier
(1631).

36. Berinthia in The Maid's Revenge, and Rosaura in
The Cardinal are driven to desperation by the injuries
done them and theirs and resort to crimes to gratify their
overwhelming desire for revenge. They and their analogues may be distinguished from those listed in Section
35 by the fact that they develop into criminals in the
course of the play while the latter are wicked at its very
opening. Theodosia in The Royal Master and Donabella
in The Imposture betray a depth of passion which might
easily lead to such criminality as that of the characters
first mentioned.

Cf. Gismunda in Tancred and Gismunda, Belimperia
in The Spanish Tragedy, Tamyra in The Revenge of Bussy
D'Ambois, Gabriella in The Triumph of Death, Edith in
The Bloody Brother, Martia in The Double Marriage, Caro-
pia in Revenge for Honor, Onaelia in The Noble Soldier
(1631).

The above analogous characters, it must be remembered,
in some cases approach the genuine wicked women of Section 35.

37. The Dukes in The Traitor, Love's Cruelty and The

Duke's Mistress, and the King in The Politician are lecherous tyrants whose lust has much to do in influencing the plots of the respective plays. The Duke in The Traitor, and the King in The Politician are weak, as well as lustful, while the Kings of The Cardinal and The Young Admiral, and the Duke in The Imposture are merely weak. Basilius in The Arcadia is lecherous but not tyrannical. Note Titus Martius in The Faithful Friends, and the King in Andromana. Usually the unworthy ruler, no matter from what source his unfitness arises, is dominated by an intriguing favorite, but this is by no means an invariable rule. Also, he is not necessarily a weak monarch.

Cf. Saturninus in Titus Andronicus, Richard III in Richard III, Claudius in Hamlet, Macbeth in Macbeth, Antiochus in Pericles, Henry III in Bussy D'Ambois, the Duke in The Revenger's Tragedy, the King in The Maid's Tragedy, Leontius in Cupid's Revenge, Wolfort in The Beggar's Bush, Valentinian in Valentinian, Rollo in The Bloody Brother, the Great Duke in The Loyal Subject, Antigonus in The Humorous Lieutenant, Clodio in The Custom of the Country, Ferrand in The Double Marriage, Frederick in A Wife for a Month, the Tyrant in The Second Maiden's Tragedy, Ferdinand in The Duchess of Malfi, the Duke in Women Beware Women, Albovine in Albovine, the Duke in The Cruel Brother.

38. The profligate young gentleman usually is wild rather than innately depraved, but occasionally he is both a villain and a debauchee. The type flourishes as well in tragedy as in comedy, although its proper place seems in a comic setting. Shirley's rakes include Hippolito in Love's Cruelty, Malipiero in The Gentleman of Venice, Lodwick in The Grateful Servant, Orseolo in The Humorous Courtier, Pisauro in The Opportunity, Luys in The Brothers, Fowler in The Witty Fair One, Lord Bonvile

in Hyde Park, Wilding and Hazard in The Gamester, Lord
Fitzavarice in The Example, Lord A. in The Lady of Pleasure. Note Marc Antonio in Love's Pilgrimage. It is
curious that nearly every one of the above reforms in the
course of the play.

Cf. Prince Henry in Henry IV, Parts I and II, Lucio
in Measure for Measure, Hippolito in Blurt, Master Con-
stable, Sebastian in The Atheist's Tragedy, Ilford in The
Miseries of Enforced Marriage, John Gresham in If You
Know not Me, You Know Nobody, Part II, Ricardo in The
Coxcomb, Young Loveless in The Scornful Lady, Valentine
in Wit Without Money, Rutilio in The Custom of the
Country, Mirabel in The Wild Goose Chase, Wellborn in
A New Way to Pay Old Debts, Ubaldo and Ricardo in The
Picture, Ferentes in Love's Sacrifice, Nick in The Weed-
ing of the Covent Garden, Careless in A Mad Couple Well
Matched, Wat in The Damoiselle, Asotus in The Jealous
Lovers, Careless in A Fine Companion, Ergasto in The
Lost Lady (1637?), Hipparchus in The Prisoners (1637),
Lorece in The Obstinate Lady (1638–39).

39. The rough blunt soldier is met with in Shirley's
Sforza in The Maid's Revenge, Aquinus and Reginaldus
in The Politician, Mauritio in The Young Admiral, and the
Captain in The Doubtful Heir. Pallante in The Duke's
Mistress possesses some of the characteristics of this type,
while Antonio in The Sisters has all the elements save the
military profession. As a rule, in the earlier drama especially, the blunt soldier, who is a faithful friend to the
hero, acts as a link between the main plot of the play, in
which he displays his courage and enlivens the dialogue
with rough wit, and the comic relief where he takes part
in more or less horse-play. Shirley, however, does not
emphasize all the typical sides of the character except perhaps in The Doubtful Heir. Note the merry young man

like Mercutio in Romeo and Juliet, as a related figure,
and observe that not all the analogous characters below are
soldiers.

Cf. the Bastard in King John, Kent in King Lear,
Enobarbus in Antony and Cleopatra, Menenius in Coriolanus, Downright in Every Man in his Humor, Martell
and De Vitry in Thierry and Theodoret, Dion and the
Old Captain in Philaster, Melantius in The Maid's Tragedy, Ismenus in Cupid's Revenge, Mardonius in A King
and No King, Jacomo in The Captain, Hubert in The Beggars' Bush, Dubois and Longueville in The Honest Man's
Fortune, Petillius in Bonduca, Pontius and Æcius in Valentinian, Hamond in The Bloody Brother, Theodore in The
Loyal Subject, Chilax in The Mad Lover, Norandine in
The Knight of Malta, Leontius in The Humorous Lieutenant, the Boatswain in The Double Marriage, Sceva in
The False One, Piniero in The Island Princess, Maximinian
in The Prophetess, Tibalt du Pont in The Sea Voyage,
Plenty in The City Madam, Romont in The Fatal Dowry,
Belgarde in The Unnatural Combat, Baltazar in The Noble
Soldier (1631), Timillus in Claricilla (1636), the Lieuten-
ant in The Princess (1637).

40. The witty young woman is represented by Hilaria
in Love Tricks, Aurelia and Macrina in The Duke's Mis-
tress, the Duchess and Laura in The Humorous Courtier,
Jacinta in The Brothers, Penelope and Violante in The
Witty Fair One, Carol in Hyde Park, Penelope in The
Gamester, Jacinta in The Example, Celestina in The Lady
of Pleasure. Note also the Lady in The Noble Gentle-
man, Lucina, Rosamond, and Honoria in The Ball, Alathe
in The Nightwalker, and the Sister in Captain Underwit.
Jane in The Wedding displays some relation with this type.
Note also the clever waiting-women: Flavia in The Young
Admiral, Sensible in The Witty Fair One, Scutilla in The

Ball, and Dorothy in Captain Underwit. The best examples of the clever, mischievous young lady occur in those plays in which she perversely lays counterplots against the schemes of her persistent, and rebuffed, but secretly favored, suitor. However, she may cut but a minor figure in the play, as in The Duke's Mistress.

Cf. Beatrice in Much Ado about Nothing, Rosalind in As You Like It, Aurelia in The Case is Altered, Violetta in Blurt, Master-Constable, Rossaline in Antonio and Mellida, Crispinella in The Dutch Courtesan, Hippolita and Violetta in The Isle of Gulls, Emilia in Law Tricks, Florimel in Humor out of Breath, Maria, Livia, and Bianca in The Woman's Prize, Oriana in The Woman Hater, Mary and Dorothea in Monsieur Thomas, Galatea in Philaster, the Lady in The Scornful Lady, Clora and Frank in The Captain, Lady Hartwell in Wit without Money, Calis, Cleanthe, and Lucippe in The Mad Lover, Celia (or Enanthe) in The Humorous Lieutenant, Lamira and Anabell in The Little French Lawyer, Oriana, Rosalina, and Lillia-Bianca in The Wild Goose Chase, Juletta in The Pilgrim, Estifania in Rule a Wife and Have a Wife, Lilly in The Elder Brother, Dionysia in All's Lost by Lust, Alphonsina in The Wonder of a Kingdom.

41. The woman disguised as a man is reversed several times by Shirley. A feminine disguise is assumed by Antonio and Gorgon in Love Tricks, Pandolfo in The Imposture, Pyrocles in The Arcadia, Morello in The Bird in a Cage, and Caperwit's Page in Love in a Maze. Note also Jacques in The Noble Gentleman. The man as a woman is always a comic figure, and usually an agent in some gulling plot.

Cf. Cupid in Gallathea, Stesias in The Woman in the Moon, Libanio in The Wars of Cyrus, Tom in Orlando Furioso, Wily in George-a-Greene, Flute in A Midsummer

Night's Dream (in the play within the play), the Page
in The Taming of the Shrew (induction), Falstaff and the
two Boys in The Merry Wives of Windsor, Robin Hood in
Look About You, Jupiter in The Golden Age, Hercules in
The Brazen Age, the Bishop of Ely in The Downfall of
Robert, Earl of Huntington, Walgrave in Englishmen for
My Money, Antonio in Antonio and Mellida, Pippo in
What You Will, Lucretio in May-Day, Snip in The Blind
Beggar of Bednal Green, Joculo in Law Tricks, Lisan-
der and Manasses in The Isle of Gulls, Justiniano in West-
ward Ho, Phylocles in The Dumb Knight, Thomas in Mon-
sieur Thomas, Welford in The Scornful Lady, Veramour
in The Honest Man's Fortune, Young Archas in The Loyal
Subject, Chilax in The Mad Lover, Lucio in Love's Cure,
the Page in Epicœne, Wittipol in The Devil is an Ass,
"Frank" in The New Inn (really a girl), Follywit in A
Mad World, My Masters, "Ansaldo" in The Widow (really
a woman), Bold, Frank, and Feesimple in Amends for
Ladies, Catso in The Poor Man's Comfort, Conchylis in
Sicelides, the Page in The Hector of Germany, Tibaldo in
The Wonder of a Kingdom, Gilla in The Lover's Melan-
choly, Popinjay in The Hollander (1635), Sabelli in The
Ladies' Privilege, Valentine in Wit in a Constable (1639),
Sir Timorous in The Floating Island (1636), the Boy in
Cartwright's Siege (1637), Young Gudgeon in The Fool
Would Be a Favorite (in a play within the play) (1638).

42. The avaricious old man who seeks to prevent a young
woman dependent upon him (daughter, niece, or ward)
from marrying the man of her choice and who often attempts to direct her affections to a suitor of his own selection is introduced by Shirley in Rufaldo in Love Tricks,
Don Carlos in The Brothers, Sir George Richley in The
Witty Fair One, Sir John Woodhamore in Love in a Maze,
Sir Richard Hurry in The Gamester (ostensibly), Hornet

in The Constant Maid. Rufaldo furthermore attempts to marry a young wife. The King in The Cardinal, it should be noticed, pushes Rosaura's match with Columbo. Note also the King in The Court Secret, the Duke in The Bird in a Cage (and Mrs. Goldsworth in Love in a Maze), as interfering in their daughter's love-affairs. In all of the plays in which the opposition to the lady's marriage is sincere, the officious old man (or woman) is outwitted and the true lovers are united.

Cf. Cleander in The Supposes, Gripe in Wily Beguiled, Curvetto in Blurt, Master-Constable, Sir Bounteous Progress in A Mad World, My Masters, Hoard and Lucre in A Trick to Catch the Old One, Russell in A Fair Quarrel (ostensibly), Lorenzo in May-Day, Corbaccio in Volpone, Richer Pennyboy in The Staple of News, Pandolfo in Albumazar, Bloodhound in A Match at Midnight. Certain of these characters are more especially misers, while some, like Rufaldo, are in search of a young wife. The list is not, by any means, a complete one.

For the attempts to regulate the affections of the young ladies in the above plays of Shirley's by the characters named, cf. The Two Gentlemen of Verona, A Midsummer Night's Dream, The Merry Wives of Windsor, Romeo and Juliet, Hamlet, Wily Beguiled, Englishmen for My Money, The Phœnix, The Changeling, Women Beware Women, The Duchess of Malfi, The Devil's Law-case, Match Me in London, Women Pleased, Wit at Several Weapons, The Knight of the Burning Pestle, A New Way to Pay Old Debts, 'Tis Pity She's a Whore, A Fine Companion, The Novella, The Hollander, Argalus and Parthenia, The Shepherds' Holiday, The Lost Lady. This is not intended as a complete list of analogues.

43. The comic old man, who is generally garrulous, and whose folly furnishes amusement for the other characters,

is only approximated by Shirley in Mercutio in The Opportunity. Certain elements of this type seem present in Rufaldo in Love Tricks, and Old Barnacle in The Gamester. There is a relationship between the representatives of this type and the blunt old man such as Antonio in The Sisters (who falls in another class). Note Dorilaus in The Lovers' Progress and Sanchio and Alphonso in Love's Pilgrimage as variants.

Cf. Capulet in Romeo and Juliet, Polonius in Hamlet, Calianax in The Maid's Tragedy, Alphonso in The Pilgrim, Miramont in The Elder Brother, and Durazzo in The Guardian as typical.

44. Very frequently Shirley's witty young woman is courted by one or more foolish suitors, generally under middle age, who act as foils to her cleverness and serve as butts to her and to the other characters of the play. Frequently their gulling is the theme of the subplot. Even where there is no especially brilliant female personage, however, the foolish male character often is introduced. Also, he is not invariably depicted as in love. He may be a man of rank, a gentleman, a citizen or a boor: whatever his station and breeding may be, to a certain extent he usurps the functions of the clown of the earlier drama. To this class belong Bubulcus in Love Tricks, Montenegro in The Maid's Revenge, Depazzi in The Traitor, Sueno and Helga in The Politician, Fabio in The Young Admiral, Thomazo in The Gentleman of Venice, Bertoldi in The Imposture, Don Pedro in The Brothers, Volterre in The Humorous Courtier, Morello, Dondolo, and Grutti in The Bird in a Cage, Rawbone in The Wedding, Venture and Rider in Hyde Park, Vainman and Pumicestone in The Example, Scentlove, Kickshaw and Littleworth in The Lady of Pleasure, Startup in The Constant Maid. Note Lamount, Travers, Bostock, and Barker in The Ball, and Lambstone,

Weatherwise, Pepperton, and Overdone in No Wit, No Help like a Woman's. (See under Section 44 following for additional examples.)

Cf. Ralph Roister Doister in Roister Doister, Armado in Love's Labor's Lost, Thurio in The Two Gentlemen of Verona, Slender and Shallow in Henry IV, Part II, Slender, Caius and Shallow in The Merry Wives of Windsor, Sir Andrew Aguecheek in Twelfth Night, Rosenkranz, Guildenstern and Osric in Hamlet, Roderigo in Othello, Cloten in Cymbeline, Peter Plodall in Wily Beguiled, Jerom in Hoffman, Rowl in An Humorous Day's Mirth, Innocentio and Giovanelli in May-Day, Simonides and the Courtiers in The Old Law, Young Strowd in The Blind Beggar of Bednal Green, Scilicet and Phylantus in Every Woman in her Humor, Balurdo and Castilio in Antonio and Mellida, Simplicius in What You Will, Puff and John Ellis in Jack Drum's Entertainment, Matthew and Master Stephen in Every Man in his Humor, Sogliardo and Fungoso in Every Man Out of his Humor, Asotus in Cynthia's Revels, La Foole and Daw in Epicœne, Kastrel in The Alchemist, Cokes in Bartholomew Fair, Pennydub, Muckhill and Tipstaff in The Puritan, Goosecap, Rudesby and Foulweather in Sir Giles Goosecap, Oliver in The London Prodigal, Petoune in The Fleire, Moroso in The Woman's Prize (advanced in years), Hylas in Monsieur Thomas, Cacafogo in Rule a Wife and Have a Wife, Sir Abraham and Frederick in A Woman is a Weathercock, Bubble and Scattergood in Greene's Tu Quoque, Wealthy in The Hog hath Lost his Pearl, Shallow in The Heir, Dotterel in The Old Couple, Graccho in The Duke of Milan, Sylli in The Maid of Honor, Asotus in the Bondman, Tim in A Match at Midnight, Ticket and Ruffit in The City Wit, Widgeon and Nonsense in The Northern Lass, Clotpoll in The Weeding of the Covent Garden, Swayne in The Court Beggar

(1632 or '40), Nehemiah in The New Academy, Tim and Tom Hoyden in The Sparagus Garden, Sir Amphilus in The Damoiselle (1637–38), Innocent Lambskin and Speedwell in A New Wonder: A Woman Never Vexed, Andrew in The Ordinary, Crackby and Sir Geoffrey in The Lady Mother, Shallow-wit and Holdfast in Wit in a Constable (1639), Gudgeon in The Fool Would Be a Favorite (1638), Pupillus in The Noble Stranger (1638), Timothy in The City Match (1639).

45. Often the gull or foolish suitor is attended by a servant as witless or as gullible as he, as Depazzi and Crispino in The Humorous Courtier, Lodam and Camelion in The Wedding, Treedle and his Tutor in The Witty Fair One, Simple and Thump in Love in a Maze, Young Barnacle and Dwindle in The Gamester. Note Sir Pergamus and Dindimus in The Faithful Friends, Freshwater and Gudgeon in The Ball, Underwit and Thomas in Captain Underwit.

Cf. Strumbo and Trompart in Locrine, Slender and Simple in The Merry Wives of Windsor, Tim and his Tutor in A Chaste Maid in Cheapside, Sir Gregory and Pompey in Wit at Several Weapons, Onos and his Tutor in The Queen of Corinth, Sancho and Soto in The Spanish Gipsy, Chough and Trimtram in A Fair Quarrel, The Ward and Sordido in Women Beware Women, Lothario and Borachio in The Cruel Brother, Bergetto and Poggio in 'Tis Pity She's a Whore, Capritio and Miscellanio in Holland's Leaguer (1632), Asotus and Ballio in The Jealous Lovers (1632), Dungworth, and Ralph and Dobson in Covent Garden (1632), Tub and Hilts in A Tale of a Tub (1633).

46. The clown was almost an essential figure in the earlier Elizabethan drama. Generally he was a servant, sometimes a fool or jester, sometimes he was a rustic, but always he was a member of the lower ranks of society.

In the later drama he is superseded to a considerable degree by either the foolish gentleman (who is often from the country), the parvenu citizen, or the poltroon. Consequently there are only six really well defined clowns in Shirley's plays. They are Pazzorello in The Young Admiral, Bombo in The Royal Master, Rodamant in St. Patrick for Ireland, Georgio in The Gentleman of Venice, Pimponio in The Opportunity, Piperollo in The Sisters. Note also Mochingo in The Laws of Candy, the Artizans in The Faithful Friends, Base and Galoshio in The Nice Valor, Jacques in The Noble Gentleman, Buzzano in Dick of Devonshire, Toby in The Nightwalker, Lancelot in The Lovers' Progress, Thomas in Captain Underwit, Pickadill in No Wit, No Help like a Woman's. It is worth observing that in the following lists the characters of this type who have no definite names occur chiefly in plays produced before 1615, and that the nameless clowns in plays after that date are the creation of dramatists whose first work was done before 1600.[5]

Cf. the Clowns (and Fools) in Titus Andronicus, All's Well that Ends Well, King Lear, Othello, Timon of Athens, Antony and Cleopatra, The Winter's Tale, A Lookingglass for London, Sir Thomas More, Doctor Faustus, The Wounds of Civil War, Nobody and Somebody, The Golden Age, The Four Prentices of London, The Rape of Lucrece,

[5] The clowns and similar comic characters in the Elizabethan drama have been exhaustively discussed by Eckhardt, Die lustige Person. See especially Part V, "Die Narren," and Part VI, "Die Clowns"; pp. 262-299, and 371-453 are of especial interest in connection with the list given above. For Shirley's clowns, etc., see particularly pp. 386 (Dametas), 398-400 (Pimponio, Bombo, Piperollo), 435-36 (Rodamant). It will be noted that Eckhardt does not consider Pazzorello or Georgio in his study. Also, his lists of the comic characters which are grouped above under the generic name "clown" differ from those here given.

Fortune by Land and Sea, The Captives, The English Traveller, A Maidenhead Well Lost (1633), Love's Mistress, A Challenge for Beauty, The Birth of Merlin, The Trial of Chivalry, The Thracian Wonder, The Pilgrimage to Parnassus, The Miseries of Enforced Marriage, If You Know Not Me, You Know Nobody, Parts I, II, Match Me in London, The Mad Lover, The Fair Maid of the Inn, The Bloody Banquet, Appius and Virginia, The Martyred Soldier, The City Nightcap, A New Wonder: A Woman Never Vexed, Lady Alimony (a Country Boor) (1637).

Cf. also Ambidexter in Cambyses, Subtle Shift in Sir Clyomon and Sir Clamydes, Tom Miller in Jack Straw, Adam in A Looking-glass for London, Ralph Simnell and Miles in Friar Bacon and Friar Bungay, Bullitbrumble in Selimus, Jenkin in George-a-Greene, La Fue in The Distracted Emperor, Piston in Soliman and Perseda, Costard in Love's Labor's Lost, the two Dromios in The Comedy of Errors, Speed and Launce in The Two Gentlemen of Verona, Quince, Bottom, Flute, Snout, Snug and Starveling in A Midsummer Night's Dream, Launcelot in The Merchant of Venice, the Servant, Sampson, Gregory, and Peter in Romeo and Juliet, Dogberry and Verges in Much Ado about Nothing, Touchstone in As You Like It, Feste in Twelfth Night, Thersites in Troilus and Cressida, the Cobbler, etc., in Julius Cæsar, Pompey in Measure for Measure, the Grave-diggers in Hamlet, the Old Shepherd in The Winter's Tale, the Porter in Macbeth, Trinculo, Stephano, and Caliban in The Tempest, the Friar, Jack and John in Edward I, Corebus in The Old Wives' Tale, Will Summer in Summer's Last Will and Testament, Trotter in Fair Em, Mouse in Mucedorus, Hodge in Thomas, Lord Cromwell, Puppy and Curtall in The Wounds of Civil War, Chub and Hobs in Edward IV, Part I, Socia in The Silver Age, Gallus in The Brazen Age, Thersites in The

Iron Age, Parts I, II, Fiddle in The Fair Maid of the
Exchange, Clem in The Fair Maid of the West, Parts I,
II, Cock in The Royal King and Loyal Subject, Stilt in
Hoffman, Will Cricket in Wily Beguiled, Haunce in The
Wisdom of Doctor Dodypoll, Dick Bowyer in The Trial of
Chivalry, Pipkin in How a Man May Choose a Good Wife
from a Bad, Much and Ralph in The Downfall of Robert,
Earl of Huntington, Much in The Death of Robert, Earl of
Huntington, Frisco in Englishmen for My Money, Coomes,
Hodge and Nicholas in The Two Angry Women of Abing-
ton, Barnaby in A Shoemaker a Gentleman, Babulo in Pa-
tient Grisel, Shadow in Old Fortunatus, Gnotho in The
Old Law, Plain Dealing in The Whore of Babylon, Scum-
broth in If This Be Not a Good Play, The Devil Is in It,
Bilbo in Match Me in London, Cargo in The Wonder of a
Kingdom, Swash in The Blind Beggar of Bednal Green,
Joculo and Adam in Law Tricks, Dametas in The Isle of
Gulls, Kemp in The Travails of Three English Brothers,
Grim in The Lovesick King, Passarello in The Malcontent,
Dondolo in The Fawn, Bunch in The Weakest Goeth to the
Wall, Frog in The Fair Maid of Bristow, Bassiolo in The
Gentleman Usher, Argus in The Widow's Tears, Dondolo
in The Revenger's Tragedy, Gumwater in A Mad World,
My Masters, Neatfoot in The Roaring Girl, President in
The Dumb Knight, Rabshake in A Christian Turned Turk,
Surdo and Catso in The Poor Man's Comfort, the Beggars
and Boors in The Beggar's Bush, Shorthose in Wit with-
out Money, Villio in The Double Marriage, Penurio and
Bomby in Women Pleased, Bobadilla in Love's Cure, the
Servant in The Wild Goose Chase, Geta in The Prophetess,
Bustopha in The Maid in The Mill, Tony in A Wife for
a Month, Trincalo in Albumazar, Cancrone and Serocca in
Sicelides, the Englishman and Frenchman in The Hector
of Germany, Ambler in The Devil is an Ass, Fly in The

New Inn, Jacques in All's Lost by Lust, Sim in A Match
at Midnight, Gazet in The Renegado, Calandrino in The
Great Duke of Florence, Hilario in The Picture, Berecinth-
ius in Believe as You List, Gothrio in The Bashful Lover,
the Dwarf in The Raging Turk, Rollano in Fuimus Troes,
Trollio in The Lover's Melancholy, Jeffrey in The Queen's
Exchange, Andrea in The Queen and Concubine, Cornego
in The Noble Soldier, Bromius and Mopsus in Randolph's
Amyntas, Scrub in Love Crowns the End (1632), Slip in
Tottenham Court (1633), Mopas and Bufo in The Queen,
Suckabus in The Seven Champions of Christendom, Trapolin in Trapolin Supposed a Prince. Observe that this type
is closely related to the gull (Sections 43 and 44), the
poltroon (Section 46) and the page (Section 47).

47. The gull, boor, or clown is usually a poltroon whose
cowardice supplies some of the comic passages in the plays
in which he figures. Bubulcus and Orlando Furioso in
Love Tricks, Montenegro, Depazzi (The Traitor), Sueno
and Helga, Fabio, and Pazzorello, the Citizens in The
Doubtful Heir, Bertoldi, Mendoza in The Court Secret,
Don Pedro, Depazzi (The Humorous Courtier), Morello,
Piperollo in The Sisters, Lodam, Rawbone, Young Barnacle, Rapture in The Example, Scentlove, Startup, Polybrontes in The Contention of Ajax and Achilles are Shirley's cowards. Note Lapet and the Gallant in The Nice
Valor, Jacques in The Noble Gentleman, Bostock in The
Ball, and Toby in The Nightwalker. There is no discrimi-
nation in regard to rank among the characters of this type.
The poltroon may be a nobleman like Don Pedro, a citizen
like Young Barnacle, or a servant like Pazzorello. The
type in its later form is a development of the earlier *miles
gloriosus*.

Cf. the poltroons already listed among the foolish personages, such as Roister Doister, Aguecheek, Daw, La

Foole, etc., with Sir Topas in Endymion, Huanebango in
The Old Wives' Tale, the Braggart in Nobody and Some-
body, Basilisco in Soliman and Perseda, Falstaff and Bar-
dolph in Henry IV, Parts I, II, and The Merry Wives of
Windsor, Pistol in Henry IV, Part II, Henry V, and The
Merry Wives of Windsor, Nym in Henry V, and The
Merry Wives of Windsor, Parolles in All's Well that Ends
Well, Bragadino in The Blind Beggar of Alexandria,
Quintiliano in May-Day, Bobadill in Every Man in his
Humor, Buffone in Every Man out of his Humor, Tucca
in The Poetaster, Tipto in The New Inn, Matzagente and
Balurdo in Antonio and Mellida, Herod in The Fawn,
Lazarillo de Tormes in Blurt, Master-Constable, Gullio in
The Return from Parnassus, Part I, Furor Poeticus in The
Return from Parnassus, Part II, Protaldy in Thierry and
Theodoret, Humphrey in The Knight of the Burning Pes-
tle, Nicodemus in The Triumph of Honor, Pharamond in
Philaster, Timantus in Cupid's Revenge, Bessus in A King
and No King, Lodovico and Piso in The Captain, Judas
in Bonduca, Timentes in The Swisser.

48. The clever page as a comic character had become
rare by 1625. He still was a figure on the stage, but he
seldom played any other part than that of a servant. Day
had expressed what was apparently the general sentiment of the dramatists, twenty or more years earlier,
when he said that pages were "clean out of the fashion,"
Law Tricks, IV, 1. Shirley's pages have very little to do
with the plots of the plays in which they appear, but in
one or two cases they recall the clever Boys of Lyly
and Shakespeare. His representatives of the type are
Jocarello in Love Tricks, Didimo in The Young Admiral, Celio in The Court Secret, Lysippus and Didymus in
The Contention of Ajax and Achilles, and the Pages in
Love's Cruelty, Love in a Maze, Hyde Park, The Gamester,

and The Example. Ascanio in The Opportunity is a clever boy, but not a page.

Cf. the Pages in Endymion, Campaspe, Sapho and Phao, Midas, Captain Thomas Stukeley, Selimus, The Taming of the Shrew, Timon of Athens, Jack Drum's Entertainment, The Fawn, The Malcontent, Eastward Ho, Blurt, Master-Constable, The Isle of Gulls, Law Tricks, Humor out of Breath, Lingua, The Return from Parnassus, Part II, The Poetaster (two "Pyrgi"), Epicœne, All Fools, Monsieur D'Olive, The Hector of Germany, The Queen of Corinth, The Mad Lover, The Fatal Dowry, The Maid of Honor, The Unnatural Combat, The Combat of Love and Friendship (1636).

Cf. the Boys in The Merry Wives of Windsor, Henry IV, Part II, Henry V, An Humorous Day's Mirth, The Two Angry Women of Abington, Every Woman in her Humor, Satiromastix, The Return from Parnassus, Part I, The Woman Hater, The Wild Goose Chase, Lady Alimony (1635).

Cf. Jack and Will in Damon and Pythias, Orgalio in Orlando Furioso, Moth in Love's Labor's Lost, Halfpenny and Lucio in Mother Bombie, Catso and Dildo in Antonio and Mellida, Bydett, Pippo, Phylus, and the other Pages in What You Will, Joculo, Frisco, and Mopso in The Maid's Metamorphosis, Snip in The Blind Beggar of Bednal Green, Joculo in Law Tricks, Bullaker, Jack and Will in Sir Giles Goosecap, Pantofle in The Turk, Veramour in The Honest Man's Fortune, Conchylio in Sicelides, Pacheco in Match Me in London, Allworth in A New Way to Pay Old Debts, Dorylus in Randolph's Amyntas, Paegnium in The Jealous Lovers (1632), Nitido in The Fancies Chaste and Noble (1635).

The above lists of pages, boys, etc., are not exhaustive,

but aim to include those characters of the general type who are more especially distinguished for wit, mischief, etc. For an interesting character of a page, see John Stephens the Younger's Essays and Characters, Bk. II, Character 24.

# CHAPTER V

## LOVE TRICKS AND THE MAID'S REVENGE

"The drama had become conventionalized. The dramatists were no longer searching for new themes and characters in a wide range of stories; they were inventing their plots, but were restricted in their materials. The ingredients of early plays served Shirley's purpose and by a few new devices or changes in motive he gave his fashionable ladies, his lustful monarchs, scheming favorites and exiled heroes new names and adventures, and so produced a play. The cleverness of the plot occupies your attention, or occasionally a beautiful passage or a fine conception of character arrests the mind" (Thorndike, Tragedy, p. 231).

What Professor Thorndike says of Shirley's tragedies is equally applicable to his comedies and tragi-comedies. From the array of parallel devices of one kind or another in the preceding chapter we see that certainly the drama had become conventionalized, and that out of these more or less hackneyed devices, grouped about several of the leading themes and situations discussed in Chapter III, Shirley built his plays. In the present chapter the attempt will be to show how he went about the construction of his plays, as far as internal evidence adduced nearly two hundred and ninety years after their composition can explain their author's methods. Love Tricks and The Maid's Revenge have been chosen as fairly representative of Shirley's methods of dramatization. Moreover, they are his earliest extant efforts in comedy and in tragedy, and while, of course, in later plays occasionally Shirley departs from

116

his practice as shown in the composition of the dramas
just mentioned, yet, in general, up to The Court Secret, his
last regular play, he follows the same formula.   These two
early plays have the advantage of being based on novels,
not on plays, so that the dramatist's selection and rejection
of material may be observed—how it accords or does not
accord with the dramatic conventions of the time.   The
discussion of these two plays will be somewhat fuller than
that of those in the following chapters.   There the emphasis will be upon Shirley's sources, general and particular;
here it is rather upon his treatment of his sources.

## I.  Love Tricks

Love Tricks, which was licensed February 10, 1624–25,
bears every indication of having been composed during
Shirley's residence at St. Albans.   As Schipper says
(James Shirley, p. 20) it is a comedy "welches zwischen
verschiedenen Arten der Komödie, der Intrigen-Komödie,
der Posse und der Pastoral-und Sitten-Komödie hin-
und herschwankt."   This curious mixture of types, together
with the matter, would serve to identify the play as the
work of a young scholar of considerable reading and not
much actual practical knowledge of the drama.

The main plot—the story of the loves of Infortunio and
Selina—is derived from Of Phylotus and Emilia, the
eighth novel of Barnabe Riche's Farewell to Military Profession.[1]   A number of elements from other sources which

[1] The title of the play (which suggests Day's Law Tricks) may
be derived from Wit at Several Weapons, IV, 2 ("Love-tricks break
out, I see"), or from Grim, the Collier of Croydon, V, 1 ("Wanton
love-tricks").  The expression is also found in Law Tricks, II, 1,
The Maid's Tragedy, V, 2, The Guardian, III, 6, The Royal Slave,
II, 4 (1636) (used in another sense).  The subtitle (The School
of Compliments) perhaps suggested the title of The Academy of

also enter into the play will be pointed out in the course of
the discussion. Riche's characters have all been renamed
and new characters have been introduced to the number
of twelve besides the shepherds and shepherdesses. Thus
Riche's Alberto = Shirley's Cornelio, Phylotus = Rufaldo,
Flavius = Infortunio, Philerno = Antonio, Emilia = Selina, and Brisilla = Hilaria. The new characters added
are Gasparo, "a gentleman, lover of Felice," Bubulcus, "a
rich gull, in love with Hilaria," Jenkin, "a Welshman,"
Jocarello, "his page," Gorgon, "Antonio's servant," Ingeniolo, "a justice's clerk," Orlando Furioso, "a roarer,"
"an Old Countryman," Oaf, "his son," Felice, sister to
Selina, Delia, "a chambermaid," and Medulla, "a country
gentlewoman." Various elements have been introduced
such as the social and literary satire and pastoralism.[2]

The play may be briefly outlined as follows:

Infortunio is in love with Selina who loves Rufaldo,
an old man. Unable to win her, Infortunio goes mad.
Selina on the eve of her wedding discovers that she really
loves Infortunio, and so, disguised as a shepherd, she flees
into the forest. Her brother Antonio, though pretending to
search for her, dresses himself in her clothes, and is married
to Rufaldo in her place. Antonio loves Hilaria, the daughter of Rufaldo, whom her father designs to marry to
Bubulcus, a cowardly fool. Bubulcus, who has been beaten
by Antonio, pretends to have slain him in a duel, and is
arrested, since Antonio has apparently disappeared. In
the meantime, Selina in disguise is residing with some shepherds among whom is her sister, Felice, who had run away
sometime before in order to escape an obnoxious marriage.
The mad Infortunio comes to them, and is cured by Felice.

Compliments, a poetical miscellany published in 1640, to which
doubtless Brome alludes in The Jovial Crew, II.

  [2] Baskerville, Mod. Lang. Notes. XXIV, 100-101.

Gasparo, Felice's early lover, appears, and discovers her identity and Selina's. They wonder to hear that Selina is thought still to be in the city. Selina's father, Cornelio, Rufaldo, and the others are invited to witness the rustic sports of the shepherds. They go and discover the deception. Felice and Gasparo, Selina and Infortunio, Hilaria and Antonio are united. Some additional comic passages are furnished in the play by the long episode of the Compliment School, by the humors of Jenkin, Selina's Welsh suitor, and by the clever pranks of Gorgon, Antonio's servant, who follows Gasparo through the play.

Only a few of the characters require discussion. Rufaldo has been treated in Chap. IV, Sect. 42. Infortunio in character somewhat resembles Aurelio in May-Day. His name seems derived from The Hector of Germany, III, 3. There, Young Fitzwater has run away with Floramel, his father's betrothed. She has left a page in her clothing who goes to the church with the old man (II, 4). Fitzwater and Floramel being wrecked on the French coast, the latter gives her name as Infortuna and her husband's as Infortunio. Gasparo has a few of the traits of Lemot in An Humorous Day's Mirth, Ludovico in May-Day, Macilente in Every Man out of his Humor, the Colonel's Friend in A Fair Quarrel, and similar humorists. Among the characters in English drama who are parallels to the clever Gorgon are Matthew Merrygreek in Roister Doister, Dulipo in Supposes, Skink in Look about You (a combination of the clever servant and the clown), Tranio in The Taming of the Shrew, Pisanio in Cymbeline, Angelo in May-Day, Brainworm in Every Man in his Humor, Mosca in Volpone, the Butler in The Miseries of Enforced Marriage, Cricca in Albumazar, Launce in Wit without Money, Sim in A Match at Midnight, Jeremy in The City Wit (1629), Pate in The Northern Lass (1630), Urinal in The

Hollander (1632), Grimes in The Lady Mother (1635), Crochet in A Fine Companion (1635). Shirley uses the type later in Diego in The Maid's Revenge, Carlo in The Bird in a Cage, Brains in The Witty Fair One, Close in The Constant Maid. Note Savorwit in No Wit, No Help like a Woman's. Gorgon and Diego, who are both young, are not far from the witty page (see Chap. IV, Sect. 48).

Jenkin, the comic Welshman, is an example of a very common humorous figure in Elizabethan drama—the foreigner whose broken English and display of what passed for national characteristics make him amusing. In The Nightwalker, Maria, as a Welsh girl, uses the dialect for pathetic rather than for comic effect. The fourth stanza of Shirley's poem Upon the Prince's Birth (VI, 424 ff.) contains a use of the dialect. Other Welsh figures in the drama are the various Welsh characters in Edward I, Glendower in Henry IV, Part I, Sir Hugh Evans in The Merry Wives of Windsor, Fluellen in Henry V, Owen, Gough and Davy in Sir John Oldcastle, Sir Vaughan in Satiromastix, Captain Jenkin in Northward Ho, Bristle in Bartholomew Fair, the Welshwoman in A Chaste Maid in Cheapside, the Welsh Madman in The Changeling, the Welshman in The Royal King and Loyal Subject, and Randall in A Match at Midnight.[3]   For other Welsh characters, see Eckhardt, Die Ausländertypen (Materialien,

---

[3] Out of three hundred and sixty-six jests in A Banquet of Jests, or Change of Cheer, ten concern the Welsh. Cf. also Character 14, Bk. II, A Wrangling Welsh Client, in Essays and Characters, by John Stephens, the Younger; On a Welshman's Devotion, and a Welshman in Wit Restored; epigrams On a Welshman and an Englishman, On a Welshman (two of the same title), epitaphs On a Welshman (two in number), The Welshman's Praise of Wales and Hur in Love in Wit's Recreations. Note also Jonson's masque, For The Honor of Wales.

XXXII), p. 23 ff., and for a discussion of various attributes
of the stage Welshman, see *ibid.*, p. 12 ff.[4]  Observe that
Jenkin is the generic name for the Welshman, as Sandy is
for the Scotchman, and Patrick, or Teague, for the Irish-
man.  Frisk and Winfield (as a Frenchman) in The Ball
are examples of the occurrence of another nationality than
Welsh in the plays in which Shirley had a hand.  Note
Ascanio as a Swiss in The Opportunity.  Orlando Furioso,
the roarer, is treated with the poltroons in Chap. IV, Sect.
47, and Bubulcus, the foolish lover is considered in the
same chapter, Sect. 44.  Joculo, Jenkin's page, is treated
in Chap. IV, Sect. 48.  Only Hilaria, among the female
characters, need be mentioned here.  She is a very faint
foreshadowing of the witty young lady of Hyde Park, etc.
(see Chap. IV, Sect. 40).

Act I, Sc. 1.  Not in the novel.  Antonio here is shown
residing at his father's house, and a suitor to Hilaria, not
a stranger to both as in Riche.  Shirley has added Gasparo
and Felice, his lost mistress, and sister to Antonio.  Gasparo's remarks on newsmongers suggest The Staple of
News, but seem prior in date.  Cf. also The Gamester,
III, 3, The Example, IV, 1.  Other attacks on newsmongers occur in News from the New World Discovered in
The Moon, Wit without Money, II, 4, and The Fair Maid
of the Inn, IV, 2.  "A page to wait on him in quarto"
(p. 9) is an example of a common figure.  Cf.  "A gentleman in folio," III, 5; "A very devil in decimosexto," The
Gamester, IV, 1; "I'll fight with you myself in this small
volume Against your bulk in folio," Captain Underwit,

4 In Eckhardt's valuable and comprehensive study of foreign types
in the drama, which came into the present writer's hands after the
completion of this book, are noted apparently all the references to
foreign manners, etc., in the Elizabethan plays to which its author
had access.  The reader must be referred to this volume for Shirley's
allusions of such a nature.

V, 1 (1635?); "Though bound up in decimosexto for carriage, yet a wit in folio for cosenage," Mother Bombie,
II, 1; "Whoreson proverb-book bound up in folio," The
Two Angry Women of Abington, II, 1; "Your two little
pages which are less by half than two leaves have more
learning in them than is in all their three volumes," Sir
Giles Goosecap, II, 1; "My dancing braggart in decimosexto," Cynthia's Revels, I, 1; "A slave in folio," The
Turk, I, 2; "My little wit in decimosexto," The Unnatural
Combat, III, 2; "One Bound up in decimosexto," The Maid
of Honor, II, 2; "He lies in loose sheets, everywhere," Wit
without Money, II, 3; "I had rather walk in folio," Love's
Cure, II, 2; "Bound in decimosexto," The City Nightcap,
V, 1; "The rest were made But fools in quarto, but I find
myself an ass in folio," Wit in a Constable, II, 1 (1639).
See Adams, Materialien, XXVII, 80 (edition of The
Turk).[5]

Infortunio's quibbling on the coldness of his heart (p. 11)
seems possibly a satirical use of the metaphysical poets'
employment of the conceit. Antonio's offer to him to kick
Selina is reminiscent of passages in The Sisters, III, 2,
The Gamester, II, 1, and The Constant Maid, II, 3. Cf.
The Woman's Prize, IV, 5, The Woman Hater, II, 1, III, 1,
Monsieur Thomas, IV, 2, The Captain, III, 3, Love's Cure,
IV, 1, Microcosmus, III. For the eavesdropping of him
and Gasparo (p. 10 ff.), see Chap. IV, Sect. 30 (cf. also
p. 13 ff., II, 1, III, 2). In the novel Emilia's youthful
suitor, Flavius, is loved by her from the first, but she does
not become acquainted with him until she is betrothed to
the old Phylotus.

Gorgon's making Rufaldo believe himself rejuvenated
(p. 14 ff.) is used again in regard to Basilius, The Arcadia,

[5] For the mention of "Knights of the post" (p. 9), see under
The Ball, II, 2.

II, 1, in as far as the renewing of youth goes. It is related
also to Fowler's being persuaded that he is dead, The
Witty Fair One, IV, 4, V, 1, 3 (see under these scenes for
analogues). Other rejuvenations occur in Wily Beguiled,
p. 318, The Old Law, III, 2, May-Day, I, 1, Albumazar, I, 2,
Sicelides, II, 3, IV, 4, The Old Couple, IV, The Heir, III,
Albovine, IV, 1 (1626), Love's Sacrifice, II, 2 (1630), A
Fine Companion, II, 4 (1633), The Lady Mother, I, 2
(1635), The Antiquary, I, 1 (1636).

Act II, Sc. 1. Entirely Shirley's. For Antonio's
eavesdropping, see under I, 1. Bubulcus' threats against
Antonio are related to Montenegro's conduct, The Maid's
Revenge, I, 2. Cf. also Kastril and Surly, The Alchemist,
IV, 4. Cf. for the general situation, The Witty Fair One,
II, 2; and see also The Constant Maid, II, 1. Device's at-
tempt at bullying Courtwell on hearing from the Sister
that the latter was a coward (Captain Underwit, IV, 3) is
based apparently on Hilaria's trick in this scene. For
Antonio's beating Bubulcus, see Every Man in his Humor,
IV, 5, Every Man out of his Humor, V, 3, 4, The Poetaster,
III, 1, The Fair Maid of the West, Part I, II, 3, Ram
Alley, IV, 1. Note the cowardice of Scentlove, The Lady
of Pleasure, V, 1.

Sc. 2. Shirley's scene. In the novel Emilia is forced
to betroth herself to the old Phylotus; here her father tries
to dissuade Selina, but she has a passion for Rufaldo, and
is determined to marry him. A situation roughly paralleling that here is found in the love of Phillis for the
Cripple, The Fair Maid of the Exchange, p. 31. A hint
for Cornelio's advice to his daughter (p. 27) occurs in the
novel, p. 194. Shirley seems to have reversed in Selina's
anticipations (p. 29) the usual order of things when an
old man is about to marry a young bride. A reference to
Narcissus occurs, p. 32 (see Chronology, Chap. II). The

intercepted letter (p. 32–33) occurs again in The Maid's
Revenge, III, 1, The Wedding, IV, 1, and The Witty Fair
One, II, 2. The device is also found in Love's Labor's
Lost, IV, 1, 2, The Two Gentlemen of Verona, III, 1, Ham-
let, V, 1 (reported), Othello, V, 2, King Lear, IV, 6,
Every Man in his Humor, I, 1, The Fair Maid of the
Exchange, p. 45, The Knight of Malta, I, 3 (pretended),
Women Pleased, III, 2, A Wife for a Month, I, 2.

For the madness of Infortunio, cf. Belfare in The Wedding, V, 1, and Ajax in The Contention of Ajax and
Ulysses. Note that the Passionate Lord in The Nice Valor,
Rosaura in The Cardinal, and the Niece in The Constant
Maid pretend madness, as does Engine in Captain Underwit. Infortunio's rending the letter and his hallucinations
are a recollection of the distracted Hieronymo and the
petitions, The Spanish Tragedy, III, 13. Cf. also Pasquil
and the bonds, Jack Drum's Entertainment, III. Other
mad characters occur in the persons of Isabella in The
Spanish Tragedy, Venelia in The Old Wives' Tale, Aber-
dine in The Wisdom of Doctor Dodypoll, Titus in Titus
Andronicus, Cassandra in Troilus and Cressida, Ophelia in
Hamlet, Lear in King Lear, Lady Macbeth in Macbeth,
Timon in Timon of Athens, Pandora in The Woman in the
Moon, Orlando in Orlando Furioso, Lucibell in Hoffman,
Dowsecer in An Humorous Day's Mirth, Palemon in The
Thracian Wonder, the mad persons in Northward Ho, Cor-
nelia in The White Devil, Ferdinand and the Madmen in
The Duchess of Malfi, the Madmen in The Honest Whore,
Part I, Anne Ratcliffe in The Witch of Edmonton, Pasquil
and Mammon in Jack Drum's Entertainment, Tangle in
The Phœnix, the Madmen in The Changeling, Carracus in
The Hog hath Lost his Pearl, Ricardo in The Coxcomb,
the Gaoler's Daughter in The Two Noble Kinsmen, Alinda
and the mad persons in The Pilgrim, Memnon in The Mad

Lover, Sigismund and Gisbert in The Poor Man's Comfort, Troubleall in Bartholomew Fair, the Richer Pennyboy in The Staple of News, Cassandra and Orestes in Goffe's Orestes, Overreach in A New Way to Pay Old Debts, Leonora in A Very Woman, Melander in The Lover's Melancholy, Penthea in The Broken Heart, Antharis in The Swisser (1631), Aramant in The Inconstant Lady (1633), (Genest, VIII, 445), Cloe and Gloriana in Love Crowns the End (1632), Fancy in The Floating Island (1636), Spinola in Imperiale (1639).

Act III, Sc. 1, consists of a soliloquy by Rufaldo on his wedding-morn.

Sc. 2 is partially founded on Riche. Jenkin's discovery of Selina in disguise fleeing from her father's house is based on a servant's witnessing Emilia's flight. However, Emilia's escape is made in male clothing supplied by her lover, Flavius, and she seeks refuge in his house. Also she does not flee on the morn of her wedding. For Selina's disguise as a shepherd, see Chap. IV, Sect. 32. Cf. her seeking shelter among the shepherds with As You Like It, II, 4 (which is probably the source), and Sir Clyomon and Sir Clamydes, p. 516. Note also similar episodes in Cervantes' Galatea and in the pastoral portions of Don Quixote. For the sudden reversal of her feelings toward Rufaldo, cf. Serena in The Thracian Wonder, V, 2, and see A Woman is a Weathercock, III, 2. For Jenkin's eavesdropping during the scene, see under I, 1.

Sc. 3 differs from the novel in having Antonio present at the discovery of Selina's flight. The latter too, is not seen by a servant, as she leaves the house. Shirley introduces another variation in Antonio's asking Hilaria's aid in the working out of his trick upon their respective fathers. Cf. Duke Frederick's discovery of the flight of Rosalind and Celia, As You Like It, II, 2.

Sc. 4 is preparatory to Jenkin's subsequent urban and rural adventures.

Sc. 5. The Compliment School is Shirley's addition. The Academy of Compliments, mentioned earlier in this chapter, is thus described in a list of "Choice poems with excellent translations by the most eminent wits of this age," appended to Moseley's edition of Osmond, the Great Turk (1657): "The Academy of Compliments wherein ladies, gentlewomen, scholars, and strangers may accommodate their courtly practice with gentle ceremonies, complimental, amorous, high expressions and forms of speaking or writing of letters, most in fashion and additions of many witty poems and pleasant new songs." This applies as well to Shirley's scene as to Moseley's handbook.

Various sources have been suggested for the general idea of the School of Compliment. Gosse believes that Shirley may have had in mind the Nubes of Aristophanes (Best Plays of James Shirley, p. xii). Schelling suggests for sources Epicœne and The Staple of News (Eliz. Dram., II, 287, note). The latter could not very well be a source since Love Tricks preceded Jonson's play. Miss Kerr mentions The Devil is an Ass, IV, 1, as a basis (Influence of Ben Jonson, p. 49). Cynthia's Revels, II, 1, III, 1, 3, V, 2, should be noted as a possible original for the scene also. In addition to the above, cf. May-Day, I, 1 (Innocentio's wishing to be entered at an ordinary so as to learn to converse), IV, 1, and A Fair Quarrel, IV, 1 (a school of roaring is introduced in a shorter, less elaborate scene with less broadly applied satire). As a matter of fact, this scene of Shirley's is based on no one scene in a preceding play but apparently on all of them taken together.[6]

[6] The idea is employed later in The New Academy, IV, 2 (1628?) The Sparagus Garden (1638) (Hoyden's being made a gentleman),

For the verses furnished Bubulcus, see Chap. IV, Sect. 22. Koeppel (Shakespeare's Wirkung, p. 56), follows the Shakespeare Allusion Book (I, 357), and Gifford's note (p. 56–57) in considering the line "O that I were a flea upon thy lip!" (p. 43), not a parody on a line in Romeo and Juliet, II, 2. Donne's Flea and On a Flea on his Mistress' Bosom together with Drummond's Happiness of a Flea, and On the Same should be compared. As a matter of fact, the various speeches or compliments furnished by Gasparo have undoubtedly some satirical application (cf. The Poetaster, III, 1).

There may possibly be an allusion in the name of Delia, the chambermaid, to Daniel's sonnet-cycle, Delia. The dialogue between Gorgon and her (p. 46) was undoubtedly suggested by some romance. The speech made for the Country Magistrate (p. 45) is an early form of the more extended parody on addresses in courts of law which occur in The Traitor, III, 1, and Chabot, III, 2, V, 2.

Orlando Furioso's speech (pp. 47–48) is a parody on the tearing of a passion to tatters, which is commonly met with in early Elizabethan tragedies. For the sort of speech here burlesqued see Tamburlaine to Theridamas, Tamburlaine, Part I, I, 2, and Tamburlaine, ibid., V, 2, Part II, II, 4 (on Zenocrate's death), V, 1 (on the conquest of Babylon), Alphonsus in Alphonsus, King of Arragon, the Moor in The Battle of Alcazar, Orlando in Orlando Furioso, Furor Poeticus in The Return from Parnassus, Part II, IV, 2, Tactus in Lingua, V, 7, Hercules in The Silver Age, [III], p. 145, [V], pp. 158–59, Muleasses in The Turk, II, 1, Borgias and Timoclea, ibid., IV, 1, Nero in Nero, IV, 5. Shirley has a similar burlesque in Love in a

and The Noble Stranger, IV (1638) (Pupillus' being made a wit). Cf. also the "Academy" in The Variety, II, 1, by the Duke of Newcastle and Shirley (?).

Maze, IV, 3. The uncertain dates of Goffe's Orestes, Raging Turk, and Courageous Turk prevent one from doing more than suspect Shirley of hitting at the outrageous vaunting frequent in them.[7]

What the source of Ingeniolo's honeyed speech (pp. 48–49) is cannot be determined. It seems evident that it is directed at the authors who made persons employ a diction superior to their positions in society. Jenkin's desire for an "amorous pastoral" since he is going among the shepherds satirizes the conventional pastoralism of a slightly earlier day. This mild satire is rather peculiar as occurring here, when compared with the Shepherds' speeches in IV, 2. Cf. Captain Jenkin's visit to Bellamont for verses in Northward Ho, IV, 1. Medulla's dialogue with Gasparo has no recognizable application.

The masquerading before the mad Infortunio which terminates the scene brings to mind The Nice Valor, II, 1. Cf. also The Mad Lover, IV, 1, and A Very Woman, IV, 2. More or less analogous incidents occur later in Shirley's Example, V, 1, and in The Lover's Melancholy, III, 3, IV, 2 (1628). The idea of damned souls in hell recalls Los Sueños of Quevedo, Dekker's News from Hell, Dekker his Dream, Tom Telltroth, etc. (cf. Cam. Hist. Eng. Lit., IV, 403). Note also the medieval visions of hell. Infortunio's quizzing Gasparo's clients recalls Ralph and the inmates of Barbaroso's cave, The Knight of the Burning Pestle, III, 4. The characters which they give of themselves seem based on Spark's description of hell, The Fleire, V (p. 54 ff.).[8] Cf. also The Honest Whore, Part I,

[7] Note Marmion's Bravo, The Antiquary, V, 1, as perhaps deriving some speeches from this passage.

[8] Suckabus in The Seven Champions of Christendom, III (1634) gives characters by opposites. Fowler in The Witty Fair One, V, 1, gives characters of those he meets in "heaven."

V, 2 (characters of madmen), and If This Be Not a Good Play, the Devil Is in It, p. 351 ff. The subjects of the characters given to Infortunio are derived seemingly from Overbury's Characters, of which there were ten editions by 1622. Overbury's "devilish usurer" = Gasparo as "a usurer"; "A Chambermaid" = Delia, "a chambermaid"; "A Sergeant" = Ingeniolo, "an undersheriff" (cf. also Character 1, Bk. II, A Jailor, John Stephens the Younger's Characters and Essays, and Earle, Microcosmography, XIX (A Constable); this book was circulated in MS.); "A Very Woman," and "Her next part" = Medulla, "a country justice's wife"; "An arrant horse-courser" = Bubulcus, "a horse-courser"; "A braggadocio Welshman" = Jenkin, "damned for her valor." Only Gorgon, "a watchman," and Oaf, "a younger brother," have no parallels in Overbury, but cf. the latter with his Elder Brother, and see Microcosmography, VIII (A Younger Brother). Cf. these characters and the ones given of the clients on their entrances during the scene with those listed in Chap. IV, Sect. 21. Note also Infortunio's mention of Owen Glendower, and Jenkin's claim of relationship with that worthy (p. 56) who, it seems, had to do with the devil (Henry IV, Part I, III, 1).

Act IV, Sc. 1, is from the novel for the greater part. Shirley's chief contributions are Hilaria's knowledge of the true sex of her pretended stepmother, the introduction of Gorgon and Bubulcus, and the explanation of Antonio's disappearance by the supposition that he has gone in search of his sister. For Antonio's disguise, see Chap. IV, Sect. 41 (cf. Gorgon disguised, V, 1, 3). Note that the substitution of brother for sister occurs in Twelfth Night, and Love's Cure. Antonio as his sister suggests Thomas in Monsieur Thomas, IV, 6, 7, 8, etc. For Bubulcus' boasts, see under II, 1. For his "challenge," cf. Coomes and

Francis, The Two Angry Women of Abington, III, 2, and Innocentio and Giovenelli, May-Day, III, 1. Cf. his verses (p. 59) with those referred to in Chap. IV, Sect. 22. Gorgon's parting words (p. 60) seem a quotation. For Rufaldo's making love to the disguised Antonio, see Chap. IV, Sect. 7. For Rufaldo's marriage to Antonio as Selina, cf. Hylas, and Thomas as Dorothy, Monsieur Thomas, V, 9 (reported). See under V, 3, following. Cf. the false Selina's forcing Rufaldo to grant the terms imposed with The Fawn, V, The Puritan, IV, 1, The Woman's Prize, II, 6, Rule a Wife and Have a Wife, II, 3, Ram Alley, III, 1, The City Madam, II, 2. Shirley's probable source is the granting of the disguised Emilia's conditions by the old sharper and money-lender Lurdo, in Law Tricks, III, [1]. There is a slight suggestion of the incident in the novel, however. Later occurrences of similar conditions are found in Love in a Maze, III, 1, The Northern Lass, I, 6 (1630), The Jealous Lovers, V, 8 (1632), A Fine Companion, II, 4 (1633), The Ordinary, IV, 3 (1634), Wit in a Constable, IV, 1 (1639). Koeppel derives Antonio's "little world of man" (p. 62) from the Gentleman's "his little world of man," King Lear, III, 1 (Shakespeare's Wirkung, p. 56). Shirley's only mention of Phylerno's sending a courtesan to Phylotus to perform the duties of a wife is in Antonio's remark, "Keep a whore under my nose; nay, I will allow it" (p. 63). Antonio's going to bed with Hilaria in his feminine disguise is paralleled in Englishmen for my Money, V, 3, The Scornful Lady, V, 2, Amends for Ladies, III, 3. Cf. also The Arcadia, III, 4.

Sc. 2 is Shirley's addition entirely. It is probably derived from As You Like It, II, 4, etc., as Gosse suggests (Best Plays of James Shirley, p. xii. Cf. also Schelling, Eliz. Dram., II, 287). Cf. The Maid's Metamorphosis, The Downfall of Robert, Earl of Huntington, III, 2, etc.,

The Thracian Wonder, The Coxcomb, III, 3, The Pilgrim, V, 6, for more or less similar scenes.[9]   The disguise of Felice recalls Angelica as a poor woman in Orlando Furioso, p. 101, while Selina's disguise as a shepherd suggests Neronis in Sir Clyomon and Sir Clamydes, p. 520 (see under III, 2).   The celebration of the pastoral life by the three shepherds suggests Tasso's Aminta, I, 2 (chorus), Il Pastor Fido, II, 5, IV, 9 (chorus), Mucedorus, IV, 3, The Maid's Metamorphosis, I (Silvio's contest with Gemulo), The Faithful Shepherdess, The Tempest, II, 1 (Gonzalo's ideal commonwealth), The Bondman, IV, 2 (Pisander on the golden age), Character 25, Bk. II, "An Honest Shepherd," in John Stephens, the Younger's Essays and Characters, and the Passionate Shepherd group of poems (for the last, see under Love's Cruelty, II, 2). Note The Brothers, IV, 2.   The metre of this passage resembles that of parts of Fletcher's pastoral, but is less varied.   The mad Infortunio's appearance recalls that of Alinda, mad and disguised as a boy, The Pilgrim, III, 6. Felice's curing him of his distemper (which takes place between this scene and V, 1) is based probably upon the cures wrought by Clorin in The Faithful Shepherdess.   Cf. also the mad Orlando in Orlando Furioso, together with Eusanius and Radagon in The Thracian Wonder, Orlando in As You Like It, and Hippolito and Francisco in Humor out of Breath, as dwelling among the shepherds, or in the forest.   Cf. also Serena and Palemon, The Thracian Wonder, V, 2.

Scs. 3 and 4, which are not based on the novel, suggest

9 Greg, Past. Poet. and Past. Dram., p. 408, commenting on the pastoral elements in Love Tricks, calls attention to the genuine pastoral tone and feeling in parts of this scene. The disguised sisters who become a shepherdess and shepherd and who are followed by their lovers suggest a pastoral influence.

in Jenkin's search for Selina, Ascanio's seeking Eurymine, The Maid's Metamorphosis, II. The echo-dialogue cannot be traced back to any one original, notwithstanding Gifford's making its source The Hog hath Lost his Pearl, IV. Too many parallels exist, such as Shirley's own Narcissus (VI, 465, 480), The Arraignment of Paris, III, 2 (a variation on the usual form), The Old Wives' Tale, p. 450, The Maid's Metamorphosis, IV, The Wounds of Civil War, III, 4, The Iron Age, Part I, V, 1, Old Fortunatus, I, 1, If This Be Not a Good Play, the Devil Is in It, p. 325, Cynthia's Revels, I, 1, An Humorous Day's Mirth, p. 45 (quoted), The Return from Parnassus, Part II, II, 2, Law Tricks, V, 1, The Turk, V, 1 (counterfeit), The Duchess of Malfi, V, 3, Anything for a Quiet Life, V, 2. We find the device used later in The Queen's Exchange, II, 3 (1632), and Love's Mistress, I, 1, II, 1 (1634). Examples of it are found in Sidney's Arcadia, pp. 226–27 (end of Bk. II), and Stirling's Aurora. See also Il Pastor Fido, IV, 8.[10]

Sc. 5, which owes nothing to Riche, is as Gifford says, probably drawn principally from Every Man in his Humor, II, 2, 3, III, 1, IV, 3, 4. Shirley uses the counterfeit soldier again in The Imposture, V, 1, and The Sisters, IV, 2. Parallels are found in Every Man out of his Humor, III, 1, The Blind Beggar of Bednal Green, II, 1, Sophronisba, II, 2, The Atheist's Tragedy, II, 1, Wit at Several Weapons, I, 2, The Captain, II, 1, IV, 5, A Woman is a Weathercock, III, 3, The Roaring Girl, V, 1, The City Wit, II, 1 (1629). Gasparo's bringing back Gorgon's sight with kicking him suggests the recovery of Simpcox, Henry VI, Part II, II, 1. Gasparo's deciding to turn shepherd suggests Don Quixote's resolving to become a shepherd when he has ceased

---

[10] An article upon the echo-dialogue in Elizabethan literature is in preparation by Elbridge Colby, Proudfit Fellow in Letters in Columbia University.

to be a knight-errant (Don Quixote, Part II, Chap. LXVII).

Sc. 6 is not found in Riche. Bubulcus' boastful account of his "slaying" of Antonio is based on Every Man out of his Humor, IV, 4, according to Miss Kerr (Influence of Ben Jonson, p. 48 ff.). Too many analogues, more or less close, occur, however, to allow one single source to be fixed. Among these are Henry IV, Part I, II, 4, V, 4 (Falstaff's stories of the robbery, and the death of Hotspur), The Fair Maid of the West, Part I, III, 2, Your Five Gallants, III, 5, Amends for Ladies, IV, 2, The Maid in the Mill, IV, 2 (Bustopha's story), Fuimus Troes, III, 1 (1625). Later uses of the same incident occur in A Fine Companion, IV, 4, The Fool Would Be a Favorite, IV (1638). Shirley employs it again in The Imposture, III, 2, The Wedding, IV, 3, Honoria and Mammon, I, 1, and it also occurs in The Faithful Friends, III, 2, The Ball, IV, 1, and Captain Underwit, V, 1. Koeppel finds Bubulcus' contradictions as to his sword and rapier reminiscent of Bobadill, Every Man in his Humor, III, 1 (Ben Jonson's Wirkung, pp. 135–36). For the arrest of Bubulcus as Antonio's murderer, together with V, 2, cf. Every Man out of his Humor, V, 3 (see also Hartwell's arrest, The Constant Maid, V, 1, 3).

Act V, Sc. 1. The greater part of this scene is Shirley's. See under IV, 2, for various parallel pastoral scenes. Infortunio's proposing to stay among the shepherds suggests As You Like It, II, 4, etc. His finding Selina like herself recalls the same play, V, 4. His desiring to court her as a mistress and thereby to forget himself seems drawn from As You Like It, III, 2 (Orlando's asking Rosalind as Ganymede to act as Rosalind). Cf. also Gallathea, IV, 4, and see The Doubtful Heir, IV, 2. For Gasparo and Gorgon in this scene and V, 3, cf. Pheander in The Thracian

Wonder, IV, 1, and Autolycus, The Winter's Tale, IV, V.
Note the name "Mopsa" as assumed by Gorgon in disguise
as derived from Sidney's Arcadia (see also The Winter's
Tale). For Gorgon's feminine disguise, see Chap. IV,
Sect. 41, and also IV, 1. Gasparo's identification of Felice
recalls Hubert and Jaculin, The Beggar's Bush, IV, 2.
For his fortune-telling, cf. Lancelot in The Lovers' Progress, II, 2, George-a-Greene in George-a-Greene, p. 261, and
Pheander in The Thracian Wonder, IV, 1. Note Manly,
The Witty Fair One, III, 4. When Selina reveals herself,
it is Gasparo who is incredulous and suspects witchcraft,
not Infortunio—who corresponds to Flavius in the novel
(this is the sole use of Riche in this scene). For surprises
of a similar nature, see Scs. 2 and 3, following, and The
Imposture, III, 1. For the by-play between the shepherds
and the disguised Mopsa, cf. Rufaldo and Antonio as
Selina, IV, 1 (see also V, 3). This seems a reversal of
Phebe and Rosalind in disguise, As You Like It, III, 5,
V, 2.

Sc. 2 is Shirley's. Miss Kerr derives Bubulcus' confession of cowardice from Shift's, Every Man out of his
Humor, V, 3 (Ben Jonson's Influence, p. 49). However,
cf. Falstaff's admitting that he had lied concerning his
robbery, Henry IV, Part I, II, 4. Antonio's surprise
at hearing a report of his presence in the country parallels Selina's surprise near the end of the preceding
scene.

Sc. 3 is partly founded on the novel. For Jenkin's fear
of being enchanted, see The Young Admiral, V, 3, and The
Bird in a Cage, I, 1. Cf. Koeppel, Reflexe der Ritter-
Romane im Drama, p. 219, note. There is a recollection
in Jenkin's wanderings, perhaps, of Don Quixote on the
Sierra Moreña. Cf. Jocarello's interest in the preparations for the shepherds' festival with Sancho Panza and

Comachio's wedding festivities, Don Quixote, Part II, Chaps. XX, XXI.

The festival itself is a necessary part of nearly every pastoral and of many rustic scenes. Cf. The Arcadia, I, 3, Love's Metamorphosis, I, 2, Love's Labor's Lost, V, 2, As You Like It, V, 4, The Winter's Tale, IV, 4, The Thracian Wonder, II, 2, The Faithful Shepherdess, I, 1, V, 5, The Two Noble Kinsmen, III, 5, Women Pleased, IV, 1, The Prophetess, V, 3, The Maid in the Mill, II, 2, The Witch of Edmonton, III, 4. Note also Argalus and Parthenia, I, 2, IV, 1 (1638). For the masque (p. 81) see Chap. IV, Sect. 18, and under The Grateful Servant, IV, 4, 5. The identification of Antonio and Selina is, of course, from Riche. However, in the novel the *dénouement* comes at Alberto's house in the city. For another tangling of the identity of brother and sister, see Twelfth Night, V, 1. Antonio as Selina and Selina as Antonio confronting each other have parallels more or less close in The Comedy of Errors, V, 1, The Taming of the Shrew, V, 1, The Silver Age, II, 1, The Fair Maid of the Exchange, p. 84, Albumazar, IV, 7, 8, The Maid in the Mill, III, 2, and, later, A Fine Companion, V, 2 (1633). See also under Shirley's Imposture, III, 1, 3, and note The Opportunity, IV, 1, The Sisters, IV, 5, The Witty Fair One, V, 3. Cf. the discovery of Antonio's true sex with Love in a Maze, V, 5, The Merry Wives of Windsor, V, 5, Epicœne, V, 1, The Honest Man's Fortune, V, 3. See also The New Inn, V, 1 (1629), where a "boy" disguised as a girl turns out to be really a girl. For the use of the title of the play in this scene (p. 94) and in 2 (p. 87) (cf. also the epilogue), see Chap. IV, Sect. 31. For the resurrection of Antonio (as far as Cornelio is concerned) in this scene and the preceding, see Chap. IV, Sect. 29.

As Baskerville points out (Mod. Lang. Notes, XXIV,

100–101) the gulling of Bubulcus by Gorgon as Mopsa is drawn from Epicœne's confounding of La Foole and Daw, Epicœne, V, 1. Shirley repeats this incident in Love in a Maze, IV, 3, V, 5. Cf. also Shallow in The Heir, V, and note the influence of the present incident upon the fortunes of Don Pedro, The Brothers, V, 3.

The contest between comic characters as to which should speak the epilogue seems derived from Every Man out of his Humor (see also the later Staple of News). Comic epilogues occur in The Cardinal, The Imposture, The Brothers, The Sisters, No Wit, No Help Like a Woman's, Satiromastix, The Knight of the Burning Pestle, and in the later News from Plymouth (1635).

## II. THE MAID'S REVENGE

Whether The Maid's Revenge was Shirley's second *play* or only his second tragedy depends upon the interpretation put upon a passage in the dedication prefixed to the quarto edition. There Shirley calls it the "second birth in this kind which I dedicated to the scene." This has always been taken to mean that The Maid's Revenge was its author's second play, but it seems more likely that "kind" refers to "tragedy" than to plays in general. However, no record of an earlier tragedy exists, unless the non-extant St. Albans be the play in question (see Chap. VI). To all intents and purposes, The Maid's Revenge may be regarded then as Shirley's earliest tragedy.

The Maid's Revenge is based upon Antonio and Berinthia, a Spanish History (in the index, more properly, A Portugal History) which is the seventh "history" in John Reynolds' Triumphs of God's Revenge against the Crying and Execrable Sin of Murder. Shirley makes quite free with his source in this play, Gifford to the contrary notwithstanding. He has introduced new material and

changed the old to a considerable degree, although not so
much as in Love Tricks. Characters are added, the principal one of which is Castabella, sister to Antonio, and in
love with Sebastiano. There is a hint for her in Reynolds
(p. 84) where Antonio's *two* sisters are mentioned as lamenting their brother's death. That is their only part in
the story. Count de Montenegro, "a braggart," who is
a suitor to Catalina, is Shirley's invention. In the scenes
at Elvas he plays the part of Villandras in the story.
Velasco's name is suggested by Reynolds' Belasco; Shirley's character is, however, Antonio's rival, not his friend,
as in the novel. Sharkino's man, Scarabeo, is Shirley's
addition. The Nurse who appears in the *dramatis personæ*,
but nowhere else, is not found in Reynolds.

Certain changes are also made in the characters taken
from the novel. Sforza, a "blunt soldier," is the Belasco
of the tale more definitely characterized. Villandras is
transferred from the faction of Sebastiano to that of Antonio. Sarmiata, who appears as Sharkino in The Maid's
Revenge, is here less a villain than a quack. The other
personages of the play are practically the same as their
originals in the story.[11]

The Maid's Revenge may be thus briefly outlined:

Sebastiano invites his friend Antonio to Avero to meet
his sisters, Catalina and Berinthia. Antonio falls in love
with the younger, Berinthia. On asking her hand from
her father, Vilarezo, he is refused on the ground that her
elder sister must be married the first. In the meantime,
Catalina has fallen deeply in love with Antonio. The latter uses Catalina as a blind for his continued courtship of
her sister, but she discovers the trick, and in order to get
her rival out of the way, engages Velasco, another suitor

---

[11] It is worth noting, perhaps, that Castabella and Sebastian both
are names of characters in The Atheist's Tragedy.

of Berinthia's, to abduct his mistress.  Catalina then tells
her father of Antonio's pursuit of Berinthia, who is then
placed in her custody.  Diego, Antonio's servant, who pretends to be a suitor to Ansilva, the sisters' maid, brings a
letter to Berinthia from Antonio, who has returned to his
home at Elvas.  Berinthia loses the letter.  It is found by
Catalina, who reads it, and, fired with jealousy, plans with
Velasco the details of her sister's abduction.  Then in a
soliloquy Catalina announces her intention of poisoning
Berinthia just before the abduction.  Diego, who has opportunely overheard these plans, warns Berinthia, and then
returns to tell Antonio.  Antonio with some friends comes
to Avero, and is admitted to Vilarezo's house in the dark,
as Velasco.  He carries away Berinthia to Elvas.  Velasco
arrives, finds the bird flown, and raises the alarm.
Antonio is immediately suspected, so Sebastiano goes to
Elvas.  He finds his sister there, and she tells him of
Catalina's plot against her.  He returns to Avero, but
Catalina, who has been warned by her lover, Montenegro,
of what Sebastiano will charge her with, defends herself
to her father so skilfully that he refuses to believe Berinthia's story, and sends his son to revenge the stealing of
his sister and to bring her back.  Sebastiano returns to
Elvas, challenges Antonio, and kills him.  Velasco and Villandras, their respective seconds, are also slain.  Berinthia
is taken back to her father's house, where she meditates
revenge.  An opportunity comes when, after overhearing
Montenegro bribing Ansilva to give Catalina a love powder,
she substitutes poison for the powder.  Then finding Sebastiano asleep, she stabs him, but is detected by his page.
As Berinthia gloats over her deed Catalina enters dying
of the poison, and dragging Ansilva who is also poisoned.
Berinthia taunts her sister and then stabs herself.  Vilarezo enters with his household and the sisters die, con-

fessing their crimes. Then Sebastiano's page discovers herself to be Castabella, sister to Antonio, who had fallen in love with Sebastiano at Elvas, and who now had followed him in disguise, since no other course was open to her toward the slayer of her brother.

For analogues to Catalina, the wicked woman, Velasco, her accomplice, Berinthia, who is driven to crime by desire for revenge, Montenegro, the poltroon, and Sforza, the blunt soldier, see Chap. IV, Sects. 35, 34, 36, 47, 39. Diego, the clever servant, has been mentioned in the discussion of Love Tricks. Scarabeo, the servant of Sharkino, the "shirking [qy. "sharking?"] doctor," is the necessary companion of such a character in an Elizabethan play. However, he has so little clownery in his part (unlike most of his *confrères*) that he has not been listed among the clowns in Chap. IV, Sect. 46. Cf. Sharkino with Forobosco in The Fair Maid of the Inn, the Empiric Doctor in The Emperor of the East, and Pynto in The Queen, among others. Cf. Scarabeo with Peter in Gallathea, Miles in Friar Bacon and Friar Bungay, Nano and Androgyno in Volpone (II, 1), Face in The Alchemist, and Firestone in The Witch. Didimo in The Young Admiral (IV, 1), and Carlo in The Bird in a Cage are Shirley's other characters of this sort. For Scarabeo's personal appearance, cf. Camelion in The Wedding, Manes in Campaspe, Shadow in Old Fortunatus, Pachieco in The Woman Hater, Penurio in Women Pleased, the Slave in A Very Woman, III, 1 (described). Note also the Uncle's description of Onos, The Queen of Corinth, IV, 1. Sharkino and his man suggest Doctor Cleander (Doctor of Laws) and Carion in The Supposes. Sharkino suggests the Doctor in The White Devil (II, 1).

Act I, Sc. 1. Almost entirely based upon Reynolds' story. Shirley's only variation lies in that he does not make Sebastiano praise one sister more than the other. This scene is the source of The Brothers, I, 1 (Luys' taking Alberto home with him as a suitor to Jacinta). A similar incident occurs in The Opportunity, I, 2 (Aurelio as Borgia regarding himself and Cornelia), which is drawn from another source.

Sc. 2. The first part of the scene is Shirley's. For Montenegro's boasts, see under Love Tricks, II, 1, IV, 1. Cf. his mention of the Donzel del Phebo (p. 107) with The Bird in a Cage, III, 2, The Gamester, III, 2, The Ball, I, 1, and see Koeppel, Reflexe der Ritter-Romane im Drama, p. 212, note. His reference to Rosiclere is paralleled in The Young Admiral, III, 1, The Bird in a Cage, III, 2, The Faithful Friends, II, 2 (cf. Koeppel, as cited above).

Gifford derives Montenegro's allusion to Hercules and the Pygmies (p. 107) from Jonson's masque, Pleasure Reconciled to Virtue. However, this masque was produced in 1618–19, and was not printed until 1641, so, as Shirley in all likelihood was not present at its production, and probably saw no MS. copy, he would seem not to have used it here. A similar reference is to be found in The Opportunity, II, 1. For Montenegro's presenting verses not his own to his mistress, cf. Bubulcus, Love Tricks, IV, 1. See also The Witty Fair One, III, 2. Montenegro on satire (p. 109) suggests the dialogue of Horace and Trebatius, The Poetaster, III, 2 (cf. also Castruchio [George Wither] in the early part of The Cruel Brother [1627]). Other criticism more or less analogous is to be found in The Humorous Courtier, II, 2, The Bird in a Cage, IV, 2, The Sisters, IV, 2, The Wedding, III, 2, Love in a Maze, II, 2, Every Man in his Humor, The Poetaster, I, 1, The Parliament of Bees, Character V, The Noble Soldier, III, 2 (1631), Love's Mistress, I, 1, II, 1 (1634).

Vilarezo's determination not to marry his younger

daughter before the elder is drawn from Reynolds, as is also Antonio's resolving to use Catalina as a blind. A parallel to the former point occurs in The Taming of the Shrew, I, 1.

Act II, Sc. 1, owes very little to Reynolds. Catalina's discussion of Antonio with Ansilva is an employment of a common device in Elizabethan plays which is akin to the Character (see Chap. IV, Sect. 21). Similar discussions are found in The Two Gentlemen of Verona, I, 2, The Merchant of Venice, I, 2, The Four Prentices of London, p. 91, A Challenge for Beauty, II, 1 (1635), The Malcontent, V, 3, What You Will, IV, 1, May-Day, II, 1, Amends for Ladies, III, 3, Catiline, II, 1, Monsieur Thomas, I, 3, The Captain, I, 2, The Honest Man's Fortune, V, 3, The Wild Goose Chase, III, 1, The Elder Brother, I, 1, The Fair Maid of the Inn, III, 1, 'Tis Pity She's a Whore, I, 2, Randolph's Amyntas, I, 1, The Combat of Love and Friendship, I, 2 (1636).[12] Shirley employs the device again in The Cardinal, I, 2. See also The Faithful Friends, II, 2.

There is a very slight suggestion in the novel of the stolen meetings of Berinthia and Antonio (see God's Revenge, p. 75). There they meet secretly early in their acquaintance, and Catalina is not told of their love. Diego's courtship of Ansilva here is a variation of Shirley's.

Sc. 2 is Shirley's principally. Catalina's eavesdropping (cf. III, 1, 5, V, 2, and see Chap. IV, Sect. 30), Antonio's pretense of love for her (see Chap. IV, Sect. 6), and Castabella's letters (p. 121) are Shirley's introduction. Diego's starting to work into Ansilva's confidence (drawn from Reynolds) is used again in The Constant Maid, I, 2. Diego's suit to Ansilva is from the novel also, but in the play he personally asks leave to visit her, and not through

12 See also Deloney's Jack of Newbury, Chap. I.

his master, as in the story. Moreover Antonio is not present at Diego's pressing his suit. Reynolds' elaborate leave-taking has been cut down and simplified by the dramatist. Antonio departs for Elvas, not for Lisbon, as in the story.

Sc. 3 is entirely Shirley's. Catalina's arousing Velasco's jealousy is strongly reminiscent of Iago and Othello in Othello. Cf. also The Doubtful Heir, IV, 2, The Royal Master, III, 2, The Witch, III, 2, Love's Sacrifice, III, 3.

Sc. 4 is likewise Shirley's. Here Castabella falls in love with Sebastiano from her brother's description of him (cf. Love's Cruelty, I, 1).

Sc. 5. The placing of Berinthia in the custody of her sister is from the novel, but there it does not occur until after her correspondence with Antonio has been discovered. Cf. also Imogen and the Queen, Cymbeline, I, 1. Velasco's following Catalina's advice (Sc. 3) in asking for Berinthia's hand is Shirley's addition. For Velasco's eavesdropping, see Chap. IV, Sect. 30.

Act III, Sc. 1, is based on Antonio and Berinthia, but contains a number of deviations from it, together with some additions. The discovery of Antonio's letter to Berinthia results from the latter's losing it, not from Catalina's accidentally finding it in her sister's pocket, as in the novel. Berinthia, as has been noticed, is already in confinement in the play. Diego in this scene eavesdrops and overhears Catalina's plots, instead of learning them from Ansilva, as in Reynolds. The letter, too, is here the first that passes between the lovers. For the intercepted letter, see Love Tricks, II, 2. See Chap. IV, Sect. 30, for Diego's eavesdropping. For the betrayal of the plot, cf. The Two Gentlemen of Verona, III, 1 (a reversal). The plot of Catalina and Velasco for the abduction of Berinthia has been drawn on by Shirley in The Brothers, IV, 2.

Sc. 2. Shirley has based this scene upon the merest

hint in the novel. Reynolds does not introduce Sarmiata at this juncture; his first appearance is after the flight of Berinthia, and then he furnishes the poison with which Catalina despatches Ansilva. By virtue of his claims to reading the past (p. 143) Sharkino falls among Shirley's characters who pretend to dealings with the supernatural, and hence for analogous scenes, Chap, IV, Sect. 24, must be consulted. For the comic fortune-telling, cf. The Sisters, III, 1, The Lovers' Progress, II, 2, The Variety, II, 1, The Supposes, I, 2, The Merry Wives of Windsor, IV, 5, Antony and Cleopatra, I, 2, The Pilgrim, V, 4, The English Moor, IV, 5. For the reference to a poisoned fig (p. 141), cf. The Court Secret, I, 1, IV, 1, The Brothers, III, 2, Henry V, III, 6, The Fleire, IV, The White Devil, IV, 1, The Duchess of Malfi, II, 3, The Noble Soldier, V, 4 (1631). A non-extant tragedy called The Spanish Fig was acted about 1602. In the preceding list of references, the allusions may sometimes be to a contemptuous gesture and not to a method of administering poison. The episode of Montenegro and the servingmen is apparently based on some popular story. The entrance of a Maid with a urinal (p. 145) parallels The Wise Woman of Hogsdon, II, 1 (see also Monsieur Thomas, II, 5, A Wife for a Month, II, 1, The City Wit, III, 1, The Virgin Widow, V, 1). For the "High Germans" (p. 147), see under The Opportunity, III, 1. Scarabeo's eating spiders and toads (pp. 147–148) seems the source for Quibble's similar diet, the effects of which he removes with his medicines, in The Virgin Widow, IV, 1.

Sc. 3, which is very short, is based on Reynolds. The poison which Ansilva obtains in the novel, however, is to operate within a limit of three days, and not twelve hours, as here. Shirley, too, has only one attempt at poisoning Berinthia, while the novelist has two.

Scs. 4, 5, and 6, which represent Berinthia's flight, in so far as Antonio's part is concerned, are founded on the novel, as are also Vilarezo's suspicions concerning his complicity, and Sebastiano's pursuit of him. Shirley differs from Reynolds in having Berinthia's escape discovered immediately, and not the next morning. Velasco's contemplated abduction of her is Shirley's addition. Ansilva's mistaking Antonio for Velasco recalls May-Day, III, 1. The stealing away of Berinthia has been drawn on by Shirley in The Imposture, II, 3. Cf. The Guardian, III, 5, for an abduction and The Variety, V, 1, for an attempt at the same. Sebastiano's situation in regard to his friend's conduct has been paralleled by that of Honorio, The Imposture, II, 3.

Act IV, Sc. 1, is entirely Shirley's up to the entrance of Sebastiano and Montenegro. The greater part of the remainder of the scene is based upon Reynolds' save that Montenegro plays the part of Villandras in the novel. Reynolds does not mention Villandras by name as one of the two companions of Sebastiano who are admitted to the castle. The falling in love of Sebastiano and Castabella (which is Shirley's) suggests Romeo and Juliet, in so far as they are members of two hostile families. Sebastiano's conflict between love and paternal duty, or ideals of honor (cf. also Scs. 3 and 4), suggests that in the later Brothers, III, 1 (see Chap. III).

Sc. 2 is drawn chiefly from the novel. Montenegro's warning Catalina of the charges against her and Velasco is Shirley's. The dramatist is responsible, also, for Vilarezo's command to Sebastiano to kill Antonio. Reynolds gives Sebastiano a choice between law and force as methods of recovering Berinthia.

Sc. 3 is in part from Antonio and Berinthia. In the story Sebastiano does not remain at Antonio's castle as he does in the play, but returns to Elvas to await Villandras' return. The banquet and the presence of the ladies at the giving of the challenge are, therefore, Shirley's. In the novel, the challenge is written, and not oral as in the play. The only hint for the scene is Vilarezo's letter to his son. For the masque see Chap. IV, Sect. 18. The manner of giving the challenge is copied in The Court Secret, III, 3. It suggests a recollection of Henry VI, Part II, II, 1, or The Captives, I, 2. Note also The Distresses, IV, 1 (1639). Sforza seems to refer to "my old lad of the castle," Henry IV, Part I, I, 2, in his "Knights of the castle" (p. 170).

Sc. 4 differs from the tale in that female spectators view the duel. Shirley has Castabella and Berinthia watch the combat from the castle walls, and has Velasco, who has accompanied Montenegro back from Avero, take part in the fighting after the latter has saved himself. The duel between two persons who are connected by blood or by love, as are Sebastiano and Antonio, occurs in Shirley's Imposture, III, 3, Court Secret, IV, 2, Coronation, II, 2, 3 (no combat actually), and Example, V, 2. Cf. The Lovers' Progress, II, 3. Similar incidents are found in The Honest Man's Fortune, IV, 2, The Maid in the Mill, I, 1. See also The Island Princess, IV, 3. The source of Shirley's management of the scene may be Love's Cure, V, 3. Here we have two ladies of hostile houses, each of whom loves the other's brother. The feud is to be decided by a combat between the two lovers. However, a reconciliation is effected through the women, thereby differing from The Maid's Revenge. The begging for the lives of characters dear to them, by interrelated characters occurs also in The Royal King and Loyal Subject, V, 1. Montenegro's part in the duel suggests Love Tricks, IV, 6 (cf. also The Wedding, IV, 3).

Act V, Sc. 1, is an addition of Shirley's. For Castabella's disguise as a page, see Chap. IV, Sect. 32. Her entering the service of her former lover, Sebastiano, as a page, is Fletcherian. Cf. Lelia in The Faithful Friends, Leocadia and Theodosia in Love's Pilgrimage, Julia in The Two Gentlemen of Verona, Euphrasia in Philaster, Aspatia in The Maid's Tragedy, Urania in Cupid's Revenge, Alinda in The Pilgrim, Cleanthe in The Obstinate Lady (1638–39). Note also Imogen in Cymbeline and Maria in The Bashful Lover (1635). See under The Court Secret, V, 1, for parallels to the sister who loves her brother's slayer. Pulcheria in The Sisters, is a character modeled on Castabella.[13]

Sc. 2 is Shirley's. In the novel Berinthia's revenge does not extend to her sister. For her eavesdropping, see Chap. IV, Sect. 30. The love-potion or powder (procured in III, 2) is found again in The Arcadia, IV, 3 (cf. The Humorous Lieutenant, IV, 4). Berinthia's exchanging the two powders is perhaps derived from the exchanged swords in Hamlet, V, 2.

Sc. 3. The death of Sebastiano is drawn from the novel excepting that there the page, "Philippo," is not in his master's room when the latter is stabbed, and there is no evidence of the murder's taking place early in the morning. The remainder of the scene is Shirley's. The fate of Ansilva may indeed have been suggested by the manner of her death in the novel, but there Catalina poisons her, while Sebastiano is pursuing Antonio and Berinthia.. Her death is not indicated in the play. In the novel, Catalina, after having been struck by lightning, dies a penitent, confessing her sins, and receiving the forgiveness of her sister. Berinthia does not kill herself in the novel, as in the

13 Note in Howell's Familiar Letters, I, 317, a mention of "Madame of Lorain" following "Monsieur" to Brussels through hostile territory in a page's disguise.

play, but conceals the death of Sebastiano as long as she can. She is finally condemned to perpetual imprisonment. Sharkino drops out of the play after the one scene in which he appears, whereas Reynolds has Sarmiata hanged. For the death of Catalina by poison and the accompanying agonies, see Chap. IV, Sect. 11. In the final slaughter there is a suggestion of the later Love's Cruelty, V, 2. For the use of the title of the play in the text (p. 184), see Chap. IV, Sect. 31.

It has been shown in the preceding pages that Shirley did not follow his source very closely. The plots which he borrowed, he revised to suit his taste. Not only does he alter the incidents, but the personages as well. These latter, often, he not only renames, but recharacterizes. New incidents and new characters, too, are added in each play. Nearly all these changes tend toward a further complication of the plot.[14] In Love Tricks, for instance, a new pair of lovers is introduced, as well as two new suitors for Selina. In The Maid's Revenge another pair of lovers is added, and each sister is given a suitor who either is altogether an invention of the dramatist's, or else is not mentioned as a lover in the novel. Humorous scenes are added, which in the case of Love Tricks, at least, represent an additional complication.

Shirley's additions are drawn from various sources, of which plays furnish by far the greater number. Scenes and parts of scenes are derived from the playwrights with more or less alteration, and characters, too, are modeled on those in earlier dramas.

---

[14] In these plays the source is a novel. Note, however, that in The Opportunity and The Young Admiral (which are from the Spanish) the original plays have undergone simplification, especially in the case of the latter. Shirley seems in them to have emphasized character, rather than incident, as in the originals.

The majority of Shirley's borrowings from plays, however, cannot be traced to one direct source. A score or
more of analogues to a single passage often present themselves, of which nearly any one might plausibly be considered its source. In such cases it seems that the dramatist
did not draw on one single play or passage in a play, but
rather on the aggregate of all such plays or passages. In
other words, the particular device had become conventional,
and so was used by Shirley with probably no reference to
any single earlier play. In several cases analogues in
plays have been cited for incidents which rest directly upon
the main source of the play under discussion. The existence of these parallels proves Shirley often to have selected
and retained those parts of the original story which had
been brought on the stage more or less frequently already.
An incident or character must be popular in order
to be so often repeated as to become conventional, and the
knowledge of this fact seems to have been the principle
on which he acted, both in the introduction of new material
and the retention of the old.

But while we can find dozens of parallels for a number
of the incidents and characters in these two plays, it can
not be said that either resembles any one play very closely.
There must then be some sort of originality in them de-
spite their author's use of hackneyed material. This originality is obviously in the combination of material, and
in the little variations from the conventional which Shirley has made here and there in his incidents or characterizations.

In some instances the use of the same incident or character several times over in Shirley's plays has been noted.
This is an important point. The author not only borrows
from others individually and collectively, but from himself as well, and of these debts, as of the others, it can be

said nearly with equal propriety, that he often so recombines and retouches his borrowings from himself, as to make them appear at least not to be mere slavish copies.

Judging from the two plays examined in this chapter, the following statement of Shirley's methods of dramatic composition may be drawn up for use in the study of his later plays: He found his plot, cut it down, often leaving conventionalized elements, and altered it to his taste.[15] Then he introduced incidents, slightly altered, even scenes, sometimes, from earlier plays, or more often conventional incidents from what was the common stock of all dramatists of the time. Additional complications are created through the introduction of new characters and the doubling of the love-affairs. New motives too are brought in through the new characters, as well as through the new incidents. Humorous material, including comic scenes, satirical touches (such as burlesques and general criticism) often allusions to contemporary events, is added. The characters are shifted about, and re-characterized to suit the altered plot, generally imitating at the same time either a particular figure in a preceding play, or a conventionalized character. Only occasionally do we find an incident or a personage who can not be paralleled. These revised and added elements he combined with those in the original plot, in such a way as to give the casual reader the impression of a considerable degree of originality—the originality, in fact, consisting of management, not of materials.

[15] In the case of the two plays discussed, the plots were drawn from novels, but as sources for later plays, we have other dramas, either foreign or domestic, and in some cases it may be that Shirley invented his plots. Whatever the origin of the plot may be, however, the treatment does not vary save in the case of The Arcadia.

# CHAPTER VI

## THE TRAGEDIES

### I. St. Albans

The Tragedy of St. Albans was entered in the Stationers' Register as Shirley's, February 14, 1639–40. No other direct reference to it has ever been found. There is no extant edition, and there is no record of its ever having been licensed for performance. It may be, however, that Malone through an oversight or a defect in the original MS. failed to note the licensing of St. Albans in his extracts from Herbert's Officebook. It is practically certain, nevertheless, that the play was never printed, and it has been commonly thought that it was produced in Ireland.

As a matter of fact, however, it is not unlikely that St. Albans is Shirley's earliest tragedy. In the dedication to the 1639 edition of The Maid's Revenge, the author says of that play, "It is a tragedy which received encouragement and grace on the English stage; and though it came late to the impression, it was the second birth in this kind which I dedicated to the scene." Plainly, "kind" refers to "tragedy" and not to plays (that word or an equivalent nowhere occurs in the passage), as has been always supposed. Hence we have a tragedy of Shirley's produced before February 9, 1625–26 (the date of the licensing of The Maid's Revenge) and after February 10, 1624–25 (when Love Tricks was licensed) to account for. All of Shirley's other tragedies can be accounted for

(unless we accept Fleay's elaborate but groundless dissocia-
tion of The Politic Father and The Politician), except St.
Albans.  Furthermore, we know that Shirley had spent
several years in, or near, the town of St. Albans, both as
an Anglican clergyman, and as a schoolmaster.  Therefore,
what more probable than that he dramatized an event connected by tradition with his place of residence?

As to the subject of St. Albans, a few theories which
seem obviously wrong have been advanced.  Fleay suggests that the tragedy treated the life of Clanrickard, Earl
of St. Albans, or that of Francis Bacon, Viscount St.
Albans (Biog. Chron., II, 244).  Nissen conjectures that
the town itself or the life of Hubert de Burgh, Earl of
St. Albans (Fleay's Clanrickard) furnished the material
for the play (James Shirley, p. 8).

Nissen's second hypothesis appears most nearly to state
the probable facts in the case.  It seems likely that St.
Albans was a sort of miracle play—influenced by The Virgin-Martyr of 1620 (printed 1622),—based on the life and
death of Alban, the first British martyr, who suffered
under Diocletian.  In support of this theory are the facts
that Shirley resided in or near the town of St. Albans
which derives its name from the early saint, and that at
the end of the sixteenth century legends concerning him
were still connected with the town as is shown in Henry VI,
Part II, II, 1.[1]  Furthermore, Shirley's clerical profession,
his conversion to Catholicism, and the influence of The
Virgin-Martyr, together with the existence of St. Patrick
for Ireland make still stronger the presumption that this
tragedy dealt with a saint's life.  As a possible source
Bede's Historia Ecclesiastica, Bk. I, Chap. 7, may be cited
(see under The Maid's Revenge for a word on the dating of

[1]For an account of the foundation of churches to commemorate
St. Alban, see the Victoria History of Hertfordshire, II, 483 ff.

that play, and under St. Patrick for Ireland on other miracle plays). It should be remembered also that William Rowley had touched upon the martyrdom of St. Alban in A Shoemaker a Gentleman (acted 1610; printed 1638).[2]

In any event, whether the play was produced in 1625, as appears most probable, or in Ireland between 1636 and 1639–40, it seems likely from the date of its entry that Shirley, finding the tragedy about to be published on his return from Ireland, suppressed it, possibly on account of dissatisfaction with the play (a fact which, when compared with his criticism of The Maid's Revenge as an early play in the dedication affixed to it, would point toward its early composition).

## II. The Traitor

There seem to be no adequate grounds for the ascription of the earliest version of The Traitor to Anthony Rivers, a Jesuit who died in Newgate. Both Dyce and Ward consider the play Shirley's. However, Halliwell (Dict. O. E. Plays, p. 250) follows Motteux (The Gentleman's Journal, April, 1692), as quoted by Dyce (Account, xv), in ascribing the tragedy to Rivers, and in giving credit for alterations in it to Shirley. Halliwell has a separate entry for the 1692 edition of The Traitor with its changes and assignment to Rivers. Schipper believes that doubts had been thrown on the true ownership of the play in Shirley's time and that to these doubts Atkins' verses prefixed to the first quarto refer (James Shirley, p. 45). It seems likely, however, that had there been any controversy then over the authorship, some less dubious allusion to it would be extant.

2 There is always the possibility that the entry of 1639-40 in the Stationers' Register may refer to an attempt to reissue Rowley's old play under a different title and with Shirley as author.

The source of The Traitor has been generally considered to be Novel XII of the Heptameron, which is a version of the story of the assassination of Duke Alessandro de Medici by his cousin, Lorenzino. While it is possible that the first hint for the plot of the play came from this story, it is practically certain that some Florentine historian, or historians, furnished the dramatist with material. Certainly the Heptameron was not the sole source. No names are given in the French story. The *dramatis personœ* of the tragedy gives "Alexander, duke of Florence," and "Lorenzo, his kinsman and favorite." Furthermore, the play corresponds more closely to the historian's account of the murder than to the novelist's. What historian Shirley drew upon is a matter of doubt, for they agree fairly closely in their narratives. Segni's Istorie Fiorentine seems, however, the most probable source, since it contains a germ for the relationship of Amidea and Sciarrha in the play.[3]

An outline of the plot of The Traitor follows:

Lorenzo, favorite and kinsman of Alexander, Duke of Florence, plots to depose the latter. The Duke is warned of his machinations, but Lorenzo convinces him of his rectitude. On the Duke's behalf, Lorenzo asks Sciarrha, a noble, to bring his sister Amidea to the Duke's bed. Sciarrha spurns the proposition and the two plot the death of Alexander. After Lorenzo's departure, Sciarrha opens the matter to Amidea as a test. She proves virtuous. The Duke visits Sciarrha, and, although his impending fate is presented in an allegorical masque, he is not warned, but goes to meet Amidea. She repulses his advances, and threatens suicide. The Duke becomes repentant. Lorenzo's contemplated treason is revealed by Sciarrha, but the

[3] For an account of the reign and death of Alessandro de Medici, see Napier, Florentine History, Bk. III, Chap. 1.

former again successfully deceives Alexander and continues in favor. Sciarrha then slays Pisano who has jilted Amidea as he is on his way to marry Oriana whom his friend, Cosmo de Medici, has resigned to him. Lorenzo, who has again influenced the Duke to the pursuit of Amidea, offers Sciarrha his life in return for Amidea's honor. Sciarrha on refusing is told that he will be killed and his sister ravished. He then agrees. However, he slays her after testing her virtue and fortitude, and sends her body to the Duke's palace where it is laid on a bed. The Duke enters, embraces the corpse, and discovers Amidea to be dead. As he mourns, he is set upon by Lorenzo and Petruchio, the latter's accomplice. Sciarrha enters and fights with Lorenzo. Each slays the other. A guard which Petruchio has summoned and most of the characters yet alive enter and Cosmo is proclaimed Duke. The comedy is furnished by the fears of Depazzi, a cowardly accomplice of Lorenzo's.

The characters in the tragedy agree with the historical personages thus: Alexander, Duke of Florence = Alessandro de Medici; Lorenzo = Lorenzino de Medici; Amidea = Luisa Strozzi, Caterina Ginori, and Laldomine Salviati; Cosmo = Cosimo de Medici; Sciarrha = Lorenzino and Scoronconcolo; Florio = Giuliano de Medici; Depazzi = Francesco de' Pazzi; Petruchio = Scoronconcolo.[4] Francesco and Lorenzo de' Pazzi are mentioned by Segni (Istorie Fiorentine, p. 226) as intimates of Alessandro. After the assault on Guiliano Salviati, for which he was imprisoned, the former fled the city. He was a friend of Lorenzino's (Varchi, Storia Fiorentina, V, 70).

The historical events around which The Traitor was built may thus be summarized:

[4] A speech in the first edition of the play (IV, 2) is given to "Piero." Scoronconcolo is sometimes called Piero di Gioanabate (Napier, Florentine History, Bk. III, Chap. 1).

Alessandro besought Lorenzino to make an assignation for him with the latter's aunt, Caterina Ginori. Finally Lorenzino agreed to bring a meeting about. He told the Duke that it was arranged, and that the two were to meet secretly at his house for the sake of the lady's reputation. Lorenzino left the Duke in his chamber after securing his sword and fastening the door, and with a bravo called Scoronconcolo (whom he had prepared to commit a murder for him) set upon the Duke and killed him in spite of his struggles. The two then fled. Cosimo de Medici who was not quite eighteen, was chosen to succeed Alessandro (Napier, Florentine History, Bk. III, Chap. 1. Based on Varchi).

Segni (Istorie Fiorentine, p. 314) says that Lorenzino promised to procure his sister Laldomine, widow of Alemanno Salviati, for the Duke, who wished for a son whom he could be certain was his own. Lorenzino promised to bring the two together when his mother was absent. She had left Florence on the day of the assassination to visit her younger son, Guiliano.

Varchi (Storia Fiorentina, V, 106) says that Luisa Strozzi, to whom Alessandro made advances, was poisoned by her relatives in order to save her from him.[5]

From these accounts Shirley has built up his play with the aid of various lesser points which will be indicated in the course of the discussion.

Dessoff in his comparison of The Traitor and Enciso's Los Médicis de Florencia is of the opinion that the two dramatists used a common source (Studien zur vergleichenden Litteraturgeschichte, I, 421 ff.). In spite of the rad-

---

[5] In Appendix C (II, 221, note), the Heptameron, Bibliophilist's Society edition, the following additional authorities on the murder of Alessandro de' Medici are given: Nerli, lib. XII; Adriani, lib. I; Ammirato, lib. XXXI; Paulus Jovius, Hist., lib. XXXVIII; Guazzo, Istorie, fol. 159.

ical difference in plot of the plays, he finds eight or nine parallels, which are: an attempt to kill the Duke, which is prevented by a lady, Cosimo's resignation of a mistress to a friend, the taking of an oath to free Florence from Alessandro, a lady's threatening to stab herself, the Duke's letting Lorenzo read the letter accusing him of treason, a scrap of conversation between the Duke and Lorenzo, the promising of an assignation to the Duke and his assassination when separated from his retinue, Cosimo's being proclaimed Duke and marrying the lady whom he had renounced. However, on separating the parallels due to a common use of Florentine history from those which seem to come from some other source, it seems hardly safe to assume that such generally used romantic material as the latter class consists of would be necessarily drawn from any single given original.

The historical Lorenzo seems to have had no definite motive for his crime. He may, it seems from the historians, have been actuated by ambition, patriotism, personal revenge, or innate depravity. Shirley makes the first-named his prime motive. In the play he is a fine example of the Machiavellian false favorite (see Chap. IV, Sect. 33). Shirley's Cosmo, while he is noted for his old head on young shoulders (I, 1), and while he seems a trifle cold-blooded in his giving up Oriana (II, 2, p. 127), is not much like the crafty Cosimo of history who became ruler of Florence at less than eighteen, and very speedily its despot. In Alessandro, Shirley has drawn the typical conventional weak lustful sovereign (see Chap. IV, Sect. 37). Cf. Sciarrha and Floria with Melantius and Diphilius in The Maid's Tragedy. Depazzi (cf. Depazzi in The Humorous Courtier) is the conventional poltroon, and Petruchio, the villain's tool (for both, see Chap. IV, Sects. 33, 47). Amidea is the steadfastly virtuous heroine, while

Oriana, who is yielded to Pisano by the friendly and politic Cosmo, is akin to the deserted mistress (as in Amidea).

Act I, Sc. 1. Cosmo's renunciation of Oriana after
learning of Pisano's love for her (see also II, 2, IV, 2)
is drawn from The Grateful Servant, IV, 2 (cf. Chap. IV,
Sect. 4). Petruchio's owing his escape from the gallows
as referred to here and in V, 2, is based on Lorenzino's
having saved Scoronconcolo from that fate (Napier, Florentine History, Bk. III, Chap. 1; Varchi, Storia Fiorentina, V, 268). Cf. Bosola as having been released from
prison through the Cardinal, The Duchess of Malfi, I, 1.
The scene is entirely Shirley's as are all those dealing with
the subplot of Cosmo and Oriana.

Sc. 2 is based partly on the fact that Alessandro is
said to have been often warned against Lorenzino, who used
great boldness in defending himself and who pretended to
have been a spy on the Florentine exiles (Napier, Florentine History, Bk. III, Chap. 1). An analogue occurs in
I, 1, of The Cruel Brother, in which the Duke shows dis-
trust of Lucio, his favorite. The letters from Castruchio
in exile are suggestive of Davenant's Castruchio, "a satirical courtier," who stands by and comments during the
scene. Cf. Lorenzo's defense of himself with that of Melantius, The Maid's Tragedy, IV, 2. The mention of the death
of Cardinal Ippolito de Medici (who was Duke Alessandro's
cousin, not his brother as Shirley has it) and of Cardinal
Salviati's alliance with the Florentine exiles against the
Duke show Shirley to have drawn on some other account
than that of the Heptameron.

Act II, Sc. 1, may have been suggested remotely by the
French novel or may be based upon the historians. Lorenzo presses the Duke's suit for Amidea to Sciarrha as,
in the other accounts, Alessandro himself urges Lorenzino

to bring him and Caterina or Laldomine together. There
is a strong suggestion of an indebtedness to Lussurioso and
Vendice, The Revenger's Tragedy, I, 3, and Vendice and
Gratiana, *ibid.*, II, 1. Parallels occur in The Gamester, I,
1, Edward III, II, 1, Women beware Women, II, 1, A Wife
for a Month, I, 1. Koeppel (Shakespeare's Wirkung, p.
57) considers there to be an influence of Measure for Measure in this scene and those following which show the Duke's
pursuit of Amidea. The parallel must be admitted, but
Tourneur's influence is stronger than Shakespeare's, especially in the scene under discussion.

The plotting of the Duke's death is doubtless derived
from Lorenzino's preparation of Scoronconcolo for Alessandro's murder (cf. the later Politician, III, 1). The
patriotism and love of liberty simulated by Lorenzo may
have been suggested to Shirley by Lorenzino's Apologia.
The comparison of Lorenzo by Sciarrha with the ancient
Romans is based on the terming of Lorenzino, the "Florentine Brutus" (Segni, Istorie Fiorentine, p. 345). Cf.
also V, 3, Alessandro's "Thus Cæsar fell by Brutus." See
under The Young Admiral, I, 2.

The conversation between Sciarrha, Florio, and Amidea
is based on The Revenger's Tragedy, II, 1. Similar scenes
between near relatives, one of whom acts, or pretends to
act, as a pander occur in The Gamester, II, 1, Edward III,
II, 1, A Woman Killed with Kindness, V, 1, The Revenger's Tragedy, II, 1, The Second Maiden's Tragedy,
II, 1, Women beware Women, II, 1, The Loyal Subject,
III, 4, A Wife for a Month, I, 1, The Cruel Brother, III,
1.

The test has been discussed in Chap. IV, Sect. 15. Here
possibly it is a reminiscence of Vendice's trial of his mother,
Gratiana, The Revenger's Tragedy, II, 1. Gratiana urges
Lussurioso's suit to Castiza, who pretends her mother is

not herself, the course taken with Sciarrha by Amidea, who warns Florio from him as being a changeling. Cf. The Gamester, II, 1.

Sc. 2 (see I, 1). Cf. Morosa's part in this scene with that of Gratiana in The Revenger's Tragedy, II, 1.

Act III, Sc. 1. For trial scenes, see Chap. IV, Sect. 17. Mock trials paralleling that in this scene are to be found in The Family of Love, V, 3, The City Madam, III, 1, The Staple of News, V, 2, The Northern Lass, V, 8, Holland's Leaguer, IV, 5 (1632), Covent Garden, V, 6 (1632), Lady Alimony, II, 5 (1635), Trapolin Supposed a Prince, I, 2 (before 1640). Cf. also Falstaff as the King, Henry IV, Part I, II, 4. Rogero's absorption in his part recalls Chilax as Memnon, The Mad Lover, II, 2. Note also Rawbone's apprehensions as to the future, in The Wedding, IV, 3, in connection with Depazzi's terror. Rogero's speech recalls that made by Gasparo for the Country Magistrate, Love Tricks, II, 5, and harks forward to those of the Advocate, Chabot, III, 2, V, 2. The mention of the plot "to poison his highness' hunting-saddle" is possibly drawn from the supposed plot of Dr. Lopez against Queen Elizabeth in 1594 (Lee, D. N. B., XXXIV, 132 ff.).

The relations of Depazzi, Rogero, and Lorenzo, as shown in this scene and I, 2, are reminiscent of Lothario, Borachio, and Castruchio in The Cruel Brother. Depazzi, however, drops out of sight in IV, 1, whereas in Davenant's play Lothario slays the Duke. Lorenzo's letter to Depazzi parallels Richard's instructions to Buckingham, Richard III, III, 5.

Sc. 2. The masque may be derived from The Revenger's Tragedy, V, 3, although not used as a vehicle for a crime as there (see under The Cardinal, III, 2). The allegorical masque occurs again in The Coronation, IV, 3. Note also the play within the play, Hamlet, III, 2. See Chap.

IV, Sect. 18. For Amidea's intention of converting the Duke, see under The Grateful Servant, III, 4.

Sc. 3. Cf. The Custom of the Country, I, 2, with the Duke's presence in Amidea's chamber. His courtship of her suggests that of Titus Martius in The Faithful Friends, IV, 4. Marcus Tullius, like Sciarrha and Florio, is concealed in the room. Their eavesdropping also suggests that of Vendice and Hippolito, The Revenger's Tragedy, III, 4 (see also Chap. IV, Sect. 30). Parallels to the Duke's attempt on Amidea and her defense are noted in Chap. IV, Sect. 9. Her use of a weapon in defending herself (indirectly) is paralleled in The Duke's Mistress, V, 1, St. Patrick for Ireland, IV, 1, Edward III, II, 2, Lust's Dominion, V, 3, Westward Ho, IV, 2, A Woman Killed with Kindness, V, 1, Sophronisba, IV, 1, The Triumph of Honor, Sc. 4, The Custom of the Country, I, 2, The Little French Lawyer, IV, 6, Rule a Wife and Have a Wife, V, 4, The Second Maiden's Tragedy, V, 1, Catiline, II, 1, The Poor Man's Comfort, IV, All's Lost by Lust, I, 1 (reported), The Lovesick Court, IV, 2, The Novella, V, 1, The Jealous Lovers, III, 10 (1632). Note also The Example, III, 1.

For the conversion of the Duke, see Chap. IV, Sect. 10. An especially close parallel occurs in Edward III, II, 1, 2, in which the King first repents of his pursuit of the Countess of Salisbury, then resumes it, and again repents. Cf. Lorenzo's convincing the Duke of his loyalty in the face of Sciarrha's accusations with Melantius concerning the charges made by Calianax, The Maid's Tragedy, IV, 2. Observe Shirley's skilful use of surprise during the entire scene (see Chap. III).

Act IV, Sc. 1, opens with a typical villain's soliloquy such as occurs, for instance, in The Cardinal, V, 1, The Imposture, V, 3, The Court Secret, III, 2, Dick of Devon-

shire, IV, 1, The First Part of Jeronymo, p. 460, Lust's
Dominion, I, 2, 4, Henry VI, Part III, III, 2, V, 6, Richard III, I, 1, 3, Othello, I, 3, II, 1, 3, V, 1, King Lear,
I, 2, V, 1, Two Tragedies in One, I, 1, 3, 4, etc., Volpone, III, 1, Sejanus, II, 2, III, 2, V, 1, 4, The Dumb
Knight, I, 1, The Turk, I, 2, 3, II, 2, 3, III, 4, IV, 1,
The Knight of Malta, I, 1, The Deserving Favorite, II,
1, A Maidenhead Well Lost, I, 1 (p. 105), Imperiale, I,
3.

As far as the falseness of the repentance goes, Lorenzo's
penitence may be paralleled in The Insatiate Countess, III,
Valentinian, II, 6.

Sc. 2. For Amidea's renunciation of Pisano, cf. I, 1,
II, 2. Sciarrha's halting the bridal procession for a quar-
rel closely parallels I, 1, of The Little French Lawyer.
Analogous incidents occur in The Shoemaker's Holiday,
V, 2, The London Prodigal, III, 3, The Insatiate Coun-
tess, I, A Woman is a Weathercock, II, 1, Women beware
Women, IV, 3. See also The Old Law, V, 1 (comic), The
Two Noble Kinsmen, I, 1, The Maid of Honor, V, 2. For
Death as Amidea's husband, cf. The Witch of Edmonton,
III, 3. See also The Constant Maid, IV, 2.

The conditions under which Lorenzo guarantees Sciarrha's immunity from punishment for the death of Pisano
recall Measure for Measure, II, 4 (cf. Koeppel as earlier
cited). See also under II, 1, and under Love's Cruelty,
III, 3. Note Frederick and Valerio, A Wife for a Month,
IV, 2, and the King and Leucothoë, The Heir, IV.
Lorenzo's suggestion that the Duke might ''discharge his
Duchess with a quaint salad'' recalls the vengeance of the
President of Grenoble in Novel XXXVI, the Heptameron
(the source of a part of Love's Cruelty). The elevation
of Amidea hinted at parallels Frederick's offer to Evanthe,
A Wife for a Month, I, 1, and points forward to The

Duke's Mistress, II, 2. Note also The Wise Woman of Hogsdon, V, 4.

Act V, Sc. 1. Sciarrha's presentation of his predicament to Amidea seems derived from Measure for Measure, III, 1. Her death at the hands of Sciarrha to prevent any harm befalling her seems suggested by that of Luisa Strozzi, as related by Varchi, Storia Fiorentina, V, 106. Analogues more or less close are found in The Distracted Emperor, V, 3, The Second Maiden's Tragedy, III, 1 (planned by Govianus but executed by the Lady), The Cruel Brother, V, 1, The Distresses, IV, 1 (a threat) (·1639?).

Sciarrha's resolve to kill his sister when she is "nearest Heaven" is the antithesis of Hamlet's attitude toward Claudius, Hamlet, III, 3 (cf. The Cardinal, IV, 1), The Triumph of Death, Sc. 6, The Maid's Tragedy, V, 2, The Jealous Lovers, III, 9 (1632). Satiromastix, p. 249 ff., The Bloody Banquet, IV, 3, parallel Sciarrha's resolution.

Sc. 2. Lorenzo's stabbing Alexander's picture and his allusion to the belief as to bewitching a person by sticking pins in his image or his picture recall references to this superstition in The Whore of Babylon, p. 226, The Witch, V, 2, The Virgin-Martyr, III, 1, Goffe's Orestes, III, 6. Cf. Howell's Familiar Letters, I, 52. Lorenzo's reference to the Duke's "youth and beauty" are touches of the poet's, for Alessandro de Medici was the son of a mulatto slave and possessed the quadroon's complexion with woolly hair and thick lips. He was, however, a young man at the time of his death.

The arrangements for Amidea's visit to the Duke in secret were drawn doubtless from the stipulations for the meeting of Alessandro, and Laldomine Salviati or Caterina Ginori (Nápier, Florentine History, Bk. III, Chap. 1; Segni, Istorie Fiorentine, p. 314; Varchi, Storia Fiorentina, V, 268). The same occur in The Grateful Servant,

IV, 4, The Witty Fair One, IV, 3, 4, V, 3, The Gamester, III, 1, IV, 1, V, 2, The Lady of Pleasure, IV, 1.  Cf. also The Gentleman of Venice, II, 1, III, 3, IV, 3.  The same stipulation lies at the bottom of the complications of The Wedding.  Cf., for parallels, All's Well that Ends Well, IV, 2, Measure for Measure, IV, 1, The Fair Maid of the West, Part II, II, 1, Sophronisba, IV, 1, The Insatiate Countess, II, The Witch, II, 2, III, 1, The Bloody Banquet, II, 3, The Parliament of Love, III, 3, The City Nightcap, I, 1, Albovine, III, 1.

Sc. 3.  Amidea's body "discovered on a bed prepared by two Gentlewomen" is a distinct borrowing from "Vendice, with the skull of his betrothed dressed up in tires," The Revenger's Tragedy, III, 4.  The Duke's entrance and approach to the corpse are from the same play, with perhaps a hint from The Atheist's Tragedy, IV, 3.  Parallels are found in The Distracted Emperor, II, 1, Sophronisba, III, 1, The Second Maiden's Tragedy, V, 2, The Duke of Milan, V, 2.

The Duke's desiring death after he discovers Amidea to be lifeless suggests the offer of his life by the Duke to Foreste and Lucio in The Cruel Brother, V, 1.  They do not take advantage of the offer, however.  A closer parallel occurs in Alphonsus, Emperor of Germany, IV, 2.  Mentz in grief cries out for death; Alexander stabs him, excusing himself with, "It was my duty to obey you, sir."  The Duke's "Oh spare me to consider; I would live a little longer," is reminiscent of Mentz's "O, stay awhile."  Whether Shirley, or the author of Alphonsus, is the debtor is uncertain as the priority of that play to The Traitor is considered doubtful.  The Duke's cry of "Treason!" when he is attacked is based on Alessandro's exclamation of "Ah traditore!" (Segni, Istorie Fiorentine, p. 315).  The dismissal of his train agrees with the historical accounts in

that Alessandro took only two followers with him. One
he dismissed; the other after waiting without Lorenzino's
house grew tired and went home (cf. Napier, Florentine
History, Bk. III, Chap. 1).

Sciarrha's death seems drawn from that of Foreste in
The Cruel Brother, V, 1. Both die at the hands of the
two Dukes' instruments, Castruchio and Lorenzo, respectively. Castruchio does not fall as does Lorenzo but, like
Petruchio, attempts to escape, and is brought in as a prisoner at the end of the play. Cosmo assumes control of
the situation, as does Dorido. Cf. Lysippus' taking charge
of affairs in The Maid's Tragedy, V, 2. The death of
Lorenzo is unhistorical, of course. In reality he survived
the death of Alessandro about twelve years. Both he and
his accomplice escaped safely to Venice.

### III. LOVE'S CRUELTY

Two sources are offered for Love's Cruelty by Langbaine: Novel XXXVI of the Heptameron of Marguerite
of Navarre, and Novel 6, Decade III, of the Heccatomithi
of Cinthio (Dramatic Poets, pp. 480–81).[6] The French
version occurs in English as Novel 58, Part I, of Painter's
Palace of Pleasure, under the title of A President of
Grenoble. Miss Ott is of the opinion that it is probable
that Shirley used this translation (Die Italienische Novelle
im Englischen Drama, p. 113). Painter's translation is so
faithful to the original, however, as to preclude any positive statement on that point.

As a matter of fact, however, it seems nearly certain
that, while certain positions of Love's Cruelty are based
upon A President of Grenoble or its original, we must go
for the general source of the tragedy to A Woman Killed

---

[6] See also Les Cent Nouvelles Nouvelles, Novel LXVII.

with Kindness. The two plays correspond in details of the main plot which do not occur in the novels, and there is furthermore, a resemblance in their underplots.[7] It appears probable, indeed, that Shirley worked over Heywood's play, introducing the French story into his rewritten form of the earlier tragedy for the purpose, perhaps, of emphasizing Bellamente's regard for his honor.

It should be noted that between 1625 and 1636 nine plays of Heywood's were produced at the Cockpit to one at any other theatre, and that during this time Shirley wrote nearly exclusively for the Queen's Men at this theatre. This fact, together with the popularity of Heywood's plays, makes it extremely probable that Shirley was acquainted with the older man's most famous play. As to Queen Marguerite's novel, we find Shirley in two other plays using stories which are to be found in her collection, so it seems likely that he utilized the novel for certain scenes of his tragedy.

Love's Cruelty may thus be briefly summarized:

Bellamente praises his friend Hippolito to Clariana, his betrothed, so highly, and in such a manner as to arouse her curiosity concerning him. She visits Hippolito's apartments to see what sort of man he really is. Being called away by a message from the Duke, Hippolito locks her in. Bellamente is sent by his friend—who does not know who his visitor is—to release the lady. His jealousy is awakened, but he is appeased. The marriage of Bellamente and Clariana takes place. Clariana and Hippolito now yield to their passions, and are discovered together by a servant who reports to his master what he has seen. Bellamente,

[7] The source of the story of Mountford and Acton in A Woman Killed with Kindness is the Palace of Pleasure, Part II, Novel 30. Shirley's underplot, however, is nearer Heywood's play than it is to Painter's tale.

after assuring himself of the couple's guilt, by a ruse makes the servant think he has been mistaken. After some debate, he allows the pair to go unpunished. A little time after, Clariana, hearing of Hippolito's intended marriage sends for him secretly. On their meeting, she attempts to dissuade him from his marriage. Bellamente who surprises them together suspects a renewal of their previous intimacy. As he rushes out to alarm his servants, Clariana stabs Hippolito, who, in turn, kills her. Bellamente, on returning, falls dead. Hippolito dies of his wound after Eubella, his betrothed, has arrived. The underplot deals with the Duke's pursuit of Eubella, the virtuous daughter of Sebastian, an old honest lord, whose favor the Duke tries to win by heaping favors upon him. Hippolito, who is a former lover of hers, attempts to win her for the Duke, but, as a result of her firm defense of her chastity and his own experiences with Clariana and Bellamente, is converted and receives her hand from the Duke who also repents. At the end of the play, after Hippolito's death, the Duke proposes marriage to Eubella, and she seems not unfavorable to his suit.

Shirley's characters correspond thus with Heywood's: Bellamente = Frankford; Hippolito = Wendoll; the Servant = Nicholas; Clariana = Mrs. Frankford; and in the underplots, Sebastian = Sir Charles Mountford; the Duke and Hippolito = Sir Francis Acton; Eubella = Susan Mountford.

These characters are of a more or less stereotyped nature as they appear in Love's Cruelty. Bellamente, the high-minded lover and husband, Hippolito, the wild young man who repents, the lustful sovereign who repents likewise, Clariana, the wicked woman, Sebastian, the blunt honest old man (for the last four, see Chap. IV, Sects. 38, 37, 35, 39, and 10), and Eubella who successfully defends her chastity through all sorts of trials are familiar figures. Bovaldo, the loose-moraled old courtier, who is an added character of Shirley's, is to some extent reminiscent of Sophronius in The Second Maiden's Tragedy.

It is a significant fact that Shirley has laid the scene of his play in Italy at a petty court, and has made some of his characters courtiers. He has also changed the motivation of the husband's refusing to take vengeance upon his wife and her lover. Heywood's Frankford relies upon the guilty parties' consciousness of their guilt as a punishment, while Bellamente is influenced in addition by the desire of keeping his dishonor concealed. These two important changes in the play are directly in line with the practice of romanticizing plays by laying their scenes at court in a foreign country, by making their characters persons of rank, and by introducing various elements of the Spanish code of honor.

Act I, Sc. 1. Hippolito's refusal to see Clariana, as related to her by Bellamente, recalls Roderigo's similar refusal, The Spanish Gipsy, I, 5. Cf. also Nevill and Scudmore, A Woman is a Weathercock, I, 1.

Sc. 2. For social criticism, expressed directly and indirectly in the discussion of means of rising at court, or of life at court, see III, 1, following, and note The Royal Master, IV, 3, The Gentleman of Venice, II, 1 (Bellaura), The Grateful Servant, I, 1, 2, II, 1, III, 4, V, 1, The Humorous Courtier, IV, 1, V, 3 (in a broad way the entire play is an attack on court life), The Bird in a Cage, I, 1, II, 1, The Lady of Pleasure, IV, 2. Note that The Ball was expurgated before its acting was allowed, because of direct satire upon certain courtiers. See also As You Like It, II, 2 (indirectly), All's Well that Ends Well, II, 2, Timon of Athens, II, 2, The Old Law, II, 1, Every Man out of his Humor, II, 1, The Woman Hater, I, 3, Valentinian, III, 2, The Elder Brother, V, 1, The Renegado, II, 1 (pimping as a road to preferment), The Picture, I, 2, The Emperor of the East, I, 2, May's Cleopatra, II, The Fancies Chaste and Noble, II, 1, 3. The Duke's attempt to make Sebastian an agent in securing Eubella's compliance with his desires suggests Lorenzo and Sciarrha, The Traitor, II, 1. Cf. also A Woman Killed with Kindness, IV, 2. Examples of the honoring of a father by a prince who designs the daughter's ruin are to be found in The Downfall of Robert, Earl of Huntington, III, 1, The Second Maiden's Tragedy, II, 3, Match Me in London, IV, The Virgin Widow, I, 1.

Act II, Sc. 1. Hippolito's fencing-lesson in his apartment should be compared with Bobadill and Matthew, Every Man in his Humor, I, 4. Clariana's visit and her remaining in Hippolito's lodgings (II, 3), recall Constantia at Don John's apartment, The Chances, I, II. For the allusion to Lindabrides, a lady of easy virtue in The Mirror of Knighthood, cf. Honoria and Mammon, I, 2, and see Koeppel, Reflexe der Ritter-Romane in Drama, p. 212, note.

Sc. 2 is somewhat reminiscent of I, 1, A Wife for a Month. Hippolito corresponds to Soranzo, the Duke to Frederick, and Eubella to Evanthe. There is also a certain resemblance to The Traitor, II, 1. For courtship by proxy, see Chap. IV, Sect. 3. Hippolito's enumeration of the delights which would be Eubella's should she yield to the Duke's suit belongs to the "invitation to love" group which seems to date from Marlowe's Passionate Shepherd to his Love, and Donne's Bait. Analogues occur in The Doubtful Heir, IV, 2, The Grateful Servant, IV, 5, The Lady of Pleasure, V, 1, The Triumph of Beauty, pp. 336–37, Captain Underwit, II, 2, Mucedorus, IV, 3, Friar Bacon and Friar Bungay, p. 165, Lust's Dominion, I, 1, The Blind Beggar of Alexandria, p. 17, Volpone, III, 6, The

Turk, V, 3, The Elder Brother, III, 5, IV, 3, Believe as
You List, IV, 6, Microcosmus, III, Hannibal and Scipio,
IV, 5 (1635), Cartwright's Siege, II, 6, V, 4 (1637), The
Obstinate Lady, IV, 2 (1638–39). See also Shirley's Narcissus (Poems, VI, 477–79), and note the joys of the rustic
life, Love Tricks, IV, 2. Burlesques occur in The Lady
of Pleasure, V, 1, Captain Underwit, II, 2, Wit in a Constable, II, 1 (1639). This passage of Shirley's in Love's
Cruelty is remarkable in being entirely in prose. Florid
verse is the usual medium of expression. For Eubella's
defense of her virtue, see Chap. IV, Sect. 9. A particular
parallel, however, occurs in A Woman Killed with Kindness, V, 1 (Sir Francis Acton and Susan). Shirley's compliment to Jonson in this scene should be compared with
the dedication to The Grateful Servant and the prologue
to The Sisters. Steevens' assertion that Shirley's commendatory verses to Love's Sacrifice (printed 1633) contain an attack on Jonson is not founded on fact (see the
Shakespeare Variorum, I, 405). Prynne is certainly
Shirley's mark. Cf. A Prologue to the Alchemist Acted
there [Ireland] (VI, 490–91).

Sc. 3 has no analogues save the remote one noted under
II, 1.

Act III, Sc. 1. See Chap. IV, Sect. 26, for the drinking-
scene. The entrance of fiddlers, or other entertainers, to
scenes of conviviality, as here, is found in The Gamester,
II, 2, as well as in The Jew of Malta, IV, 5, A Cure for a
Cuckold, IV, 1, Wit in a Constable, V, 1 (1639). For
the satirical dialogue between Bovaldo and Sebastian upon
rising at court, see I, 2.

Sc. 2. A Woman Killed with Kindness, II, 3, seems the
source. Both scenes begin with a soliloquy by the false
friend (Wendoll and Hippolito, respectively) in which each
laments his treachery toward the trusting husband. In

each play the false wife then enters, and at her sight the lovers' compunctions vanish. In both plays the woman mentions her husband's absence from home, and desires her lover to stay to keep her company. In Love's Cruelty, however, it is Clariana who makes the advances, whereas Wendoll does the lovemaking in A Woman Killed. The entrance of Nicholas in the latter play and the rousing of his suspicions, together with his voicing of them in a soliloquy, are used in Shirley's tragedy in the appearance of Hippolito's Page and Bellamente's Groom, the latter of whom suspects Hippolito of undue familiarity with his mistress. Their conversation also recalls that of Jenkin and Cicely, A Woman Killed, IV, 4, in which, as in Shirley's scene, the mistress is suspected of infidelity to her husband, and the voicer of the suspicions is rebuked by his companion.

Sc. 3. Sebastian's outbreak at the Duke's proposal recalls that of Helvetius, The Second Maiden's Tragedy, II, 3, and of Valerio, A Wife for a Month, IV, 2. Cf. the Duke's suggestion as to Eubella's ransoming her father with Lorenzo's offer to Sciarrha, The Traitor, IV, 2, V, 1. An analogue occurs in The Distracted State, II, 1 (1641).

Sc. 4 has a partial parallel in A Woman Killed, yet probably the source is Queen Marguerite's novel. In III, 2, of Heywood's play, Frankford is informed by Nicholas of his wife's infidelity, while Bellamente is told of Clariana and Hippolito by a servant who had discovered them in the act. Bellamente's soliloquy near the beginning of the scene is nearly a paraphrase of Frankford's in A Woman Killed, as cited above. Shirley differs from the French story in having the servant discover the couple almost in his master's presence, and to report immediately what he has seen. Note The Fatal Dowry, III, 1. The placing of the servant at the foot of the stair with arms to prevent an escape comes from the French. For the calling a messenger with bad news a "raven," cf. Nobody and Somebody, p. 316, Macbeth, I, 5, The Raging Turk, IV, 3, A New Wonder: A Woman Never Vexed, III, 1.

Act IV, Sc. 1. The false wife and her lover in bed at the beginning of this scene is Shirley's, but cf. 'Tis Pity She's a Whore, V, 5. The song of For He Did but Kiss Her, quoted by Clariana, occurs in Robert Jones' First Book of Songs and Airs (1601), according to Ebsworth (quoted by Bullen, Old Plays, IV, 384). The song is mentioned also in The Grateful Servant, V, 1, and Every Woman in Her Humor, II, 2. In both A Woman Killed with Kindness, IV, 6 (reported), and the French novel the lover and his mistress are surprised by the latter's husband. Cf. also The Malcontent, II, 5 (narrated), The Atheist's Tragedy, IV, 5, A Christian Turned Turk, p. 231, The Fatal Dowry, IV, 2, Revenge for Honor, III, 1, The Elder Brother, IV, 4 (comic), Love's Sacrifice, V, 1. After the entrance of Bellamente the Heptameron is the chief source. The lover concealed by the husband while the servant enters and helps search for him, the dismissal of the last convinced that his eyes had deceived him, the subsequent departure of the lover unharmed—these are all from the French. Note that in A Woman Killed, III, 2, Frankford suggests that Nicholas' eyes may have deceived him. The permitting the guilty couple to escape, however, seems more due to Heywood's influence, for retribution finally comes in the novel to the pair. Bellamente, like Frankford, forswears his wife, but does not drive her from him, as Mrs. Frankford is driven away. Hippolito, too is required to keep from his former friend's sight. Bellamente's questioning of Clariana as to what deficiency she had found in him is drawn from A Woman Killed with Kindness, IV, 6. Note The Fatal Dowry, IV, 4. Shirley's emphasis on the maintenance of appearances is drawn from Queen Marguerite rather than from Heywood. The escape of an adulteress, real or supposed, with or without her paramour, more or less by the husband's connivance, is found in Bussy D'Ambois, V, 1, The Maid's Tragedy, IV, 1, The Fatal Dowry, IV, 4, The Just Italian, III, 1, The Platonic Lovers, V, 1 (1635).

Sc. 2. See Chap. IV, Sect. 9, for Eubella's defense of her chastity. Koeppel derives this incident with the similar ones in Hyde Park, V, 1, and The Example, III, 1, from Pericles, IV, 6 (Shakespeare's Wirkung, p. 58, note). This derivation shows how easy it is to find an indebtedness where none really exists. The lady who falls in love with the person who courts her for another is found also in The Royal Master, II; 1, The Sisters, IV, 4, Henry VI, Part I, V, 3, Twelfth Night, I, 5, III, 1, The Trial of Chivalry, I, 3, Every Woman in her Humor, II, 1, The Lovesick King, II. For the conversions of Hippolito and the Duke, see Chap. IV, Sect. 10. The repentance of the latter may be derived from A Woman Killed with Kindness, V, I (Sir Francis Acton and Susan Mountford).

Sc. 3 seems based in spirit on Frankford's mourning over his wife's lute in A Woman Killed, V, 2. Shirley's second marriage may account for his description of the true wife; with this passage should be compared Strozza's speech, The Gentleman Usher, IV, 1, and Valentine's, Wit without Money, I, 1.

Act V, Sc. 1. Hippolito's fear lest Clariana's letter is a snare laid by Bellamente is drawn from Nicholas' fear of the President's vengeance in Queen Marguerite's novel.

Sc. 2. See under IV, 1, and cf. The Guardian, III, 6, especially as to the part which Clariana's maid, Milena, plays (the maid who aids her mistress in arranging her assignation is a common figure, however). The source for Clariana's revenge upon Hippolito may be the attempted murder of Soranzo by Hippolita in 'Tis Pity She's a Whore, IV, 1. Here also the revenge recoils upon the avenger, but the object of it is not slain as in Love's Cruelty. The close of the play with its promise of future happiness for Eubella should be compared with the last scene of The Politician and the prospects of the widowed Albina as there intimated.

## IV. THE POLITICIAN

The identification of The Politician with The Politic Father (see Chap. II) has been disputed. In Anglia, VIII, 410, and his later works, Fleay advanced the theory that The Politician was played in Dublin and that The Politic Father is the comedy known to us as The Brothers, while the play licensed in 1626, under that title, he would have us believe to be Dick of Devonshire which Bullen assigns to Heywood. Nason (James Shirley, Chap. II) argues that The Brothers is The Politic Father of 1641, and that The Brothers of 1626 is non-extant. He does not accept Fleay's identification of The Brothers of 1626 with Dick of Devonshire. Schipper (James Shirley, pp. 242-3) and Neilson (Cam. Hist. Eng. Lit., VI, 225) seem to agree with Fleay as to the production of the play in Ireland. Ward is skeptical as to the identification of The Brothers and The Politic Father (Hist. Eng. Dram. Lit., III, 104).

There is no evidence that The Politician was not first acted in Ireland, but why it is not identical with The Politic Father is not very clear. We have the King of Norway, a father, and certainly politic, while Gotharus, who, at least, thinks himself a father, and who is, according to Shirley, a politician, has a very good claim also to the designation which furnishes the title to the latter play. The Elizabethan meaning of the word "politician" [8] describes either of these characters better than it does Don Carlos in The Brothers.

Fleay himself refers to Shirley's "habit of renaming his plays (Anglia, VIII, p. 410), so that the difference in title between The Politic Father and The Politician needs no especial attention. The fact that The Brothers was first printed in 1652 means little. To argue for the date 1641 from that circumstance would lead one to suggest that the plays printed in the Beaumont and Fletcher folio of 1647 were first produced years after the deaths of the authors.

In the article cited above Fleay states (p. 410) that The Brothers "must date in 1641 since the prologue alludes to the King's 'Spanish plot' of that year." In the first place, Shirley would not have been likely to have alluded to any such affair as the turning over of the Irish army to Spain; if he had done so, it would not have been jocularly; and thirdly, the allusion is most probably to the plot of the play which is laid in Spain. In addition, any references to a Spanish plot would have been relished more, perhaps, by an audience in 1626, than in 1641. [9]

There is no reason to suppose that Shirley did not write for the Queen's Men at Salisbury Court after 1636. In-

[8] N. E. D. (I) "A shrewd schemer"; (II) "a statesman." Cf. the use of the term in The Laws of Candy, V, 1, The Iron Age, Part I, I, 1, The Turk, II, 1, 2, IV, 1, Appius and Virginia, II, 1, The False One, *dramatis personæ*, The Distracted State, *dramatis personæ* (1641). See Characters 12 ("A Simple Politician"), and 22 ("A Sick Machiavel Politician") in Bks. I and II, respectively, The Essays and Characters of John Stephens, the Younger.

[9] See Clarendon, Hist., I, 492 ff.; Gardiner, Hist. of Eng., IV, 373-74, X, 10. The so-called plot was formed between May 10, 1641, and the latter part of August of that year.

deed, The Gentleman of Venice seems to have been produced there in 1639. It is surely as reasonable to believe him to have written two plays for that company as one. For Fleay's statement that The Politic Father was licensed for the King's Men at Blackfriars (Stage, p. 361) there seems no basis. The Politician, under whatever title it first was played, was acted at Salisbury Court by the Queen's Men. This is shown by the titlepage of the edition of 1655, and by the fact that the prologue to The Cardinal specifically mentions that play as being Shirley's first tragedy for the King's Men.

There is, moreover, no direct evidence to connect Dick of Devonshire with Shirley, or The Brothers with The Politic Father (see Chap. X for the former). Fleay's citation of "You show a provident father" (The Brothers, I, 1) as a proof of the play's identity with The Politic Father is of no particular value, for the expression is not identical with the title (see Chap. IV, Sect. 31). Nissen's idea (James Shirley, p. 13, note) that the dedication to The Brothers shows it to be dated after 1640 is based apparently on a misunderstanding of the English. Shirley says, "This composition [The Brothers], which, after its birth, had in my thoughts, a dedication to your name, although it but now took the boldness to wear it in the forehead." These words do not refer to the dedication of the play *at* "its birth" in 1626, to Thomas Stanley, then an infant in arms, but to its dedication *after* its birth to that gentleman, who was past twenty-five years of age in 1652. The fact that The Brothers seems to have been produced by the King's Men at Blackfriars has no especial significance in the dating of the play, for Shirley may as well have written for them in 1626 as in 1641. The evidence of the titlepage of The Brothers is against Fleay's statement (Stage, p. 333) that this comedy was licensed for the Queen's Men at the Cockpit. Nothing seems to support Fleay save that nearly all of Shirley's early plays were acted by that company. Neither The Brothers nor The Politician was in the list of plays claimed by Beeston, in 1639 for the Cockpit Company (Collier, Hist. Eng. Dram. Poet., II, 91–92, note), so that they must either have been produced subsequent to that date, or have been the property of another company.

That The Brothers was the property of the King's Men is conclusively shown not only by the titlepage of the early edition, and by Moseley's list bound up therewith (Nason, James Shirley, Chap. II), but by contemporary documentary evidence. In a list of sixty unpublished plays belonging to the King's Men which is appended to a warrant of the Lord Chamberlain, the Earl of Essex, The Brothers stands forty-fifth, with The Doubtful Heir, The Imposture, and The Country Captain, forty-first, forty-second and forty-third, respectively.[10] Certainly it seems improbable to say the least, that in this list dated August 7, 1641, ten weeks after the licensing of The Politic Father, that that play should appear with a new title in an official enumeration. Many of these plays are very old ones. Twenty-seven are Beaumont and Fletcher's. What so remarkable then that Shirley's Brothers should remain unpublished fifteen years after its first presentation when Beaumont and Fletcher's Woman's Prize, produced thirty-five years earlier also was in the player's hands in MS.?

The fact of the matter seems to be that The Brothers of 1652 is The Brothers of 1626, which was produced by the King's Men, and that The Politician of 1655 is The Politic Father of 1641 which was presented by the Queen's Men. In 1652 Shirley was probably first able to secure

10 Edited by Chambers, Malone Society Collections, I, 364 ff.

the rights of publication of his King's Men plays, or perhaps the actors themselves designed to publish in one volume all the plays Shirley wrote for them.

According to Langbaine, a story resembling the plot of The Politician occurs in the first book of The Countess of Montgomery's Urania [11] (Dramatic Poets, p. 481). As in Hoffman, the non-extant Danish Tragedy, Hamlet, The Loyal Subject, The Costly Whore, Albertus Wallenstein, and Brennoralt (the list is incomplete), the scene of The Politician is laid in northern Europe. A leading theme of the play is the intrigue of the ambitious favorite, Gotharus (for whom see Chap. IV, Sect. 33). The wicked stepmother, Queen Marpisa (whose name may be from Sidney's Marpesia, The Arcadia, Bk. III, p. 366), occurs in the play as in Andromana, Cupid's Revenge, and Cymbeline (see Chap. IV, Sect. 35). Her relations with Gotharus which play an important part are paralleled in Titus Andronicus, Henry VI, Part II, The Malcontent, The Mayor of Queenborough, The Revenger's Tragedy, Nero, Albovine, among others. This triangular relationship in The Politician—the King, Queen and Gotharus,—is complicated by Albina, the wife of Gotharus whom the King admires. Turgesius, the Prince, relates the tragedy to those plays in which ingratitude to a successful commander plays a part,

[11] The Countess of Montgomery's Urania, by Lady Mary Wroth, niece to Sir Phillip Sidney, was entered in the Stationers' Register, July 13, 1621, and was published the same year; hence why Neilson should think that the priority of The Urania to The Politician needs "further examination" (Cam. Hist. Eng. Lit., VI, 225) is a mystery. On account of the satiric treatment of the amorous adventures of certain courtiers, the sale of the book was stopped. The Urania seems now to be an extremely rare volume, probably because of this attempt at suppressing it. For information concerning it and its author, see Horace Walpole, Noble Authors, I, 485; Sir Sidney Lee, D. N. B., LXIII, 161 ff.

as The Young Admiral, Coriolanus, The Loyal Subject, Albertus Wallenstein, etc. Besides these general relationships, the influence of Sejanus seems strong in some portions of the play.

The plot of The Politician follows:

The King of Norway, while his son Turgesius is absent on a campaign, marries Marpisa, who has been, and still is, the mistress of Gotharus, the King's favorite, who neglects for her Albina, his virtuous wife. Marpisa and Gotharus plot to make Haraldus (her son by a former marriage, who is thought by Gotharus to be his child) heir to the throne in place of Turgesius. They make the King jealous of his son by representing him to be ambitious of becoming King. Letters forged by them and the expostulations of Olaus, the King's uncle, at his marriage increase his anger at the Prince. When Turgesius returns, he is harshly received by his father. Aquinus, an honest soldier, pretends to be suborned by Gotharus to murder the Prince. The populace and soldiery rise at the supposed death of Turgesius. Gotharus, who is pursued by them, is poisoned by Marpisa who considers him responsible for the death of Haraldus. The Prince is found to be alive, the King in atonement to his son offers to abdicate, Marpisa poisons herself and dies penitently, while only the virtuous characters are left alive at the end of the play.

Haraldus, the young son of Marpisa, whose part it is to supply a pathetic element in the play, parallels Young Lucius in Titus Andronicus, Young Talbot in Henry VI, Part I, and the various Princes, etc., in Parts II, III, Arthur in King John, the Princes in Richard III, Lucius in Julius Cæsar, Fleance and Macduff's Children in Macbeth, Young Marcus in Coriolanus, Mamillius in The Winter's Tale, Ned in George-a-Greene, Mahomet in Selimus, the true and false Ascanii in Dido, Queen of Carthage, Edward

III in Edward II, the children of Antony in The Virtuous
Octavia, the Boy in A Warning for Fair Women, the
Younger Bruce in The Death of Robert, Earl of Hunting-
ton, Pertillo in Two Tragedies in One, Julio in Antonio's
Revenge, Astor, Phillippo and the Boys in The Devil's
Charter, Urania in Cupid's Revenge, Hengo in Bonduca,
the Boy in Sir John Van Olden Barnavelt, Lucio in The
Double Marriage, Giovanni in The White Devil, Edward
and Maria in Anything for a Quiet Life, the Babes in The
Bloody Banquet, Aegrothus' Boy in Goffe's Orestes, Alad-
din's Children in The Courageous Turk, Britannicus in
Agrippina, Sebastian in The Noble Soldier, Gonzago in
The Queen and Concubine.

For the fops (and poltroons) Sueno and Helga, cf.
Fabio in The Young Admiral, note Sycophant in Nobody
and Somebody, the lord described by Hotspur, Henry IV,
Part I, I, 3, and see Chap. IV, Sect. 47. For the blunt
old Olaus, see Chap. IV, Sect. 39, and cf. Ismenus in
Cupid's Revenge. Cf. Aquinus with Pallante in The
Duke's Mistress, Claudio in The Imposture, and note Pon-
tius in Valentinian.

The list of "characters" appended to the names in the
*dramatis personæ* is found again in The Gentleman of
Venice. Cf. Every Man Out of his Humor and The New
Inn. For the use of the title of the play in the *dramatis
personæ*, cf. The Young Admiral, etc. See also I, 1, IV,
5, V, 2, following.

Act I, Sc. 1, opens as does Sejanus, I, 1. Two "honest
courtiers" enter and discuss conditions at court with special reference in both to the favorites, Gotharus and Sejanus. Then in both plays a virtuous character and a
wicked one (Drusus and Albina, Sejanus and Gotharus)
pass over the stage separately and are commented on by
the courtiers. Gotharus, as he enters, is besieged by peti-

tioners; Sejanus is beset by flatterers and placehunters. In both plays the probable removal of the heirs to the crown is discussed. The marriage of Marpisa and the King recalls that of Margaret and Henry VI, Henry VI, Part I, V, 3, 5, Part II, I, 1. Petitioners are also introduced in The Sisters, IV, 2. Parallels occur in The Spanish Tragedy, III, 13, Henry VI, Part II, I, 3, Timon of Athens, I, 1, Nobody and Somebody, p. 280, Edward IV, Part I, p. 81, The Malcontent, I, 5, The Mayor of Queenborough, I, 1, The Prophetess, III, 1, The Lovesick Court, I, 1, The Queen and Concubine, II, 3, The Emperor of the East, I, 2, III, 2, Believe as You List, I, 2.

Gotharus' plot against Turgesius is the same as Cesario's against Vittori, The Young Admiral, I, 1. More or less close analogues are found in The Faithful Friends, II, 1, David and Bethsabe, p. 468 ff., Lust's Dominion, III, 2, Hamlet, III, 1 (narrated in V, 2), Cupid's Revenge, II, 2, All's Lost by Lust, I, 1. Howell, Familiar Letters, I, 208, relates a somewhat similar story of the Duke of Ossuna. The jealousy of the successful general in The Royal King and Loyal Subject, and Albertus Wallenstein is related to the feelings of Gotharus.

Characters crossing the stage while other personages comment on them (often furnishing ''characters'' of them) occur in Hyde Park, I, 1, The Gamester, III, 3, The Example, I, 1, Antonio and Mellida, I, Cynthia's Revels, II, 1, Sejanus, I, 1, V, 8, Troilus and Cressida, I, 2, Pericles, II, 2, Henry VIII, IV, 1, The Dumb Knight, II, 1, The Turk, I, 1, Philaster, I, 1, The Loyal Subject, IV, 2, A Wife for a Month, V, 2, Ram Alley, I, 1, The White Devil, II, 4, The Changeling, V, 2, Nero, I, 1, The Partial Law, I, 5, The Novella, I, 1, Lady Alimony, II, 2.

For Albina's defense of virtue and Gotharus' eavesdropping, see Chap. IV, Sects. 9 and 30. His jealousy (partly pretended) recalls Othello, IV, 2, while his soliloquy is based apparently on that of Iago, *ibid.*, I, 3. Cf. also Lust's Dominion, I, 4. Haraldus' desire of attending the University at Wittenberg and Gotharus' attempts at dissuasion recall Hamlet, I, 2. Jerom in Hoffman, I (p. 9), is mentioned as having been a student at Wittenberg. For the dialogue of Marpisa and Gotharus at the end of the act, Livia and Sejanus, Sejanus, II, 1, should be compared. Further analogues are Roxena and Horsus, The Mayor of Queenborough, III, 1, and Isabella and Mortimer, The Fall of Mortimer.

Act II, Sc. 1. The beating of Sueno (cf. III, 1) is paralleled by Sejanus, I, 2 (Drusus striking Sejanus). Cf. also Henry VI, Part II, I, 3, Nobody and Somebody, pp. 298, 316. For Helga's fooling over the telling of news see I, 1, of The Young Admiral. Koeppel (Shakespeare's Wirkung, p. 60) derives Fabio's tediousness in that play from Polonius, Hamlet, II, 2. There is no direct source, however, for either of Shirley's incidents, for the same is to be found in Romeo and Juliet, II, 5, III, 2, Henry IV, Part II, V, 3, The Case is Altered, I, 2, A Tale of a Tub, III, 1, Westward Ho, II, 2, A King and No King, II, 1, The Lovesick Court, I, 2. An analogue for the King's jealousy of Turgesius as displayed in this scene (and III, 1) is that of Almanzor towards Abilqualit in Revenge for Honor, II, 1, which, like the King of Norway's, is created and fed by a wicked favorite. Cf. Cupid's Revenge, III, 4, and The Bloody Brother, II, 1.

For the conversation of Haraldus and Gotharus (with IV, 3), cf. Hamlet and his mother, Hamlet, III, 4. The question of Haraldus' legitimacy parallels that of Phillip, Lust's Dominion, I, 3, etc. Olaus' upbraiding of the King on account of his marriage again suggests Hamlet, III, 4. Kent's attack on Lear, King Lear, I, 1, should be compared, as well as Lust's Dominion, II, 1, and The Costly Whore, III, 1. As the King goes out he refers, apparently, to Cynthia's Revels.

Act III, Sc. 1. Sueno's plucking a hair from Reginaldus' beard and being beaten therefor seems derived from Young Barnacle and Hazard, The Gamester, II, 2, V, 1; see also The Imposture, V, 1. The conversation between Marpisa and Albina is founded on that between Ardelia and Euphemia in The Duke's Mistress, II, 2.

Sc. 2. The orders given by the King to raise forces to oppose Turgesius are a reminiscence of Cesario's commands in The Young Admiral, I, 1, and parallel The Loyal Subject, II, 1. The inciting of Aquinus to the murder of Turgesius by Gotharus is an echo of Valerio and Pallante, The Duke's Mistress, III, 3. Cf. also The Traitor, II, 1, The Coronation, III, 2, The Iron Age, Part II, V, 1, The Malcontent, III, 3, The Insatiate Countess, IV, The Phœnix, IV, 1, The Witch, II, 2, The Changeling, II, 2, Othello, IV, 2, The Spanish Curate, V, 1, Albovine, IV, 1, 'Tis Pity She's a Whore, II, 2, The Lady's Trial, III, 4, The Distracted State, IV, 1 (1641). For Gotharus' quotation from The Spanish Tragedy, II, 1, see under The Constant Maid, I, 1.

Sc. 3. Ward (Hist. Eng. Dram. Lit., III, 98, note) derives this scene from Cassio's intoxication, Othello, II, 3. The resemblance is merely general, as it is to the drinking scenes listed in Chap. IV, Sect. 26. The scene is related more closely to The Young Admiral, IV, 1, and its analogues, as the purpose of the intoxicating of Haraldus is to remove his melancholy (a specific treatment for a temperamental ailment). Haraldus' throwing a glass of wine in the face of one of his companions recalls The Gamester, II, 2, The Imposture, V, 1, Fortune by Land and Sea, I, 1, The New Inn, IV, 2.

Sc. 4 (with IV, 2). The return of a victorious force to a hostile court is drawn from The Young Admiral, I, 2. Parallels are Titus Andronicus, I, 1, The Loyal Subject, II, 1, and Appius and Virginia, I, 3, 4. As in The Young Admiral, a forcible entry to the city is advised, which is dismissed with a reproof by the commander. Cassandra's account of affairs at court in The Young Admiral is paralleled by Olaus' story in the earlier scene.

Act IV, Sc. 1. The dialogue between Gotharus and the King at the beginning of this scene is based on The Young Admiral, II, 1, in which Vittori is discussed by Cesario and the King of Naples. The reported illness of Haraldus seems, like the illness and death of Mamillius, The Winter's Tale, III, 2, a sort of visitation for the wickedness of his parents. Cf. the "death" of Gonzago, The Queen and Concubine, IV, 6.

Sc. 2. See III, 4. The pretended murder of Turgesius by Aquinus is based upon Claudio's attempt on Honorio's life, The Imposture, IV, 4. Cf. Pallante's plot against the Duke in The Duke's Mistress, IV, 1, V, 1. Lust's Dominion, II, 4, should also be compared.

Sc. 3 (see II, 1) seems a combination of Hamlet, III, 4 (Hamlet and his mother), and A King and No King, V, 4 (Arbaces, Arane and Gobrias). The question of a son's legitimacy is put to his mother by the Bastard in King John, I, 1. Parallels for Haraldus' death have been cited under Sc. 1 of this act; to these should be added that of Urania in Cupid's Revenge, V, 3. The rebellion, the breaking out of which Hormenus reports, is a device used by many Elizabethan dramatists to aid in bringing about the end of a play. Revolts are thus employed in The Doubtful Heir, V, 4, The Coronation, IV, 3, Philaster, V, 3, The Loyal Subject, IV, Cupid's Revenge, IV, 3, 4, The Double Marriage, V, 1.

Sc. 4. Marpisa's revenge upon Gotharus, whom she holds accountable for Haraldus' death, is accomplished by means of a box of poison under the guise of medicine. There seems a relationship here to Berinthia's substitution of poison for a love-potion in The Maid's Revenge, V, 2. A possible source is Aglaura, V, 3. Cf. The Cardinal, V, 3, and Cymbeline, I, 5, etc. For other poisonings, see Chap. IV, Sects. 11 and 12. Albina's surprising her husband with Marpisa repeats I, 1, and is a reversal of Love's Cruelty, IV, 1.

Sc. 5. Gotharus' escape from the rebels seems derived from Timentes' attempted escape from a pretended pursuit in The Swisser, III, 1 (Timentes, however, dies of fear, not by poison, as does Gotharus). Analogues occur in Locrine, II, 5, The Iron Age, Part II, V, 1, Henry IV, Part I, V, 4, The Turk, IV, 1, Alphonsus, Emperor of Germany, II, 3 (this play contains not only the feigning of death but an exchange of clothing also), The Prisoners, III, 5.

Sc. 6. For the resurrections of Turgesius and Aquinus, see Chap. IV, Sect. 29.

Act V, Sc. 1. The quarrel between the King and Marpisa seems without parallels.

Sc. 2 seems related, as far as the adjustments of difficulties, righting of wrongs, etc., go, to Philaster, V, 4, 5. Gotharus' squalid death is paralleled by that of Suffolk, Henry VI, Part II, IV, 1. The rebels' desire for fragments of Gotharus' body is drawn either from the threats towards Pharamond, Philaster, V, 4, or the description of the mutilation of Sejanus, Sejanus, V, 10. Note the parcelling out of the body of St. Hugh, A Shoemaker a Gentleman, IV, 2. The King's humility at his entrance suggests Richard II, IV, 1, and Edward III, V. Marpisa's entrance and her tirades before her repentant death seem related to the death of Bacha, Cupid's Revenge, V, 3. Cf.

Artesia's defiance in The Birth of Merlin, V, 2 (she, however, does not escape punishment for her crimes as do
Marpisa and Bacha), and the Queen, Cymbeline, V, 5 (reported). Eleazar's dying curses in Lust's Dominion, V, 6,
ought also to be noted.

## V. The Cardinal

As Dyce in his Account (p. xxxix) says, The Cardinal
was plainly written under the influence of The Duchess of
Malfi. The stories of the two plays touch in several points,
but there is no plagiarism or close borrowing. The revenge tragedy as a class contributes something to The Cardinal, while plays in which Church dignitaries figure, such
as Henry VIII, furnish hints for various incidents.

The plot of The Cardinal runs as follows:

The Duchess Rosaura, a young widow, loves, and is loved
by, Alvarez, a young Navarrese noble. The Cardinal, who
is the King's favorite, induces his master to press her to
marry Columbo, the Cardinal's nephew. Rosaura is betrothed to him against her will. While Columbo is on a
campaign, she writes him a letter asking for her release
from their engagement. Columbo misinterprets the letter,
as the Duchess intends, and releases her. Rosaura then
obtains permission of the King to marry Alvarez. On Columbo's return, he plans a revenge upon the Duchess, and
accordingly murders Alvarez during the celebration of his
wedding. Rosaura now meditates revenge on Columbo,
and allies herself with Hernando, a soldier unjustly disgraced by Columbo. Hernando slays Columbo in a duel.
The Cardinal, in pursuing his revenge upon Rosaura for
Columbo's death, attempts a rape upon her while she is
simulating madness, and is wounded by Hernando, who
then stabs himself. The Cardinal, mistakenly believing
himself dying, poisons Rosaura and himself.

For the Cardinal as a wicked favorite, see Chap. IV, Sect. 33, and cf. the Cardinals in Henry VI, Parts I, II, The Duchess of Malfi, Henry VIII, The Distracted State (1641). Cf. the Duchess with Berinthia in The Maid's Revenge, the Duchess in The Duchess of Malfi, Katherine in Henry VIII, the Duchess in More Dissemblers besides Women, Onaela in The Noble Soldier. Hernando, who corresponds to Bosola in the latter part of The Duchess of Malfi, suggests Hamond in The Bloody Brother, Adorni in The Maid of Honor, Stephanos in The Roman Actor, Baltazar in The Noble Soldier, Zorranes in Aglaura. As an avenger he recalls Sciarrha in The Traitor, Vendice in The Revenger's Tragedy, etc. He approaches the blunt, honest soldier type (Chap. IV, Sect. 39). Cf. the King of Navarre with Duke Ferdinand in The Duchess of Malfi and see Chap. IV, Sect. 37, for other weak rulers. Alvarez corresponds to Antonio in The Duchess of Malfi. Cf. Columbo with Fulgentio in The Maid of Honor. For the use of the title of the play in the prologue, see Chap. IV, Sect. 31.

Act I, Sc. 1. For the discussion of matters at court and the character of the Cardinal, note as a source Delio's character of Webster's Cardinal, The Duchess of Malfi, I, 1. Cf. also The Politician, I, 1, The Doubtful Heir, IV, 1, The Court Secret, III, 1, The Coronation, I, 1, The Opportunity, II, 2, Chabot, I, 1, The Triumph of Death, Sc. 2, Henry VIII, I, 1, The Distracted State, I, 1 (1641).

Sc. 2. For the discussion of the merits of Alvarez and Columbo by Rosaura and her waiting-woman, see under The Maid's Revenge, II, 1, and for Rosaura's pretense of affection toward Columbo, see Chap. IV, Sect. 6.

Act II, Sc. 1. The council of war and the quarrel of Columbo and Hernando is a borrowing from The Rebellion, II, 1 (produced 1639, printed 1640). Here Machvile and

Antonio fall out over plans for the conduct of the campaign. Antonio is accused of cowardice because of the cautious nature of his advice and a *mêlée* follows. Shirley's habit of introducing variations from his source should be kept in mind here. Ward (Hist. Eng. Dram. Lit., III, 94, note) suggests an indebtedness of Shirley in this scene to Henry V, IV, 3, in the discussion of the comparative strength of the several armies. Columbo's rage directed toward the bearer of Rosaura's letter recalls Cesario in The Young Admiral, I, 1, and Macbeth, Macbeth, V, 3.

The letter and Columbo's misinterpretation of it are related to the equivocal speech and misunderstood message which Shirley has used in a number of earlier plays (see Chap. IV, Sect. 27). As to Columbo's conception of the letter as a test, see Chap. IV, Sect. 15. For the conversation of the officers on the Duchess' early first marriage, see The Grateful Servant, I, 1.

Sc. 2 seems to have no parallels.

Sc. 3. The accusations and recriminations of the Duchess and the Cardinal here and in IV, 2, parallel those of Queen Katherine and Cardinal Wolsey in Henry VIII, II, 4, III, 1. At the end of the scene Gifford notes an obvious allusion to contemporary conditions in England.

Act III, Sc. 1, seems without parallels.

Sc. 2. The comic scene in which servants preparing for some sort of feast or celebration figure, such as we find at the opening of Sc. 2, occurs in many plays. Cf. The Wedding, II, 1, The Grateful Servant, II, 1, A Yorkshire Tragedy, Sc. 1, No Wit, No Help like a Woman's, II, 1, IV, 2. If there is a specific source for this part of the scene in The Cardinal, it is in The Gentleman Usher, II, 1, in which a masque is being prepared for presentation. There is also a resemblance to The Antipodes, II, 1, 2. Scenes of a similar nature are found in The Supposes,

III, 1, Romeo and Juliet, I, 5, Coriolanus, IV, 5, The Case
is Altered, I, 1, The Poetaster, II, 1, The New Inn, III, 1,
An Humorous Day's Mirth, p. 34, The Gentleman Usher,
I, 1, The Widow's Tears, III, 1, A Woman Killed with
Kindness, III, 2, The Honest Whore, Part II, I, 1, The
Maid's Tragedy, I, 2, The Honest Man's Fortune, V, 3,
The Bloody Brother, II, 2, The Humorous Lieutenant, I, 1,
Appius and Virginia, IV, 2, The Platonic Lovers, I, 1.

For the masque within a play, see Chap. IV, Sect. 18.
The masque in a play had already been used as a vehicle
for a crime in Antonio's Revenge, V, 5, The Revenger's
Tragedy, V, 3, Women Beware Women, V, 1, 'Tis Pity
She's a Whore, IV, 1, Love's Sacrifice, III, 4, Alphonsus,
Emperor of Germany, III, 1, while masques with a tragic
element are to be found in The Malcontent, V, 3, The
Duchess of Malfi, IV, 2, and The Broken Heart, V, 2
("revels").

Act IV, Sc. 1. Hernando's resolution of killing the
Cardinal when he is deepest in sin is a reversal of Sciarrha
and Amidea, The Traitor, V, 1. Hamlet regarding his
uncle, Hamlet, III, 3, is in accord with Hernando. For
analogues, see under The Traitor, V, 1.

Sc. 2. Columbo's threats in his dialogue with the
Duchess suggest Fulgentio in The Maid of Honor, II, 2.
The discussion of their revenge upon him by Rosaura and
Hernando recalls Julia, Domitella and Stephanos in The
Roman Actor, III, 1, concerning their vengeance on Do-
mitian. The conversation of the Duchess and the Cardi-
nal has already been referred to Henry VIII (see under
II, 3). The Cardinal's penitent tone should be compared
with that of Lorenzo in The Traitor, IV, 2, or of the King
in Aglaura, IV, 4. There seems a reminiscence, too, of
Ursini's pleading for Borgia's pardon, The Opportunity,
I, 2.

Sc. 3. The duel between Columbo and Hernando and the former's death suggests Adorni's revenge on Fulgentio, The Maid of Honor, III, 2, 3. The revenge in Massinger's play, which is wholly on the lady's (Camiola's) account, is not represented on the stage.

Act V, Sc. 1. For the villain's soliloquy delivered by the Cardinal, see under The Traitor, IV, 1.

Sc. 2. For the disguised avenger, Hernando, cf. Antonio in Antonio's Revenge, IV, 1, etc., and Vendice in The Revenger's Tragedy, I, 3. Antonio's wish that Hernando and the Cardinal were on some promontory together, which is a repetition of Arcadius' wish concerning Seleucus, The Coronation, II, 2, suggests Edgar and Gloster, King Lear, IV, 6.

Sc. 3. The pretended madness of the Duchess (planned IV, 2) suggests Titus, Titus Andronicus, III, 2, etc., Hamlet in Hamlet, Edgar in King Lear, III, 4, etc., Antonio in Antonio's Revenge, IV, 1, Brutus in The Rape of Lucrece. See under Love Tricks, II, 2. Hernando's position behind the arras during the Cardinal's interview with Rosaura recalls Sciarrha and Florio, The Traitor, III, 3. See Chap. IV, Sect. 30, for eavesdropping. For the Cardinal's attempted rape of Rosaura, see under St. Patrick for Ireland, III, 2. For deaths by poison, see Chap. IV, Sects. 11 and 12. The administration of poison as medicine in The Politician, IV, 4, and the analogues cited for that incident should be noted. Cf. also The Noble Soldier, V, 4. The King's closing reflections upon the abuses to which sovereigns are subject from unworthy favorites perhaps allude to contemporary political troubles in England.

Epilogue. For the comic epilogue, see under Love Tricks. This is an early use of the comic epilogue with a tragedy. Note that The Cardinal is called Shirley's first tragedy for the King's Men.

# CHAPTER VII

## THE TRAGICOMEDIES

### I. THE YOUNG ADMIRAL

That The Young Admiral was esteemed in its own day we learn from Sir Henry Herbert's Officebook in which it is favorably mentioned because of its freedom from obscenity and profanity (Shakespeare Variorum, III, 232–33). In his dedicatory epistle Shirley says, "It hath been grateful to the stage and graciously entertained at court by their Majesties" (on the King's birthday, November 19, 1633, Shakespeare Variorum, III, 234). Epigram XVI, in Wit's Recreation, To Mr. James Shirley on his Comedy, viz., The Young Admiral, attests its popularity.

Stiefel in an article in Romanische Forschungen, V, ascribed the play to a Spanish source, Lope de Vega's Don Lope de Cardona. Later Stiefel proved the indebtedness in Die Nachahmung spanischer Komödien in England unter den ersten Stuarts, III, which appeared in Archiv für das Studien der neueren Sprachen und Literaturen, CXIX (1907).[1]

The plot of The Young Admiral runs thus:

Cesario, Prince of Naples, and Vittori, the Young Admiral, are rivals for Cassandra's hand. On her account Cesario breaks off a match with Rosinda, Princess of Sicily. The Sicilians, enraged at the insult, attack Naples. Ce-

[1] The following discussion of The Young Admiral, in so far as the Spanish source is concerned is based upon Stiefel's valuable article.

190

sario, in hope that Vittori will be killed, sends him as commander against the hostile fleet. To the Prince's disgust he is victorious. On his return, Vittori finds the gates of the city closed. Cassandra meets him and tells him of his father's imprisonment for resenting an insult from the Prince. Warned by the King of danger to Cassandra and himself, Vittori flees with her and his father, Alphonso, who has been released. Alphonso is recaptured, however, and Vittori and Cassandra are shipwrecked and made prisoners by the Sicilians who are preparing to besiege Naples. The King of Sicily offers Vittori a choice between Cassandra's death and his entering the service of Sicily. He chooses the latter. He learns then that Alphonso will be beheaded if his son serves in the enemy's forces. It is proposed that father and son fight as champions for Naples and Sicily. Cesario, however, is lured to the enemy's camp by a letter from Cassandra, where he is captured. Rosinda, who has accompanied her father on the campaign, goes to Naples and gives herself up. The Sicilians threaten to execute Cesario, whereupon the Neapolitans allege that they will retaliate by executing Rosinda. Peace is now made. Rosinda is married to Cesario, and Cassandra to Vittori (who has suspected her fidelity because of her letter to Cesario). The comic element is supplied by the gulling of Pazzorello, Rosinda's cowardly servant.

There are comparatively few translations of Lope's language in The Young Admiral. The debt is one of plot chiefly, and Shirley has not hesitated to vary from the Spanish play. He has substituted Naples for Arragon and has left no Spanish element whatever visible in his tragicomedy. Unity of place and time is more nearly attained in The Young Admiral than in Don Lope. In the latter the action begins in Arragon, changes to Sicily, then back to Arragon, and ends in Sicily. The Young Admiral is laid in Naples and its vicinity. As a result, the time of the action is shortened. The last act of Don Lope de Cardona has been much simplified and compressed by Shirley. Besides the lack of a radical change of scene as in that play, there is no supposed death of Cassandra, no madness of Vittori, no carrying of the war into Sicily, no disguise of Cassandra as a man, and no resurrection scene. Inasmuch as some of these devices are particular favorites of Shirley's, we must conclude that the lack of space, together with his practice of not subordinating characterization to mere incident, prevented his introducing them. As it is, he has written a drama of average length mainly upon the first two acts of the earlier play.

Only three of Lope's names are taken over by Shirley: Cassandra, Rosinda (Princess of Sicily in the English play, her attendant in the Spanish), and Fabricio (Fabrichio in Shirley). Cassandra becomes Vittori's betrothed, whereas in Lope's play she is Don Lope's wife. The English author has substituted the King of Naples for Don Alonzo of Arragon, the King of Sicily for Don Roxenio of Sicily, Cesario for Don Pedro, Vittori for Don Lope, Alphonso for Don Bernardo, Mauritio for Captain Urea, Rosinda for Clenarda, and Flavia for Rosinda. He has added Julio, Alberto and Fabio as Neapolitan nobles, and Horatio and Trivulsi as Sicilians, besides Didimo, Pazzorello, and several other minor characters, while he has omitted Lope's Secretary to Don Alonzo, Felix, Leonardo, Lupercio and the five fishers. It should be noted that his characters are given Italian names.

We have some familiar characters: the weak monarch (see Chap. IV, Sect. 37) influenced by his headstrong passionate son, the unjustly treated commander (a model of honor and amativeness), the faithful heroine, loving and

beloved, the sentimental heroine who is ready to sacrifice
herself for him who has forsaken her, the exquisite, who is
a poltroon as well as a fop, the blunt soldier, the mischievous page and the clown (see Chap. IV, Sects. 47, 39, 48,
46, for the last four characters). Of these the first five
are fairly closely derived from the Spanish play, while
the others are Shirley's addition. All, however, are frequently met with in the English drama.

Act I, Sc. 1. Founded on Don Lope de Cardona, I, 2,
as far as material goes. For jealousy of the successful
commander, see under The Politician, I, 1. Cesario's
hatred of Vittori is caused by rivalry in love more than by
ambition, however. Cesario's desertion of Rosinda (based
on Lope) is a source for the forsaking of Pulcheria, daughter of the Sicilian Viceroy as related in The Sisters, V, 1
(not precisely a following of The Young Admiral), and
Julio's transfer of his affections from Isabella to Clara in
I, 1, The Court Secret. In the three plays the lady follows her recreant lover and wins him finally. For Fabio's
inability to tell his news, see under II, 1, The Politician
(cf. V, 2, following). As to Cesario's orders concerning
Vittori's reception, see under II, 1, The Politician. Alphonso's arrest seems a source for the management of
Piracquo's arrest, The Court Secret, II, 1. In Lope's play
Don Bernardo is neither arrested on the stage, nor is he
charged with treason.

Sc. 2. See III, 4, IV, 2, The Politician, for the un-
grateful treatment of the victorious general. This inci-
dent and Cassandra's warning are from Don Lope, I, 2.
See Coriolanus, V, 3, for the entrance of ladies in mourn-
ing garments. For Vittori's allusion to Brutus and his
Genius (p. 106), cf. Julius Cæsar, IV, 3, and see Plutarch,
Lives, Julius Cæsar, p. 107, Marcus Brutus, p. 163. Cf.
Sciarrha's allusion to the Romans, The Traitor, II, 1, and

note that an edition of North's Plutarch's Lives appeared in 1631. In the Spanish play the Admiral's interview with the King takes place in the city, I, 5, but here it is outside the gates. The two interviews correspond, with the exception that Don Bernardo is freed in Don Pedro's presence, while Shirley's King in his son's absence releases the prisoner, and issues his sentence of exile.

Act II, Sc. 1. Founded on I, 8, of Don Lope. Shirley uses the Prince's upbraiding of his father for having freed Don Bernardo and his obtaining permission to pursue the fugitives, but makes Cesario already to have ordered a search for them. The fact of the capture of Don Bernardo and the escape of his son and Cassandra is drawn from Don Lope, I, 11. The approach of the Sicilian fleet is based upon II, 1, of the Spanish play.

Sc. 2. The opening conversation is Shirley's. The entrance of the Princess and her attendant seems based on II. 4, Don Lope de Cordona. There, however, Cassandra is the companion of the Princess. The comedy between Didimo and Pazzorello is Shirley's. The storm and the consequent capture of Vittori and Cassandra are variations upon I, 14, of the Spanish play. There, the fugitives fall in with the royal hunting-party in Sicily before the departure of the avenging fleet.

Act III, Sc. 1. Didimo's offer to Pazzorello to insure him against gunshots and sword-thrusts is Shirley's introduction. In view of the indebtedness in IV, 1, it is probably based on The Alchemist, I, 1, in which Subtle and Face provide for Dapper's introduction to his ''aunt of Fairy'' who is to give him a charm to secure good luck in gaming. The Gamester, I, 1, The Imposture, II, 2, and The Politician, II, 1, seem based on, or related to, this scene in The Young Admiral. The making a coward appear brave had been used in The Humorous Lieutenant, III, 5,

Love's Cure, III, 2, and it occurs in the same form as in The Gamester in The Combat of Love and Friendship, IV, 4 (1636). The word "slick-free," on which Gifford has a note, is paralleled as "stick-free" in Holland's Leaguer, V, 4,[2] and is there used in connection with "an old witch at Sweden." "Shot-free" occurs in The Variety, I, 1, The New Inn, IV, 3, and in Covent Garden, III, 3.

Horatio's courting of Cassandra in this scene and in IV, 3, is Shirley's introduction. Vittori's struggle between love and loyalty is merely suggested by Lope de Vega in II, 4, of his play. Florello's desertion to the Pisans in III, 1, of Davenant's Siege should be compared with Vittori's action. Love causes both defections. Like Bertolina in the earlier play, Cassandra tries unsuccessfully to dissuade her lover from carrying out his plan. Florello, however, has accomplished his desertion before Bertolina learns of it. Inasmuch as Shirley has borrowed in a later scene from The Siege, it is probable that his conflict of love and honor here is derived also from it. Cf. The Two Gentlemen of Verona, II, 6.

Sc. 2. The dialogue of Mauritio, the bluff soldier, and the poltroon, Fabio, which is Shirley's, suggests Fletcher (cf. Mardonius and Bessus, A King and No King). The conversation of the King and Cesario is based upon II, 1, Don Lope. Vittori's entrance as a herald, with the subsequent portion of the scene, is derived from *ibid.*, II, 2, 5. The mention of the disgraced soldier (Alphonso) as commander against a hostile army is paralleled in The Loyal

---

2 Gifford is wrong concerning the form of the word. As Potter says, the proper spelling is "stick-free," and it is cognate with German "stichfrei" = invulnerable (Mod. Lang. Notes, XXVII, 199). See The Anatomy of Melancholy, Part I, Sec. II, Mem. I, Subsec. 3 (cited by Potter).

Subject, I, 4, 5. Vittori's announcement of his own presence in the Sicilian army has a suggestion in it of the news
of Coriolanus' presence in the army of Aufidius, Coriolanus, IV, 6. Vittori's consequent predicament—leading
troops against a king in whose power his father is, and by
whom he is held as a pledge—is that of Don Lope in II, 5,
of the Spanish play. The same situation occurs in The
Four Prentices of London, pp. 96, 97.

Act IV, Sc. 1. The exchange of confidences by Cassandra and Rosinda at the beginning of this scene comes from
Don Lope de Cardona, II, 6, as does also the setting under
way of their plot against Cesario. The remainder of the
scene, which is Shirley's introduction, is concerned with
Pazzorello's encounter with Rosinda's maid, Flavia, disguised as a witch. As Gifford notes, this is derived from
The Alchemist, III, 2, V, 2 (cf. III, 1, preceding). Pazzorello, like Dapper, empties his pockets, and gives up his
diamond ring as does Dapper his love-token. In each
play the victim is soundly pinched. In Davenant's Siege,
IV, 1, two arrant cowards, Ariotto and Lazaro, become
brave as a result of engaging in a duel, it should be remembered. See also The Politician, III, 3, The Imposture,
III, 2, V, 1, The Gamester, II, 2, Amends for Ladies, III, 4,
The Noble Stranger, IV (1638) (based as to management
perhaps on this scene in The Young Admiral), for related
incidents, and see under III, 1, preceding. For parallels
to Flavia's reference to Mephistopheles, see Koeppel's Marlowe, Kyd [etc.] im Spiegel des Dramas, p. 15, note.
Pazzorello's conduct after his ''enchantment'' recalls La
Writ's after his first taste of duelling in The Little French
Lawyer (II, 2, 3, etc.), as well as that of the other cowards
made brave in the plays cited above.

Sc. 2. The nomination of Alphonso as Neapolitan
champion is drawn from Don Lope, II, 9, in which Don

Bernardo is chosen as Arragonese champion. His lamentation over Vittori's treason comes from Sc. 8 of the same act. Shirley does not utilize the actual meeting of father and son on the field which occurs in Don Lope de Cardona, II, 10. In The Thracian Wonder, V, 2, father and son actually fight as hostile champions, before they discover each other's identity. Note the death of a son at his father's hands in Titus Andronicus, I, 1, and the duel between father and son in The Unnatural Combat, II, 1. Cf. the O. H. G. Hildebrandslied, and its analogues and derivatives. Fabricio's appearance with Cassandra's letter (II, 11, of the Spanish play) occurs during Cesario's interview with Alphonso in this scene.

Sc. 3. Horatio's suit to Cassandra is Shirley's (cf. III, 1). See also Chap. IV, Sect. 9, on defenses of chastity. Rosinda's anxious waiting for the Prince is drawn from Don Lope, II, 12.

Sc. 4 is an addition by Shirley. Pazzorello's "lying perdu," with his dialogue with the Sergeant, is borrowed from the scene between the Town Perdue and the Sergeant in Davenant's Siege, III, 1. Both Pazzorello and the Town Perdue are to stand guard for two hours, both refer to the bullet's noise, and imitate their whistle. The making of their wills is mentioned in both plays, and in each the bullets are contrasted with sugar-plums. Pazzorello's reference to being shot into the town by a cannon is suggested by a speech in The Siege, V (p. 429). His repetition of the word "perdu" and the designation of Davenant's character also help to point out the indebtedness. There are suggestions of All's Well that Ends Well, IV, 1, in this portion of the scene. Pazzorello's guiding Cesario to the ladies is drawn from the Perdue's capture of Florello (who coughs and discovers himself as does Pazzorello) in The Siege as cited.

Sc. 5 is based principally upon the Spanish play, II, 14, 15. Pazzorello's claim to the credit of Cesario's capture suggests Falstaff's "slaying" of Hotspur, Henry IV, Part I, V, 4. Cassandra's letter, which is now read, is longer and more calculated to arouse Vittori's suspicions than that in Don Lope. Shirley utilizes II, 15, in which Don Lope reads the letter. Vittori's jealousy is manifested in a different manner from Don Lope's.

Act V, Sc. 1. The opening of the scene by Rosinda and Flavia is based on Don Lope, III, 5, in which Clenarda and Rosinda discuss Don Pedro's imprisonment. The Princess' revelation to Vittori of her plan for securing Cesario's freedom comes from III, 12, of the Spanish play in which her act is represented.

Sc. 2. The King of Naples' despair at his son's loss is drawn from Don Lope, III, 4, 5. Vittori enters, but voluntarily and in his right mind, and accompanied by Rosinda who offers herself as a hostage for Cesario. Don Lope, III, 12, is the source with the difference that it is to Cassandra who is disguised as a Portuguese knight that the Princess of Sicily surrenders herself. Vittori's giving himself up parallels Florello's return to the Florentines in Davenant's Siege, IV, 1, after his earlier desertion of them.

Sc. 3. The conversation between Cesario and Cassandra in the Sicilian camp is drawn from Don Lope, III, 6, in which Don Pedro learns of Clenarda's love for him. Don Pedro's knowledge is gained, however, in another way. The King of Sicily's angry threats are based on Don Lope, III, 7. The sentence of death passed on Florello in The Siege, IV, 1, should also be noted. Alphonso's entrance as an ambassador is founded on III, 10, of the Spanish play. There, however, he does not announce the presence of the Princess in Naples, but returns unsuccessful from his mission. The embassy takes the place of Lope's III, 14, in which Clenarda's death is threatened in revenge for Don Pedro's. The comic ending of the scene is Shirley's.

Sc. 4 is an equivalent to the last scene of Don Lope de Cardona, rather than an imitation of it. In both, peace is ratified, and final adjustments of relations take place which secure the happiness of all.

## II. THE DUKE'S MISTRESS

There seems to be no single definite source for The Duke's Mistress, but rather a general indebtedness to plays built about the theme of the neglected wife. Chief among the plays to which Shirley's tragicomedy appears related is Brome's Queen and Concubine which appeared in the same year. Brome's Queen Eulalia is superseded by Alinda in the King's affections, is banished, and after various trials, is taken back by her repentant husband. Shirley's Leontio is to a certain extent, paralleled by Brome's Ludovico. A Wife for a Month, as far as the relationships of the characters are concerned, presents a striking similarity also. Shirley's Dionisio, Euphemia, Ardelia, and Fiametta correspond to Fletcher's Frederick, Maria, Valerio, Evanthe and Cassandra. Davenant's Fair Favorite (1638) seems to owe something to The Duke's Mistress.

An outline of The Duke's Mistress follows:

The heart of the Duke of Parma is attracted from his Duchess, Euphemia, by Ardelia, who is betrothed to Bentivolio, a young gentleman who is on his travels. Bentivolio, on returning to Parma with Horatio, whose humor of courting ugly women furnishes the low comedy, mistakenly suspects her fidelity. She proves her virtue to him by a ruse. In the meantime, Euphemia has displeased the Duke and has been placed in the custody of Leontio, the Duke's favorite and heir. Leontio, who loves her, makes advances which are repulsed. With Valerio and Pallante, a disaffected soldier, he plots the Duke's death. Bentivolio is drawn into the conspiracy. Learning of the love of Bentivolio and Ardelia, Valerio threatens to the latter to betray them to the Duke, and exacts her chastity as the price of silence. She pretends to consent, but when he visits her she draws a pistol. Bentivolio's entrance forces Valerio to hide behind the arras. The former, believing him to be the Duke, stabs him through the hangings. The Duke is thought dead, so Bentivolio, Horatio and Ardelia are imprisoned. The Duke, however, who has been warned by Pallante, appears, is reconciled with Euphemia, overcomes Leontio, who is fatally wounded, frees Bentivolio, his mistress, and his friend. The lovers are united, and all ends well for them.[3]

The characters are conventional in most respects with the exception of Ardelia, who seems rather an experiment on Shirley's part. The lustful Duke (see Chap. IV, Sect. 37) who neglects his virtuous wife, his rival (who is unusual in not having the customary respect for royalty), his bluff friend, the Machiavellian villain, and the honest soldier are met with in The Duke's Mistress. It should be noted that the plotting Leontio and the astute Valerio both perform the functions of the villain (see Chap. IV, Sect. 33). In Horatio who loves none but ugly women we have a humorist of the Jonsonian sort. Pallante, the unjustly treated soldier, suggests Pallantus in H. Killigrew's Conspiracy (1634) who is scorned for his rough exterior (see Chap. IV, Sect. 39).

Act I, Sc. 1. Cf. the entrance of Leontio in thought with that of Gotharus, The Politician, I, 1. The entrance

---

[3] This play is really as much a tragedy as The Politician is and is so termed on the early titlepage. However, the usual classification as a tragicomedy has been followed here.

of Pallante, the poverty-stricken soldier, brings to mind Davenant's similar characters in Albovine, II, 1, The Just Italian, I, 1, The Siege, I, 1, The Wits, I, 1, Love and Honor, II, 1, News from Plymouth, I, 1 (sea-captains) (1635), and The Unfortunate Lovers, II, 1 (1638). See the quarrel between the Courtier and the Soldier, A Contention for Honor and Riches, Sc. 2 (p. 302). Note the discontent of Seleucus, The Coronation, III, 2, IV, 1. Cf. the soldiers in The Faithful Friends, in Thierry and Theodoret, The Loyal Subject, The Humorous Lieutenant, The Royal King and Loyal Subject, The Unnatural Combat, and see also Disraeli, Curiosities of Literature, History of Charles I and his First Parliaments, on the disbanded soldiers. For the Duke's suggesting that Pallante buy new clothes, cf. the Steward and Belgarde, The Unnatural Combat, III, 1. In the Duke's courtship of Ardelia, after Pallante's dismissal, is a borrowing from Doctor Faustus, V, 3,

". . . With one smile exalt again
His heart to heaven, and with a kiss breathe in me
Another soul fit for thy love,"

an idea used before by Arcadius, The Coronation, III, 2.

Act II, Sc. 1. Horatio's preference for an ugly mistress because with such a one there are no grounds for jealousy suggests Burton's advice: "If thou wilt avoid them, take away all causes of suspition and jealousie, marry a coarse piece, fetch her from Cassandre's temple which was wont in Italy to be a sanctuary of all deformed maids, and so thou shalt be sure no man will make thee cuckold but for spight" (Anatomy of Melancholy, Part III, Sec. 3, Mem. 4, Subs. 2). For Horatio's description of his ideal mistress, see under III, 2, and for the reference to monsters, see under The Bird in a Cage, II, 1. His reference to Lapland witches recalls Flavia, The Young Admiral, IV, 1.

Sc. 2. Euphemia's indignation at Ardelia recalls Maria and Evanthe, A Wife for a Month, I, 1. There is no reconciliation between the two as in Fletcher's play, however. Eulalia and Alinda in The Queen and Concubine, II, 2, ought also to be noted. Leontio's asides in Shirley's scene remind one of Lodovico's in The Queen and Concubine, as cited, as well as in the scene preceding. The appointment of Lodovico as the Queen's gaoler (*ibid.*, I, 7) is paralleled by Leontio's designation for a similar duty by Duke Dionisio.

The meekness of Euphemia manifested at the beginning of the scene recalls that of Juliana towards Virolet, in The Double Marriage (III, 3, etc.), as well as that of Brome's Eulalia. Shirley's Albina, Mrs. Wilding, Astella, etc., are off the same piece. The Queen and Jane Shore in Edward IV, Part II, p. 126, and the Queen and Floramel, The Hector of Germany, IV, 5 (here it is the latter who is meek), should also be noted. The Fair Favorite, III, 1, seems indebted to Shirley here.

Act III, Sc. 1. The device by which Ardelia convinces Bentivolio of her chastity is a utilization of The Curious Impertinent, as employed in Amends for Ladies, V, 1. Here Sir John Loveall by overhearing Subtle unsuccessfully court his wife, the Lady Perfect, is convinced of her virtue, and repents of his previous suspicions.

Sc. 2. As Gifford suggests in a note, Horatio's song is doubtless that printed among Shirley's poems as On One that Loved None but Deformed Women. With this poem Suckling's The Deformed Mistress and Suckabus' Song in The Seven Champions of Christendom, V, should be compared. For the grotesque description of Fiametta together with Horatio's ideal mistress as described in II, 1, and the

grotesqueness in IV, 1, see Chap. IV, Sect. 20. Horatio's
reference to "good madam Kickshaw" may refer to The
Lady of Pleasure in which there is a character named
Kickshaw. The reference by the same character to platonic love alludes to a courtly fashion of the day on which
in the same year (O. S.) Davenant had founded his play,
The Platonic Lovers. The prologue to that drama and the
explanation of platonic love in I, 1 (p. 17), in it and
Howell's definition, Familiar Letters, I, 317 (June 3,
1634), should be noted. The fashion is attacked, II, 6, of
Lady Alimony (1635). Semanthe, a Platonic Lady, occurs
in Aglaura (1638).

Sc. 3. Leontio's courtship of Euphemia suggests Ludovico's love for Eulalia, The Queen and Concubine, I, 7,
III, 3. The former, however, loses his respect for the lady
and the scene becomes one of Shirley's favorites with its
virtuous lady repulsing the too daring lover. Similarly
in The Duke of Milan, II, 1, Francisco who has been entrusted by the Duke with his Duchess attempts her honor,
and suggests that they make way with the Duke and with
his own wife, and ascend the throne. Marcelia, like Euphemia, spurns the proposition. Leontio meditates seriously on crimes, as does Francisco, and at once begins to
plot the Duke's death, obtaining the aid of the disaffected
Pallante (see under The Politician, III, 1).

Act IV, Sc. 1. The nose of wax, Gifford states, is drawn
from an epigram in the Greek Anthology. The "running
at tilt" of the "two devils" brings to mind the quarrel of
Gammer Gurton and Dame Chat, Gammer Gurton's
Needle, III, 3. "Scolopendra" as a cant term applied to
a woman of bad reputation, occurs in The Siege, V (p.
426). Cf. Deloney, Jack of Newberry, Chap. I (p. 19).
For analogues to this part of the scene, see Chap. IV,
Sect. 20. Fiametta's revelation to the Duke of the love

of Ardelia and Bentivolio is reminiscent of Cassandra's treachery, A Wife for a Month, I, 2.

The attempt on virtue and the defence of chastity which are represented in the dialogue between Valerio and Ardelia have been treated in Chap. IV, Sect. 9. Valerio's hold over Ardelia as a result of his having learned of her love for Bentivolio resembles De Flores' use of his knowledge of Beatrice's secret in The Changeling, III, 4. Secrets are employed as goads in The Lovers' Progress, III, 6, The Fair Maid of the West, Part II, I, 1, The Second Maiden's Tragedy, IV, 1, The Witch, III, 1, Albovine, IV, 1, The Sparagus Garden, II, 6. A mortgage is used as a weapon against Lady Peregrine in The Example, I, 1. This scene seems employed in The Fair Favorite, III, 1 (1638). For Valerio's "You shall lead destiny . . . ," cf. Captain Underwit, II, 3.

The conspiracy for the death of the Duke and, incidentally, of Bentivolio, which is now further revealed, should be compared with The Coronation, IV, 1, Julius Cæsar, II, 1, Catiline, III, 3, while Bentivolio's employment as a tool by Leontio seems based on the use of Sciarrha by Lorenzo, The Traitor, II, 1, IV, 1.

Act V, Sc. 1. For Valerio's attempted rape of Ardelia, see under St. Patrick for Ireland, III, 2. Ardelia's defense of herself with a pistol when Valerio returns to claim his price has been mentioned with analogues under The Traitor, III, 3. The probable source of Valerio's death at Bentivolio's hands is Hamlet's slaying of Polonius behind the arras, Hamlet, III, 4. Law Tricks, III, [1], should be compared. Other deaths as a result of mistaken identity are to be found in The First Part of Jeronymo, p. 467, The Rape of Lucrece, V, 4, The Revenger's Tragedy, V, 1, The Turk, IV, 1, The Duchess of Malfi, V, 4, All's Lost by Lust, IV, 2, The Double Marriage, V, 2, The City Nightcap,

V, 1, The Cruel Brother, V, 1, The Distracted State, IV, 1, Aglaura, V, 1, 2 (1637), Imperiale, III, 4 (reported). An interesting variation is to be found in Cartwright's Siege, III, 1, in which the stabbing takes place in a dream.

Sc. 2. Pallante's pretense of remorse at the murder which he claims to have committed suggests that of the Second Murderer in Richard III, I, 4, and of Tyrrell in the same, IV, 3. Bentivolio's confession of the murder of the Duke, together with Horatio's admission of complicity in the deed in the next scene, seems a source for Hartwell's confession of the slaying of Startup, The Constant Maid, V, 1, 3 (see under that play).

Sc. 3. Analogues to Horatio's false self-accusation, mentioned in connection with the preceding scene, are found in The Insatiate Countess, III, Goffe's Orestes, IV, 5, The City Nightcap, V, 1, and The Lady Mother, V, 1, 2 (1635). Horatio's remark that his "humor's out of breath" may refer to Day's Comedy, Humor out of Breath.

Sc. 4. For the penitence of the Duke, see Chap. IV, Sect. 10. The Fair Favorite, V, 1 (1638), seems indebted to this incident. For the resurrection of the Duke, see Chap. IV, Sect. 29. Cf. The Fair Favorite, V, 1. Leontio's surprising the Duke with Euphemia seems the basis for *ibid.*, III, 1 (p. 244 ff.). The survival and happiness of the virtuous characters should be noted.

For the epilogue in prose (save a couplet at the close) see under The Wedding.

## III. THE ROYAL MASTER

From the dedication to the Earl of Kildare which Shirley affixed to The Royal Master it would seem that that tragicomedy was his first play to be produced in Ireland (Schipper, James Shirley, p. 191; Fleay, Anglia, VIII, 408). It may reasonably be dated 1637 (see Chap. II).

According to Stiefel (Romanische Forschungen, V, 196, note) the source of The Royal Master is a Spanish play. Miss Ott derives the story of Domitilla and the King from the Decameron of Boccaccio, X, 7 (Die Italienische Novelle im Englischen Drama, pp. 43–44). However, in some places The Royal Master parallels The Great Duke of Florence so closely that it seems certain that the resemblance cannot be accidental. There seems also to be some relationship to A Maidenhead Well Lost.

The scene of The Royal Master is laid in Naples.

The King of Naples, a widower, entertains his brother-in-law, the Duke of Florence, at his court as a suitor to his sister. Montalto, the King's favorite, who loves the Princess strives to break off the match. He contrives so that the Duke shall meet Domitilla, a beautiful young girl who lives secluded in the country. The King, who designs Domitilla as a wife for Montalto, broaches the matter to her. She misunderstands him and thinks he woos for himself. Domitilla and her mother are ordered to court. Montalto tells the Duke that Theodosia loves the first, and pretends to confide to his enemy, Riviero (in the Duke's service in disguise), that she is not a maid. This the Duke learns, and tells the King, who questions his sister. She denies the charge. Montalto has informed Theodosia of the Duke's transfer of his love to Domitilla. She confronts the girl, and learns of her love for the King. Growing suspicious of Montalto, the King suggests that he marry the Princess to patch up her honor. Montalto falls into the trap and offers to do so, whereupon the King proposes that he pretend to frown upon his favorite, and orders him under arrest. The Duke woos Domitilla while the Princess eavesdrops. He is cured of his temporary passion and is reconciled with Theodosia. Montalto and his parasites are exposed to the King by Riviero and his

friends.  To break off Domitilla's affection for him, the
King pretends to court her for a mistress.  She indignantly
repulses him, and is upheld by Octavio, Riviero's son.  As
a result the King concludes a match between her and Octavio.

The parallels in incident between The Royal Master,
The Great Duke of Florence, and A Maidenhead Well
Lost will be pointed out in the detailed discussion which
follows, as they are not brought out well by an outline.
In A Maidenhead Well Lost, as well as in The Great Duke
of Florence, we have an Italian scene, with a Duke of
Florence in the action who, however, does not play the
part of Shirley's Duke.  The King of Naples in Shirley's
play = Heywood's Duke of Milan, and Massinger's Duke of
Florence; Montalto = Stroza and Sanazarro; Theodosia =
Julia and Fiorinda; the Duke of Florence = the Prince of
Parma and Giovanni; Domitilla = Lauretta and Lidia;
Simphorosa = Lauretta's Mother and Charomonte; Bombo,
Domitilla's "Secretary" = the Clown (who is the Mother's
gentleman-usher) and Calandrino.  Of course, the plays
of Massinger and Heywood differ widely in some points
from The Royal Master.  Shirley's chief deviations from
the earlier authors are in the character of the King and in
his conduct towards Domitilla.

For Montalto, the intriguing favorite, see Chap. IV,
Sect. 33.  Unlike Sanazarro, in The Great Duke, Montalto
is strong and a villain.  Domitilla, the charming little
country maiden, in her innocence and simplicity recalls
Margaret in Friar Bacon and Friar Bungay, Margaret in
The Gentleman Usher, Imogen in Cymbeline, Perdita in
The Winter's Tale, Miranda in The Tempest, and Reginella
in The Goblins.  The disguised Philoberto (Riviero) seems
a reminiscence of Philenzo as Rolliardo in The Bird in a
Cage.  He resembles also Phœnix in The Phœnix, and

Hercules as Fawn in The Fawn. For Bombo, the clown, see Chap. IV, Sect. 46. Cf. also Lovell in The Lady Mother. Schipper unadvisedly compares Bombo with Falstaff and Malvolio (James Shirley, p. 199). "Bombo" is one of the names of Pride in Pathomachia, IV, 4. Note also Rimbombo, the Cyclops, in Sicelides, and Bomby in Women Pleased.

Act I, Sc. 1. For the King's mourning the dead Queen Cæsaria, cf. The Great Duke of Florence, I, 2. Shirley used this previously in regard to Lord A., The Lady of Pleasure, III, 1. The relations of the Duke of Florence and Theodosia, as shown here, parallel closely those of the Duke and Duchess in The Humorous Courtier, and in The Opportunity. At the opening of The Great Duke, also, the match between Sanazarro and Fiorinda had been already arranged. An allusion to The City Nightcap occurs, p. 107. The reference to Montalto as a colossus (p. 110) may be paralleled in Chabot, II, 1, IV, 1, Bussy D'Ambois, I, 1, Sejanus, I, 2, Julius Cæsar, I, 2, The Turk, IV, 1, V, 3, Appius and Virginia, III, 1, Albertus Wallenstein, I, 1, V, 1 (1634–38), Hannibal and Scipio, IV, 2.

Sc. 2. For Bombo's entry with a book here and in II, 1, see under Chap. IV, Sect. 23. Cf. Guido's arrival with the news of the King's approach with Contarino, The Great Duke, I, 1. For Guido's conversation with Bombo, cf. Sanazarro and the servants, *ibid.*, II, 2; note, too, in this connection Calandrino's simplicity, *ibid.*, I, 1. The preparations for the King's visit recall The Grateful Servant, II, 1, The Gentleman Usher, I, 1, A Mad World, My Masters, II, 1, 2 (the visitor is not of royal rank in the last), The Great Duke, IV, 2, A Maidenhead Well Lost, III. See under The Cardinal, III, 2, for general analogues. Octavio's complimenting Domitilla is reminiscent of Sanazarro's falling in love with Lidia, The Great Duke, II, 3.

Octavio's eulogy of life at court suggests Arcadius in The Coronation, II, 1, and is repeated in substance later by Giovanni, The Gentleman of Venice, II, 1. Cf. also Aimwell concerning Violetta, The Witty Fair One, I, 2, III, 3, and Playfair, The Constant Maid, IV, 3.

Act II, Sc. 1. Gifford finds a satirical allusion in Bombo's remarks on court masques to the "court-poet of the day," and, of course, to Inigo Jones. Cf. Love in a Maze, IV, 2, A Contention for Honor and Riches, Sc. 1, and Honoria and Mammon, I, 1. See also The Maid's Tragedy, I, 1, and The Elder Brother, II, 2, for similar references to the constituents of court masques. For the reference to the appearance of Cupid in masques, see under The Coronation, IV, 3, and cf. Chap. IV, Sect. 18. For Bombo's drunkenness, see Chap. IV, Sect. 26, and cf. especially The Two Angry Women of Abington, I, 2, II, 2, The New Inn, II, 2, III, 1, The Lady Mother, III, 1. The reference to "Venus' dandiprat" is paralleled in The Arcadia, I, 3, where Dyce derives the word from Stanyhurst's translation of l. 719, Bk. I, of the Æneid. See The Constant Maid, IV, 3. It is applied also to Didymus, a page, in The Contention of Ajax and Ulysses, Sc. 1. Bombo's use of military terms in his drinking, as well as in III, 3, is paralleled in May-Day, IV, 1, The New Inn, III, 1, Microcosmus, III, The Ordinary, II, 1. Cf. the wooing of Domitilla by the King and her misunderstanding him with the Prince of Florence and Lauretta, A Maidenhead Well Lost, III. For courtship by proxy and misinterpretations, see Chap. IV, Sects. 3, and 27.

Sc. 2. With III, 1, cf. The Great Duke of Florence, III, 1, and A Maidenhead Well Lost, I, 1, III, for slandering a lady. Note also The Wedding, I, 4. Analogues are Hoffman, II, Much Ado About Nothing, III, 2, Cymbeline, II, 4, The Queen's Arcadia, III, 4, The Woman Hater,

III, 1, IV, 1, Philaster, II, 4, The Partial Law, II, 2, The Duke of Milan, IV, 3, The Deserving Favorite, II, 1, The Costly Whore, I, 1, The Platonic Lovers, II, 1 (cf. especially Fredeline's telling of his love for Eurithea), The Lady Mother, I, 3. Montalto's insidious attacks upon the Duke here and in IV, 1, suggest Iago in Othello, III, 3, IV, 1. For Domitilla's being ordered to court, cf. The Loyal Subject, II, 6, and The Royal King and Loyal Subject, II, 1.

Act III, Sc. 1. For the resurrection of the supposedly dead Riviero here and in V, 2, see Chap. IV, Sect. 29. Cf. the comparison of Montalto to a comet (p. 140) with similar figures in The Court Secret, I, 1, The Imposture, V, 3, The Great Duke of Florence, I, 1, The Picture, II, 1, and Stroza concerning Sforza, A Maidenhead Well Lost, I, 1. Disraeli quotes Sir Dudley Digges in opening the impeachment proceedings against the Duke of Buckingham as comparing the Duke to a "meteor exhaled out of putrid matter" (Curiosities of Literature, The Secret History of Charles I and his first Parliaments).

Sc. 2. Montalto attempts to divert Theodosia's thoughts from the Duke by betraying the new passion of the last for Domitilla; cf. II, 2, III, 1. See also The Doubtful Heir, IV, 2, for a later use by Shirley. Cf. Stroza and Julia, A Maidenhead Well Lost, I, 1. Contrast Theodosia's jealousy with Fiorinda's meekness, The Great Duke, V, 2. The inquiries concerning the Duke's whereabouts recall Fiorinda and her maid, ibid., II, 1.

Sc. 3. For Bombo on court-life, see under Love's Cruelty, I, 2. His refusal to entertain Domitilla's suggestion that he become a lay-friar, and his reasons for it are utilized by the Bard, St. Patrick for Ireland, V, 1. Cf. Bombo's wish that he were a fool with Dogberry, Much Ado about Nothing, IV, 2, and note Startup, The Constant

Maid, V, 3. See also The Late Lancashire Witches, II. Cf. Domitilla's " 'Tis your humility" with Shylock, The Merchant of Venice, III, 1. For Bombo's military figures, see under II, 1. His being called to go as ambassador suggests Monsieur D'Olive. Castles in the air such as Domitilla's (p. 147–48) are found in The Grateful Servant, II, 1, The Humorous Courtier, IV, 1, V, 2, Honoria and Mammon, II, 1, IV, 2, Twelfth Night, II, 5, The Miseries of Enforced Marriage, IV, Ram Alley, III, 1, A Trick to Catch the Old One, IV, 4, Albumazar, II, 4, The Parliament of Love, II, 1, Believe as You List, III, 2, The Ordinary, II, 3, Cartwright's Siege, II, 2 (1637). Domitilla's disquisition on a subject's rising to the regal rank through virtue has more or less close parallels in the passages on true nobility and on rising by virtue in The Bird in a Cage, II, 1, The Coronation, IV, 1, Hyde Park, V, 1, The Ball, IV, 1. Cf. also Every Man in his Humor, I, 1, Catiline, II, 1, The Duchess of Malfi, II, 1, The Custom of the Country, II, 1, The Shepherds' Holiday, IV, 3, Albertus Wallenstein, IV, 1 (1634–38), The Queen of Arragon, III, 1 (1640). Cf. also Chaucer's Wife of Bath's Tale, ll. 1109–1206.

Act IV, Sc. 1. Koeppel derives the Duke's comparison of Theodosia to a fallen star (p. 154) from Henry VIII, IV, 1 (Shakespeare's Wirkung, p. 61). The King's interrogation of Theodosia concerning Montalto's charges against her resembles Theander's examination of his sister, Ariola, concerning her relations with Phylomont, The Platonic Lovers, III, 1. There, however, the point at issue is not the lady's chastity. Theodosia's jealousy of Domitilla expressed in the scene between the two recalls Love in a Maze, II, 2 (see also II, 3). Note the later Imposture, V, 2, 3, 5, and Court Secret, II, 2. Cf. Love's Pilgrimage, III, 2, Fair Em, II, 2, A Midsummer Night's Dream, III, 2,

Match Me in London, III, A Maidenhead Well Lost, I, 1, and contrast The Great Duke, V, 3. Montalto's hesitating to stab the Duke (p. 163) is reminiscent of Antonio's Revenge, III, 2, Hamlet, III, 3, and Humor out of Breath, I, 2.

Cf. Bombo's scene following with Calandrino and Giovanni, The Great Duke of Florence, III, 1. Calandrino, like Bombo, enters "fantastically dressed," and in the course of the dialogue, makes some satirical remarks on court-life. Cf. also Short-hose in Wit Without Money, II, 3, and the Clown (who is "gallant") in A Maidenhead Well Lost, III. For Bombo's allusion to the "lady of Leander's lake," cf. Koeppel, Reflexe der Ritter-Romane im Drama, p. 197, note. Bombo's definition of honor (p. 166) should be compared with The Nice Valor, III, 2, Henry IV, Part I, V, 1, Bussy D'Ambois, II, 1, Valentinian, III, 3. Cf. also Richard III, I, 4, Othello, II, 3, The City Wit, I, 1, The Fancies Chaste and Noble, I, 1, 3, for similar burlesque definitions and commentaries. Note the King's definition of conscience, The Noble Soldier, IV, 2. See under The Sisters, I, 1.

For the King's test of Montalto, see Chap. IV, Sect. 15. Cf. the King's suggesting the marriage of Montalto and Theodosia with Wilding's forwarding the match between Hazard and Penelope, The Gamester, V, 1. The pretended disgrace of Montalto recalls the arrest of Sanazarro, The Great Duke, V, 1. The King's concealment of his knowledge of Montalto's machinations parallels the Duke's suppressing his knowledge of the deceit of Sanazarro and Giovanni, ibid., III, 1.

Act V, Sc. 1. Bombo, like Calandrino in The Great Duke (III, 1), returns to the country after showing himself in his gay attire. For Theodosia's eavesdropping (p. 173 ff.), see under Chap. IV, Sect. 30. For the Duke's return to Theodosia, cf. The Coronation, IV, 3, and see

Chap. III, for Shirley's fickle lovers. Cf. Fiorinda's forgiveness of Sanazarro, The Great Duke, V, 2. The Duke's soliloquy before Theodosia's appearance corresponds with Sanazarro's soliloquy, *ibid.*, V, 1, and his repentance, as expressed at the end of the scene recalls Sanazarro's (*ibid.*).

Sc. 2. The presentation of petitions to the King by Riviero, Andrugio, and the others brings to mind Phœnix in disguise presenting to his father accounts of the various crimes of which he has learned, The Phœnix, V, 1. For Montalto's disgrace, cf. Sejanus, V, 10, The Gentleman Usher, V, 1, The Phœnix, V, 1, A Maidenhead Well Lost, V (the victory over Stroza). For the use of the title of the play in the text, see Chap. IV, Sect. 31. Miss Ott, as quoted, Neilson (Cam. Hist. Eng. Lit., VI, 230), and Ward (Hist. Eng. Dram. Lit., III, 116, note), agree in finding the source for the King's curing Domitilla's love for him by pretending to woo her to unchastity in the Decameron, Day X, Novel 7. There is no need of going to Italian novels for a source for this incident. In The Deserving Favorite, II, 1, Lysander, who desires his mistress, Clarinda, to transfer her affections from him to the Duke, pretends to make advances to her. She, however, unlike Domitilla, suspects his sincerity and tests him. Also in The Faithful Shepherdess, IV, 5, occurs a reversal. Clorin, by pretending to yield to Thenot's suit, cures him of his love for her. For her defense of her chastity against the pretended advances of the King, see Chap. IV, Sect. 9. For the public announcement of Riviero's being in life, cf. III, 1, and see Chap. IV, Sect. 29.

## IV. THE DOUBTFUL HEIR

The date of The Doubtful Heir is fixed, approximately, by the references in the Dublin prologue to Claricilla and

Aglaura, the first of which appeared in 1636, and the second in 1637. It therefore may be dated after Shirley's return to Ireland in 1637, possibly in the latter part of that year or the early part of 1638. Its Irish production was under the title Love's Victory.[4] As Rosania, it was licensed in England, June 1, 1640, and it was printed as The Doubtful Heir in 1652.

The Doubtful Heir is one of Shirley's most Fletcherian plays, and therefore falls in the same class as The Grateful Servant and The Coronation, for instance. But another fact connects it with The Coronation. Shirley has drawn upon the earlier play for much of the plot of The Doubtful Heir. Through the two earlier plays, also, the influence of A King and No King and of Philaster may be traced.

The plot of the play runs as follows:

Ferdinand, heir to the Murcian throne, who has been thought to have died in infancy, has been brought up in Valencia, in fear of his unscrupulous uncle's designs. When he reaches manhood, Ferdinand attempts to seize the throne which is occupied by his cousin, Olivia, but is defeated and captured with his mistress, Rosania, who is in page's clothing. He is tried for treason. Olivia, who presides at the trial, falls in love with him and offers him her hand, although she is betrothed to Leonario, Prince of Arragon. Ferdinand prudently accepts her hand, but does not claim his conjugal rights after their marriage. Angered, the Queen in revenge woos Ferdinand's page, Tiberio, who is Rosania disguised, and arranges a meeting for them in her chamber. Ferdinand and Rosania plan then that the former shall break in, and surprise his wife, thus obtaining ground for a divorce. Ferdinand's plan

---

[1] Halliwell, Dict. O. E. Plays, p. 156, confuses Shirley's Love's Victory with a MS. pastoral with the same title.

is carried out, but Olivia, who has learned ''Tiberio's'' real sex defies her husband, and exposes his conspiracy. Ferdinand and Rosania are then imprisoned, but are released by Leandro, an old lord, who possesses proofs of Ferdinand's right to the throne. Ferdinand then deposes Olivia. In the moment of his triumph troops appear which are thought to be those summoned from Arragon by Leonario. However, they are Valencian allies of Ferdinand, led by Rosania's father. The play ends with the uniting of Ferdinand and Rosania, and of Leonario and Olivia.

Thus it will be seen that Sophia in The Coronation, supposed Queen of Epire = Olivia in The Doubtful Heir, supposed Queen of Murcia; and, proceeding through the *dramatis personæ*, Lisimachus, betrothed to Sophia = Leonario, betrothed to Olivia; Demetrius and Leonatus, heirs to the throne of Epire, concealed in infancy, and thought dead = Ferdinand; Polidora, betrothed to Demetrius = Rosania; Eubulus and Macarius, who are supposed to be the father and uncle, respectively, of Demetrius and Leonatus, and who know the secret of their birth = Leandro, who knows the true derivation of Ferdinand; also Cassander, who sets up Leonatus as a pretender = Leandro, who reasserts Ferdinand's title. The incidents from The Coronation which are utilized in The Doubtful Heir will be considered in the discussion of the play (see also Nason, James Shirley, Chap. XVI).

There is some resemblance between the situation of Ferdinand and Rosania, and that of Perkin and Katherine, Perkin Warbeck, IV, 3, etc. Ferdinand's predicament when wedded to Olivia although betrothed to Rosania recalls Amintor in The Maid's Tragedy, who marries Evadne, though betrothed to Aspatia (who, like Rosania, assumes male clothing in the course of the play). For analogues to the lost child motive, see under The Gentleman of Venice, V, 4.

For parallels to the fickle Olivia in Shirley's other plays, see Chap. III. For the girl in male costume (Rosania), and the blunt soldier (the Captain), see Chap. IV, Sects. 32 and 39.

Act I, Sc. 1.[5] The dunning of the Captain by the two Citizens suggests The Merchant of Venice, III, 3, IV, 1, If You Know not Me, You Know Nobody, Part II, p. 328, Alboine, II, 1, III, 1, and The Unfortunate Lovers, II, 1, III, 1 (1638). Note also Character IV of The Parliament of Bees, and see under The Duke's Mistress, I, 1. For the report that Ferdinand is alive, cf. the confirmation of the same, V, 4, and see Chap. IV, Sect. 29. For the account of the false burial of the infant Ferdinand, cf. The Coronation, III, 2, V, 3. See also Believe as You List, II, 2.

Act II, Sc. 1, is devoted almost entirely to an expository soliloquy by Leandro.

Sc. 2 shows the Captain and his two creditors, whom he had tricked into enlisting at the end of I, 1, as returned from the war. There is some satire on broken soldiers' setting up as courtiers.

Sc. 3. For the parallels to the prison setting, and to Rosania's male disguise, see Chap. IV, Sects. 14 and 32. Shirley differs from the majority of dramatists who have ladies in male clothing follow their lovers in that Ferdinand knows the true sex of his seeming page. The love-scene between Ferdinand and Rosania corresponds in a general way to that between Demetrius and Polidora, The Coronation, II, 1. Analogues to the master in prison attended by a faithful page occur in The Ladies' Privilege, III, and Sir John Van Olden Barnavelt, III, 4, 6.

[5] For the occurrence of the early titles in the Dublin prologue, see Chap. IV, Sect. 31.

Sc. 4. For analogous trials in courts of law, etc., see Chap. IV, Sect. 17. Ferdinand's defense of himself and his motives (p. 304 ff.) suggests Perkin, Perkin Warbeck, II, 1. Cf. also, The Ladies' Privilege, IV. For Ferdinand's account of his page (p. 307), cf. The Grateful Servant, I, 2, Philaster, I, 2, The Lover's Melancholy, I, 1. Olivia's falling in love with Ferdinand during the scene, as manifested by her asides, is paralleled in The Humorous Courtier, I, 1 (pretended), The Opportunity, I, 2, The Coronation, II, 3, The Iron Age, Part I, I, 1, Wit without Money, I, 2, The Prophetess, III, 3, The Maid of Honor, IV, 4, Nero, IV, 5. Olivia's pardoning of Ferdinand and leaving the stage, escorted by him, is drawn from Sophia's choosing Demetrius as her husband, The Coronation, II, 3. For a queen's falling in love with a rebel and marrying him, cf. The Queen, I. For Olivia's practically offering her hand to Ferdinand, see Chap. IV, Sect. 1. Ferdinand's apparent desertion of Rosania for the Queen is based on the conduct of Demetrius towards Polidora, The Coronation, II, 3. Ferdinand, however, intends to temporize, while Demetrius is led on by ambition. Cf. also A King and No King, III, 1, The Double Marriage, II, 3, The Prophetess, II, 3, The Fair Maid of the Inn, IV, 1, All's Lost by Lust, II, 6, The Maid of Honor, IV, 4. He is in the same predicament as Antonius in The Virgin-Martyr, I, 1.

Act III, Sc. 1. The discussion of the marriage-night of Ferdinand and Olivia, although in a different tone, recalls passages in The Maid's Tragedy, III, 1, and A Wife for a Month, IV, 2. The following comic scene between the Captain and the Citizens is perhaps based on Florello, Punto, and Staccata, The Just Italian, IV, 1. Cf. also Mardonius, Bessus, and the Swordmen, A King and No King, IV, 3, V, 3, and Romont and the Creditors, The Fatal Dowry, I, 1. See Nason, James Shirley, Chap. XVI.

For the Captain's eavesdropping and that of Ferdinand, see Chap. IV, Sect. 30. See Chap. IV, Sect. 8, for Olivia's pretending to make love to Rosania disguised as a page. The incident may be derived directly from Anything for a Quiet Life, III, 1, etc., in which Mrs. Knavesby pretends love for Mrs. Cressingham who is clothed as a page. Note also that an analogue occurs in No Wit, No Help Like a Woman's, II, 3, V, 1, for which Shirley wrote a prologue in 1638. In The Antiquary, IV, 1, Æmilia woos Angelia as a page, while Lorenzo, the former's husband, eavesdrops, as does Ferdinand. See also James IV, V, 1. For Ferdinand's spying, cf. The Maid's Revenge, II, 2. Langbaine derives either this scene or IV, 2, from The English Adventures, Part III (Dramatic Poets, p. 484). Cf. the conversation of Rosania and Ferdinand after Olivia's exit with The Coronation, IV, 3, and note A King and No King, IV, 2. For Ferdinand's abstaining from Olivia's bed, cf. Alphonso and the Queen, The Queen, I, II.

Act IV, Sc. 1. The misgivings of the courtiers regarding the relations of the Queen and Rosania as Tiberio are drawn probably from Philaster, II, 4, III, 1, but cf. The Grateful Servant, II, 1, III, 1. Cf. the comments on Ferdinand's rise at court with The Opportunity, II, 2. Ferdinand's lines, "Had she more ornament . . ." (p. 327), seem derived from Marlowe's "If all the pens that poets ever held . . . ," Tamburlaine, Part I, V, 2, but cf. The Iron Age, Part II, V, 1. For Rosania's offering to resign Ferdinand to Olivia in order to secure his comfort, see Chap. IV, Sect. 4. Cf. especially, The Sea Voyage, IV, 2, and The Double Marriage, III, 3. Cf. Ferdinand's plot against the Queen with Cornari and Florelli, The Gentleman of Venice, IV, 3.

Sc. 2. Leonario's telling Olivia of what he has learned of the relations of Ferdinand and Rosania from the eaves-

dropping Captain suggests Montalto and Theodosia in The
Royal Master, III, 2. Leonario's motives, however, are
honorable. Cf. also The Witch, III, 2, Love's Sacrifice,
III, 3, The Lady's Trial, II, 3. Olivia's imagining Ro-
sania disguised as Tiberio to be a woman, and herself a
man suggests Love Tricks, V, 1, Gallathea, IV, 4, As You
Like It, III, 2, etc. For Olivia's mention of Venus and
Adonis, cf. The Sisters, III, 2, Every Woman in her Humor,
II, 1, The Return from Parnassus, Part I, III, 1 (quoted),
IV, 1, The Fair Maid of the Exchange, p. 55, A Mad
World, My Masters, I, 2, The Dumb Knight, III, 1, The
Bondman, I, 2, The Noble Stranger, IV (1638). Olivia
approaches in her mock courtship, the invitation to love
for which see under Love's Cruelty, II, 2. Cf. Ferdinand's
surprising the disguised Rosania in Olivia's chamber with
No Wit, No Help like a Woman's, V, 1, and The Lover's
Melancholy, III, 2. See also Philaster, IV, 3, and Brennoralt, V, 2 (1639). The dressing of Rosania in woman's
clothes to ''disguise'' her seems based upon Philippa's
similar device in The Widow, V, 1. The disclosure of
Rosania's true sex suggests Philaster, V, 5, while Olivia's
defending herself against Ferdinand's charge of infidelity
by a countercharge recalls The Antiquary, IV, 1.

Act V, Sc. 1, represents the setting on foot by Leandro
of a plot to restore Ferdinand to the throne of Murcia.
Cf. The Coronation, IV, 1.

Sc. 2. For the prison setting, and for Ferdinand and
his book, see Chap. IV, Sects. 14 and 23. The combination
of prison, book, and soliloquy recall Bertoldo, The Maid
of Honor, IV, 3. Each receives his freedom after he
soliloquizes. For the recognition of Ferdinand as King,
cf. The Coronation, III, 2, IV, 1. As has been noted, the
stories of the concealment of the respective infants correspond very closely.

Sc. 3. The performances of the Captain and the Citizens are partially based on Bessus, Bacurius, and the Swordmen, A King and No King, V, 3. The Citizens' discovery that they are not altogether cowards suggests strongly Ariotto and Lizaro in Davenant's Siege, IV, 1. Cf. also The Little French Lawyer, II, 2.

Sc. 4. For the revolt, see under The Politician, IV, 3 (a timely revolt is as useful in a romance as a resurrection for untangling complications). A notable surprise comes at the close of the play in the discovery that Alfonso, who had entered the city as an Arragonese ally of Olivia, is, in reality, a Valencian, a friend of Ferdinand's, and the father of Rosania.

### V. ST. PATRICK FOR IRELAND

St. Patrick for Ireland, Part I, was acted only in Dublin, apparently, since there is no record of its having been licensed for the London stage. The date of its performance may be set at about 1639, the date given by Chetwood on the titlepage of his reprint of the play in 1751. Whether or not Chetwood had any authority for this date is a matter of conjecture. In any case, he cannot be far wrong. The second part promised in the prologue and epilogue seems never to have materialized.

Ward suggests as possibly related to St. Patrick, Kirke's Seven Champions of Christendom, or Calderon's El Purgatorio de San Patricio (Hist. Eng. Dram. Lit., III, 100, note). The Seven Champions which was produced at the Cockpit before 1636 (Fleay, Biog. Chron., II, 25), is a strange hodge-podge, apparently from its structure and character a reworking of a very early play. Shirley may have got the idea of St. Patrick from it; certainly there are some parallels between The Seven Champions and Shirley's play. There seems no indebtedness to El Purga-

torio in St. Patrick. The two differ widely in characters
and plot. The Spanish play, which begins with Patrick's
becoming a slave after a shipwreck, covers many years.
One character journeys through Purgatory. However, in
both plays the saint has a vision (in which his future mission is foretold by an angel), a miraculous escape from
death, and he performs a resurrection. Likewise, a profligate and ravisher takes part in both plays. Good and bad
angels are characters in common. In both a character
sinks into the ground, in El Purgatorio to purgatory, in
St. Patrick presumably to hell.

Probably St. Patrick was written as a sort of concession
to the tastes of the Dublin populace. Its source seems
to have been some common account of the life of St. Patrick with perhaps hints from various other sources. It
should be noted that Shirley's St. Albans perhaps was
of much the same character as St. Patrick. Other plays
besides The Seven Champions which deal with saints'
lives are A Shoemaker a Gentleman (printed 1638), The
Virgin-Martyr, and The Martyred Soldier. For more or
less analogous supernatural elements, cf. also Doctor
Faustus, The Wars of Cyrus, Friar Bacon and Friar
Bungay, The Wisdom of Doctor Dodypoll, Grim, the Collier of Croydon, The Devil is an Ass, Bussy D'Ambois,
Macbeth, The Tempest, If This Be Not a Good Play, the
Devil Is in It, The Triumph of Death, The Prophetess,
The Devil's Charter, The Picture, Trapolin Supposed a
Prince. As examples of the spectacular, which have some-
thing, therefore, in common with St. Patrick, Heywood's
five Ages (printed 1611, 1613, 1632) should not be over-
looked. The name of Archimagus suggests a recollection
of The Faery Queen.

The plot of St. Patrick follows:

St. Patrick comes to Ireland attended by a guardian

angel, Victor, and a number of priests. He drives before him the hostile spirits of Archimagus, the pagan chief priest. Dichu, an Irish courtier, is converted to Christianity. Leogarius, King of Ireland, who is inimical to St. Patrick, condemns Dichu's sons, Ferochus and Endarius, to death. To escape this fate, they play the part of idols in the temple at the connivance of Archimagus. Leogarius attempts to poison Patrick who is preserved by his sanctity. Rodamant, Archimagus' servant, drinks part of the poison, and dies, but is revived by the saint. Leogarius' Queen is converted by this miracle. Milcho, Patrick's former master, sets fire to his house in which are the saint, the Queen, and a Bard. They are preserved, but Milcho perishes. In the meantime, Corybreus, elder son to the King and a rival to his brother, Conallus, in the affections of Milcho's daughter, Emeria, receives from Archimagus a magic bracelet which confers invisibility upon the wearer and by its aid, in the guise of a god, ravishes Emeria. When he repeats his visit, she stabs him to death. Rodamant secures the bracelet and employs it in some comic scenes. The various characters then all meet in the forest. Archimagus, as a last resort, causes all the venomous reptiles in Ireland to attack Patrick who banishes them from the island. Archimagus then is swallowed up by the earth, the King, Endarius, Fedellus, and the rest are converted, while the unhappy Emeria founds a convent.

The characters in St. Patrick thus roughly correspond to those in The Virgin-Martyr; Dioclesian and Theophilus = Leogarius; Theophilus = Dichu; Dorothea = St. Patrick; Angelo = Victor; Harpax = Archimagus; Spungius and Hircius = Rodamant and the Bard; Calista and Christeta = Fedella and Ethne. In The Martyred Soldier of Henry Shirley (before 1627) we have St. Eugenius, an

Angel, a Clown, converted persecutors, and court ladies.

St. Patrick also recalls the Hermit in The Birth of Merlin, St. Dunstan in Grim, the Collier of Croydon, and the various saints in A Shoemaker a Gentleman. Victor, his angelic attendant, is paralleled by the Good Angel in Doctor Faustus, the Angel of Winifred's Well in A Shoemaker a Gentleman, the Angels in If You Know Not Me, You Know Nobody, Part I, the Genius in The Queen's Exchange, the Genius in The Queen and Concubine, the Attendant Spirit in Comus.

Cf. Archimagus as a magician with Brian Sansfoy in Sir Clyomon and Sir Clamydes, Faustus in Doctor Faustus, the Magician in The Wars of Cyrus, Sacrapant in The Old Wives' Tale, Friar Bacon, Friar Bungay and Vandermast in Friar Bacon and Friar Bungay, Merlin and Proximus in The Birth of Merlin, Peter Fabel in The Merry Devil of Edmonton, Erectho in Sophronisba, the Witches in Macbeth, Prospero in The Tempest, Pope Alexander in The Devil's Charter, Hecate in The Witch, Mother Sawyer in The Witch of Edmonton, the Witches in The Late Lancashire Witches, Ormandine and Argalio in The Seven Champions of Christendom, Comus in Comus, Mago in Trapolin Supposed a Prince. For his Evil Spirits, cf. Mephistophelis and the Bad Angel in Doctor Faustus, La Pucelle's Fiends in Henry VI, Part I, Akercock in Grim, the Collier of Croydon, Pope Alexander's Devils in The Devil's Charter, the fiends in If This Be Not a Good Play, the Devil Is in It, Tarpax and the other spirits in The Seven Champions of Christendom, Eo, Meo, and Areo, in Trapolin Supposed a Prince. Magicians and conjurers, genuine or fraudulent, have often a clownish servant, hence Rodamant. Cf. Scarabeo in The Maid's Revenge, and Carlo in The Bird in a Cage, Wagner in Doctor Faustus, Miles in Friar Bacon and Friar Bungay, the Clown in

The Birth of Merlin, Akercock in Grim, the Collier of
Croydon, Caliban in The Tempest, Suckabus in The Seven
Champions. Cf. the Bard with the Harper in Edward
I, and note the Clowns in Doctor Faustus. For other
clowns, see Chap. IV, Sect. 46.

Act I, Sc. 1. Archimagus' receiving news of the coming
of the Christians recalls Argalio, The Seven Champions
of Christendom, IV. Cf. also The Tempest, I, 2. Archimagus' reproof of the Magicians suggests Prospero's rebuke to Ariel in the latter scene. For an employment of
the prophecy or oracle analogous to that in this scene and
V, 3, see Shirley's Arcadia, I, 1, V, 2, The Contention of
Ajax and Ulysses, Sc. 2, The Lovers' Progress, III, 5, IV,
2. Cf. also Jocasta, I, 1, III, 1, Sapho and Phao, II, 1,
Midas, II, 2, V, 3, Mother Bombie, II, 3, III, 1, 4, V, 2,
Alphonsus, King of Arragon, III, IV, Edward I, p. 383,
Henry VI, Part I, V, 3, Part II, I, 4, Part III, IV, 6, V, 6,
King John, IV, 2, V, 2, Richard III, I, 1, 3, IV, 2, V, 1,
Troilus and Cressida, II, 2, Julius Cæsar, I, 2, III, 1,
Macbeth I, 3, IV, 1, Antony and Cleopatra, II, 3, Cymbe-
line, V, 4, 5, The Winter's Tale, III, 2, Henry VIII, I, 2,
V, 5, Edward III, IV, 3, The Birth of Merlin, I, 2, III,
3, IV, 5, etc., Edward IV, Part II, p. 131, The Golden Age,
I, 1, IV, 1, The Iron Age, Part I, I, 1, II, 1, The Rape of
Lucrece, II, 2, Love's Mistress, I, 1, Lust's Dominion, III,
2, The Thracian Wonder, II, 3, V, 2, If This Be Not a
Good Play, the Devil Is in It, p. 305, Hymen's Triumph,
III, 4 (reported), Sicelides, III, 6, Bonduca, III, 1
(omens), The Mad Lover, V, 3, The Prophetess, II, 1,
Fuimus Troes, III, 3, May's Cleopatra, II (omens), Anti-
gone, III, V, The Roman Actor, V, 1, The Lovesick Court,
I, 2, Randolph's Amyntas, I, 5, The Seven Champions of
Christendom, I, III, IV, The Shepherds' Holiday, II, 1,
III, 2, The Lady Errant, V, 2, The Virgin Widow, V, 1.

The flight of Archimagus' evil spirits before St. Patrick may be drawn from the flight of Harpax before Angelo, The Virgin-Martyr, IV, 3. Cf. also Friar Bacon and Friar Bungay, p. 168, The Birth of Merlin, II, 3, The Seven Champions of Christendom, III. The striking of Dichu motionless as he attempts to attack the saint is based upon The Virgin-Martyr, IV, 1, in which Sapritius is stricken as he orders the ravishment of Dorothea. Cf. also James IV, Induction, Friar Bacon and Friar Bungay, pp. 159, 162, Doctor Faustus, V, 1, The Birth of Merlin, IV, 5, The Lovesick King, I, The Tempest, I, 2, V, 1, The Prophetess, I, 3, The Martyred Soldier, IV, 3. Cf. the unsuccessful attempts upon Patrick's life here, and in III, 1, V, 3, with Shacklesoul's temptations of the Subprior, If This Be Not a Good Play, the Devil Is in It, pp. 312 ff., 331 ff. For Dichu's conversion, cf. The Virgin-Martyr, III, 1, 2, and The Martyred Soldier, I, 2.

Act II, Sc. 1. For the entrance of Rodamant with a book, see Chap. IV, Sect. 23. Analogues also for the eavesdropping of Corybreus and Archimagus (cf. IV, 1) and the attempt of the former upon the virtue of Emeria are cited in Chap. IV, Sects. 30 and 9.

Sc. 2. For the setting in a temple, cf. Alphonsus, King of Arragon, IV, Pericles, V, 3, A Game at Chess, V, 1, Fuimus Troes, II, 6, etc., The Jealous Lovers, V, 6. The posing as idols of Ferochus and Endarius in this scene and in IV, 2, may be derived from The Mad Lover, V, 3. Note also Corybreus as a god, III, 2, IV, 1, and cf. The Trial of Chivalry, IV, 1. The moving of the "idols" recalls the statue of Hymen, The Jealous Lovers, V, 6. Cf. The Two Noble Kinsmen, V, 1, 2, 3. Parallels to Rodamant's jest on "keeping the door" are found in The Duke's Mistress, V, 4, The Opportunity, V, 1, The Constant Maid, III, 1, The Lovers' Progress, I, 1, The Brazen

Age, p. 228, Blurt, Master-Constable, II, 2, Westward Ho, V, 1, The Honest Whore, Part I, IV, 1, Part II, III, 2, The Wonder of a Kingdom, III, 1, The Revenge of Bussy D'Ambois, I, 1, Othello, IV, 2, Pericles, IV, 6, The Elder Brother, IV, 4, The Parliament of Love, IV, 3, The Martyred Soldier, IV, 3, Covent Garden, V, 2, Microcosmus, V, Osmond, the Great Turk, IV.

Act III, Sc. 1. Rodamant's passion for the Queen, as expressed in his opening soliloquy and in following scenes, recalls Suckabus' frequent references to his mother, Calib's possessions as ''Queen of Helvetia'' in The Seven Champions of Christendom (see III, for instance). Cf. also Bertoldi and Fioretta in The Imposture, and Labesha and Martia in An Humorous Day's Mirth. The scene with the Bard which follows recalls Edward I, p. 382 ff. The attempted poisoning of St. Patrick and the failure to injure the saint thereby are related, seemingly, to The Virgin-Martyr, IV, 2, in which Dorothea is whipped, but by divine intervention, suffers no injury. Cf. also The Martyred Soldier, III, 4 (the torture of St. Eugenius), and note also the escape of St. Anthony and St. Andrew from death at the hands of the Emperor of Trebizon, The Seven Champions of Christendom, II. For general analogues to the use of poison, and to the resurrection of Rodamant, see Chap. IV, Sects. 11, 12, and 29. Cf. with the latter the curing of Henrick of a scorpion's bite by St. Eugenius, The Martyred Soldier, III, 4. The conversion of the Queen by the miraculous reviving of Rodamant suggests the conversion of Theophilus, The Virgin-Martyr, V, 1. The King's ordering her into confinement recalls the punishment of Calista and Christeta for the same offense, *ibid.*, III, 2.

Sc. 2. For the use of sleeping draughts, see Chap. IV, Sect. 13 (used here differently). Note the Magician's enchanting Panthea in her sleep at the desire of Araspas, The Wars of Cyrus, II. Ward derives Corybreus' visit to Emeria as the god Ceanerachius from Josephus (Bk. XIII, Chap. IV), or from Bandello (Part III, Novel 19) (Hist. Eng. Dram. Lit., III, 100, note). Miss Ott suggests Bandello as the source (Die Italienische Novelle im Englischen Drama, p. 78 ff.). The incident is found in varying forms, as in the story of Mundus and Paulina, Confessio Amantis, Bk. I, ll. 761–1059; the story of Nactabanus, *ibid.*, Bk. VI, ll. 1789–2366; and in various other versions of the story of the parentage of Alexander the Great. See also Geoffrey of Monmouth, Historia Regum Britanniae, Bk. VIII, Chap. 19 (the parentage of King Arthur); Friar Onion as the angel Gabriel in Tarlton's News out of Purgatory; Boccaccio, Decameron, Day IV, Novel 2. Cf. the reversal of the disguise (Jupiter as a mortal) in Amphitruo, I, 3, etc., and The Silver Age, II, 1. For disguises as gods, see II, 2, IV, 1, 2, and cf. The Nice Valor, II, 1, The Triumph of Honor, Sc. 2, The Mad Lover, V, 3. Emeria's cry of "Who is't calls Emeria?" (p. 403) suggests Hieronymo, "Who calls Hieronymo?" The Spanish Tragedy, II, 4. Cf. Lust's Dominion, III, 3, The Trial of Chivalry, II, 3, Antigone, V, and see under The Constant Maid, I, 1.

Note particularly in relation to Corybreus' rape of Emeria the attempted ravishment of Dorothea, The Virgin-Martyr, IV, 1. Parallels occur in Dick of Devonshire, II, 2, Double Falsehood, II, 1 (reported), Titus Andronicus, II, 3, 4, The Golden Age, II, 1, The Rape of Lucrece, IV, 3, The Mayor of Queenborough, III, 2, The Spanish Gipsy, I, 3, The Death of Robert, Earl of Huntington, I, 3 (reported), Valentinian, II, 6, III, 1, The Queen of Corinth, I, 4, II, 1, V, 2, All's Lost by Lust, II, 1, The Unnatural Combat, V, 1, The Cruel Brother, IV, 1, The Unfortunate

Lovers, V, 1 (reported), The Swisser, III, 3, Imperiale,
V, 5 (reported). Rape is attempted in The Cardinal, V,
3, The Duke's Mistress, V, 1, The Example, III, 1, The
Wars of Cyrus, II (threatened), The Two Gentlemen of
Verona, V, 4, The Tempest, I, 2, The Woman Hater, V,
5 (pretended), The Faithful Shepherdess, IV, 3, V, 3,
The Poor Man's Comfort, II, IV, The Lovesick Court,
IV, 2, The Court Beggar, III, 1 (reported), The Deserv-
ing Favorite, IV, 1, Love Crowns the End, p. 11, The
Bashful Lover, III, 3, The Shepherds' Holiday, V, 2.
Ravishment is pretended in Lust's Dominion, V, 1, The
Queen of Corinth, V, 2, Revenge for Honor, III, 1, Osmond,
the Great Turk, III.

Act IV, Sc. 1. Milcho's advising Emeria to forsake
Conallus for Corybreus is a reminiscence of Don Carlos'
instructions to Jacinta, The Brothers, II, 1. For the
Bard's song before Emeria, see The Queen of Corinth,
III, 2. The dialogue between Emeria and Conallus in
which she tells him of her violation suggests Castiza and
Vortiger, The Mayor of Queenborough, III, 3. There,
however, Vortiger has been his wife's real ravisher. For
Emeria's revenging her dishonor upon the pretended deity,
see under V, 1, The Duke's Mistress. The consequent exposure of Corybreus is somewhat like that of the Governor
in The Island Princess, V, 5. For Rodamant's verses to
the Queen (p. 415), see Chap. IV, Sect. 22. Cf. also
Suckabus' lines to his mistress, The Seven Champions of
Christendom, V. Milcho's attempt at immolating St. Patrick, the Queen, and the Bard, with which the scene closes,
recalls the attempt at torturing Dorothea, The Virgin-
Martyr, IV, 1, 2 (cf. St. Patrick, III, 1). Note also St.
Patrick's mentioning his having walked through fire, The
Seven Champions of Christendom, IV. Cf. Milcho's leap-

ing into the flames with Dido, Queen of Carthage, V, 2, and The Brazen Age, p. 253.[6]

Sc. 2. Cf. Ferochus and Endarius as idols with the same in II, 2. Together with V, 1, the pranks of Rodamant who has Corybreus' magic bracelet and who now walks invisible suggest the mockery of Harpax in the study of Theophilus, The Virgin-Martyr, V, 1. See The Witty Fair One, V, 1. Cf. also the use by Suckabus of the spells taught him by his father, Tarpax, in The Seven Champions of Christendom, III, and employed by him in V. Note Ariel and the three servants, The Tempest, III, 2. Other parallels are Doctor Faustus, III, 2, A Midsummer Night's Dream, III, 2, Grim, the Collier of Croydon, IV, 1. Cf. also The Puritan, IV, 2. Shirley's only "ghosts" now appear—Ferochus and Endarius, as their own spirits. Cf. Mrs. Arthur in How a Man May Choose a Good Wife from a Bad, p. 60 ff., Maria in The Nightwalker, III, 2, Chilax in The Mad Lover, V, 4, Maria in The Bashful Lover, IV, 2, Milesia in The Lost Lady, IV, 1, Philanthus in The Fool Would Be a Favorite, V. Cf. Chap. IV, Sect. 24. Note the actual ghosts of the Earl and Countess of Coventry (the father and mother of St. George) in The Seven Champions of Christendom, I.

Act V, Sc. 1. Rodamant's entry in the forest intent on hanging himself because of the supposed death of the Queen suggests particularly Edward I, pp. 406-7. Cf. also Cupid and Death, pp. 351, 362, David and Bethsabe, p. 480, An Humorous Day's Mirth, p. 43, Cæsar and Pompey, II, 1, The Downfall of Robert, Earl of Huntington, V, 1, All's Lost by Lust, V, 3. In The Seven Champions of Christendom, II, St. Anthony and St. Andrew, after being

6 These two parallels were suggested by Mr. J. Frank Dobie of Columbia University.

condemned to death are permitted to choose their execu-
tioners, a fact presenting some analogies to Rodamant's errand.   Note also Depazzi's search for a death that suits him,
The Humorous Courtier, V, 2.   Rodamant's trip to the forest
suggests Bertoldi in the later Imposture, V, 4.   For his
pranks upon the soldiers (by which he rescues Emeria),
see under IV, 2.   Here, The Tempest, III, 2, seems the
source.   For the resurrection of St. Patrick, the Queen,
and the Bard, with those of Ferochus and Endarius in V,
2, see Chap. IV, Sect. 29.   Cf. the Bard's refusal to become a Christian with Bombo, The Royal Master, III, 3.

Sc. 2.   Gifford derives Dichu's cave from that of Bel-
larius, Cymbeline, III, 6, IV, 2.   Note also the caves in
Locrine, IV, 4, Timon of Athens, IV, V, Cupid's Revenge,
V, 3, The Knight of Malta, IV, 1, which might as well be
sources.

Sc. 3.   Cf. St. Patrick's prophecy with I, 1.   Cf. the
future of Conallus, as revealed, with that of Banquo, Mac-
beth, IV, 1.   St. Patrick's vision resembles that of
Theophilus, The Virgin-Martyr, V, 2.   Note also the visions of St. Dunstan in Grim, the Collier of Croydon, I, 1,
V, 1, and of St. Eugenius, The Martyred Soldier, III, 2.
Analogues are found in The Wounds of Civil War, V, 5,
The Triumph of Death, Sc. 4, Henry VIII, IV, 2, The
Raging Turk, V, 9, Love Crowns the End, p. 23, The
Queen and Concubine, III, 2, Messallina, II, 1.   Sophos
in Wily Beguiled, p. 278 ff., has a dream not of a religious
nature.   The attempt of Archimagus to destroy the saint
with aid of the reptiles seems certainly drawn from a popular life of St. Patrick.[7]   The fate of Archimagus—he sinks
into the earth—seems to have suggested that of Phantasm,

[7] The absence of poisonous reptiles in Ireland is mentioned in
Fuimus Troes, III, 1.   See Dyce's Middleton's Works, III, 177,
note, IV, 495, note.

Honoria and Mammon, V, 1. It parallels the disappearances of Harpax in The Virgin-Martyr, V, 1, 2, and of Calib in The Seven Champions of Christendom, I. Cf. Doctor Faustus, V, 4, Grim, the Collier of Croydon, V, 1, The Devil's Charter, V, 6, If This Be Not a Good Play, the Devil Is in It, p. 348, The Martyred Soldier, V, Messallina, V, 1, The Virgin Widow, V, 1. Note also the sinking into the earth of Queen Eleanor, Edward I, p. 408. The conversion of Leogarius resembles somewhat that of Theophilus, The Virgin-Martyr, V, 1. Their places in the two plays correspond. Note that Hubert, on assuming the crown, in The Martyred Soldier, V, announces his conversion.

### VI. THE GENTLEMAN OF VENICE

Langbaine conjectures, regarding The Gentleman of Venice, that the intrigue between Florelli, Cornari, and Claudiana was borrowed from a novel in Gayton's Festivous Notes to Don Quixote, Bk. IV, Chaps. 6, 7, 8 (Dramatic Poets, p. 479). According to Ward, however (Hist. Eng. Dram. Lit., III, 117, note), this book was not published until 1654,[8] so that another source must be sought. Dibdin asserts that the plot is from Don Quixote (History of the Stage, IV, 46), but, although the intrigue above mentioned resembles, somewhat, that of The Curious Impertinent, there seems to be no indebtedness. There is some suggestion of the story of the King and the Steward's Wife, Confessio Amantis, Bk. V, ll. 2643–2825. The part of The Gentleman of Venice which treats the love of Giovanni and Bellaura may be related to Lope de Vega's El Hombre por su Palabra which it seems to resemble, as the Spanish play is outlined in Von Wurtzbach's Lope

---

[8] Langbaine probably confused the date of publication (1655) of The Gentleman of Venice with that of its presentation.

de Vega und seine Komödien, pp. 222-23. There is also some likeness to A Mad Couple Well Matched, and to The Rebellion.

The Gentleman of Venice may be outlined thus:

Cornari, "a gentleman of Venice," because of the debauchery of his nephew and heir, Malipiero, resolves to alienate his inheritance from him at any cost. Being childless, Cornari conceives the fault to be his own, and so, finding that his wife Claudiana admires a brilliant Englishman, Florelli, then in Venice, he resolves that Florelli shall act as a sort of proxy for him. He has the Englishman kidnapped and brought to his house where he is introduced to Claudiana. Thinking the deed done, Cornari resolves to kill Florelli so as effectually to hide his dishonor, but finds by a ruse that the two have really spent their time together in prayers for him. He conveys Florelli back then to the place where he was seized and releases him. Malipiero, who has been imprisoned for stealing crown-jewels and for treasonable plans, repents and is pardoned by his uncle. The other story is that of the love of Giovanni, a gardener, for Bellaura, the Duke's niece. Giovanni goes to war, wins glory, and is ennobled by the Duke. He asks the hand of Bellaura as a reward for his services. It is refused because of his humble origin. His supposed mother, Ursula, however, to save the life of Thomazo, the supposed son of the Duke and Malipiero's fellow-conspirator, confesses that she had exchanged her child for the Duke's in the cradle, and that Giovanni is really the Duke's son. Thus the way is smoothed for the marriage of Bellaura and Giovanni.

It will be seen that at least one of the two practically separate plots of the play helps to place it, as Ristine says, in the small group of tragicomedies the subject of which is Italian domestic life and in which are included The City

Nightcap, The Just Italian, and The Twins (English Tragi-comedy, p. 140).

Examples of a person's rising from an early obscure position to eminence, either through his own achievements, or through the discovery of his true identity, or both, as Giovanni does, are not uncommon in Elizabethan drama. Characters whose fortunes parallel those of Giovanni are Careno in The Supposes, the sons of the Earl of Boloign in The Four Prentices of London, Simon Eyre in The Shoemaker's Holiday, Ferdinando in The Weakest Goeth to the Wall, Thornton in The Lovesick King, Helena in All's Well that Ends Well, Marina in Pericles, Perdita in The Winter's Tale, Golding in Eastward Ho, Antonio in A Very Woman, Marullo in The Bondman, Cicely in Tottenham Court, Archigenes in The Shepherds' Holiday. Note also Mucedorus in The Arcadia, Mucedorus in Mucedorus, Offa and his brother in A Shoemaker a Gentleman, Honorio in The Noble Stranger, and especially Sebastiano as Giovanno, a tailor, in The Rebellion. For analogues to Malipiero, the dissipated gentleman, Thomazo, the clownish poltroon, and Georgio, who is close to the comic servant type of clown, see Chap. IV, Sects. 38, 47, and 46. Cf. Thomazo especially with Cloten in Cymbeline.

As in The Politician, and the analogues there cited, brief characters are affixed to the *dramatis personæ*. The title of the play is attached to Cornari's name, as it is to that of Gotharus in The Politician. For this and the occurrences of the title in I, 1, and IV, 2, see Chap. IV, Sect. 31.

Act I, Sc. 1. Cf. the quarrel of Cornari and Malipiero over the latter's demands for money with Flowerdale and his Uncle, The London Prodigal, I, 1, John Graham and his Uncle, If You Know Not Me, You Know Nobody, Part II, p. 254, Jamie and Henrique, The Spanish Curate, I,

1, Philargus and Parthenius, The Roman Actor, II, 1, Careless and Dotario, A Fine Companion, I, 7, Sir Geoffrey and Crackby, The Lady Mother, I, 2. Malipiero's invitation to Cornari to a debauch is based on a speech of Luys to his father, The Brothers, V, 3. Cf. Lodwick and the Duke, The Grateful Servant, I, 1. Claudiana's childlessness suggests that of Labervele's Countess, An Humorous Day's Mirth (p. 25), of Violante, The Spanish Curate (I, 1), and of Lady Thrivewell, A Mad Couple Well Matched (II, 1).

Cornari's getting a son by proxy may come from Careless' courtship of Lady Thrivewell, A Mad Couple Well Matched, III, 1. Cf. The Spanish Curate, I, 3, Henrique and Violante seeking how to deprive Jamie of his inheritance, and cf. Jamie's claims of Ascanio's supposititiousness, *ibid.*, III, 3. Note that in A Fine Companion, I, 7, Dotario announces that he will not make Aurelio, brother to the prodigal Careless, his heir, but will get a son. Note Morose's deciding on marriage in order to cut Dauphine out of his estate, Epicœne, I, 1. Cf. Cornari's wishing Claudiana to go abroad more with Lavervele and his Countess, An Humorous Day's Mirth, p. 25. The tone of their conversation suggests Bartolo and Amaranta, The Spanish Curate, II, 2, and Corvino and Celia in Volpone, II, 3.

Sc. 2. For Roberto on Ursula's reception of Giovanni's reading the story of Xantippe, cf. The Wife of Bath's Prologue, 1. 711 ff. (particularly ll. 727–32). Note the references (p. 13) to Amadis de Gaul, Don Quixote, and Guzman de Alfarache. See for allusions to the first, Koeppel, Reflexe der Ritter-Romane in Drama, p. 217, note, and for references to Don Quixote, cf. Honoria and Mammon, V, 1, and The Triumph of Peace. Cf. The Triumph of Peace for a use of Don Quixote. Note Florelli, as described, p. 13, and I, 3, as being a counterpart of the

"Admirable Crichton." There seems to be, as Gifford notes, some satire on the fantastic gardening of the day (p. 14). Ursula's reminiscences concerning Thomazo as her foster-child recall the Nurse, Romeo and Juliet, I, 3, and the Nurse, A Mad Couple Well Matched, II, 1.

Sc. 3, which is expository, begins the systematic contrasting of Giovanni and Thomazo which continues through the play.

Act II, Sc. 1. For Cornari and Claudiana, cf. Volpone, II, 3. Georgio's finding meanings in the flowers is paralleled in Richard II, III, 4, Hamlet, IV, 5, The Winter's Tale, IV, 4, All Fools, II, 1, Law Tricks, III, 2, Philaster, I, 2 (reported), The Two Noble Kinsmen, II, 1, A New Wonder: A Woman Never Vexed, III, 1. See also A Handful of Pleasant Delights, p. 3. For Giovanni on courts, cf. Octavio, The Royal Master, I, 2. Bellaura's replies suggest the advice of Foscari, The Grateful Servant, I, 2 (see also under Love's Cruelty, I, 2). For Cornari's Bravos here and in IV, 3, V, 2, 3, see The Antiquary, III, 1, and note Verdugo in Imperiale. Cf. the kidnapping of Florelli with The Picture, III, 3. The secrecy with which Florelli is brought to Cornari's house is related to the stipulations of Amidea as reported, The Traitor, V, 2 (see the analogues to that scene).

Act III, Sc. 1. For the day-dreams of Thomazo and his companions, cf. The Arcadia, III, 1. The original source is Henry VI, Part II, IV, 2, 6, 7. In connection with the reference to "Scanderbeg" (p. 33), note "Squanderbag" as a military figure in Honoria and Mammon, IV, 1, etc. For similar allusions see The Shoemakers' Holiday, III, 1, Satiromastix, p. 233, Every Man in his Humor, I, 2, The Dumb Knight, I, 1. A play, The True History of George Scanderbeg, was entered in the Stationers' Register in 1601, as by Marlowe. For the references to the Amster-

dam sectaries (p. 37), note The Family of Love and The
Alchemist, and cf. Every Woman in her Humor, I, 1, Sir
Giles Goosecap, II, 1, Wit in a Constable, II, 1.

Sc. 2. Note the contrast between Thomazo in the preceding scene and Giovanni in this. Giovanni's preparations to leave for the seat of war may have been suggested
by Sebastiano and his fellow tailors in The Rebellion, I, 1.
Cf. also Offa in A Shoemaker a Gentleman, III, 2, and
Silvio in Women Pleased, IV, 1, 2, 4.

Sc. 3. Cf. Florelli's being brought in blindfolded with
The Lady of Pleasure, IV, 1, and The Picture, III, 5. Cf.
also The Witch, III, 1, The Bloody Banquet, III, 3, IV, 3,
The Fool Would Be a Favorite, III. In the last play cited,
Philanthus who is blindfolded and led to Lucina's house
suspects enchantment, as Florelli thinks himself dreaming
(cf. The Constant Maid, IV, 3). An apparent inconsistency in Shirley's scene occurs in Florelli's telling Cornari
who seems still to be masked that he has a good face (p. 45).

Sc. 4. For analogous drinking scenes, see Chap. IV,
Sect. 26. Similar scenes in the apartments of prostitutes
are found in The Jew of Malta, IV, 4, 5, Henry IV, Part II,
4 (Doll is a guest at the tavern), Blurt, Master-Constable,
II, 2, III, 3, etc., Your Five Gallants, II, 1, Westward Ho,
IV, 1, The Honest Whore, Part I, II, 1, Northward Ho,
III, 1, If You Know Not Me, You Know Nobody, Part II,
p. 307 ff., The Royal King and Loyal Subject, III, 1, The
Dutch Courtesan, II, 1, The Fair Maid of Bristow, I, 3
(perhaps not indoors), Greene's Tu Quoque, p. 544 ff. (at
a tavern), The City Madam, III, 1, IV, 2, Holland's
Leaguer, IV, 2, The Weeding of the Covent Garden, I, 1,
IV, 1, The Jealous Lovers, III, 5, Messallina, I, 1. The
Novella, V, 1, is laid in the apartment of a pretended
courtesan. Malipiero's calling Rosabella "Lady Gui-
nevere" (a nickname for women of doubtful character) is

paralleled in The Sisters, IV, I, and The Gamester, V, 1
(cf. Koeppel, Reflexe der Ritter-Romane im Drama, p. 197,
note).

Marino's part in the scene recalls Bellamont and Doll,
Northward Ho, III, 1.  Note Thomazo's references to the
"Queen of Carthage" and to "Cleopatra" (p. 49).  The
attempt to sell the stolen crown jewels recalls Ithamore's
blackmailing Barabas, The Jew of Malta, IV, 4, 5.  Malipiero's nautical figures are strongly suggestive of Young
Geraldine's account of Young Lionel's debauch, The English Traveller, II, 1.  See also The Anatomy of Melancholy,
Part I, Sec. 2, Mem. 4, Subsec. 7, and Howell's Familiar
Letters, II, 459.  Thomazo's remarks on the instability of
his brains (p. 53) are later paralleled by Haraldus, The
Politician, III, 3.  The entrance of the officers summoned
by Marino recalls The City Madam, IV, 2.

Act IV, Sc. 1.  Cf. the conversation of Cornari and
Claudiana with Volpone, III, 6, Anything for a Quiet Life,
II, 1, The Custom of the Country, I, 1 (a test).  Note also
an experience of Jonson's, Conversations with Drummond,
Sect. XIII, and see A New Way to Pay Old Debts, III, 2.
There seems to be a reference to The Just Italian, p. 57.

Sc. 2.  Cf. the news of Giovanni's gallantry with that of
Silvio's conduct, Women Pleased, V, 1.  Giovanni's requesting Bellaura's hand as a reward for his deeds may be
drawn from "Giovanno's" asking Antonio for Evadne,
his sister, in return for having saved his life, The Rebellion,
II, 1.  Note also Helena, All's Well that Ends Well, II,
1, 2.  This incident is utilized in The Imposture, I, 1, in
regard to Leonato's reward for his services.  For love between a man and a woman really or apparently much his
superior in rank, cf. Mucedorus and Pamela, The Arcadia,
Philenzo (Rolliardo) and Eugenia, The Bird in a Cage,
Mucedorus and Amadine, Mucedorus, Offa and Leodice, A

Shoemaker a Gentleman, Ferdinando and Odillia in The
Weakest Goeth to the Wall, Silvio and Belvidere in Women
Pleased.

Cf. Georgio's comments on Giovanni's reward and his
disgust at his master's simplicity with the remarks of
Sapritius, The Virgin-Martyr, I, 1. Cf., also, Comachio
in The Humorous Courtier, IV, 1.

Sc. 3. Cf. Cornari's informing Florelli of the part he is
expected to perform with Lodwick and Piero, The Grateful
Servant, IV, 1, Contarini and Giotto, The Humorous
Courtier, III, 1. Note also Ferdinand and "Tiberio," The
Doubtful Heir, IV, 1. See The Merry Wives of Windsor,
II, 2, The Triumph of Honor, Sc. 3, The Coxcomb, II, 1,
The City Nightcap, I, 1. Observe the other dramatic ana-
logues to the Curious Impertinent. Cf. Confident's willing-
ness to prostitute his wife to his patron, The Example,
IV, 1. Cf. the introduction of Claudiana with that of
Carintha and Giotto, The Humorous Courtier, IV, 3. Note
also Volpone, III, 6, Anything for a Quiet Life, II, 1, III, 1.
Florelli's attitude towards Claudiana suggests Wittipol and
Mrs. Fitzdottrel, The Devil is an Ass, IV, 3 (opening of
the scene).

Act V, Sc. 1. Cf. Ursula's hint as to a mystery concerning Giovanni with Lady Goldenfleece's hints, No Wit,
No Help Like a Woman's, I, 1, and those of Garrula, The
Lovesick Court, I, 2, etc. Cf. her hearing of the con-
demnation of Thomazo with The Shepherds' Holiday, IV, 2.

Sc. 2. For the imaginary cuckoldom of Cornari, see
Chap. IV, Sect. 25. His use of a friar's garb and the rite
of confession as a means of arriving at the true state of
affairs has the following analogues: Edward I, p. 412, If
This Be Not a Good Play, the Devil Is in It, p. 339 ff., The
City Nightcap, III, 1, The Emperor of the East, V, 3, The
Bashful Lover, IV, 2. Note also Queen Eleanor's Confes-

sion, Kittredge and Child's Ballads, No. 156, Du Chevalier
qui fist sa femme confist, Montaiglon, No. 16, Les Cent
Nouvelles Nouvelles, No. 78, Decameron, Day VII, Novel 5.
The device is referred to in Anything for a Quiet Life, II, 1.
An overheard confession is employed in The Mayor of
Queenborough, III, 3, and is contemplated in The Sad
One, IV, 3. A mock confession is planned in The Ordinary,
V, 3. Friar's habits are used as disguises in The Fair
Maid of Bristow, V, 2, The White Devil, V, 3, The Island
Princess, IV, 1, etc. (a Moorish priest), The Wonder of a
Kingdom, V, 1, A Very Woman, IV, 2, The Bashful Lover,
IV, 2. The fact that Florelli, apparently a seventeenth
century Englishman, asks for a confessor is worth noting.
Contrast Dick of Devonshire, IV, 2. Florelli's account of
how he and Claudiana had spent their time together recalls
Hazard's account of his reception by Mrs. Wilding, The
Gamester, V, 2.

For Florelli's affirmation to Cornari of his wife's chas-
tity, cf. The Grateful Servant, V, 1, The Humorous Court-
ier, V, 3, The Wedding, IV, 4 (a variation), The Gamester,
V, 2. Other parallels are met with in The Fawn, IV, The
Insatiate Countess, V, The Woman's Prize, IV, 5, The
Spanish Curate, V, 2, The Dumb Knight, V, 1, The Roaring
Girl, IV, 2, The Hector of Germany, V, 5, The City Night-
cap, III, 1, Albovine, V, 1, The Cruel Brother, V, 1, The
Queen, V, The Antipodes, V, 5.

For the conversion of Malipiero expressed by letter, p. 79,
and in person, Sc. 4, see Chap. IV, Sect. 10. Especially
close parallels are the reformations of Quicksilver, Eastward Ho, V, 1, Young Flowerdale, The London Prodigal,
V, 1, Nick, The Weeding of the Covent Garden, V, 3, Wat,
The Damoiselle, V, 1, Young Lionel, The English Traveller,
IV, 6.

Sc. 3. Note Florelli's reference to Endymion, and to

the fairies. The former is mentioned in The Example,
I, 1. Cf. The Variety, V, 1, and The Downfall of Robert,
Earl of Huntington, III, 1.

Sc. 4. Roberto's references to a pear-tree in connection
with the froward Ursula recall similar allusions in The
Gamester, V, 1, and in Timon of Athens, V, 1. Ursula's
confession of her substitution of her child for the Duke's
recalls Vicina's similar statement, Mother Bombie, V, 3.
Cf. also No Wit, No Help like a Woman's, V, 1, A King and
No King, V, 4, Thierry and Theodoret, III, 1 (Brunhalt's
story), The Fair Maid of the Inn, III, 2, The Queen's Ex-
change, IV, 1 (Edith's story), The Magnetic Lady, IV, 1,
V, 6, The Virgin Widow, V, 1. Morulla's confession, The
Sisters, V, 2 (reported) is based on Ursula's. Cf. also The
Court Secret, IV, 3, V, 3.

For the clearing up of Giovanni's parentage, cf. Phillis
of Scyros, V, 9, The Supposes, V, 5, The Comedy of Errors,
V, 1, Cymbeline, V, 5, Pericles, V, 1, The Winter's Tale,
V, 2 (reported), The Case is Altered, V, 4, The New Inn,
V, 1, The Weakest Goeth to the Wall, V, 3, The Maid's
Metamorphosis, V, Monsieur Thomas, V, 10, The Triumph
of Love, Sc. 8, The Beggar's Bush, V, 2, The Humorous
Lieutenant, V, 5, The Maid in the Mill, V, 2, The Fair Maid
of the Inn, V, 3, The Heir, IV, V, The Captives, IV, 1, The
Lovesick Court, V, 3, The Antipodes, V, 6, The Jovial Crew,
V (1641), The Deserving Favorite, V, 1, Tottenham Court,
V, 7, The Jealous Lovers, IV, 9, V, 7, Perkin Warbeck, II, 1
(doubtful), The Shepherds' Holiday, V, 4, Love's Riddle,
V, 1, The Princess, V, 8, The Prisoners, V, 3, The Goblins,
V, 5, The Obstinate Lady, V, 6, The Rebellion, V (1641)
(Sebastiano reveals himself).

## VII. The Imposture

The Imposture seems to be a reworking of parts of earlier

plays of Shirley, interspersed with hints from the works of other dramatists.

The plot of the play follows:

The Imposture opens with Mantua in a state of siege. Leonato, Prince of Ferrara, raises the siege. For his aid he is promised the hand of Fioretta, Princess of Mantua, who, by the advice of Flaviano, the Duke's favorite, himself in love with her, has been sent, ostensibly to a nunnery, but, in fact, to the house of Flaviano's mother. When Leonato demands his bride, he is told that she is vowed to spend a year in the convent. He insists on seeing her. Juliana, a novice who had been seduced by Flaviano, is engaged to act as a substitute for the Princess. She pretends to refuse the request of Leonato that she leave the convent, but in reality advises him to abduct her. This he does. Just before his arrival at Ferrara, Fioretta who has left her retreat arrives there incognita. Honorio, her brother, who is ignorant of the imposture, appears in search of his sister, and, meeting Leonato, fights with him. Flaviano and Claudio, who now arrive at Ferrara, seek to assassinate Honorio. Claudio betrays Flaviano, and frustrates his plot. Having compunctions of conscience, Juliana confesses her identity to Leonato, but not her relations with Flaviano. To spite the Mantuans, Leonato announces that he will marry Juliana. Claudio, however, unfolds the plots of Flaviano to Leonato and tells of Juliana's past. Flaviano attempts to flee, but is taken, banished, and his estate confiscated for the use of the convent into which Juliana must retire. Leonato marries Fioretta; Honorio marries Donabella, sister to Leonato. The comic element is furnished by the pursuit of Florelia, a wealthy widow, by two soldiers, Volterino and Hortensio. She offers her hand to him who will make her cowardly son, Bertoldi, brave. The soldiers attempt to make Bertoldi at least ap-

pear courageous, but are unsuccessful. Finally, nevertheless, Florelia gives her hand to Hortensio.

From the preceding summary it will be seen that The
Imposture embodies elements of The Royal Master and
The Maid's Revenge. From The Royal Master comes the
love of Flaviano for Fioretta and his attempt to break off
her match with Leonato (cf. Schipper, James Shirley, p.
270). From The Maid's Revenge comes the visit of Honorio to Ferrara to avenge the false Fioretta's abduction,
and to take her back to Mantua. Certain other elements
from the earlier plays not shown in the summary will be
taken up later.

For the Machiavellian Flaviano, see Chap. IV, Sect. 33.
Cf. Montalto in The Royal Master. Donabella and Fioretta suggest Theodosia and Domitilla in The Royal Master with certain of their characteristics and relations inter-
changed. Juliana suggests her namesake in Measure for
Measure, as well as Mariana in the same play. Note, in
regard to her relations with Flaviano, that Romelio admits
in The Devil's Law-case, III, 3, having got a nun with
child. For Bertoldi, see Chap. IV, Sect. 47. Cf. his passion for Fioretta with Rodamant and the Queen, St. Patrick for Ireland, and Labervele and Martia, An Humorous
Day's Mirth. Cf. Florelia and her suitors with Lady
Goldenfleece and hers in No Wit, No Help Like a Woman's,
and with the Widow and her followers in The Widow.

Act I, Sc. 1. The pretense of sending Fioretta to a convent, but in reality sending her away so as to escape the
match with Leonato recalls The Merry Devil of Edmonton,
I, 1. Milliscent in The Merry Devil, however, is really
placed in a convent. Note that the terms for which they
are immured, or are supposed to be, are the same (see
Sc. 2). In The Turk, I, 1, Borgias pretends to the Dukes
of Florence and of Venice that Julia has died; his design

is to prevent the marriage of either with her. Cf. Flaviano's feelings toward Fioretta as shown in this scene with those of Montalto toward Theodosia, The Royal Master, I, 1. For his desire to remove Honorio from his path (p. 188) see under The Politician, I, 1.

Sc. 2. For the return of a victorious army from battle, cf. The Politician, III, 4, The Young Admiral, I, 2. Note also Titus Andronicus, I, 1, Coriolanus, II, 1, Edward I, p. 377, and More Dissemblers besides Women, I, 3, The Roman Actor, I, 4. Many early plays, such as the two parts of Tamburlaine, contain similar spectacles. Flaviano's ornate speech to the conquering Leonato, as Gifford notes, is obviously studiously insincere. In this respect, it resembles D'Amville's lamentation, The Atheist's Tragedy, II, 4, Macbeth, Macbeth, II, 3, Frank to Susan, The Witch of Edmonton, II, 2, and the Governor of Verona to Albovine, Albovine, I, 1. Note also Contarini to Paulina in Shirley's later Sisters, II, 2.

Cf. the account of Bertoldi's conduct in battle (p. 192) with the pages concerning Balurdo, Antonio and Mellida, II. Note Ariotto and Lizaro in Davenant's Siege, II, 1. Bertoldi's entrance laden with arms is drawn probably from Sir Pergamus and his trophies, The Faithful Friends, III, 2. Cf. also Falstaff with Hotspur's body, Henry IV, Part I, V, 4, Bessus in A King and No King, II, 1, and A Fine Companion, IV, 4. This incident is related to Device's presenting to the Sister Courtwell's sword which he has stolen, Captain Underwit, V, 1. Note that Bertoldi does not expatiate on his feats of arms. Fioretta's "vow" to remain a year in the convent suggests Thaisa's vow to remain a year unmarried, Pericles, II, 5 (cf. The Merry Devil of Edmonton, I, 1). The fact that the Duke attempts to prevent the unsatisfactory marriage of his daughter suggests The Bird in a Cage, I, 1, and Women Pleased, I, 1.

For the rage of Leonato at the slight put upon him, cf. Don Pedro in The Brothers, V, 3, and the Duke of Siena, Women Pleased, III, 3.

Act II, Sc. 1. Cf. the convent setting with The Merry Devil of Edmonton, III, 1, Measure for Measure, I, 4, The White Devil, IV, 1. Note The Grateful Servant, V, 2. Flaviano's pretense that the Prince does not love Fioretta (p. 200) is related to The Royal Master, II, 2, 3 (Montalto's assurances that Theodosia does not love the Duke). The contriving to pass off Juliana as Fioretta may be derived from A Maidenhead Well Lost, IV, in which the Duke of Milan plots with Stroza to substitute Lauretta for Julia in the nuptial bed of the Prince of Florence. Flaviano's arranging the substitution with Juliana recalls Heywood's play as cited above, p. 149 ff. (Stroza and Lauretta). For mock conversions such as Flaviano's, see under Chap. IV, Sect. 10.

Sc. 2. For the plot to make Bertoldi brave, see under The Young Admiral, III, 1, IV, 1. Cf. his frequent and promiscuous offers of his mother's hand here and throughout the play (as in IV, 2), with Simpleton's similar offers, The Variety, V, 1, and with Mrs. Tongueall's allusions to her daughter Jenny, in Covent Garden.

Sc. 3. Cf. Juliana as a Princess (Fioretta) with Seleucus (who is really a King), The Coronation, IV, 1, Pimponio in The Opportunity, II, 1, Frapolo in The Sisters, IV, 4, the Cousin in The Constant Maid, III, 2, Hoffman in Hoffman, II, the Courtesan in The Mad Lover, V, 4. For Juliana's hints to Leonato, see Chap. IV, Sect. 28. The source here is probably The Witty Fair One, I, 3. Cf. May-Day, II, 1, The Fawn, III, IV, The Family of Love, I, 2, Wit Without Money, V, 3. For the abduction of Juliana, cf. The Maid's Revenge, III, 4, 5, 6, The Merchant of Venice, II, 6, Othello, I, 1, The Merry Devil of Edmon-

ton, III, 2, IV, 1.  Honorio's situation (p. 210) is based
on that of Sebastiano, The Maid's Revenge, IV, 1 (a struggle between the desire to avenge the kidnapping of his
sister and his sense of the relationship in which he stands
to the kidnapper).  Honorio, however, does not hesitate
as long as does Sebastiano.

Act III, Sc. 1.  Fioretta's learning of the arrival of the
false Fioretta at Ferrara together with Honorio's meeting
the latter in Sc. 3 following is a variation on the actual
meeting of a character with an impostor who is impersonat-
ing him.  Cf. Love Tricks, V, 1, 3, The Opportunity, IV, 1,
and the later Sisters, IV, 5, V, 2.  Parallels occur in The
Supposes, IV, 5, Sir Clyomon and Sir Clamydes, p. 531,
The Comedy of Errors, III, 1, V, 1, The Taming of the
Shrew, V, 1, Look about You (very frequently), What You
Will, IV, 1, The Fair Maid of the Exchange, p. 84, Al-
bumazar, IV, 7, 8, The Maid in the Mill, III, 2, The Just
Italian, III, 1, Love and Honor, IV, 1, The Novella, V, 1,
The Queen's Exchange, III, V, 1, Trapolin Supposed a
Prince, V, 4.  See under Love Tricks, V, 3, for other ana-
logues.

Sc. 2.  For Volterino's account of Bertoldi's ''courage''
in battle, see under Love Tricks, IV, 6.  Cf. especially Sir
Pergamus, The Faithful Friends, III, 2, and Bessus, A
King and No King, II, 1.  Bertoldi's cowardice after Hor-
tensio's entrance recalls the fright of Bubulcus at the end
of Love Tricks, IV, 6.  Cf. also The Gamester, II, 2, V, 1,
Every Man in his Humor, IV, 5, Every Man out of his
Humor, V, 3, 4, A King and No King, III, 2, The Court
Beggar, III, 1.  See under I, 2.  Florelia's offering her
hand to the suitor who will fulfill her conditions recalls
Jacinta in The Example, IV, 2, Lucina in The Ball, III, 1,
Quisara in The Island Princess, I, 3.

Sc. 3.  Cf. the duel between Honorio and Leonato with

that in The Maid's Revenge, IV, 3. Note that the situation here is that of a brother fighting the abductor of his sister (pretended), and that the first later falls in love with the sister of his opponent. The duel is halted by the entrance of the sisters (real and pretended) of the combatants. For Honorio's surprise at Juliana's appearance as Fioretta, see under Sc. 1 of this act. See Chap. IV, Sect. 31, for the occurrence of the title of the play in the text (p. 226).

Act IV, Sc. 1, contains an interchange of half-confidences between Fioretta and Donabella.

Sc. 2. Cf. Bertoldi's willingness to assist Flaviano and Claudio in the murder of Honorio with Piperollo's eagerness to help in the robbery of his parents, The Sisters, I, 1. His promiscuous offers of Florelia's hand have already been noted under II, 2.

Sc. 3. For Florelia's pretense of eavesdropping, cf. V, 2, and see Chap. IV, Sect. 30. Her making game of Volterino and Hortensio recalls Hyde Park, I, 1, and The Ball, II, 3, etc. The proposal of Hortensio to make Bertoldi brave on wine is paralleled later in The Politician, II, 1.

Sc. 4. Claudio's sudden change of heart, and refusal to kill the Prince is drawn from The Duke's Mistress, V, in which Pallante who has been entrusted with the assassination of the Duke proves not to have done it (see under The Politician, IV, 2, 5).

Sc. 5 is concerned with Juliana's sudden contrition, her half-confession to Leonato, and his defiance of Honorio.

Act V, Sc. 1. For drinking scenes, see Chap. IV, Sect. 26. For an analogue to Hortensio's description of the legend of Arion and his dolphin (p. 248), see the Clown on the legend of Troy, Love's Mistress, II, 1. Cf. Pandolfo as a soldier with Gorgon in Love Tricks, IV, 5. The quarrel of Bertoldi and Pandolfo is based on those of Young Barnacle, The Gamester, II, 2, IV, 1, V, 1. The language of Pandolfo suggests an indebtedness to Pistol in Henry IV, Parts I, and II, Henry V, and The Merry Wives of Windsor, and to Bobadill in Every Man in his Humor. For the throwing of wine in the faces of Bertoldi and Florelia in disguise, see under The Politician, III, 3. For Florelia's male garb, see Chap. IV, Sect. 32. For the use of "sandiack" (p. 250), cf. "sanzacke," The Renegado, III, 4.

Sc. 2. Donabella's overhearing Honorio and Fioretta suggests The Maid's Revenge, II, 2, in its effect upon her. For the eavesdropping, cf. IV, 3, and see Chap. IV, Sect. 30. The jealousy of Donabella suggests strongly that of Theodosia, The Royal Master, IV, 1 (cf. Sc. 5), when she falsely thinks Domitilla her rival.

Sc. 3. For Flaviano's villain's soliloquy (p. 255) see under The Traitor, IV, 1. For his comparison of Claudio to a comet, see under The Royal Master, III, 1. Koeppel derives his "If I but meet him handsomely, I'll make him fix'd as the north star" from Cæsar's "I am as constant as the northern star" (Julius Cæsar, III, 1) (Shakespeare's Wirkung, p. 62).

A reference seemingly to The White Devil occurs, p. 256. The conversation between Fioretta and Juliana is modeled seemingly on that between Theodosia and Domitilla, The Royal Master, IV, 1 (see also Sc. 2 of this act). In both the Princess attacks the woman of lower rank whom she thinks her rival. Note another use of this incident in The Court Secret, II, 2.

Sc. 4. Flaviano's predicament (bound to a tree by Hortensio and the Friar) suggests Protaldye, Thierry and Theodoret, V, 1. For Bertoldi in the forest and his fears, see St. Patrick for Ireland, V, 1. The description of Volterino's mother (Pandolfo in disguise) is based on The Duke's Mistress, II, 1, III, 2, IV, 1, with a touch perhaps from Flavia's disguise, The Young Admiral, IV, 1. See also Chap. IV, Sects. 20 and 21. Koeppel parallels Volterino's "I left her in a sieve was bound for Scotland" (p. 264) with the First Witch's "In a sieve, I'll thither sail," Macbeth, I, 3 (Shakespeare's Wirkung, p. 62). For Pandolfo's disguise as an old woman, see Chap. IV, Sect. 41. Cf. Bertoldi's readiness to marry the supposed woman with Rufaldo's predicament, Love Tricks, IV, 1.

Sc. 5. All the characters gather. Note the clamoring of the three women for justice (p. 266), and cf. The Laws of Candy, V, 1. Flaviano's disgrace is based upon that of Montalto, The Royal Master, V, 2. Cf. also The Gentleman Usher, V, 1. Bertoldi's crying out for justice since Leonato is about to marry his "mistress," Fioretta, is based, perhaps, on Pazzorello's injudicious claims for Cæsario's ransom, The Young Admiral, IV, 5. For comic epilogues, see under Love Tricks, and The Cardinal.

## VIII. THE COURT SECRET

The Court Secret, which was apparently not finished until after the closing of the theatres in 1642 (see the titlepage of the old edition), was therefore first presented after the Restoration when Pepys saw it as a new play August 18, 1664 (Diary, IV, 206; cf. also Langbaine, Dramatic Poets, p. 475).

The intricate plot of The Court Secret may thus be summarized:

Carlo, supposed Prince of Spain, who is betrothed to Isabella, Princess of Portugal, falls in love with Clara, daughter to Duke Mendoza. His rival (whom Clara loves) is Manuel, supposed son to Piracquo, a noble, who had been banished many years earlier, and who had turned pirate, but who has now been pardoned. Maria, the Infanta of Spain, loves Manuel, but is contracted to Antonio, Prince of Portugal and brother to Isabella. Manuel and Carlo quarrel. The former is imprisoned, but is released by Carlo's efforts. Carlo, finding Manuel to be his rival, resolves to fight him. The Prince reveals his passion for Clara to her father, but is discouraged. Clara, Manuel, and Carlo meet. Manuel offers to renounce Clara to Carlo, but she refuses to allow the renunciation. Carlo challenges Manuel, and in the resulting duel the former is dangerously wounded, but is generally thought to have been slain. Manuel, who gives himself up, is imprisoned. Mendoza now confesses that Carlo is really his own son, Julio, who had been passed off as the Prince, when the last had been stolen in childhood from his Governess, Mendoza's Duchess. Clara now is in the predicament of loving the man who had supposedly killed her brother. Manuel and Clara bewail their lot in the presence of Maria, who finally renounces Manuel. Next, Carlo, or Julio, is discovered to be alive. Piracquo confesses now to have stolen the infant Prince from Mendoza's house, and reveals Manuel to be the kidnapped child. Thus all ends happily; the various plots of Roderigo, the King's brother, which have no very important part in the play, are frustrated; and the various pairs of lovers, Manuel (or Carlo) and Clara, Antonio and Maria, Carlo (or Julio) and Isabella are united.

The Court Secret in its extraordinary complexity of plot and in its various surprises goes beyond even Love in a Maze. The several pairs of lovers, their misfit affections and the final adjustment of relationships suggest the typical pastoral plot. Hints from The Maid's Revenge and The Young Admiral seem evident here and there. As in The Coronation, A King and No King, and The Lovesick Court, diverted incest plays a part in the action (see under I, 1). The relations of the Spanish and Portuguese recall The Spanish Tragedy. There is no main source for the plot. Schipper surmises that it is founded on a foreign novel or play (James Shirley, p. 289).

For Roderigo, whose intrigues are indeed not very prominent, see Chap. IV, Sect. 33. Piracquo's name may be derived from The Changeling. Other pirates occur in Elizabethan plays, as Purser and Clinton in Fortune by Land and Sea, the Pirates in Pericles, Menecrates and Menas in Antony and Cleopatra, Ward, Danziker, etc., in A Christian Turned Turk, the Duke of Sesse in The Double Marriage, Albert in The Sea Voyage, Grimaldi in The Renegado, the Pirates in A Very Woman, Manlius and Tullius in Claricilla, Gillippus in The Prisoners, and Bragadine in The Princess. Maria suggests Theodosia in The Royal Master, but Clara is more angelic than Domitilla in the same play—somewhat like Rosania in The Doubtful Heir. The most interesting characters are the timid Mendoza with his "court secret," and the mischievous Pedro who plays on his fears. Mendoza's continual apprehensions recall Sir Solitary Plot in The Example. His harping on his secret suggests Garrula in The Lovesick Court.

Act I, Sc. 1. Maria's dropping her jewel and refusing to take it from Manuel who picks it up is allied to the hint, as found in The Imposture, II, 3. The immediate source is probably Calantha's similar business with a ring, The Broken Heart, IV, 1. Cf. also The Opportunity, IV, 1, The Spanish Tragedy, I, 3, Twelfth Night, II, 2, The Fawn, III, The Fair Maid of the West, Part II, IV, 1, The Scornful Lady, III, 1, Wit Without Money, IV, 4, The Spanish Curate, II, 4. For Mendoza's eavesdropping, cf. II, 2, and see Chap. IV, Sect. 30. For the "fig" he mentions (p. 437), see under The Maid's Revenge, III, 2. See Chap. IV, Sect. 15, for Roderigo's pretended test of Piracquo (cf. III, 3, following). Cf. The Royal Master, III, 1, for Roderigo's comparison of Piracquo to a comet (p. 438).

As analogues to the brothers and sisters who are in love, but who are ignorant of their blood-relationships (Maria with Manuel, Carlo with Clara) we may cite Sophia and Demetrius in The Coronation, II, 3, Celia and Thyrsis in Phillis of Scyros, I, 5, Silena and Accius in Mother Bombie, V, 3, Bella Franca, Charles and Eustace, The Four Prentices of London, p. 82, Phœnixella and Camillo, in The Case is Altered, III, 3, Eudina and Philocles, The Lovesick Court, II, 1, Faustina and Philautus, Holland's Leaguer, III, 4, Bellamy and Sam, Tottenham Court, III, 3, Silvia and Cleander in The Shepherds' Holiday, III, 2. A possible source for the double entanglement here is the love of Pamphilus for his sister, Techmessa, and of Tyndarus for his sister, Evadne, in The Jealous Lovers. For reversals of this situation—supposed brothers and sisters in love—see under The Opportunity, I, 2. Note that Annabella and Giovanni in 'Tis Pity She's a Whore, I, 3, etc., are aware of their relationship, as are Juno and Jupiter, The Golden Age, III, 1.

The entrance of Roderigo with Antonio and the latter's jealousy on seeing Maria and Manuel recalls The Maid's Revenge, II, 2, and The Imposture, V, 2. Roderigo's attempt at rousing the jealousy of Antonio suggests Catalina and Velasco, The Maid's Revenge, II, 3, and Montalto's stories, The Royal Master, II, 2, III, 2. Carlo's forsaking Isabella of Portugal as shown in this scene, her following him to Spain, III, 1, and their reconciliation, V, 3, are drawn from The Young Admiral, I, 1, II, 2, V, 4. Cf. The Sisters, V, 1. Koeppel derives Manuel's comparison of Clara's hand to a shrine (p. 445) from Romeo's similar figure, Romeo and Juliet, I, 5, and notes Montalto concerning Domitilla, The Royal Master (not The Traitor, as Koeppel says), I, 2 (Shakespeare's Wirkung, p. 63).

Act II, Sc. 1. For the King's wavering between Roderigo and Carlo, cf. The Young Admiral, I, 2. For the entrance of Manuel and Antonio fighting, cf. Henry VI, Part II, III, 2. For the arrest of Piracquo on his supposed son's account, cf. The Young Admiral, I, 1. For the King's test of Carlo's honor, see Chap. IV, Sect. 15.

Sc. 2. For Pedro's eavesdropping, see Chap. IV, Sect. 30, and cf. I, 1. Mendoza's planning to rid himself of Pedro here and in IV, 1, is based probably on The Young Admiral, I, 1, etc. Cf. also The Politician, I, 1. For the scrap of Spanish (p. 455), see under The Humorous Courtier, II, 2.

Sc. 3. The rivalry of Maria and Clara here displayed may be drawn from Love in a Maze, II, 2. See under The Royal Master, IV, 1.

Sc. 4. For the prison setting together with that in V, 1, 2, see Chap. IV, Sect. 14. The scene between Manuel and Carlo parallels that just preceding (Sc. 3) between Clara and Maria.

Act III, Sc. 1. The character of Roderigo given here is based on that of The Cardinal, I, 1. See under The Politician, I, 1. Although the preparation for the banquet is not meant to be especially humorous, yet see under The Cardinal, III, 2.

Sc. 2. For Roderigo's villain's soliloquy, see under The Traitor, IV, 1. It seems derived from Lorenzo's soliloquy in that scene. For Mendoza's misinterpretation of Carlo, see Chap. IV, Sect. 27. Mendoza's opposition to Carlo's suit to Clara recalls Themele's attempts at hindering the suit of Philocles to Eudina (his sister), The Lovesick Court, II, 1. Note the King's attempt at directing the affections of Maria toward Antonio, and see Chap. IV, Sect. 42.

Sc. 3. Manuel's offer to give Clara her freedom so that she may accept Carlo brings to mind II, 2, The Traitor, since in both the lady is present at the renunciation. As

in The Grateful Servant, IV, 2, the rival of the self-sacri-
ficing lover is (or seems to be) of high rank. Cf. Maria's
renunciation of Manuel, V, 2, following. See also Chap.
IV, Sect. 4. Cf. with Clara's refusal to allow Manuel to
give her up, Cellide and Valentine, Monsieur Thomas, II, 5,
and Matilda and Hortensio, The Bashful Lover, V, 2. The
manner and circumstances of Carlo's challenge of Manuel
are based on The Maid's Revenge, IV, 3. For the pretense
of a test, see under I, 1, and cf. Chap. IV, Sect. 15.

Act IV, Sc. 1, is taken up by Pedro's playing on the
fears of Mendoza. Cf. II, 2, and note Garrula, The Lovesick Court, II, 1, etc.

Sc. 2. Carlo's device for overcoming Manuel's rever-
ence for royalty so as to insure a duel seems original with
Shirley. Cf., however, Aspatia (in disguise) and Amintor,
The Maid's Tragedy, V, 4. See under The Example, IV, 3,
and The Wedding, II, 2. Moorish disguises occur in The
Parliament of Love, The English Moor, and The Lost Lady
(female characters). Cf. Manuel's superstitious regard
for Carlo's rank with Amintor, The Maid's Tragedy, II, 1,
etc. Cf., however, Chap. III. For the duel itself and the
relationships of the combatants, The Maid's Revenge, IV, 3,
affords a parallel. Additional complications of relationships are introduced in The Court Secret. Note also
Philocles and Philargus, The Lovesick Court, IV, 2, and
Philatel, Torcular, and Samorat, The Goblins, I, 1.

Sc. 3. For Mendoza's confession of the substitution of
Julio for Carlo, see under The Gentleman of Venice, V, 4.
Cf. The Lovesick Court, V, 3, and The Shepherds' Holi-
day, III, 2, and note V, 1, 3, of the present play.

Act V, Sc. 1. See under II, 4, for the prison here and
in the next scene. As an analogue to this comic passage
in prison, Twelfth Night, IV, 2, should be compared. Note
also the servants on their way to execution, The Bloody

Brother, III, 2. Cf. Pedro's ballad with their song at the end of the scene cited. For the use of the title of the play in the text (p. 499) see Chap. IV, Sect. 31. Note Mendoza's repetition to Clara of the story of the substituted children (cf. IV, 3, V, 3, and The Gentleman of Venice, V, 4). The situation of Clara—in love with the supposed slayer of her brother—is modeled upon that of Castabella, The Maid's Revenge, V. Cf. Ursini and Cornelia, The Opportunity, I, 2, etc., and Sabrina, Samorat and Orsabrin, The Goblins, II, 2. Cf. Romeo and Juliet, III, 2. Note Maria in Sc. 2, following.

Sc. 2. For the setting, cf. II, 4, V, 1, and see Chap. IV, Sect. 14. Cf. Clara's playing the rôle of Maria (in earnest, as a sister whose brother has been slain by her lover) with the various representations of one person by another in A Looking-glass for London, p. 123, Henry IV, Part I, II, 4, As You Like It, IV, 1, Troilus and Cressida, I, 3, III, 3, Cynthia's Revels, III, 3, The Poor Man's Comfort, III, The Mad Lover, II, 2, The Bondman, II, 3, The Ordinary, V, 3. Cf. Maria's renunciation of Manuel with III, 3, note The Gamester, IV, 2, and see Chap. IV, Sect. 4.

Sc. 3. For the resurrections of the true Julio and the true Carlo which have been under way during IV, 3, V, 1, and which are consummated in this scene, see Chap. IV, Sect. 29. Note also, in connection with Carlo, the appearance of Torcular, who has been thought slain by his sister's lover, in The Goblins, V, 5. Cf. Piracquo's confessing having stolen the infant Carlo with Ursula in The Gentleman of Venice, V, 4, and Morulla in The Sisters, V, 2. For analogues to the recovery of lost children, see under The Gentleman of Venice, V, 4. An adjustment of relationships occurs also in The Distresses, V, 1.

# CHAPTER VIII

## THE ROMANTIC COMEDIES

### I. The Brothers

The Brothers, which was licensed November 4, 1626, was printed as the first of a volume of Six New Plays published in 1652, as Shirley's contribution to the King's Men at Blackfriars. Because Shirley's other plays up to 1631-32 were produced at the Cockpit by the Queen's Men, Fleay in Anglia, VIII, 405-6, 410-11, advanced the theory that The Brothers is the tragicomedy called Dick of Devonshire, and that The Politic Father, a play produced in 1641 which has been identified generally with The Politician, was printed as The Brothers among the Six New Plays. In the discussion of the identification of The Politic Father and The Politician (Chap. VI) it has been shown that a play called The Brothers was listed among the dramas of Shirley which were in the hands of the King's Men ten weeks after the licensing of The Politic Father, that no play called The Politician or The Brothers was among the plays claimed by Beeston for the Queen's Men in 1639, that no importance is to be attached to the fact that The Brothers appeared in print twenty-six years after its licensing, that the dedication of the printed Brothers has been misinterpreted, that the title of The Politic Father applies at least as well to The Politician as to The Brothers, and that there is no reason to believe that Shirley wrote exclusively for the Queen's Men in 1626, and

exclusively for the King's Men in 1641. Fleay's absurd
identification of The Brothers of 1626 and Dick of Devonshire is refuted in Chap. X.

Hence, in this discussion, following Dyce and Ward,
we shall consider The Brothers as having been first acted
in 1626, and first printed in 1652. Indeed, it seems very
probable that the young playwright should have sold this
comedy to the chief company of the day, and finding that
in the future he could "do better" with the Queen's Men,
sold his other plays to them (excepting Love in a Maze)
up to the production of The Doubtful Heir in 1640. Then
it may have been that taking Massinger's place as a more
or less regular contributor to the King's Men, he wrote
for them until the closing of the theatres, in the meantime,
however, selling one play—The Politic Father, or The Politician—to the Queen's Men.

The plot of The Brothers is as follows:

Francisco and Fernando, younger and elder sons to Don
Ramyres, love Jacinta and Felisarda, respectively, the
daughter and niece of Don Carlos. Being a younger son,
Francisco pretends to devote himself to Felisarda, the
penniless companion of Jacinta, in order to deceive Don
Carlos, while his brother pretends to court Jacinta. Luys,
son to Don Carlos, returns from the university, bringing
with him a friend, Alberto, as a candidate for his sister's
hand. Don Carlos accepts Alberto as a suitor, but dismisses him when the rich Ramyres presents Fernando as
a rival. Fernando is then discarded for Don Pedro, a
very wealthy nobleman. Fernando reveals his love for
Felisarda to his father who pretends to disinherit him in
favor of Francisco. Felisarda's intimacy with Fernando
being discovered, she is sent from Don Carlos' house.
Ramyres pretends to die, cutting off Fernando with a
meagre pension. Jacinta is to be married to Don Pedro,

but she dresses Estefania, a lady to whom he had been formerly contracted, in clothing like her own; and sending her counterfeit to the church in her stead, she elopes with Francisco. At the instigation of Luys, Alberto waylays the coach in which the false Jacinta is and carries her off. Learning her identity and hearing of Jacinta's elopement, he marries Estefania. Carlos is mollified by the thought that Francisco is his father's heir. Francisco, however, offers his heritage to Fernando who refuses it. Ramyres now appears, announces that he has been testing his sons, and sanctions the marriage of Fernando and Felisarda.

The Brothers seems related in some respects to The Devil's Law-case (acted 1619; printed 1623). The test of a son by a father who gives himself out as dead occurs in The London Prodigal and The Staple of News. It is found later in The City Match (1639) (cf. Koeppel, Quellen Studien, I, 16). Some hints in the play come from The Maid's Revenge. For the grasping parent, Don Carlos, the poltroon and braggart, Don Pedro (cf. Montenegro, The Maid's Revenge), and the dissolute Luys, see Chap. IV, Sects. 42, 47, 38. Jacinta is an early sketch of the witty young lady (see Chap. IV, Sect. 40).

For the Spanish plot mentioned in the prologue, see under The Politician.

Act I, Sc. 1. The request of Don Carlos to Francisco to cease his attentions to Jacinta, and Francisco's desiring permission to pay his addresses to Felisarda as a blind for his real passion are drawn from Vilarezo's rejection of Antonio's suit, and the latter's subsequent actions, The Maid's Revenge, I, 2, II, 2. Note also Romelio's discouraging Contarino's suit to his sister, The Devil's Law-case, I, 1, and cf. Carlos' references to his brother Theodoro's losses with the reported losses of Romelio, *ibid.*, II, 1, 3. For the reference to the foot-cloth, see Adams' note, The

Turk, p. 86. The introduction of Alberto by Luys as a suitor to Jacinta is based on Antonio and Sebastiano, The Maid's Revenge, I, 1, 2. Note also Aurelio as Borgia, The Opportunity, I, 2, and cf. Romelio and Ercole, The Devil's Law-case, I, 2. The demureness of Luys and his father's thinking he has reformed recalls Monsieur Thomas and his father, Monsieur Thomas, I, 2, etc. Cf. the meeting of Fernando and Felisarda, as described by the former, with that of Alsemero and Beatrice, as related in The Changeling, I, 1. Farmer suggests that Milton borrowed Uriel's passing to and fro between heaven and earth on a sun-beam (Par. Lost, IV, 555–60, 589–91) from Fernando's description of Felisarda at vespers (p. 202) (Essay on the Learning of Shakespeare, p. 38). The dispute between the brothers in regard to the pretended rivalry of Fernando with Francisco points forward to The Court Secret, II, 4. Cf. Francisco on his brother's seniority as accidental (p. 204) with Jamie, The Spanish Curate, I, 1. For the brothers as rivals, note that three brothers court the same girl in The Fair Maid of the Exchange, pp. 14–16, etc., and that they are named Frank, Ferdinand, and Anthony.

Act II, Sc. 1. For Luys' asking Jacinta for money, see under The Gentleman of Venice, I, 1, and note The London Prodigal, I, 1, IV, 2. His trying to force Jacinta to a match with his creditor, Alberto, recalls Romelio, The Devil's Law-case, I, 2, III, 3. For the pretending of love to deceive the eavesdropping Carlos, see under Chap. IV, Sects. 6 and 30. Note the general resemblance to The Maid's Revenge, II, 2. The dismissal of Felisarda is drawn on for The Witty Fair One, III, 5. Carlos' superseding each of his daughter's suitors by a richer one is employed later in St. Patrick for Ireland, IV, 1. Note also The Taming of the Shrew, II, 1, The Merry Devil of

Edmonton, I, 1, The London Prodigal, II, 4, and The Devil's Law-case, I, 1. For the attempt at constraining the affections of Jacinta, see Chap. IV, Sect. 42.

Act III, Sc. 1. The interview between Ramyres and Fernando concerning the latter's love for Felisarda has elements in common with similar dialogues in All's Well that Ends Well, I, 3, Sejanus, III, 2, Fortune by Land and Sea, I, 2, The Roaring Girl, I, 1. Ramyres' threatening to disinherit his son suggests Fortune by Land and Sea, I, 2, III, 1. For the test of his sons, etc., by Ramyres which begins in this scene and is concluded in V, 3, see under Chap. IV, Sect. 15. For Francisco's struggle between love and paternal duty, cf. Sebastiano, The Maid's Revenge, IV, 1, 3, 4.

Sc. 2. For the dialogue between Luys and Alberto concerning the ill success of the latter's suit to Jacinta, cf. Romelio and Ercole, The Devil's Law-case, I, 2. After the entrance of Estefania [1] who is intended as a bride for Luys, the latter makes a plea to her that she will not "dote too much" on him. This is enlarged upon in Hyde Park, II, 4.

Act IV, Sc. 1. For a later use of Fernando's awaiting news from his father's bedside, see Honoria and Mammon, III, 5. This incident is paralleled in Sir Thomas Wyat, p. 7. In both plays, physicians and priests pass in and out of the sickroom. In Fortune by Land and Sea, IV, 1, Old Harding, who has prepared to disinherit his eldest son, Phillip, in favor of his younger sons, suddenly dies before he can execute his will. There is then an exhibition of charity towards the brothers by Phillip which parallels Francisco's offer to Fernando, p. 241. The letter from Jacinta is a basis for Violetta's message to Aimwell, The Witty Fair One, IV, 1.

[1] Cf. "Lady Bird's" entrance, Love in a Maze, III, 1.

Sc. 2. For Luys' planning with Alberto the abduction of Jacinta, see under The Maid's Revenge, III, 1.

Scs. 3 and 4. The confusing of Jacinta and Estefania, because of their similar clothing, and the former's escape thereby from an abhorrent match are used again in The Witty Fair One, IV, 5, 6. Note also The Opportunity, II, 3, V, 1, for cases of confusion. Jacinta's "cold" is used in The Witty Fair One, IV, 3. Parallels occur in The Comedy of Errors, The Merry Wives of Windsor, V, 5, Fair Em, III, 3, George-a-Greene, p. 260, The Mad Lover, V, 4, The Maid in the Mill, IV, 3, A Match at Midnight, IV, 1, The Guardian, III, 5 (1633). Note that Jacinta's flight is paralleled in The Devil's Law-case, V, 4, which is notable as perhaps the shortest scene in Elizabethan drama, consisting of a stage direction. Cf. the later Love in a Maze, V, 4.

Sc. 5. Felisarda's charming lines on country life (pp. 251–52) recall the glorification of pastoral pursuits, Love Tricks, IV, 2.

Act V, Sc. 1. For the wait of Don Pedro and Don Carlos at the church for the bride, see The Wedding, II, 3, and cf. The Taming of the Shrew, III, 2. Note Biondello's entrance and his description of Petruchio's appearance in connection with Alsimira's entrance. Don Pedro's remark, "the tragic voice of women strikes mine ear" appears to be a quotation from some old play. Alsimira's story is paralleled later by the action of The Witty Fair One, V, 2.

Sc. 2. Alberto's discovery of his having stolen the wrong woman and his philosophic acceptance of the fact are utilized in The Witty Fair One, V, 3. Note also Fair Em, V, 1, Wit at Several Weapons, V, 1, The Mad Lover, V, 4, A Match at Midnight, V, 1, The Guardian, IV, 2, V, 4 (1633).

Sc. 3. For Luys' invitation to his father (p. 258), see under The Gentleman of Venice, I, 1. See under The Imposture, I, 2, for parallels to Don Pedro's wrath at the loss of Jacinta. Cf. Alberto's suggestion that Don Pedro swallow his contract with Estefania, with George-a-Greene, p. 254, Sir John Oldcastle, II, 1. Note also Poins' suggesting the forcing of Falstaff to swallow his letter, Henry IV, Part II, II, 2, and Fluellen, Pistol, and the leek, Henry V, V, 1. For the resurrection of Ramyres and the conclusion of his test of Fernando and Felisarda (cf. III, 1), see Chap. IV, Sects. 29 and 15. His consenting, after this long test, to the marriage of Fernando and Felisarda is used in The Gamester, V, 2. Russell's similar action in A Fair Quarrel, V, 1, is a close parallel. Note that unlike Shirley's other profligates (save Orseolo, who is a secret debauchee), Luys does not profess penitence at the end of the play. For the epilogue by a comic character, see Love Tricks.

## II. THE GRATEFUL SERVANT

The Grateful Servant, Shirley's first attempt at pure romantic comedy, owes something to Philaster, Twelfth Night, and The City Nightcap, with some elements possibly derived from The Lover's Melancholy (produced 1628; printed 1629).

The plot of The Grateful Servant runs thus:

The betrothal between the Duke of Savoy and Leonora, Princess of Milan, is broken off, and an attempt is made to marry the latter to her uncle. Dressed as a page, and accompanied by Valentio, a friar, she flees from Milan. They are attacked by banditti, but are rescued by Foscari, a Savoyard. He takes Leonora (who has become separated from Valentio) into his service as page under the name of "Dulcino." Arriving in the capital of Savoy, Foscari who has been thought dead, sends Dulcino to Cleona, his mistress, to announce his return.  Dulcino who finds the Duke courting Cleona tells Foscari of it, and is sent back to say that Foscari is indeed dead and that the letter brought by the page on the preceding visit was forged. Foscari visits the Duke, renounces Cleona to him, and then resolves to enter a monastery.  The priest whom he consults is Valentio whom Dulcino recognizes.  They then lay plans to prevent Foscari's carrying out his design.  The court assembles at the abbey, the identity of the two candidates for admission—Foscari and Dulcino—is revealed, and the Duke returns to Leonora, with whose picture he had formerly fallen in love, while Foscari and Cleona are united. The subplot deals with the reformation of Lodwick, the Duke's profligate brother, and his reconciliation with his virtuous wife, Astella.

Foscari belongs to the same type of over-refined, chivalric lover as Philaster in Philaster, Amintor in The Maid's Tragedy, and Menaphon in The Lover's Melancholy.  His name may be derived from Foscari in Davenant's Siege, produced in 1629.  For Lodwick, the dissolute young man, see Chap. IV, Sect. 38.  As a negligent husband he is a forerunner of Wilding in The Gamester and belongs to the same class as Young Flowerdale in The London Prodigal and Matheo in The Honest Whore, Part II.  Jacomo, the foolish steward, seems based upon Malvolio in Twelfth Night, but cf. also Bassiolo in The Gentleman Usher, and note Malfort in The Lovers' Progress.

Act I, Sc. 1.  The Duke's falling in love with the picture of Leonora whom he has never seen is used again in The Opportunity, I, 2.  Parallels are found in Fair Em, I, 1, James IV, I, 3, Agrippina, II (1628), The Queen's Exchange, I, 1, II, 1 (1632), Cartwright's Siege, I, 6 (1637), and The Phœnix in her Flames (1638) (see

Schelling, Eliz. Dram., II, 358). Note also Mucedorus in
love with the reports of Amadine's beauty, Mucedorus, I,
1, Henry VI in love with Margaret similarly, Henry VI,
Part I, V, 5, and the Duke with Valentina's glove, The
Costly Whore, I, 2. Cf. the comments upon Lodwick's
early marriage (p. 8) with those on the same subject,
The Cardinal, II, 1. The Duke's deciding to marry one
of his own subjects has been drawn on in The Humorous
Courtier, I, 1, and The Coronation, II, 3. Lodwick's asking for money seems based on Luys and his sister, The
Brothers, II, 1. See under The Gentleman of Venice, I,
1. For Lodwick's inviting his brother to a debauch, see
under The Gentleman of Venice, I, 1; the source is The
Brothers, V, 3. See under Love's Cruelty, I, 2, and note
also Foscari, I, 2, Jacomo, II, 1, V, 1, Grimundo, III, 4,
as regards Lodwick's hits at court life. For the eavesdropping here, and in II, 1, III, 1, V, 1, see Chap. IV,
Sect. 30.

Sc. 2. See Chap. IV, Sect. 32, for Leonora's disguise
as Dulcino, a page. For Foscari's warning Dulcino
against the court, cf., together with Lodwick's satire in
the preceding scene, with the analogues listed under Love's
Cruelty, I, 2. Note Bellaura, The Gentleman of Venice,
II, 1, and cf. Philaster, II, 1. For Foscari's sending a
message to Cleona by Dulcino, cf. Twelfth Night, I, 4,
and Philaster, II, 1. See under The Doubtful Heir, II,
4, for Foscari's account of his meeting with Dulcino, and
note Love's Pilgrimage, II, 2, as a close parallel. Cf.
Grimundo's informing Foscari of the Duke's suit to
Cleona with Pisano and Cosmo in the later Traitor, I, 1.

Act II, Sc. 1. See under The Cardinal, III, 2, for the
comic preparations for the reception of the Duke. For
Jacomo's dreams of greatness, see under The Royal Master, III, 3. Note as possible sources Malvolio in Twelfth

Night, II, 5, and Jacques in The Noble Gentleman, III, 1. The conversation of Dulcino and Cleona resembles a little that of Arethusa and Bellario, Philaster, II, 3. Jacomo's by-play with Dulcino regarding Cleona's present suggests Maffe and Bussy, Bussy D'Ambois, I, 1. Jacomo's suspicions of Cleona and Dulcino (see III, 1, and note his opinion of Astella and Piero, V, 1) are utilized seriously in The Doubtful Heir, IV, 1. For the source, see Philaster, II, 4, and The Lover's Melancholy, III, 2. Cf. The Duke's finding something familiar in the face of Dulcino (p. 31, for instance) with the banished Duke and "Ganymede," in As You Like It, V, 4. Cf. Lodwick and Cleona (p. 34 ff.) with the Duke and Ardelia, The Duke's Mistress, II, 2, and Wilding and Penelope, The Gamester, I, 1. Lodwick's conversation with his neglected wife, Astella, who has been eavesdropping (cf. I, 1, III, 1, and V, 1, and see Chap. IV, Sect. 30) is paralleled in All's Well that Ends Well, II, 3, The Fair Maid of Bristow, III, 3, How a Man May Choose a Good Wife from a Bad, The Phœnix, I, 2, II, 2, The London Prodigal, III, 3, The Honest Whore, Part II, II, 1, etc., A Yorkshire Tragedy, Sc. 2, The Triumph of Death, Sc. 1, The Miseries of Enforced Marriage, V, 1, The Poor Man's Comfort. Lodwick's desire for his wife's death (p. 34) suggests Young Arthur's wish expressed on p. 11 of How a Man May Choose a Good Wife.

Sc. 2. Foscari's sending Dulcino to Cleona to report his death is a variation upon Twelfth Night, I, 4. There Orsino despatches Viola as Cesario to Olivia with instructions to plead his suit. Here Foscari purposes to remove himself as an obstruction to the marriage of Cleona to the Duke for whose sake Dulcino, or Leonora, had fled from Milan. Dulcino, like Cesario, is forwarding a rival's suit. Shirley uses this situation with variations in Love in a Maze, II, 1, and The Sisters, III, 2. See Chap. IV, Sect. 5, for parallels.

Act III, Sc. 1. For Jacomo's dreams [2] and for his suspicions of Cleona and Dulcino, see under II, 1, V, 1. For his eavesdropping, cf. I, 1, II, 1, V, 1, and see Chap. IV, Sect. 30. Note Philaster, II, 2. The scene between Cleona and Dulcino suggests *ibid.*, II, 3. The tone there is not so serious as here, however. Dulcino's pressing the Duke's suit is based probably upon Twelfth Night, I, 5, III, 1. Note the renunciatory love-agent in Chap. IV, Sect. 5, and observe the relationship, in this case, to love-making by proxy (see Chap. IV, Sect. 3, for parallels).

Sc. 2 is principally comic. Note Jacomo's desire to be seen by the Duke as contrasted with Bombo's "modesty," The Royal Master, I, 2, etc.

Sc. 3 is concerned with Foscari's resolving to enter a monastery. For his opening soliloquy, note the later Love in a Maze, IV, 1. The list of eminent persons who had entered his order which Valentio gives suggests the list of the fallen at Agincourt, Henry V, IV, 8. Cf. the casualties at the siege of Troy, The Iron Age, Part II, III, 1 (printed 1632). Gifford conjectures from this glorification of the Benedictines that Shirley's confessor was a member of that order.

Sc. 4. The plot for the reforming of the rakish Lodwick which Grimundo sets under way is based on Penelope's reformation of Fowler, The Witty Fair One, III, 4, IV, 4, V, 1, 3. In the later Gamester, II, 1, etc., Wilding is reclaimed by his wife, Penelope and Hazard. Note The Traitor, III, 2, 3, The Lady of Pleasure, II, 1, All's Well that Ends Well, III, 2, Measure for Measure, III, 1, Women Pleased, III, 4, IV, 3, The Parliament of Love,

---

[2] Cf. Jacomo's toothpick (p. 43) with similar allusions in The Constant Maid, III, 2, and see under The Ball, I, 1.

III, 3, The Courageous Turk, I, II, Holland's Leaguer, II, 2, etc. Note The Wonder of a Kingdom, IV, 1 (a plan is mentioned), for incidents more or less analogous. Grimundo's pretended licentiousness suggests very strongly Malcolm's description of himself, Macbeth, IV, 3. Cf. The Noble Gentleman, I, 2, for a possible source. Note also Savile, The Scornful Lady, I, 2, Polydore, The Mad Lover, IV, 4, and the White Knight, A Game at Chess, V, 3. For the satire on courts in this scene, cf. I, 1, etc., and see under Love's Cruelty, I, 2.

Act IV, Sc. 1. Lodwick's inciting Piero to adultery with Astella is a variation of the Curious Impertinent theme. Cf. The Doubtful Heir, IV, 1, The Gentleman of Venice, IV, 3, and The Humorous Courtier, III, 1, for other variations on it by Shirley. Note also The Mayor of Queenborough, III, 1, Amends for Ladies, I, 1, The Coxcomb, II, 1, The Second Maiden's Tragedy, I, 2 (the Wife mentions to Votarius her husband's estrangement), The City Nightcap, I, 1.

Sc. 2. Note the contrast between the preceding scene and this. For the renouncing of Cleona to the Duke by Foscari, see Chap. IV, Sect. 4. A close parallel occurs in The Deserving Favorite, I, 1 (printed 1629). Lysander pleads with his mistress, Clarinda, for his rival, the Duke, because of his own poverty as opposed to the wealth of the last. Florello's yielding up Bertolina to Soranzo, his rival, in Davenant's Siege, V (acted 1629) should also be noticed. Neilson says that Foscari's romantic generosity recalls Heywood (Cam. Hist. Eng. Lit., VI, 229).

Sc. 3 shows the meeting of Dulcino and Father Valentio, and their recognition of each other.

Scs. 4 and 5, which deal with the assignation arranged by Grimundo for Lodwick, are best taken together. For

the question of assignations, see under The Traitor, V, 2
(unlike the parallels to that scene there is no attempt at
secrecy here). Greg considers the satyrs, nymphs and Sil-
vanus to be of pastoral origin (Past. Poet. and Past.
Dram., p. 408). Note too The Triumph of Peace, p. 273.
For the use of music, see also The Witty Fair One, IV, 3,
The Lady of Pleasure, IV, 1, The Wonder of a Kingdom,
IV, 1, The Picture, III, 5, News from Plymouth, IV
(1635). Belinda's pretense of being a devil is used in
The Lady of Pleasure, IV, 1. Cf. Erectho as Sophronisba,
Sophronisba, IV, 1, the Succubus, A Mad World, My Masters, IV, 1 (results in conversion of a rake), Anne, A
New Trick to Cheat the Devil (Schelling, Eliz. Dram., II,
261). See also Howell's Familiar Letters, I, 98 (Jaquette
and the she-devil). For Belinda's incitements to love, see
under Love's Cruelty, II, 2. Her allusion to Ariadne's
crown (p. 78), recalls a similar figure in The Blind Beggar of Alexandria, p. 12.

Act V, Sc. 1. For Piero's attack on the chastity of
Astella and her defense of her honor, see Chap. IV, Sect.
9. Cf. Jacomo's eavesdropping with I, 1, II, 1, and III,
1, and see Chap. IV, Sect. 30. For his suspicions of Piero
and Astella, cf. II, 1, and III, 1. After hearing Jacomo's
scandalous suggestions, Lodwick thinks himself a cuckold,
for which, see Chap. IV, Sect. 25. For Jacomo's mention
of the song, For I did but Kiss Her, see under Love's
Cruelty, IV, 1. Cf. Lodwick's comment on Piero's melancholy with The Coxcomb, IV, 8; contrast Contarini,
The Humorous Courtier, V, I, and Wilding, The Gamester, IV, 1. Note Protaldye's comment on Thierry's light-
heartedness, Thierry and Theodoret, III, 1. Cf. Piero's
claiming to have succeeded with Astella with Subtle's like
claim, Amends for Ladies, V, 1. His expression of penitence should be compared with Lodwick's in the follow-

ing scene (see Chap. IV, Sect. 10). For his affirmation of Astella's virtue, see under The Gentleman of Venice, V, 2. Jacomo's mention of Fortune my Foe (p. 87) has parallels in The Merry Wives of Windsor, III, 3, The Maid's Metamorphosis, II, Every Woman in her Humor, III, 1, The Return from Parnassus, Part I, I, 1, Lingua, III, 7, The Knight of the Burning Pestle, V, 3, The Custom of the Country, I, 1, The Two Merry Milkmaids, The Noble Soldier, III, 2 (mentioned as a "hanging tune"), Love and Honor, II, 1, The Antipodes, III, 5, The Anatomy of Melancholy (see Davenant's Dramatic Works, III, 117, note). The words of the song are found in Ebsworth's Bagford Ballads, Part IV, pp. 962–63.

Sc. 2.   For the setting, cf. The Imposture, II, 1, 3.   For the resurrection of Foscari, cf. I, 2, II, 1, and see Chap. IV, Sect. 29.   For the conversion of Lodwick, cf. Sc. 1 preceding, and see Chap. IV, Sect. 10.   Note Young Arthur's conversion, How a Man May Choose a Good Wife from a Bad, p. 74.   For Leonora's (or Dulcino's) use of the title of the play, see Chap. IV, Sect. 31.

### III.   THE ARCADIA

There is no record of the licensing of The Arcadia for performance, although the titlepage of the edition of 1640 states that it had been "acted by her Majesty's Servants at the Phœnix in Drury Lane." Fleay advances the theory that the play was written by command and produced at court on the King's birthday, November 19, 1632 (Biog. Chron., II, 239). That Shirley was commissioned to produce this dramatization of Sidney's romance seems likely, first, because of the great interest in pastoral and pastoral-romantic drama at the court of Charles I; and secondly, since, contrary to his usual methods of composition, he has followed his source with extreme fidelity and has given a practically complete acting version of the main plot of The Arcadia. The date which Fleay assigns for the play cannot, however, be justified on the evidence which he advances as a means of determining it. In the first place, the reference by the rebels to Basilius' "majestical birthday" in III, 1,[3] has no reference to King Charles' birthday, for in Sidney's romance (p. 137) the day preceding that on which the revolt broke out is mentioned as Basilius' birthday. Certainly, too, had Shirley written the play for any such occasion as Fleay asserts he did, he would not have placed the allusion to it in the mouth of a rebel. Furthermore, Fleay alleges that there is an allusion to the actor who played Mopsa in Nabbes' Covent Garden, which was presented in 1632. This "allusion" is as follows:

*"Jerker.*—Methinks she's very beautiful. What pinken eyes! What a sharp chin! Why her features transcend Mopsa's in The Arcadia!

*Jeffrey.*—Hath she not studied it, cousin, think you? And is transported to a humor of loving every man she sees?" (I, 6).

From the second speech we see that the allusion was to a printed book, and, as Nabbes' play was published in 1638 and The Arcadia in 1640, it must be not to Shirley's play but to the original Arcadia of Sidney. Fleay has neglected to mention the additional "allusion" in III, 2, of Nabbes' comedy, which runs thus:

*"Susan.*—Now Mr. Spruce hath studien [sic] The Arcadia. He says, 'Oh that I had this Warrant here! I would cut him into atoms, that wheresoever the sun shines, the trophies of my renowned victory might be visible!' "

[3] Fleay has here been led astray by the carelessness of Dyce's editorial work. The scene is 1, but is numbered 2 at the top of p. 205.

Plainly Nabbes here refers again to Sidney's Arcadia.

Fleay appears to have dropped the idea which he advances in Anglia, VIII, 406-7, that Shirley's Arcadia was the play presented at court by the Queen and her ladies to which occasion the disrespectful language of Prynne was considered to refer, for he later says that Montague's Shepherds' Paradise was the pastoral presented by the noble actresses (Stage, pp. 344-45, Biog. Chron., II, 118).

The theory that Carew's four choruses and two Songs in the Play ("A Lover in the disguise of an Amazon is dearly beloved of his mistress" and "A Lady, rescued from death by a Knight, who in the instant leaves her, complains thus") (Fleay, Biog. Chron., II, 239) were written for use in this play cannot be a correct one, for, as Vincent in a note in his edition of Carew's Poems, p. 249, says, they are inappropriate as parts of Shirley's Arcadia, not only in matter, but as far as the two songs go, in regard to the occasions on which they were sung. There is no evidence of Pyrocles' having a song in IV, 3, or later, and nowhere in the play does a knight rescue a lady and immediately leave her.

No date can be advanced for The Arcadia with any great degree of certainty save the unsatisfactory one of "before 1640." It may have been omitted accidentally from Malone's list of the licenses for Shirley's plays, or it may have been presented in Ireland,[4] or not at all at a public performance, in spite of the titlepage of the old

[4] It does not occur in the list of plays belonging to the Queen's Men in 1639, as given in Fleay, Stage, p. 357. There Fleay says in a note that six plays by Shirley which were performed by the Queen's Company are omitted. These must be, from his list on p. 341, The Brothers (a King's Men play, in fact), The Ball, The Bird in a Cage, The Gamester, The Duke's Mistress and The Constant Maid (produced in Ireland, probably). If we add The Arcadia we have seven plays. Why this discrepancy is inexplicable.

edition. Since Shirley's Irish period is so well supplied with plays, we may with some justice conjecture that The Arcadia belongs perhaps to 1627, or to 1630, years in which there seem to have been no plays licensed as by Shirley. In these years it should be noted, the dramatic pastoral had begun to take on new life, and in view of that fact what more likely than that one of the first sources to be drawn on would be the often-reprinted Arcadia of Sidney? At any rate, for the purposes of this study the play will be placed tentatively between the years 1627 and 1630.

As has been intimated, Shirley's version of The Arcadia lacks originality. Hardly an incident is introduced which is not based on the romance. As a result the characterization is poor and conventional. There is some attempt at differentiating the two Princesses according to Sidney's description of them (The Arcadia, p. 10), and the other figures are taken over much as Sidney created them. However, the great skill with which Shirley has performed the task of dramatization must be considered. From the five books of The Arcadia, totally eliminating the portion of the third book which deals with Amphialus and Cecropia's abduction of Philoclea and Pamela, he has made a unified and clear drama, devoid of verbosity and moving rapidly, in spite of Dibdin's assertion that it is "dull and perplexed" (History of the Stage, IV, 43).

The play is a pastoral only by virtue of its source, for the only evidence of a pastoral influence, as Greg notes (Past. Poet. and Past. Dram., p. 319 ff.), is the show or masque in I, 3. Here the rustic character of the performers is the principal pastoral element.[5]

---

[5] Other dramatizations of parts of Sidney's Arcadia are Day's Isle of Gulls, Beaumont and Fletcher's Cupid's Revenge, Glapthorne's Argalus and Parthenia, Love's Changelings Changed, J. S.'s Andro-

The plot of The Arcadia is, briefly, as follows:

On account of an oracle, Basilius, King of Arcadia, has withdrawn into the country with his Queen, Gynecia, and his two daughters, Pamela and Philoclea. They are accompanied by Pyrocles, Prince of Macedon, disguised as Zelmane, an Amazon, who is in love with Philoclea. Basilius loves Pyrocles whom he thinks a woman, while Gynecia, having discovered his true sex, also is enamored of him. Pamela is beloved by Musidorus, cousin to Pyrocles, who, as the shepherd Dorus, serves her governor, the rustic Dametas. Mopsa, the latter's daughter, is in love with Musidorus. Pressed by both the King and Queen for assignations, Pyrocles arranges a meeting for each of them at the same place at the same hour. While they are thus engaged, Pyrocles attempts to induce Philoclea to flee with him. They are overpowered by a mysterious drowsiness, however, and are discovered together by Dametas, and Pyrocles is made a prisoner. Musidorus has, in the meantime, sent Dametas, his wife, Miso, and Mopsa, on various fool's errands and has taken the opportunity of their absence to flee with Pamela. However, they are captured by certain rustics who, after an abortive rebellion, have turned outlaws, and are brought back to the King's lodge. While these events have been transpiring, Basilius has met Gynecia, thinking her the false Amazon, and, after betraying himself, has been exhorted into repentance by her. He swallows a draught which she gives him and apparently dies. Gynecia yields herself up as the cause of his death. King Euarchus of Macedon, father of Pyrocles, happening to arrive, he is invited to sit as judge upon Gynecia, Pyrocles, Musidorus, and Dametas, who are tried for the King's murder and for the unsuccessful

mana, The Arcadian Lovers (eighteenth century?), Morgan's Philoclea (see Greg, Past, Poet. and Past. Dram., p. 319 ff.).

elopements of his daughters. Euarchas condemns the first three to death, in spite of his discovery of the relationship borne to him by the two young men. Opportunely, Basilius revives from his supposedly lifeless condition, and so the prisoners are freed, the marriages of the Princes and Princesses follow and the oracle is fulfilled.[6]

Act I, Sc. 1. The expostulations of Philanax to Basilius on the latter's retirement are based on the letter of Philanax to the King, Arcadia, pp. 12–13. For the oracle, see Arcadia, p. 204 (cf. under St. Patrick for Ireland, I, 1). For men disguised as women (Pyrocles as Zelmane), see Chap. IV, Sect. 41. Cf. also Machessa in The Lady Errant (1635) and the ladies' disguises in The Amorous War (1639). Basilius' courtship of Pyrocles in this scene, together with the suit of Gynecia to the latter in II, 1, is based on Pyrocles' description to Musidorus of the passion of the King and Queen for him, Arcadia, pp. 53–54. For a man's making love to a woman as a man, see under Love Tricks, IV, 1, and cf. I, 3, II, 1, III, 3, of this play. See under The Humorous Courtier for disguised suitors.

Sc. 2. Mopsa's coyness at first when sued to by Musidorus is drawn from Arcadia, pp. 106–07. For Musidorus' wooing Pamela by pretending to court Mopsa in her presence, see Arcadia, pp. 101–2, Musidorus' account of the same to Pyrocles (cf. pretenses of love and double meanings as listed in Chap. IV, Sects. 6 and 27). The dialogue from the words "sweet madam, plead for me"

---

[6] The tenor of the oracle is that Basilius' daughters shall be stolen away and wed, one to a prince, the other to an "uncouth love," and that they shall be tried at the bier of Basilius whom they have made dead, while a foreign prince shall sit in Basilius' place, and that before these events shall occur Basilius shall commit adultery with his own wife.

(p. 179) to Dametas' entrance (p. 181) inclusive is drawn
from Arcadia, pp. 106-7. The mention of Musidorus as
Dorus, brother to Menalcas (p. 180), is based on Arcadia,
p. 67. Dametas refers to "Pericles, Prince of Tyre" (p.
181), for which see Koeppel, Shakespeare's Wirkung, p.
62. For Dametas' "when you carry an M under your
girdle," Dyce refers to Eastward Ho, IV, 1, for an analogue.

Sc. 3. The "pastorals" (mentioned p. 178) parallel
those at the end of Bk. I, Arcadia (see under Love Tricks,
V, 3). Dyce derives "dandiprat" as applied to Cupid
(p. 184) from Stanyhurst's Æneis, Sig. C (Bk. I, l. 719).
The expression occurs as similarly applied in The Royal
Master, II, 1. For Gynecia's being overcome with her
love for Pyrocles, cf. Arcadia, p. 97, and elsewhere.

Act II, Sc. 1. For the courting of Pyrocles in the arbor
by Gynecia, see Arcadia, p. 96 ff. In both Pyrocles while
playing on the lute and singing, is surprised by Gynecia
who makes love to him,[7] and is interrupted by Basilius.
She leaves the stage and Basilius courts Pyrocles. Other
meetings of Gynecia and Pyrocles occur, pp. 354 and
365 ff., Arcadia. Her expression of rivalry with Philoclea
in this scene (p. 188) is based on Arcadia, p. 354. Pyrocles' pretense of yielding to her suit is founded partly
on Arcadia, p. 354; his confession of his true sex on p. 366;
and his promises of satisfaction on p. 367. For Philoclea's
courting Pyrocles at Basilius' desire (pp. 189-90), see
Arcadia, p. 162 ff.[8] His kissing Philoclea and requesting
her not to speak of her errand (p. 190) is drawn from
Arcadia, p. 164, and his confession of his identity to her
from pp. 164-65. Philoclea's reference to Pyrocles' sav-

---

[7] For a lady's owning her love to the object of it, see Chap. IV,
Sect. 1.

[8] For love-making by proxy, see Chap. IV, Sect. 3.

ing her life is based on Arcadia, p. 68 ff. They are interrupted by Basilius instead of by Miso, as in Arcadia, p. 293 (sic; 193 properly). What Pyrocles says to Basilius concerning Philoclea's intercession (p. 191) is based on Philoclea's words with her father, Arcadia, p. 206. For the King's courtship of Pyrocles which follows, cf. Arcadia, pp. 161–62. His boasts as to his vigor are drawn from Arcadia, p. 350 (cf. also Love Tricks, I, 1). For Pyrocles' pretense of yielding to the suit of Basilius, see earlier in this scene, and cf. also The Gamester, III, 1, All's Well that Ends Well, III, 7, IV, 2, Measure for Measure, IV, 1, The Parliament of Love, III, 3. Note in this relation, III, 3, Shirley's Arcadia. Musidorus' report to Pyrocles of his success with Pamela is represented in Sidney's Arcadia, p. 103 ff. It should be remembered that nowhere in Shirley's play does Pamela pretend scorn for Musidorus as in Arcadia, p. 231 ff., etc. The stratagems by which Musidorus secures the absence of Dametas (p. 194 ff.), of Miso (p. 197 ff.), and of Mopsa (p. 198 ff.), are drawn from Arcadia, pp. 355, 356 ff., and 359 ff., respectively. Cf. also Leandro's device to remove Bartolus from his house, The Spanish Curate, IV, 3, 5.

Act III, Sc. 1. The beginning of the revolt comes from Clinias' story, Arcadia, p. 201 ff. Thumb, the miller, is found in Arcadia, p. 196. There he is killed: cf. IV, 1, of the play, "Thumb, the miller is cut off." The conversation of the rebels before the appearance of Basilius is based on Jack Cade and his fellows, Henry VI, Part II, IV, 2, 3, 6, 7. For the Arcadian rebels' discussion of the laws, see particularly Scs. 6 and 7, as cited above. Note also the orders of Castruccio as King, The Double Marriage, III, 2, and cf. The Gentleman of Venice, III, 1. For other analogues see Sir Thomas More, II, 1, 2, 4, Edward IV, Part I, pp. 10, 26, Histriomastix, V, 1, Sir John

Oldcastle, II, 2, III, 2, Sir Thomas Wyat, pp. 20 ff., 43 ff., Perkin Warbeck, II, 3, IV, 2. For revolts in general, see under The Politician, IV, 3. From "Enter Basilius, etc." (p. 204), Sidney's Arcadia (p. 195) is the source. There Basilius does not enter with the others, but, hearing the noise, comes with arms and armor. Sidney's revolt is more elaborate than Shirley's. As before noted, Basilius' birthday in the romance falls on the day preceding the revolt (cf. Sidney, p. 137, and Shirley, III, 1, p. 205). Cf. Pyrocles' beating off the rebels with Antonio, A Very Woman, V, 3 (1634?). The arrival of Philanax in the play is more opportune than in the romance (p. 204), where he does not appear until the rebellion has been suppressed. For Basilius' assignation with Pyrocles, see Arcadia, p. 376 ff.

Sc. 2. In Sidney's Arcadia Apollo's tree is not where Dametas goes "gold-finding," nor does that character find anything else than a parchment with verses on it in his search for the treasure (Arcadia, p. 404). Dametas' finding Mopsa in the tree is based on Arcadia, p. 405. She borrows literally from their conversation, as Sidney gives it (p. 406). For Miso's appearance and quarrel with Dametas and her daughter, see Arcadia, pp. 406–07.

Sc. 3. For Gynecia's assignation with Pyrocles, see Arcadia, p. 377, and for the latter's plan of taking the former's place in Basilius' bed, see p. 378. Cf. also Cleremont as supposedly in bed with Champernel, The Little French Lawyer, III, 3.

Sc. 4. The presence of Pyrocles and Philoclea in the latter's chamber is founded on Arcadia, p. 381 ff. Cf. The Lovers' Progress, III, 3, and The Island Princess, III, 3. For her confessing that she had wished he were a man, see Arcadia, p. 110. For their slumber (pp. 218–19), see Arcadia, p. 386. There Philoclea is too exhausted to flee. Dametas' entrance is founded on the romance, p. 408. For a use of the vault, cf. Tancred and Gismunda, IV, 1 (reported), Bussy D'Ambois, II, 1, The Revenge of Bussy D'Ambois, V, 1, Sophronisba, III, 1, The Bloody Banquet, IV, 3, Aglaura, V, 2.

Act IV, Sc. 1. With Sc. 2, see under The Sisters, I, 1, for the thieves. The Captain's inquiry after Thumb and the answers are based on Cade and Dick of Ashford, Henry VI, Part II, IV, 3.

Sc. 2. Cf. the escape of Musidorus and Pamela with The Weakest Goeth to the Wall, III, 5. For their capture, see Arcadia, pp. 365, 426 ff. In the play they do not sleep as in the romance (the slumber is transferred to III, 4?). Cf. also, Musidorus, III, 3, IV, 3, V, 1, The Little French Lawyer, IV, 5. The Captain's threatening Pamela is drawn from Arcadia, p. 427, and the thieves' decision to carry the fugitives back to the King from p. 428 ff.

Sc. 3. Gynecia's upbraiding Basilius for his attempted infidelity to her, her pretense of having gone to the cave to meet him, his repentance, the use of the liquor in the golden vessel and its effect, are based upon Arcadia, p. 409 ff. For parallels to the intercourse of Basilius and Gynecia, by mistake, see under The Wedding, V, 1; for the love-philtre, under The Maid's Revenge, V, 2; and for the conversion of Basilius, see Chap. IV, Sect. 10. For the apparent death of Basilius, see Arcadia, p. 412. In the play Gynecia at once surrenders herself, but in the romance (p. 413), she tries to escape, and when captured she avows her guilt (p. 414). Cf. the appearance of Philanax with Arcadia, p. 415. In the romance the rebels are executed (p. 432), whereas in the play (p. 235) they are pardoned, apparently for their capture of Musidorus and Pamela.

Act V, Sc. 1. For scenes laid in a prison, see Chap. IV,
Sect. 14. Pamela's arguing for her succession to the throne
is based on Arcadia, p. 433. The "iron age" referred to
by Dametas (p. 238) may be an allusion to Heywood's
plays, which were published 1632 (after the tentative date
assigned to The Arcadia).

Sc. 2. For the arrival of Euarchus and his being chosen
as judge, see Arcadia, p. 444 ff. There is no mention in
the play of Euarchus' election as Protector of the realm
as in the romance. The trial is drawn from Arcadia,
p. 453 ff. For the setting, see Arcadia, p. 458. For trial
scenes, see Chap. IV, Sect. 17. Philoclea's being condemned to confinement and perpetual chastity is drawn
from Arcadia, p. 461. Gynecia's checking of Philanax
and confession of her guilt (p. 242) is from Arcadia,
p. 462. Euarchus' sentence on her is from Arcadia, p. 463.
The false names given by the two Princes are those given
in the romance (p. 464) where they are used elsewhere.
The speech of Philanax against Pyrocles is a condensation
and paraphrase of the corresponding speech, Arcadia,
p. 465 ff., and Pyrocles' answer is from the corresponding
defense, Arcadia, p. 468 ff. For Philanax against Musidorus, and the latter's answer, see Arcadia, p. 472, and
pp. 473–74, respectively. Dametas, Miso and Mopsa are
called as witnesses in the romance (p. 474), and the first
is not there made an accessory, as in the play. Euarchus'
sentence of Pyrocles and Musidorus (p. 248) is based on
Arcadia, p. 477. The short speech of Euarchus, which pre-
cedes his pronouncing sentence on the Princes, is based
on Arcadia, p. 475 ff. The entrance of Calodoulus (pp.
248–49) and the discovery of the Princes' identity is
drawn from Arcadia, pp. 477–78. Euarchus' persistence
in regard to the finality of his judgment and Musidorus'
indignation thereat come from Arcadia, pp. 479–80. The

resurrection of Basilius (who is here called "Duke" in the romance) is based on Arcadia, p. 481 (see Chap. IV, Sect. 29, for parallels to his revival, and cf. The Bird in a Cage, V, 1, and Chap. IV, Sect. 13, for the sleeping-potion). For the close of the play, see Arcadia, p. 482.

## IV. The Humorous Courtier

In Malone's transcripts from Herbert's Officebook (Shakespeare Variorum, III, 231–32) there is no record of the licensing of The Humorous Courtier under that title. However, on May 17, 1631, The Duke was licensed, and since the Duke of Parma is an important figure in The Humorous Courtier, it is very reasonable to identify the latter as The Duke. It is possible, too, that The Conceited Duke mentioned in Beeston's list of plays, August 10, 1639 (Collier, Hist. Eng. Dram. Poet., II, 92, note), may be the same as The Duke and The Humorous Courtier. However, this identification of Fleay's (Biog. Chron., II, 237) may be doubted, for the play was entered in the Stationers' Register under its present title, July 29, 1639 (cf. Nason, James Shirley, Chap. IV).

According to Stiefel, The Humorous Courtier is based on a Spanish play (Romanische Forschungen, V, 196, note). However that may be, in material, structure, and characters, The Humorous Courtier shows the influence of the comedy of humors of thirty years earlier. The central point of The Humorous Courtier is the exposure of folly in various characters, which in one case is absolutely criminal. In its satirical purpose the play aligns itself with An Humorous Day's Mirth, Every Man out of his Humor, Cynthia's Revels, Volpone, The Phœnix, Michaelmas Term, Your Five Gallants, Fortune by Land and Sea, The Royal King and Loyal Subject, Humor out of Breath. As a matter of fact, The Humorous Courtier is a test which occupies five entire acts and which monopolizes all the action (see Chap. IV, Sect. 15). This connects it with The Widow's Tears and The London Prodigal.

A summary of the plot follows:

The Duke of Parma, who is a suitor to the Duchess of Mantua, pretends to leave Mantua, but, under the name of Giotto, remains disguised in the service of the Duchess. The Duchess announces that she will choose a husband from among her own subjects. Contarini, a newly married lord, Comachio, an old lord, and Volterre, a foolish lord just returned from travel, think certain speeches of the Duchess refer to them, and begin accordingly to pay court to her. Laura, a favorite of the Duchess, bears word to Depazzi, Comachio's foolish nephew, and also to Orseolo, a seeming misogynist, that they are favored by the Duchess. All five are encouraged to a certain extent in their love-making. Contarini attempts to persuade Carintha, his wife, to kill herself so as to set him free. Failing in this, he suborns Giotto to furnish him with grounds for a divorce. Orseolo is told that his hatred for women is suspected to rise from a physical disability, so he confesses to Giotto that his attitude towards the other sex has been merely a blind for his lechery. After the five suitors have made themselves sufficiently ridiculous, the Duchess assembles her court, reprimands the aspirants, and chooses as husband Giotto, who reveals his true identity. The Duke, who, as Giotto, has been suspected by Contarini of performing his part of their agreement, now confirms Carintha's chastity and so the play ends.

The title of The Humorous Courtier connects it with The Humorous Lieutenant. Orseolo, himself, appears modeled upon Gondarino in The Woman Hater, as far as his assumed character is concerned. Jacomo in The Captain is another figure of the same sort. Note also Alphonso in The Queen. The disguised Duke is found in The Fawn, The Malcontent, and Measure for Measure. In The Phœnix, we have a Prince in disguise. All four of these plays show a prince in disguise moving among the members of a court and observing their weaknesses. Shirley has a duke in disguise in The Opportunity, and a disguised prince in The Sisters, also. The suitor in disguise occurs in The Wedding, The Arcadia, and The Bird in a Cage. Note Lucentio and Hortensio in The Taming of the Shrew, Pedro in The Pilgrim, Galeazzo in The Bashful Lover, as examples of this character. The Duchess with her suitors whom she leads on to their final confusion resembles the later Carol in Hyde Park, Lucina in The Ball, Jacinta in The Example, and Lady Mammon in Honoria and Mammon. Laura and Giotto recall Maria and Sir Toby in Twelfth Night. For characters resembling, in a general way, Depazzi and Volterre, see Chap. IV, Sects. 44, and 45. Note especially in connection with Depazzi and his uncle, Comachio, Bergetto and Donado, 'Tis Pity She's a Whore. The name "Depazzi" is given to a foolish character in the practically contemporaneous Traitor. For his foolish servant, see Chap. IV, Sect. 45. The travelled Volterre resembles in some particulars Monsieur D'Olive in Monsieur D'Olive. Note also Puntarvolo in Every Man out of his Humor, Amorphus in Cynthia's Revels, Gullio in The Return from Parnassus, Part I, Eustace in The Elder Brother. Jack Freshwater in The Ball is a similar character of a lower type. Dondolo, as the name of a character, occurs in The Just Italian, and a personage called Charintha figures in the same play.

In the *dramatis personæ*, as in The Politician, etc., the name of the character from whom the play receives its title is followed by the title (see Chap. IV, Sect. 31).

Act I, Sc. 1. Orseolo's voicing his hatred of women

suggests Gondarino, The Woman Hater, II, 1. Cf. also, as
a later variation, Horatio, The Duke's Mistress, II, 1, etc.
Koeppel suggests that Orseolo's "Almost put a girdle
around the earth" (p. 534), together with Rolliardo's
"When I have put a girdle around the earth," The Bird
in a Cage, IV, 2, is derived from Puck's "I'll put a girdle
around the earth in forty minutes," A Midsummer Night's
Dream, II, 1 (Shakespeare's Wirkung, p. 60) (see Bullen,
Works of Middleton, VII, 342, note; Old Plays, II, 43,
note). Note Comachio's petitioning the Duchess to marry
in order that there may be an heir to the throne.[9] The
Duchess' answer to Comachio (pp. 540–41), if taken in
connection with her choice of Giotto, V, 3, contains a double meaning—her intention of selecting a husband from
her own court. See Chap. IV, Sect. 27, for misinterpretations, etc. Note also The Opportunity, III, 3, IV, 1,
Hyde Park, I, 1 (reported), The Ball, II, 3, IV, 3, for
more outspoken pretenses of preference on the part of a
lady toward her foolish suitors.

Act II, Sc. 1. Contarini's attempt at persuading
Corintha to kill herself so that he might marry the Duchess
seems a variation on the relations of Lodwick and Astella,
The Grateful Servant, II, 1. Note also Wilding and his
wife, The Gamester, I, 1.

Sc. 2. For Depazzi's verses, here and in IV, 1, see
Chap. IV, Sect. 22. His description of his facility of
composition recalls Montenegro, The Maid's Revenge, I, 2.
For the mention of Depazzi's "lock" (p. 549), cf. V, 2,
following, The Bird in a Cage, I, 1, The Coronation, I, 1,
The Lady of Pleasure, II, 1, Epicœne, IV, 2, Love and
Honor, II, 1. For Crispino's attentions to his master, cf.
Liladam and Young Novall, The Fatal Dowry, II, 2. It
may be remarked that Depazzi's various adventures at

[9] The parallels to this incident are not at hand.

court seem the source for Petrucio's actions, The Antiquary, III, 1, V, 1. At various places in this play occur scraps of Spanish, as in II, 1 (pp. 549, 553–54–57), III, 1 (p. 562), IV, 2 (p. 587). For Shirley's use of scraps of Spanish in other plays, cf. The Wedding, III, 2, The Example, IV, 1, A Contention for Honor and Riches, Sc. 3. See also Old Fortunatus, III, 1, The Alchemist, IV, 1, 2, The Devil is an Ass, V, 5, The Lady's Trial, IV, 2 (1638), The Obstinate Lady, III, 3 (1638–39). Depazzi's reference to a good dancer's rising at court (p. 554) seems aimed at the Earl of Somerset and the Duke of Buckingham, in the reign of James I (Clarendon, Hist., I, 15 ff.; Traill, Social England, IV, 164–65). Comachio's distress at Depazzi's addressing the Duchess (p. 555) recalls Donado's attempts at preventing Bergetto's speaking to Annabella, 'Tis Pity She's a Whore, II, 6. See also The Coronation, III, 2. Orseolo's suit to the Duchess that he be dismissed from court in order to escape meeting women is based apparently upon Gondarino's suing the Duke for justice because Oriana has invaded his house, The Woman Hater, II, 1. In this scene (p. 556) as well as in V, 3 (p. 606), Orseolo is called a "woman hater." For the use of the term, see Captain Underwit, IV, 3, The Captain, *dramatis personæ*, The Picture, II, 2, The Guardian, I, 1. There is also a resemblance to Gondarino's suggestions as to his punishment, The Woman Hater, V, 5.

Act III, Sc. 1. The playing of Laura and Giotto on the ambition of Volterre suggests Maria and Sir Toby with Malvolio, Twelfth Night, II, 5. Volterre's dancing, at their request, to show his agility, recalls Sir Andrew Aguecheek, *ibid.*, I, 3. Cf. also Valerio, All Fools, II, 1, Lurdo, Law Tricks, III, [1], and note Venture's singing in Hyde Park, IV, 3, and the Cripple and Barnard concerning Bowdler, The Fair Maid of the Exchange, p. 53. See also

IV, 2, of the present play. The instructions for his courtship which Giotto and Comachio agree to give to Depazzi
are suggestive of the School of Compliment, Love· Tricks,
III, 5. See also Every Man out of his Humor, V, 1. For
"rotten in my head" (p. 567) see under Captain Underwit, III, 3. For Contarini's suggesting to Giotto that he
debauch Carintha, see under The Doubtful Heir, IV, 1,
and The Gentleman of Venice, IV, 3.

Sc. 2. Cf. the visit of Laura and Carintha to Orseolo
with that of Oriana and her Waiting-woman to Gondarino,
The Woman Hater, II, 2. On entering, Orseolo makes an
attack on women, as does Gondarino, although the latter
has no long speech. Orseolo's real character as indicated
in his orders to Sancho (p. 573) may be related to the
Duke's suspicions of Gondarino's misogyny, ibid.

Act IV, Sc. 1. For Depazzi's speech to the Duchess,
see under II, 2, and cf. the compliments, Love Tricks,
III, 5. Note the "oration" delivered by Carol, Hyde
Park, III, 2. Cf. also Sogliardo and Saviolina, Every
Man out of his Humor, V, 2. See How a Man May Choose
a Good Wife from a Bad, p. 19, and note Gridonell's court-
ship of Amadine, The Platonic Lovers, II, 1 (1635), to
which Sciolto listens in horror as does Comachio. For
Depazzi's reference to the "black guard" (p. 575) see
The Triumph of Peace, p. 280. Note, for keeping the
door at masques, Hornet, The Constant Maid, IV, 3. For
Hercules as a "pedlar" (p. 577), cf. The Picture, III, 6
(played 1629; printed 1630). For allusions to Hercules'
amorous adventures, note also The Opportunity, II, 1, The
Malcontent, IV, 5, A Woman is a Weathercock, III, 3, The
Little French Lawyer, III, 3, A Challenge for Beauty,
III, 1, The Platonic Lovers, V, 1. For Giotto's allusion
to the remora (p. 578), cf. The Variety, IV, 1, The
Poetaster, III, 1, The Magnetic Lady, II, 1, The Witch,

I, 2, A Fair Quarrel, I, 1, Appius and Virginia, III, 4 (as
"iper"), The City Match, III, 2. See Howell's Familiar
Letters, I, 175. Depazzi's offer of a monopoly to Giotto
(p. 579) is a satire on a contemporary evil. The name
of the German painter mentioned by Orseolo (p. 580)—
Shadan Wierex—would seem to be an anagram upon the
name of some foreign painter in London in 1631. Van
Somer, Jannsens, Mytens the Elder, Rubens, and Van
Dyke, beside many other foreign artists, spent more or less
time in England during the reigns of James I and
Charles I. Rubens was knighted in 1630, and Van Dyke,
in 1632. See also The Lady of Pleasure, I, 1, II, 1, The
Ball, III, 3, and Dialogue, Poems, VI, 459 ff. For the
disclosure of Orseolo's secret debauchery, cf. Castruchio,
The Cruel Brother, IV, 1 (with Dorido's aside), and note
Gondarino, The Woman Hater, III, 1. For Giotto's sus-
picions of Orseolo (p. 583), cf. the Duke, The Woman
Hater, II, 1. For Orseolo's comment on court-prefer-
ment (p. 582), cf. V, 1, and see under Love's Cruelty,
I, 2.

Sc. 2. For the mutual misunderstanding of each other
by Volterre and Depazzi, see under Chap. IV, Sect. 27.
Analogues to the allusion to "Don Diego," which Gifford
notes as paralleled in Beaumont and Fletcher, are met
with in Sir Thomas Wyat, p. 45, The Captain, III, 3, and
The Maid in the Mill, II, 1. See under III, 1, for Volterre's practicing figures (p. 589).

Sc. 3. For Contarini's introduction of Giotto to his
wife, Carintha, see under The Gentleman of Venice, IV, 3.
Note also The Grateful Servant, IV, 1.

Act V, Sc. 1. Cf. the merriness of Carintha and Contarini's construction of it with Piero's melancholy as noted
by Lodwick, The Grateful Servant, V, 1. Note Mrs.
Wilding and Wilding, The Gamester, IV, 1. For Con-

tarini's thinking himself a cuckold, see under The Gentleman of Venice, V, 2, and note Chap. IV, Sect. 25.

Sc. 2. Cf. Depazzi at his toilet with Lord A., The
Lady of Pleasure, III, 1. For Depazzi's day-dreams, see
under The Royal Master, III, 3. Cf. his promising to
make Crispino a judge with Don Quixote and Sancho, Don
Quixote, Part I, Chap. VII. Depazzi's desiring a mode
of death to his taste is used in St. Patrick for Ireland, V, 1.
The discussion of the killing of Carintha by Contarini and
Giotto has parallels in the later Constant Maid, II, 2, and
Honoria and Mammon, III, 3. An analogue is found
earlier in The Witty Fair One, III, 4. See also The Fair
Maid of Bristow, III, 1, and Volpone, I, 1.

Sc. 3. For the baffling of foolish suitors, cf. Hyde
Park, I, 1, The Ball, III, 2, IV, 2. For the revelations of
folly or criminality, and the rebukes of the Duchess, see
Cynthia's Revels, V, 3, Volpone, V, 8, Michaelmas Term,
V, 3, The Phœnix, V, 1. The taming of Orseolo recalls
The Woman Hater, V, 5. For the mention of Orseolo as
a "woman hater," cf. II, 2. For Depazzi's satire on ris-
ing at court (p. 609), cf. IV, 1, and see Love's Cruelty,
I, 2. For the Duke's (or Giotto's) affirmation of Ca-
rintha's chastity, see under The Gentleman of Venice, V, 2.

## V. The Bird in a Cage

There is no entry of The Bird in a Cage in Herbert's
Officebook. However, it may very reasonably be considered identical with The Beauties which was licensed January 21, 1632–33. The Beauties would be as appropriate a
title for the play as that which it bears; and in I, 1
(p. 375) the word "beauties" is applied to the ladies attendant upon Eugenia. The date of printing of the play
(entered March 19, 1632–33, and printed 1633) and its
ferociously ironical dedication to Prynne would seem to

indicate that the original Beauties was renamed with particular reference to the imprisonment of that unfortunate Puritan for his seeming reflections on the Queen in Histriomastix (see Fleay, Biog. Chron., II, 239–40; Collier, Hist. Eng. Dram. Poet., II, 39 ff.). The Bird in a Cage seems to be mentioned in Dr. Smith's Ballad, in Musarum Deliciae (Mennis and Smith's Facetiae, I, 91). Novel LXXIII, Les Cent Nouvelles Nouvelles, is called L'oiseau en la Cage. There is no resemblance between the story and the play, however.

The plot of The Bird in a Cage runs as follows:

Eugenia, Princess of Mantua, loves the exiled Philenzo. Her father, who wishes to marry her to a Florentine prince, builds a castle in which he confines her with her ladies so that she may not be carried off by Philenzo or any other suitor of inferior rank. Guards are posted about the castle to prevent the ingress of any unauthorized person. Rolliardo, an eccentric, appears at court. As the result of his eulogizing the power of money, the Duke wagers him that, although given all the money he wants, he cannot obtain access to Eugenia within a month. In case he fails, Rolliardo must forfeit his head. Dondolo, Grutti, and Morello, three courtiers, by the aid of a quack (a painter, Bonamico, in disguise), who pretends to possess a recipe for invisibility, attempt to enter the castle but succeed only in being gulled. Disguised as a woman, Morello tries then to enter the castle, but is discovered and sentenced to wear his disguise for a month. Rolliardo attempts to bribe the guards, but finds them incorruptible. In despair, he employs his funds in obtaining the freedom of various poor prisoners, among whom is Bonamico. As a return for Rolliardo's bounty, he devises a plan for entering the castle. He prepares a cage in which he places a collection of birds. These, by direction of the Duke, he takes to

Eugenia. As she and her companions are performing an
extemporaneous play, the cage is carried in. When the
Princess is alone, Rolliardo emerges from a pillar in the
center of the cage, and, first as Rolliardo, and then as the
Prince of Florence, makes love to Eugenia who repulses
him. He discloses himself then to be Philenzo. The two
go to court. To the Duke's dismay, Eugenia proclaims
her love for Rolliardo. The Duke, at this, upbraids her
for having forgotten Philenzo. Rolliardo reveals his identity, and is sentenced to death. Letters from the Duke
of Florence arrive in which he announces that he has
given up the match between his son and Eugenia, because
of the pre-contract of the last with Philenzo. The order
for Rolliardo's execution is countermanded, but it is reported that he has poisoned himself. His body is brought
in. The Duke laments his hastiness, whereupon Rolliardo,
who has merely taken a sleeping-potion, awakes, and receives Eugenia as wife.

The Bird in a Cage is based apparently upon the main
plot of Women Pleased. Certain incidents are omitted,
and others are altered, but enough similarity remains to
indicate pretty clearly a use of Fletcher's play. Shirley's
comedy is very much simpler in plot than Women Pleased.
Shirley's Eugenia = Fletcher's Belvidere; Rolliardo (Philenzo) = Silvio; the Duke of Mantua = the Duchess of
Florence; Perenotto = Bartello; Morello, Dondolo, and
Grutti = Claudio and Soto (not in characterization, as to
Claudio); Bonamico = Penurio.

Shirley's Rolliardo is very reminiscent of Marston's
Altofronto (under the name of Malevole) in The Malcontent and Hercules in The Fawn. They are all in disguise
and all indulge in more or less bitter raillery on prevalent
abuses. Cf. also Feliche in Antonio and Mellida. It is
perhaps no more than a coincidence that Marston's plays

(with the exception of The Malcontent and The Insatiate Countess) were printed in 1633, the year of the publication of The Bird in a Cage. Railing characters more or less similar are Barker, the discredited cynic of The Ball (1632), Diogenes in Campaspe, La Busse in The Distracted Emperor, Thersites in The Iron Age, Parts I, II (printed 1632), Lemot in An Humorous Day's Mirth, Tharsalio in The Widow's Tears, Downright in Every Man in his Humor, Crito in Cynthia's Revels, Arruntius in Sejanus, Pennyboy Canter in The Staple of News, Acutus in Every Woman in her Humor, Vendice in The Revenger's Tragedy, Thersites in Troilus and Cressida, Casca in Julius Cæsar, Apemantus in Timon of Athens, Menenius in Coriolanus, Octavio in Humor out of Breath, Bosola in The Duchess of Malfi, Cordolente in Match Me in London, Rhetias in The Lover's Melancholy (1628), Roseilli in Love's Sacrifice (1630), Romanello and Spadone in The Fancies Chaste and Noble (1635), Andrugio in The Swisser (1631), Snarl in Holland's Leaguer (1632). Certain of these characters approach very closely the blunt type of the Fletcherian soldier (Mardonius, for example), but the fact that they are not of the military profession makes possible a clear distinction of a sort between the two classes of character.

For Dondolo, Grutti, and Morello, the foolish courtiers, see Chap. IV, Sect. 44. Note that Dondolo is the name of a "bald fool" in The Malcontent. Cf. Balurdo and Castilio in Antonio and Mellida, and Pelias and Cuculus in The Lover's Melancholy, especially. For Bonamico as a quack with his servant, Carlo, see under The Maid's Revenge, III, 2.

Cf. with the dedication for other references by Shirley to Prynne, the commendatory verses prefixed to Love's Sacrifice, and The Nightwalker, III, 3, 4. Other allusions

to this author and to Histriomastix occur in The Magnetic
Lady, I, 1, III, 4, The Sad Shepherd, I, 2, The Floating
Island, I, 2, III, 8 (1636), The City Match, II, 1, 2 (1639),
the dedications to The English Traveller, A Maidenhead
Well Lost, and Love's Sacrifice, Heywood's Prologue to
their Sacred Majesties at Hampton Court (Plays, VI, 342),
and R. C.'s commendatory verses to The Queen.

Act I, Sc. 1. For Morello's "amorous lock" (p. 372),
see under The Humorous Courtier, II, 2. The confinement
of Eugenia to avoid a match with Philenzo is derived from
Belvidere's being placed in the citadel to prevent her abduction by the Duke of Milan, Women Pleased, I, 1, II, 5
(reported). Both ladies are designed for other husbands
—Eugenia for the Prince of Florence and Belvidere for
the Duke of Siena. Cf. Shirley's Duke of Mantua's calling his daughter a "treasure" (p. 373) to be hidden "safe
from the robber" with Bartello's description of Belvidere,
as a "jewel" sent to the castle "to secure her" (ibid., I, 1).
For the latter, "all convenient pleasures are there propor-
tion'd" (ibid.) as for Eugenia "every day shall strive to
bring . . . fresh rarities" (p. 373). For other cases of
imprisonment, cf. The Malcontent, I, 4 (mentioned), and
The Isle of Gulls, I, 1. Note the Princesses in The Arcadia. Cf. the story of Danaë and Acrisius (The Golden
Age, IV, 1) which is the subject of the play presented,
IV, 2, following, and which is alluded to by Rolliardo (p.
381) and by the Duke (p. 401). Note The Imposture, I, 2,
as a variation.

For Rolliardo's satire upon court corruption, see under
Love's Cruelty, I, 2. The Duke's wager with Rolliardo
seems based upon the riddle propounded by the Duchess of
Florence to Silvio, Women Pleased, II, 5. In the Fletcherian play, if Silvio does not solve the riddle within a year
he is to be executed, while in The Bird in a Cage, Rolliardo

has a month in which to gain entrance to Eugenia's chamber and the forfeit for failure is his life. For incidents more or less parallel, see The Merchant of Venice, I, 2, II, 1, 7, 9, III, 2, Pericles, I, 1, The Parliament of Love, II, 1 (the time-limit here in which the wager is to be won is a month).[10]

Act II, Sc. 1. For Bonamico as a quack, or mountebank, see under The Maid's Revenge, III, 2. For his claims, see The Puritan, IV, 2, as a source. For Bonamico's eavesdropping here, cf. III, 4, and see Chap. IV, Sect. 30. Cf. Rolliardo's references to the "monsters," etc., exhibited in Elizabethan times (and our own, as well) with similar allusions in The Duke's Mistress, II, 1, The Constant Maid, I, 2 (a repetition), Shirley's Fairing (in Poems, VI, 412–13), Every Man out of his Humor, IV, 4, V, 4, Volpone, V, 2, The Alchemist, V, 1, Sir Giles Goosecap, I, 1, Ram Alley, IV, 1, The Winter's Tale, IV, 4, The Tempest, II, 2, Henry VIII, V, 4, The Knight of the Burning Pestle, III, 2, Believe as You List, IV, 3, Covent Garden, II, 2, The City Match, III, 1 (1639), Wit in a Constable, V, 1 (1639).

Rolliardo's unsuccessful attempt at bribing Perenotto and the guards is based probably on Silvio's trying to wheedle Bartello into admitting him to the citadel, Women Pleased, I, 1. Note also Silvio and Rodope, *ibid.*, II, 1. Cf. Perenotto's incorruptibility with that of the Captain, The Malcontent, V, 1. For Rolliardo's ill-success in his first attempt at gaining ingress to the castle, note besides Women Pleased, Clarindore's failure in his first attempt at winning his wager, The Parliament of Love, II, 3. Note a reference to the plays of The Invisible Knight, and The Ring (identified by Dodsley with The Two Merry Milk-

10 For the expression "on the ticket," as referring to indebtedness, cf. II, 1, and see under The Ball, IV, 1.

maids). For genuine invisibility, see St. Patrick for Ireland, III, 2, IV, 1, 2, V, 1. Cf. Rolliardo's jeering the
gulls (p. 400) (in III, 1, as well as here) and the Duke's
jeering him (p. 401 ff.) with Altofronto, The Malcontent,
I, 2, 3. Note also The Parliament of Love, III, 1, and see
Chap. IV, Sect. 20. For Rolliardo's lines on true nobility
(pp. 402–3) see under The Royal Master, III, 3. In this
speech, he refers to Shylock, and the pound of flesh in The
Merchant of Venice (IV, 1?). Cf. Rolliardo's laying aside
his assumed eccentricity to speak to Fulvio (pp. 403–4)
with Rhetias' similar action, The Lover's Melancholy, II, 1,
IV, 2. Note Fulvio's relations with Rolliardo as paralleling those of Celso with Altofronto in The Malcontent.

Act III, Sc. 1. Morello's attempt to enter the prison in
woman's dress, and his capture by the guard seem to have
been suggested by Women Pleased, II, 2, 3. In the first
scene is a dialogue between two soldiers, and in the second
the capture of Silvio in Belvidere's apartment. Shirley
has made broad farce of the scene. For the guards' making love to Morello as a woman, see Chap. IV, Sect. 7.

Sc. 2.[11] For Rolliardo's allusion to Rosiclere and the
Donzel del Phebo, see under The Maid's Revenge, I, 2.
For the ballad of the Devil and the Baker, cf. Hyde Park,
II, 4. For the "invisibility" of Bonamico, see under II, 1,
and cf. The Puritan, IV, 2. Cf. Rolliardo's jeering the
gulled courtiers in his turn with Clarindore and those who
had formerly jeered him, The Parliament of Love, IV, 5.
See also Chap. IV, Sect. 20, and cf. II, 1.

Sc. 3. For the planning the acting of a play by the imprisoned ladies, cf. A Midsummer Night's Dream, I, 2,
Histriomastix, IV, 1 (the play), and note Falstaff's suggestion as to a "play extempore," Henry IV, Part I, II, 4.

[11] For the use of "figary" (p. 411), cf. III, 2, see under The Ball,
IV, 2.

The acting of this "play" by the ladies, as here planned, and as shown in IV, 2, is based doubtless upon the presentation at court by the Queen and her ladies of Montague's Shepherds' Paradise, January 8, 1633, thirteen days before the licensing of The Bird in a Cage (or The Beauties) (Fleay, Stage, pp. 315, 318). Even if Shirley did not insert these two scenes after January 8, the presentation of the play by the noble actresses was doubtless no secret for some time before. At that, they may have been added to the original draft of The Bird in a Cage. There are six female characters in the play, so that would tend to show an especial effort on Shirley's part toward the introduction of the interlude. We may suppose that the Queen's Men carried regularly only three or four "female actors" at most, and that others were engaged especially for this play (if the interlude *was* acted). The above theory is practically established by Shirley's calling Prynne's attention in the dedication to the acting of the "interlude" by ladies. It is worth noticing that the little play is only episodic and is merely set in the body of the comedy. As to female actresses in England, allusions occur in The Ball, V, 1, and The Court Beggar, V, 2 (1640) (where Philomel imitates a player). The Queen spoke the prologue to Love's Mistress, November 19, 1634. La Pastorale de Florimène was presented before the Queen by *les filles françaises de la Reine*, December 21, 1635 (Fleay, Stage, p. 319). A French company with actresses was licensed November 4, 1629, to play at the Blackfriars, at the Red Bull, November 22, and at the Fortune, December 14 (*ibid.*, p. 334). According to the same authority, The Lady Errant was performed before the Queen at Blackfriars in 1632 with women taking the female parts (*ibid.*, p. 344). It is interesting to note that Mendoza's Amor con amor se paga was acted at the Spanish court by the

Queen's maids of honor who took the male as well as the female parts (Ticknor, Hist. Span. Lit., II, 319). The eagerness of Fidelia and Cassiana for parts recalls, as Gifford notes, Bottom's selection of his part in the play, A Midsummer Night's Dream, I, 2. Cf. the rehearsal, Histriomastix, IV, 1.

Sc. 4. For Bonamico's eavesdropping, note II, 1, and see Chap. IV, Sect. 30. For Bonamico's quotation from the Induction to The Spanish Tragedy, see under The Constant Maid, I, 1. Cf. Rolliardo's reference to the basket in which poor prisoners received their food with similar allusions in The Alchemist, I, 1, Eastward Ho, V, 1, The Widow, III, 1, If This Be not a Good Play, the Devil Is in It, p. 355, Greene's Tu Quoque, p. 541, The City Madam, I, 1 (noted by Gifford), A New Wonder: A Woman Never Vexed, IV, 1 (a prisoner is shown begging at the prison gate).

Act IV, Sc. 1. Morello's acting as court-jester seems to have been utilized for Comastus in H. Killigrew's Conspiracy (1634). Note Autolycus' song in The Winter's Tale, IV, 4, in connection with Gifford's note to Morello's song (p. 424). In the course of his exhibition of the birds Bonamico refers to events or persons more or less contemporary. Similar extended allusions are found in The Example, IV, 1, and The Virgin Widow, IV, 1. His reference to Bethlem Gabor is paralleled in The Opportunity, I, 1, The Ball, I, 1, the prologue to Volpone, The Staple of News, III, 1, Aristippus, p. 29, and see Howell's Familiar Letters, I, 236. Other references are to the Turks and Venetians, the death of Count Gondomar, Spinola, the siege of Bergen, and the Dunkirk privateers. For the allusions to Gondomar and Spinola, cf. The Staple of News, III, 1; and for the former, see A Game at Chess.

Sc. 2. See under III, 3. The play within the play in

various forms occurs in The Spanish Tragedy, IV, 3, Sir
Thomas More, IV, 1, James IV, Alphonsus, King of Arra-
gon, The Old Wives' Tale, A Midsummer Night's Dream,
III, 1, V, 1, The Taming of the Shrew, Hamlet, III, 2, The
Mayor of Queenborough, V, 1, A Mad World, My Masters,
V, 2, The Spanish Gipsy, IV, 3, The Downfall of Robert,
Earl of Huntington, The Death of Robert, Earl of Hunt-
ington, Histriomastix, II, 1, The Travails of the Three
English Brothers, p. 62, Four Plays in One, The Knight of
the Burning Pestle, The Roman Actor, II, 1, III, 4, IV, 2,
The Muses' Looking-glass, II, etc. (1634), The Conspiracy,
II, 1 (1634), Love's Mistress (1634), Lady Alimony, II, 1,
etc. (1635), The Fool Would Be a Favorite, V (1638), The
Antipodes (1638), The Jovial Crew, V (1640).[12] Note
that a masque occurs in Women Pleased, V, 3.

The prologue in conventional style contains a mention
of the title (see Chap. IV, Sect. 31). This version of the
story of Danaë may be a parody on The Golden Age, IV, 1,
which treats the same myth. For the verses of the ladies,
see Chap. IV, Sect. 22. For Catherina's satiric comments
on contemporary poetry (p. 432), cf. The Maid's Revenge,
I, 2, The Royal Master, II, 1, The Humorous Courtier,
II, 2, The Wedding, III, 2, Love in a Maze, II, 2, IV, 2,
Every Man in his Humor, V, 1, Love's Mistress, I, 1, II, 1
(1634). Donella in her criticism (p. 433) seems to allude
to the punishment of Crispinus, The Poetaster, V, 1. As
Mardona's verses are bombastic and rough, it may be that
here Shirley was parodying Marston (Crispinus), although
the "poetry" of some of Shirley's contemporaries presented as good a subject for burlesque.

Rolliardo's method of entering the castle suggests the
way in which Flores penetrates into the palace of the

---

[12] Certain of the plays with inductions have been omitted as hardly
being analogous to the play within a play.

Admiral of Babylon in which Blauncheflore is confined,
Flores and Blauncheflore. See under The Wedding, IV, 4.
Note also Gerardine's entering Maria's chamber in a trunk,
The Family of Love, II, 4, and the numerous analogues to
that device in continental prose fiction. Silvio's stolen
visit to Belvidere, Women Pleased, II, 3, doubtless is at the
bottom of the scene. Schipper suggests that a novel was
the source for Rolliardo's device (James Shirley, p. 84).
For Rolliardo's two tests of Eugenia, see Chap. IV, Sect. 15.
Cf. Eugenia's resistance of his advances with Maria, The
Malcontent, V, 2, and cf. Rolliardo's revealing himself with
Altofronto (Malevole), The Malcontent, IV, 5.

Act V, Sc. 1. Gifford notes an allusion to Archie Arm-
strong, the King's jester (pp. 441–42). Note the double
rhymes in Morello's song. Rolliardo's winning the wager
corresponds to Silvio's solving the riddle, Women Pleased,
V, 1. Note that neither performs his task unassisted. For
the use of the title in the text, cf. I, 1 ("Beauties") IV, 2
(prologue to the interlude), and see Chap. IV, Sect. 31.
For the anger of the Duke at Rolliardo's success, and at
Eugenia's love for him, cf. the Viceroy, A Very Woman,
V, 4 (earlier date?). Note that there orders are given
first for Antonio's torture as for Rolliardo's and then for
the death of the former as for that of the latter. Cf. Eugenia's prayers for the life of Rolliardo with Belvidere's
pleadings, Women Pleased, II, 5. The Duke's telling
Eugenia that she should have married Rolliardo (or Philenzo) had he lived, the discovery of his having taken a
sleeping-draught instead of poison, and the Duke's consent
to his and Eugenia's marriage are paralleled closely in
Antonio and Mellida, V, and A Chaste Maid in Cheapside,
V, 4. In the latter play the man and woman are both
thought dead; in the former, as in the present scene, only
the man is supposed dead. See also The Costly Whore,

V, 1 (printed 1633). For the use of the sleeping draught
as a poison, see Chap. IV, Sect. 13, but note The Arcadia,
V, 2. See Chap. IV, Sect. 29, for Rolliardo's revival.
The revocation of Rolliardo's sentence and his reconciliation with the Duke recall Silvio's being received back into
favor, Women Pleased, V, 1. Cf. also A Very Woman,
V, 6.

## VI. THE OPPORTUNITY

The Opportunity is an adaptation of El Castigo del
Penséque [13] by Tirso de Molina, as Stiefel shows (Romanische Forschungen, V, 193 ff.).[14] Of course, in the
light of Stiefel's researches, the relating of the play to
The Comedy of Errors, as Halliwell (Dict. of O. E. Plays,
p. 185) and others have done, does not stand.

A summary of The Opportunity follows:

Aurelio Androzzi of Milan and his friend, Pisauro, come
to Urbino. The former is mistaken for Borgia, a gentleman banished for slaying the brother of Ursini, the
Duchess' favorite. Aurelio assumes the identity thrust
upon him, deceiving even Mercutio, Borgia's father, and
Cornelia, his sister. The Duchess, who pardons him for
the murder, makes him her secretary. Both she and Cornelia are attracted by the false Borgia, and he by them,
but he hesitates between them, and tries to make sure of
both. He confesses his identity to the Duchess, mistaking
her for Cornelia. She leads him on and plays with him.
Finally the Duke of Ferrara, a suitor to the Duchess, who
has been at Urbino in disguise wins her, while Cornelia refuses both Aurelio and Pisauro and accepts Ursini, her con-

[13] Tirso's play is in turn from La Ocasion Perdida of Lope de Vega.

[14] The following section is based both upon an independent examination of the Spanish play and upon Stiefel's article as cited
above.

stant lover. The play develops through the opportunities
which Aurelio has of securing one lady or the other which
are lost because of his vacillation between the two and his
attempts to make sure of both. The comic relief is furnished by Pimponio, Aurelio's servant, who presents himself at court as the Duke of Ferrara and thereby comes to
grief.

As usual Shirley has departed from his source in a number of instances, altering incidents, omitting others, and
adding still others. He has transplanted the action from
Flanders to more romantic Italy. Tirso's military element
has been omitted, and the *dénouement* of the play has been
altered (for the better). The comic scenes in The Opportunity are Shirley's. As regards the characters (which
have been all re-named), Shirley's Duke of Ferrara =
Tirso's Casimiro; Aurelio = Roderigo; Ursini = Pinabel;
Mercutio = Liberio; Pimponio = Chinchilla; the Duchess
of Urbino = Diana; Cornelia = Clavela. Shirley's Lucio,
Pietro, and Julio correspond roughly to Leonelo and Roberto in the Spanish comedy. While Shirley has not used
Tirso's Floro and Lucretia, he has added Pisauro, Melinda,
and Laura (who is mentioned at the end of El Castigo),
besides Grutti and Ascanio, two comic characters. Shirley
makes Mercutio a comic figure (see Chap. IV, Sect. 43),
even introducing him in a scene in which he takes the part
of Tirso's Chinchilla in the corresponding scene in the
Spanish play. While most of the alterations in the action
are not essentially important, they are numerous enough
to show The Opportunity to be more than a mere paraphrase of El Castigo del Penséque.

The Duke of Ferrara in disguise at the Mantuan court,
while drawn from the Spanish, recalls the Duke of Parma
as Giotto in The Humorous Courtier. Aurelio as an ambitious lover brings to mind Cesario in The Fair Maid of

the Inn. Aurelio's friend, Pisauro, is a first draft for
Horatio in The Duke's Mistress (see also Chap. IV, Sect.
39). Shirley's Mercutio, the ambitious old father, is the
comic counterpart of the later Cassander in The Corona-
tion. Ursini seems the original of Lisimachus in that
play (note especially The Coronation, III, 2). Cf. the
innkeeper, Grutti (who is Shirley's) with Diego in Love's
Pilgrimage, Verone in An Humorous Day's Mirth, The
Vintner in The Queen of Corinth, and with the Hosts in
The Two Gentlemen of Verona, The Merry Wives of Windsor, The Merry Devil of Edmonton, Fortune by Land and
Sea, The Royal King and Loyal Subject, The Captain,
The Fair Maid of the Inn, The New Inn, A New Wonder:
A Woman never Vexed, and The London Chanticleers
(1637). Note the Host's Ghost in The Lovers' Progress.
For Ascanio, Grutti's son, cf. the pages (Chap. IV, Sect.
48). Cf. Pimponio, the servant of Aurelio, with Chin-
chilla in El Castigo, and with the clowns (Chap. IV,
Sect. 46).

Act I, Sc. 1. From El Castigo, I, 1, 2, 3, 4. The difference in scene between the Spanish and English plays has
been noted. In Tirso, Rodrigo is accompanied only by
his servant, whereas Pisauro is with Aurelio and Pimponio.
Rodrigo is accosted by no one, not even by Roberto who
spies him first, while three persons greet Aurelio as Borgia,
before Mercutio appears. Only Mercutio comes to meet his
supposed son, while in Tirso he is accompanied by his
household. During the scene, Aurelio is prompted by
Pisauro, not by the servant, as in El Castigo. Mercutio
informs Pisauro concerning his son's banishment, but in
the Spanish play Lucretia, a servant, relates the story
to Chinchilla. Note The Comedy of Errors, I, 2, etc.,
for confusion of persons. For the reference to Bethlem Gabor (p. 374), see under The Bird in a Cage, IV, 1,

and for the quotation (p. 376) from The Spanish Tragedy, II, 1, see under The Constant Maid, I, 1, and cf. The Politician, III, 2 (Gifford suggests for the quotation a source in Watson's Hekatompathia, or in The Paradise of Dainty Devices).

Sc. 2. From El Castigo, I, 8, 11. Aurelio and Pisauro arrive at court on the Duchess' invitation—a difference from the Spanish. Ursini's asking for Borgia's pardon from the Duchess (from Tirso, I, 8) furnishes a partial source for a speech of the Cardinal's, The Cardinal, IV, 2. For Ursini as the lover of the sister of the slayer of his brother (from El Castigo), see under The Court Secret, V, 1. For the Duchess' falling in love with Aurelio, see under The Doubtful Heir, II, 4. There is no outward manifestation of Diana's state of mind at this point in El Castigo besides her making Don Rodrigo her secretary. The falling in love of Aurelio and Cornelia is from Tirso. Cf. also the supposed brother and sister in love in A King and No King, III, 1, IV, 4 (note under The Court Secret, I, 1, parallels to the brother and sister in love, who are ignorant of their relationship). Aurelio's putting off Ursini's suit for Cornelia on the plea that his friend, "Aurelio," had fallen in love with her picture, and that he had promised her to that person is from El Castigo, I, 11. For falling in love with a lady's picture, see under The Grateful Servant, I, 1, and for the brother's providing a suitor for his sister, note The Maid's Revenge, I, 1, 2.

Act II, Sc. 1. Shirley's scene. Eckhardt (Die Lustige Person, p. 398) relates Pimponio's taking possession of his master's belongings and his assuming princely rank with Juniper in The Case is Altered, IV, 4, V, 2, 4. As Koeppel says, the resemblance is not striking (Ben Jonson's Wirkung, p. 127, note). For Pimponio's posing as a prince here and in III, 1, IV, 1, see under The Imposture, II, 3.

Note also Castruccio, The Double Marriage, III, 2, V, 1, and Vertigo, The Maid in the Mill, III, 2, as well as the genuine Spanish prince, Pharamond in Philaster, I, 1, 2, II, 2, 4. The passage (p. 392) from "I am too sober" to "Fifty trumpets" inclusive recalls the lines of Valentine "Then bring thy wife along . . . ," Wit Without Money, V, 2. For the allusion to Hercules' exploits, see under The Maid's Revenge, I, 2, and The Humorous Courtier, IV, 1.

Sc. 2. For the conversation of Julio and Lucio, regarding Aurelio's rise in favor (which is Shirley's), see under The Doubtful Heir, IV, 1. For their eavesdropping (p. 393 ff.), and that in II, 3, V, 2, following, see Chap. IV, Sect. 30. The conversation of Urbini and the Duke which they overhear is based on El Castigo, III, 12, in which Pinabel betrays the feelings of Diana toward Rodrigo to Casimiro. Shirley, however, makes the Duke's suspicions arise from his own observation and not from Ursini, while in the Spanish play, Pinabel suggests to Casimiro that Rodrigo is his rival. It should be noted that this scene occupies a different place from the corresponding one in El Castigo.

Sc. 3. With slight variations from El Castigo, II, 6, 7, 8, 10, 11. Scenes more or less paralleling this one as to setting are Romeo and Juliet, II, 2, Blurt, Master-Constable, III, 1, IV, 1, The Family of Love, I, 2, III, 2, The Two Angry Women of Abington, III, 2, The Poetaster, IV, 6, The Dutch Courtesan, II, 1, The Insatiate Countess, III, A Christian Turned Turk, p. 229, Wit at Several Weapons, III, 1, The Just Italian, IV, 1, 'Tis Pity She's a Whore, I, 2, The Antiquary, II, 1 (1636) (certain of these scenes are broadly comic). Shirley has omitted Chinchilla's part in the scene, there is no rejoicing on the part of the Duke audible after his happy departure, no meeting at the window between the Duchess and Cornelia, and the Duchess as Cornelia does not request Aurelio still to treat her as a sister. With these exceptions, the two scenes correspond very closely. The confusion of identities (which here is from El Castigo) had been employed by Shirley in The Maid's Revenge, III, 5, etc., The Brothers, IV, 3, etc., and The Witty Fair One, IV, 6, etc. Note also V, 1, following.

Act III, Sc. 1. Shirley's addition. Cf. Grutti and Ascanio (pp. 404–5) with Verone, An Humorous Day's Mirth, p. 34. Ascanio's disguise as a Swiss is drawn from the Page's masquerade as "Ancient Petarre," The Gamester, IV, 1. Note also the Duke of Sesse and his followers in The Double Marriage, and Aribert in The Swisser as a Swiss. A Swiss is a character in The Blind Beggar of Bednal Green, I. See Eckhardt, Ausländertypen (Materialien, XXXII), pp. 79–80, on Swiss characters in the drama. See under Love Tricks. Gifford says that the allusions to Ascanio in disguise as a "High German" relate to a gigantic German master of fence then in London. Allusions to perhaps the same person occur in The Maid's Revenge, III, 1, The Wedding, IV, 3, The Witty Fair One, V, 2, The Variety, III, 1, The Knight of the Burning Pestle, III, 2 (a "great Dutchman"), The Roaring Girl, II, 1, The Noble Soldier, II, 1 (see Bullen, Works of Middleton, IV, 46, note). Gifford notes also a reference (p. 407) to the victories of Gustavus Adolphus (who had been killed two years before The Opportunity was presented).

Sc. 2. Shirley's scene. Mercutio's pride in his supposed son's favor at court is shown again in IV, 1. Cf. Overreach concerning Margaret and Lovell, A New Way to Pay Old Debts, V, 1.

Sc. 3. Pisauro's accusing Cornelia of looking too favorably upon her "brother" is Shirley's. The scene following in which the Duchess leads Aurelio on is based on El Castigo, III, 5, 6, 7, 8. In Shirley's scene the business with the glove does not occur. Note as more or less analogous to the Duchess' virtual love-making, here and in IV, 1, following, the parallels listed in Chap. IV, Sect. 1. For her use of the double meaning and hint, here and in IV, 1, see Chap. IV, Sect. 28. Note in connection with this scene The Humorous Courtier, I, 1, etc. Cornelia's entrance with the news of the arrival of the Duke to claim the Duchess as his bride is drawn from Clavela's corresponding announcement, El Castigo, III, 6. The conversation of Ursini and Aurelio at the end of the scene is based upon that of Pinabel and Rodrigo, *ibid.*, III, 10.

Act IV, Sc. 1. For Mercutio's pride in Aurelio, see III, 2. This part of the scene is Shirley's. See under Love Tricks, V, 3, for the meeting of the Duke of Ferrara and Pimponio as the Duke. This is a source for The Sisters, V, 2. The bit of business with the glove (p. 429) between the Duchess and Aurelio is based on the long-drawn-out employment of the same article in El Castigo, III, 5, 6. See under The Court Secret, I, 1. Aurelio's writing the letter intended for "him that loves her best," at the Duchess' dictation, together with the contents of the letter, is drawn from El Castigo, III, 14. Note as a similar case of *double entendre* the letter in The Cardinal, II, 1. Cf. for the general features, The Lady of Pleasure, III, 1, Captain Underwit, I, 1 (a list), The First Part of Jeronymo, p. 465, Sir Giles Goosecap, IV, 1, The Gentleman Usher, III, 1, Match Me in London, IV, More Dissemblers besides Women, III, 2, IV, 2. A reference occurs (p. 433) to Wit at Several Weapons. The dialogue between the Duke and Aurelio comes from El Castigo, III, 15, 16. The expression which gains the Duchess' letter for the Duke is translated by Shirley from Sc. 16. The title

of Shirley's play occurs in the text (p. 436) and in V, 1
(see Chap. IV, Sect. 31). Rodrigo in El Castigo, III, 21,
remarks twice on the *ocasion* he has lost. Tirso's own
title occurs, III, 22, of his play.

Act V, Sc. 1. Based on El Castigo, III, 20, 21. Shirley places Aurelio's "father," Mercutio, on guard at the
gate. In the Spanish play Chinchilla is at the gate, but
not on guard. He sees Casimiro, but, thinking him to
be Rodrigo, makes no effort to stop him. Aurelio's be-
rating of Mercurio is based on Rodrigo's rage at hearing
of Casimiro's forestalling him, El Castigo, III, 21 (Rodrigo, however, does not storm at his servant especially).
See under II, 3, for the mistaking of Casimiro for Aurelio,
and under IV, 1, for the use of the title in the text.

Sc. 2. Nearly entirely Shirley's. Pisauro's telling Cornelia that Aurelio is her brother although he will attempt
to deny it is a reversal of the devices used by Livia to forward Hippolito's love of Isabella, Women Beware Women,
II, 1, and of Mildred to hold in check her brother Offa's
passion for her, The Queen's Exchange, IV, 1, V, 1. Cf.
Love in a Maze, III, 3, and The Example, II, 1, for one
suitor's slandering another. For Ursini's eavesdropping
cf. II, 2, 3, and see Chap. IV, Sect. 30. The match between
Ursini and Cornelia is Shirley's variation upon Tirso. In
El Castigo, III, 22, Rodrigo wins Clavela, while Pinabel
is consoled by the hand of Laura. The entrance of the
Duke and Duchess as married is the only part of the
scene drawn from the Spanish. Pimponio's Hue and Cry
seems a parody on Shirley's own Love's Hue and Cry,
The Witty Fair One, III, 2, and Poems, VI, 410–11.

## VII. THE CORONATION

The Coronation was licensed, apparently as Shirley's
February 6, 1634–35. On April 25, 1639, it was entered

in the Stationers' Register together with The Nightwalker, The Opportunity, Love's Cruelty, and Wit without Money, without an author's name.[15] In 1640 The Coronation appeared with Fletcher named on the titlepage as author.[16] However, in 1652 there appeared a catalogue of Shirley's published works affixed to the Six New Plays. Among these is The Coronation with the note, "Falsely ascribed to Jo. Fletcher" (see Nason, James Shirley, Chaps. III, V). Nevertheless, The Coronation was published in the second folio of Beaumont and Fletcher's plays, and even now is still included among them.[17] Langbaine lists it as Fletcher's (Dramatic Poets, p. 208).

At present the consensus of opinion is that The Coronation is Shirley's, or, at least, that it is as much Shirley's as King Lear, or Hamlet, is Shakespeare's. Possibly the play is a reworking or a completion of the sketch of a play by Fletcher. Again, there may have been dishonesty on the publisher's part—an attempt to pass off a play of Shirley's as Fletcher's,—or a case of confusion, perhaps connected in some way with the entry of one play of Fletcher's and Shirley's at the same time as The Coronation and the two other plays of Shirley.

Schipper's argument as to the date of composition of the play (1632) is invalid, although the date itself may be not far wrong. The fact that Cupid is spoken of as having "troubled every masque at court these seven years" cannot be construed as referring to the seven years following the accession of Charles I. Masques at the court of James I contained Cupids. For instance, they appear in

15 Arber's guess that these five plays are Beaumont and Fletcher's is not worth consideration (Transcript, IV, 438).

16 Nissen says the Hamburg City Library copy of this edition lacks Fletcher's name on the titlepage (James Shirley, p. 12).

17 The Coronation is contained in Glover and Waller's reprint of the second Beaumont and Fletcher folio of 1679.

the following court-masques of Jonson: The Hue and
Cry after Cupid (1608), Love Freed from Ignorance and
Folly (1610), Love Restored (1610), Christmas, his
Masque (1616), and Time Vindicated (1623) (see Schip-
per, James Shirley, pp. 159–60, on The Coronation).
"Seven years" means doubtless merely several years.

A brief outline of the plot follows:

Theophilus, King of Epire, dies, leaving two infant
sons, Leonatus and Demetrius, and a daughter, Sophia.
Fearing lest Cassander, an ambitious noble, should usurp
the throne, Theophilus provides that the boys be reported
dead. Sophia is then proclaimed queen under Cassander's
protection, and is later betrothed to Lisimachus, his son.
In the meantime, the princes have been given into the care
of Eubulus and Macarius, two nobles, the former of whom
rears Leonatus as Seleucus, his son, and the latter, Demetrius as Arcadius, his nephew (not son, as in the *dramatis
personæ*). The two brothers (who do not know their relationship) are to decide a feud between Eubulus and Macarius by single combat before the Queen. To prevent any
danger to the true King the two old men are reconciled.
Sophia, who has just dismissed Cassander as Protector,
chooses as her husband not Lisimachus but Arcadius.
Fired with ambition, he forsakes his mistress, Polidora, and
accepts the Queen's hand. The identity of Arcadius is now
revealed, and he is placed on the throne. He now seeks
to return to Polidora who refuses him, alleging that his
rank is now too high. Angered by his loss of power, and
the jilting of Lisimachus, Cassander sets up Seleucus as
a pretender to the crown, proclaiming him to be Leonatus.
Arcadius is dethroned and thereby regains Polidora.
Seleucus becomes rebellious toward Cassander who attempts to overthrow him by confessing his plot, but is
confounded by the revelation of his protégé's true identity.

A reconciliation between Sophia and Lisimachus is effected, and the play ends happily.

It seems fairly certain that The Coronation is based upon A King and No King (much as The Doubtful Heir is, in turn, based upon The Coronation). Shirley has, as usual, introduced variations of the plot of the earlier play. He has reversed the main situation: Arbaces in love with Panthea, who turns out not to be his sister, becomes Arcadius, about to marry Sophia who is revealed to be his sister. Tigranes who wavers in his love for Spaconia on seeing Panthea is repeated also in Arcadius who leaves Polidora for Sophia. Indeed, Arcadius in characterization corresponds to Tigranes and in the action of the play has the parts both of Tigranes and of Arbaces to maintain. The characterization of Seleucus is modeled after that of Arbaces with a touch of Mardonius. As to the other characters Shirley's Cassander = Fletcher's Gobrias; Nestorius = Lygones; Sophia = Panthea; and Polidora = Spaconia.[18]

Cassander is Shirley's first essay at the elderly politician, a class including besides the Cardinal in The Cardinal, Gotharus in The Politician, and Roderigo in The Court Secret. Sophia is an imperious spoiled child, like the Olivia of the later Doubtful Heir (see Chap. III), while Polidora, affectionate, but with a saving amount of pride, is as human in another way as Domitilla in The Royal Master. Because of this mixture of qualities, she stands nearly alone among Shirley's romantic heroines.

For the occurrences of the title of the play in the prologue, cf. I, 1, IV, 3, and the epilogue, and see Chap. IV, Sect. 31.

Act I, Sc. 1. For the discussion of Cassander's char-

18 The names "Seleucus" and "Demetrius" seem derived from Plutarch's Life of Demetrius, or from The Humorous Lieutenant.

acter, etc., see under The Cardinal, I, 1. Cassander with
his plan for a marriage between Lisimachus and the Queen
seems the original of the Cardinal and his projected match
between Columbo and Rosaura. Cf. the feud between
Eubulus and Macarius with the Capulets and Montagues
in Romeo and Juliet, Alvarez and Louis in The Spanish
Gipsy, Alvarez and Vitelli in Love's Cure, Julio and Bel-
lides in The Maid in the Mill. Note also The Maid's
Revenge. For Sophia's courtship of Lisimachus, cf. II,
3, and see Chap. IV, Sect. 1. A suggestion for the terms
of the combat between Seleucus and Arcadius seems derived from Love's Cure, V, I, in which Lucio and Vitelli
prepare for their combat.

Act II, Sc. 1. Cf. the dialogue between Arcadius and
Polidora with that between Tigranes and Spaconia, A King
and No King, I, 2 (the purpose of both is to demonstrate
the affection existing between the lovers). Note The
Doubtful Heir, II, 3, as founded upon this scene. Gifford
derives the three lines beginning ''Come let me take the
kiss, . . . ,'' from the three lines in Coriolanus, V, 3, beginning ''Now by the jealous queen of heaven. . . .'' Cf.,
however, The Queen of Corinth, I, 2, and The Bondman,
II, 1, IV, 3. For Arcadius' invitation to Polidora to come
to court, see under The Royal Master, I, 2 (which is derived from this passage). For analogues to his contemptuous remarks concerning court life, see under Love's
Cruelty, I, 2. His invoking a curse upon himself in case
he proves false to Polidora is drawn from Tigranes, A
King and No King, I, 2. Cf. also, however, Proteus in
The Two Gentlemen of Verona, II, 2, and Virolet in The
Double Marriage, I, 1. Note Cressida in Troilus and
Cressida, IV, 2.

Sc. 2. For Arcadius' wish that he and Seleucus were

to "tug upon some cliff," see under The Cardinal, V, 2, and note King Lear, IV, 6.

Sc. 3. For possible sources for the formal combat as arranged in the preceding scene and about to be engaged in in this scene, cf. A King and No King, I, 1, II, 1 (reported), and Love's Cure, V, 3 (where the combat does not actually begin). The reconciliation of Eubulus and Macarius in order to prevent possible bloodshed suggests a use of the reconciliation of the combatants in the latter play which is brought about by the threats of their various female relatives to kill each other if they proceed. For analogous formal combats, see Jocasta, IV, 1, V, 2 (between two brothers), Sir Clyomon and Sir Clamydes, p. 524, Henry VI, Part II, II, 3, Richard II, 1, 3, Troilus and Cressida, IV, 5, King Lear, V, 3 (between half-brothers), The Brazen Age, I, 1, A Maidenhead Well Lost, V, The Thracian Wonder, V, 2, The Two Noble Kinsmen, V, 5 (off stage), The Knight of Malta, II, 5, The Devil's Law-case, V, 6, The Blind Beggar of Bednal Green, V, Sophronisba, V, 2, The Dumb Knight, I, 1, The Poor Man's Comfort, V, The Partial Law, V, 4, The Queen, V, Argalus and Parthenia, IV, 1 (1638). Note the reconciliations in Romeo and Juliet, V, 3, and The Spanish Gipsy, V, 2.

For Sophia's announcement that she will choose a subject for her husband, see under The Grateful Servant, I, 1. Cf. her proposing marriage to Arcadius with her courtship of Lisimachus, I, 1, and see Chap. IV, Sect. 1. Note The Doubtful Heir, II, 4, as derived from this incident. For brother and sister in love while ignorant of their relationship, see under The Court Secret, I, 1. The position of Lisimachus here (forsaken by his mistress) furnishes a source for Leonario, The Doubtful Heir, II, 4. For the action of Arcadius in forsaking Polidora for a lady of higher rank, see under The Doubtful Heir, II, 4, which in this respect, however, actually does not parallel closely the situation in this scene.

Act III, Sc. 1. Polidora's lament over the fickleness of Arcadius seems a development of Spaconia's asides during A King and No King, III, 1, in which she watches the growth of Tigranes' passion for Panthea. Note in connection with her sadness that Panthea comments on Spaconia's melancholy, *ibid.*, IV, 1.

Sc. 2. For Cassander's attempting to incite Lisimachus to the murder of Arcadius, see under The Politician, III, 2. For Seleucus as a discontented soldier, cf. Pallante, The Duke's Mistress, I, 1, and for his sarcasms on the court, see under Love's Cruelty, I, 2. His allusion to dancing as a way to preferment (p. 494) is based on The Humorous Courtier, II, 2. Note in connection with the studied and artificial character of Arcadius' compliments to Sophia, Flaviano's speech, The Imposture, I, 2, Contarini's, The Sisters, II, 2, and their parallels. The ornamentation seems borrowed by Octavio, The Royal Master, I, 2. The lines, "One smile a day would stretch my life to immortality" (p. 498), may be related to Doctor Faustus, V, 3, "Sweet Helen, make me immortal with a kiss." Note that Arcadius (p. 499), after receiving a letter from Polidora, struggles between love and ambition but yields to the latter. This corresponds to the policy of Ferdinand in the later Doubtful Heir, III, 1, IV, 1. See under The Gentleman of Venice, V, 4, for parallels to the revelation of the true parentage of Arcadius, and note the similar incident in which Seleucus figures, V, 3, following. This is a reversal of A King and No King, V, 4, in which Arbaces is proved *no* king. For the story of the preservation of Arcadius as told by Macarius and the Bishop, cf. Henry VI, Part II, III, 2, Cymbeline, V, 5, The Winter's Tale,

V, 2 (reported), Perkin Warbeck, II, 1. This passage is utilized in The Doubtful Heir, I, 1, V, 2. For the resurrection of Demetrius (Arcadius) here, as well as that of Leonatus (Seleucus) in V, 3, following, see Chap. IV, Sect. 29. Cf. Humor out of Breath, V, 2, for the recognition of the rightful sovereign. Revelations of the relationship of two characters in the situation of Arcadius and Sophia are found in Mother Bombie, V, 3, The Four Prentices of London, p. 104, The Case is Altered, V, 4, The Lovesick Court, V, 3, The Deserving Favorite, V, 1, The Jealous Lovers, V, 7, as well as in the doubtfully Shirleian Phillis of Scyros, V, 9, and No Wit, No Help like a Woman's, IV, 1 (incorrect). The transfer by Arcadius of his love from Sophia back to Polidora here and in IV, 3, is used again in The Royal Master, V, 1 (see Chap. III). Cf. Proteus, The Two Gentlemen of Verona, V, 4.

Act IV, Sc. 1. Note in connection with Cassander's plotting the overthrow of Arcadius, The Traitor, II, 1, etc., The Politician, I, 1, etc., The Duke's Mistress, III, 3, IV, 1, The Court Secret, III, 2. For the soliloquy of Seleucus on true greatness, see under The Royal Master, III, 3. The decision to set up Seleucus as a pretender suggests Juliana as Fioretta in the later Imposture, II, 1, etc. Note the analogues to her position cited under that play. Ferdinand's situation in The Doubtful Heir, up to V, 2, is precisely that of Seleucus until his recognition as rightful King, V, 3. Cf. Seleucus as a pretender with York, Edward of March, Edward of Lancaster, and Cade in the Henry VI plays, Arthur in King John, Henry of Hereford in Richard II, Mortimer in the Henry IV plays, Richmond in Richard III, Antiochus in Believe as You List, Warbeck and Simnel (reported) in Perkin Warbeck. Note that Cade by York's admission (Henry VI, Part II, III, 1) acts as a sort of puppet for York. The game of crowning a king, as played here by Cassander, recalls Richard III, III, 7.

Sc. 2. For Sophia's misinterpretation of Lisimachus, cf. V, 2, following, and see Chap. IV, Sect. 27. This especial type of misunderstanding is used later in Captain Underwit, V, 1. Its source may be A Maidenhead Well Lost, III (Lauretta and the Prince of Florence).

Sc. 3. For the masque within a play, see Chap. IV, Sect. 18. The masque which deals allegorically with some event which occurs in the play is used in The Traitor, III, 2. The entertainment (which may be called Love Corrupted by Fortune) is strongly suggestive in theme of A Contention for Honor and Riches.

Cf. Lisander's comment upon the frequent appearance of Cupid in court-masques with Bombo's recipe for masque-making, The Royal Master, II, 1. Cf. The Sad One, V, 1 (1640), for similar satire. Fleay notes as court-masques with Cupid as a figure during the seven years preceding The Coronation, Love's Triumph, Chloridia, Love's Welcome (1633), Love's Welcome (1634), Love's Mistress [not a masque, however], and The Temple of Love (Biog. Chron., II, 241). Cupid figures in the masques in The Constant Maid, IV, 3, and The Ball, V, 1, as well as in Shirley's entertainments, The Triumph of Beauty, and Cupid and Death. See The Nice Valor, II, 1. For further parallels, see Chap. IV, Sect. 18.

Polidora's direct and indirect rebuke of Arcadius for his faithlessness is based upon Spaconia and Tigranes, A King and No King, IV, 2. Polidora, however, does not pardon Arcadius so readily as Spaconia does Tigranes. Cf. Bianca's refusing to receive back Cesario who had deserted her in The Fair Maid of the Inn, IV, 2. For Arcadius' transfer of his love back to Polidora, see under III, 2. Her entrance as mourning the "death" of

Arcadius is a serious employment of Penelope's lamentations for Fowler's "death," The Witty Fair One, V, 3. For the announcement of the breaking out of a revolt, headed by Seleucus, see under The Politician, IV, 3. Note also The Doubtful Heir, V, 4. The words "no king" in Polidora's speech (p. 520) and in the question of Arcadius "Must I be no King?" (p. 521), together with their occurrence in V, 1, 2, following, recall Arbaces in A King and No King, V, 4 ("I am found no King . . ."). Arbaces' joy over the loss of his throne, while founded on a different reason, is repeated in Arcadius' attitude through the remainder of the play. Arbaces, too, is proved not to be of royal birth, while Arcadius is shown merely to be no longer rightful king.

Act V, Sc. 1, which concerns Seleucus' asserting his independence of Cassander seems original in nearly all respects. For "no king" (p. 526), see under IV, 3.

Sc. 2. The misunderstanding of Sophia and Polidora parallels that of the former and Lisimachus, IV, 2 (see Chap. IV, Sect. 27 also). For the meeting of the two, note the later Royal Master, IV, 1, and Court Secret, II, 3.

Sc. 3. For the revelation of Seleucus' true identity, see under III, 2. Note that as in The Doubtful Heir the identity of Ferdinand is in doubt until V, 2, so that of Seleucus (or Leonatus) is from IV, 1, preceding, to this scene. Note A King and No King, V, 4, as a source for the general adjustment of relationships.

## VIII. THE SISTERS

The Sisters, which was licensed April 26, 1642, was the last of Shirley's plays to be produced before the closing of the theatres. It is an amusing but very light piece built upon a plot made up of farce and romance in almost equal parts. The Sisters contains a number of echoes of earlier plays, but no main source has yet been discovered.

The plot of the comedy runs as follows:

The father of Paulina and Angellina dies, making the former his sole heiress, for the latter is intended for a convent. Eaten up with pride, Paulina assumes the state of a princess, to the disgust of her uncle, Antonio, whose favorite Angellina is. The Prince of Parma sends Contarini, a noble, to view Paulina's ostentation. He makes love to her but actually falls in love with Angellina. Vergerio, his servant, is deputized to press his master's suit to Angellina, but she seems to be falling in love with him. In the meantime, Frapolo, a robber, and his band, attempt in the guise of astrologers to plunder Paulina's castle, but are driven away. Next, with Frapolo disguised as the Prince of Parma and the other banditti as his suite, they visit Paulina. The false Prince courts her, and marries her. Unfortunately, the true Prince appears on the scene, and as a result Frapolo's plan is frustrated and he and his companions are captured. Shortly after the Prince's arrival, it is discovered that Vergerio really is Pulcheria, daughter to the Viceroy of Sicily, who had been formerly betrothed to Contarini, but who had been reported dead. Contarini returns to her, and the Prince pays his court to Angellina who reconsiders her plan of entering a convent. By the confession of Morulla, her old nurse, Paulina is shown to be her own child, who had been substituted for the real Paulina at her death, so Angellina comes into her father's estate, an allowance from which she pays to Paulina.

Apparently, The Sisters is drawn, in part, from The Gentleman of Venice, The Young Admiral, and Twelfth Night, with certain elements borrowed from still other plays, such as The Elder Brother.

Paulina is the feminine counterpart of Thomazo, the

boorish changeling, in The Gentleman of Venice. Throughout the play, she is contrasted with the almost saintly
Angellina, as Thomazo and Giovanni are in the play mentioned. Her pride resembles that of Torrenti in The Wonder of a Kingdom or of Alteza in The Just Italian. The
ceremoniousness of her little court suggests that of Sancho
Panza at Barataria (Don Quixote, Part II, Chap. 47).
Paulina indeed, seems like the haughty wicked sister of
the *märchen*, as Angellina resembles the Cinderella
type.

Antonio, uncle to the sisters, who favors one niece at
the expense of the other whom he abuses heartily is evidently modeled upon Miramont in The Elder Brother.
Cf. also Antonio in The Chances, and Durazzo in The
Guardian, and see Chap. IV, Sect. 43. Olaus in The Politician and the others of the blunt soldier class listed in
Chap. IV, Sect. 39, should be compared (Antonio is not
a soldier, however).

The prologue is worth noting for the references to
Shakespeare by name (cf. Captain Underwit, I, 1, II, 1)
and to Fletcher, and Jonson (cf. the preface to Beaumont
and Fletcher's Tragedies and Comedies, and the dedication
to The Grateful Servant respectively). For an explanation of "London is gone to York" (the King's journey
north in 1642) see Clarendon, Hist., II, 290 ff. (Bk. IV).

The title of the play occurs in the *dramatis personæ* as
in The Young Admiral, The Duke's Mistress, etc. (see
Chap. IV, Sect. 31).

Act I, Sc. 1. For parallels to Frapolo and his banditti
in this scene, and in II, 1, IV, 1 (in their own shapes),
cf. The Arcadia, IV, 1, 2, The Triumph of Peace, Honoria
and Mammon, V, 2, The Nightwalker, The Lovers' Progress,
I, 2, Love's Pilgrimage, II, 3, The Two Gentlemen of
Verona, IV, 1, V, 3, 4, Henry IV, Part I, II, 2, Timon

of Athens, IV, 3, The Four Prentices of London, p. 77 ff., The Fair Maid of the Exchange, p. 7, The Fair Maid of the West, Part II, IV, 1, Sir John Oldcastle, III, 4, V, 2, The Blind Beggar of Bednal Green, III, 2, The Downfall of Robert, Earl of Huntington, III, 2, etc., The Death of Robert, Earl of Huntington, I, 1, etc., Your Five Gallants, III, 2, The Widow, III, 1, The London Prodigal, IV, 2, The Miseries of Enforced Marriage, IV, Thierry and Theodoret, V, 1, The Coxcomb, II, 1, The Pilgrim, II, 2, III, 1, 3, Love's Cure, IV, 3, Albumazar, I, 1, etc., A Cure for a Cuckold, II, 1, 2, 'Tis Pity She's a Whore, IV, 3, V, 4, 6, The Queen's Exchange, II, 3, IV, 1, V, 1, The Guardian, II, 3, V, 1, 4, The Sad Shepherd, The Goblins, I, 1, etc. Pretended thieves are found in Wit at Several Weapons, II, 4, and The Little French Lawyer, IV, 5, 6, V, 1. Cf. with Frapolo's laying down rules for the government of his men, The Downfall of Robert, Earl of Huntington, III, 2, The Beggar's Bush, II, 1, The Guardian, II, 3. Cf. Longino's "Conscience is a varlet" (p. 360) with Hamlet's "Conscience doth make cowards of us all," Hamlet, III, 1. Cf. the Second Murderer on conscience, Richard III, 1, 4, La Torch on the same subject, The Bloody Brother, II, 1, and the King, The Noble Soldier, IV, 2 (see under The Royal Master, IV, 1). Note Frapolo's allusion to trimness in religion (p. 361) (contemporary, doubtless, as are many of the other satirical allusions in this portion of the scene). Unfortunately for Shirley, as far as the modern reader's opinion of his taste goes, the cowardice of Piperollo (see II, 1, also) is without a single close parallel. Note Thomazo's setting out to rob the Duke (his supposed father), in The Gentleman of Venice, III, 1.

Sc. 2. See under The Politician, I, 1, for parallels to the crossing of the stage by Antonio and Angellina, while

they are commented on by other characters. For the
eavesdropping of Giovanni and Stephanio, see Chap. IV,
Sect. 30. For Antonio's railing upon his niece here and
in II, 2 (which was doubtless considered comic), cf. The
Duke's Mistress, III, 2, IV, 1, and see under Chap. IV,
Sect. 20. Note Miramont on Eustace, his nephew, The
Elder Brother, II, 1, III, 5, IV, 3. Antonio's "Thou hast
drunk a devil," and the three lines following (pp. 366-67)
recall Leontio's "I have drunk and seen the spider" (The
Winter's Tale, II, 1).

Act II, Sc. 1. There seem to be no parallels to this
scene. Note I, 1, and IV, 1, for other appearances of the
thieves in their own persons.

Sc. 2. For the mention of the Lords of Misrule (pp.
372-73), cf. The Insatiate Countess, III, The Royal Slave,
I, 3, and note Jonson's Christmas, his Masque. On these
dignitaries, see Chambers, Medieval Stage, I, 403 ff. For
Lords of Misrule at St. John's College, and at Gray's Inn
(of both of which Shirley had been a member) see *ibid.*,
pp. 408 ff., and 417-18, respectively. For the ornate flattery of Paulina by Contarini, see under The Imposture,
I, 2. Angellina's reception of Contarini's compliments to
her recalls Domitilla and Octavio, The Royal Master, I,
2, and Lidia and Sanazarro, The Great Duke of Florence,
II, 3. For the quarrel of Antonio and Paulina, see under
I, 2. Gifford notes that in a MS. of the play at Sion
College occurs the following additional couplet,

"For though I am no Princess, you shall see
Such state that Princess born shall learn of me,"

which he assigns to Davenant.

Act III, Sc. 1. For general analogues to this sharpers'
scene, see under The Maid's Revenge, III, 2. The source
of the disguise of Frapolo and the other banditti as as-

trologers may be Albumazar, I, 5, etc. Note especially also The Widow, IV, 2, and cf. The Alchemist. Thieves in disguise occur in The Nightwalker, III, 3, The Mayor of Queenborough, V, 1, and A Mad World, My Masters, II, 1, V, 1, 2. For their comic fortune-telling, see under The Maid's Revenge, III, 2. Cf. with Piperollo's fortune that told Dondolo in More Dissemblers Besides Women, IV, 1. The picking of the servants' pockets while their attention is elsewhere attracted is paralleled in James IV, IV, 3, Sir Thomas More, I, 2, The Mayor of Queenborough, V, 1, Your Five Gallants, I, 2, II, 1, The Winter's Tale, IV, 3, 4, The Alchemist, III, 2, Bartholomew Fair, II, 1, III, 1, IV, 1, 3, The Beggar's Bush, III, 1, and The Court Beggar, II, 1 (reported).

Sc. 2. For Antonio's "I could beat her" (p. 389), see under Love Tricks, I, 1. Contarini's sending Vergerio, a maid disguised as a servant, to court Angellina for him is founded on Twelfth Night, I, 4, in which Orsino sends Viola as Cesario (who is in love with him, as "Vergerio" is with Contarini) to plead his case with Olivia. See Chap. IV, Sect. 3, for wooing by proxy; and for a person's being sent to press a suit, by the success of which a rival would profit, see Chap. IV, Sect. 5, and note The Grateful Servant, II, 2. For the reference to Venus and Adonis (p. 392), see under The Doubtful Heir, IV, 2.

Act IV, Sc. 1. For the thieves, cf. I, 1, and II, 1. For the references to Claridiana and to Guenevere, see Koeppel, Reflexe der Ritter-Romane im Drama, p. 212, note. See under The Constant Maid, I, 1, for Piperollo's quotation from The Spanish Tragedy, II, 4 (which Gifford incorrectly prints as prose).

Sc. 2. Note how Angellina as her uncle's heiress is contrasted with Paulina in the preceding scenes as Giovanni and Thomazo are contrasted in The Gentleman of Venice.

For the character of the waiting-woman, see Chap. IV, Sect. 21. Note that in Cartwright's Siege, II, 2, is an indirect character of a waiting-woman, and cf. Bold in Amends for Ladies, I, 1, on the qualifications of a waiting-woman. Cf. Angellina's rebuke of the Scholar on his flowery verses to her with Fowler, The Witty Fair One, I, 3, and note Shirley's Friendship (Poems, VI, 452–53). Shirley parodies such compliments in The Witty Fair One, III, 2, The Humorous Courtier, II, 2, Love in a Maze, II, 2. For the kind of complimentary poem which she criticizes here, see Lovell's lines to the Lady, The Lady Mother, I, 1, Horatio's address to the Countess, Law Tricks, II [1], the compliments of Asotus and his companions to Phryne, The Jealous Lovers, III, 5, Guzman concerning Amoretta, The Lady's Trial, III, 1. For parallels in non-dramatic poetry, see Shirley's Love's Hue and Cry (VI, 410–11), To the Painter, Preparing to Draw M. H. H. (VI, 414 ff.), To One that said his Mistress was Old (VI, 417–18), A Dialogue (VI, 459 ff.). See also under The Maid's Revenge, I, 2, for various criticisms of contemporary literature by Shirley. Ward suggests that Newman's speech, Albertus Wallenstein, II, 2, is founded on Angellina's lines here (Hist. Eng. Dram. Lit., III, 123, note). However, this is not the case, as Glapthorne's play was printed in 1639. As Gifford says, the words of the Scholar and Francescina at parting allude to Sir Roger and Abigail in The Scornful Lady, IV, 1. Note The Lady of Pleasure, V, 1. The thronging of tradespeople to Angellina (p. 400 ff.) suggests Pennyboy Junior and the merchants, The Staple of News, I, 1. Cf. also The Old Law, II, 1, and A Fine Companion, I, 4. For the petitioners, or beggars, as soldiers, see under Love Tricks, IV, 5.

Sc. 3, which represents Piperollo's report to Paulina of the robbery of himself and Lucio (IV, 1), and the reported approach of the Prince of Parma, has no parallels, seemingly.

Sc. 4. Angellina's love for Pulcheria disguised as Vergerio, as shown in this scene, seems founded upon Olivia's passion for Viola as Cesario, Twelfth Night, I, 5, III, 1, in view of the apparent indebtedness in III, 2. For other parallels, see Chap. IV, Sect. 8, and note The Doubtful Heir, IV, 2.

Sc. 5. For Prince Farnese in disguise, see under The Humorous Courtier. For his meeting Frapolo posing as Prince of Parma here and in V, 2, following, see under Love Tricks, V, 2, and The Imposture, III, 1. For the disguise of Frapolo, assumed to gain entrance to Paulina's castle, cf. Follywit's disguise, etc., in A Mad World, My Masters, II, 1. Follywit executes his design, unlike Shirley's robber.

Act V, Sc. 1. Fabio's suspecting his wife, Morulla, to be mad is based on the opinion concerning Ursula, The Gentleman of Venice, V, 4. The discovery of ''Vergerio's'' sex, and her reconciliation with Contarini seem, with due allowance for the variations necessary for the variations in plot, to be based upon Orsino and ''Cesario,'' Twelfth Night, V, I. Pulcheria—daughter to the Viceroy of Sicily, —who has followed Contarini recalls strongly Rosinda, daughter to the King of Sicily who follows her lover, Cesario, and like Pulcheria wins him from another lady, The Young Admiral, II, 1, etc. Cf. Isabella and Carlo in the later Court Secret. For the resurrection of Pulcheria and for her disguise, see Chap. IV, Sects. 29 and 32. Her following her lover as his servant recalls Castabella, The Maid's Revenge, V, 1, 3. See Chap. III, on the fickle lover, which type Contarini approaches.

Sc. 2. Note the reference to The Knight of the Burning Pestle, p. 418. Cf. Longino's betrayal of his com-

panions with Falconbridge and Spicing, Edward IV, Part
I, p. 35.   For Piperollo's calling for a lion to decide which
is the true Prince, note The Noble Gentleman, V, 1, Henry
IV, Part I, II, 4 (in spite of Gifford), The Mad Lover,
IV, 5.   Note that Frapolo, like Pimponio in The Opportunity, IV, 1, and to a certain extent, Juliana in The Imposture, III, 3, attempts, by mere impudence, to outface
the true Prince, but again, like the characters named, is
forced to beg for mercy.   Cf. this situation with IV, 5,
and see under Love Tricks, V, 3.   The discovery of
Paulina's parentage is based on The Gentleman of Venice,
V, 4.   The stories of Morulla and Ursula are practically
the same.   Note Frapolo in this scene as a trickster tricked.
For the epilogue by a comic character, see under Love
Tricks.

# CHAPTER IX

## THE REALISTIC COMEDIES

### I. THE WEDDING

The Wedding seems not to have been licensed under that name, or possibly it was omitted by accident from Malone's transcripts from Herbert's Officebook. Fleay assigns the play, on the strength of the reference to "the last day of the first merry month, and in the second year of the reign of King Cupid" (III, 2), to presentation in May, 1626 (Biog. Chron., II, 236). While we do not know that Shirley identified Charles I with "King Cupid," yet Fleay's explanation of the phrases quoted seems at least plausible, and does not conflict with any other evidence as to the date of the comedy (there is none, by the way, save the fact of its publication in 1629). No record of the entry of The Wedding for publication appears in the Stationers' Register, yet editions of it came out in 1629 and 1633.

Stiefel offers a Spanish source for The Wedding (Romanische Forschungen, V, 196, note). It is worth noting then that Shirley had begun, probably in 1626, certainly before 1629, his borrowings from the literature of Spain, and, moreover, had utilized this foreign material in his first genuine comedy of manners. Whatever the Spanish influence amounted to, there are evidences of the influence of the Falstaffian plays of Shakespeare and Twelfth Night in the underplot of The Wedding, besides a strong suggestion of indebtedness to Much Ado About Nothing in the more romantic main plot.

322

The story of the comedy is as follows:

Gratiana, daughter of Sir John Belfare, is about to be married to Beauford. Beauford's kinsman, Marwood, tells him Gratiana has been unchaste within his own personal knowledge. Beauford breaks off the match, challenges Marwood, and wounds him, leaving him for dead on the field. He then shuts himself up in his lodgings, where he awaits arrest, and mourns Gratiana whom he thinks to have committed suicide. Milliscent, a servant, posing as a kinsman of Marwood's, brings a chest to Beauford which ostensibly contains Marwood's body, but in which Gratiana is instead. Milliscent reveals to him the reasons for Marwood's accusations and thus reconciles the lovers. Beauford is arrested and taken before Justice Landby. Marwood, whose body had disappeared from the scene of the duel, now appears as having been healed by a skilful surgeon, and clears Beauford of the charge of murder. Gratiana's innocence is then established by the confession of her maid, Cardona, who had been bribed to betray her mistress to Marwood, but who had substituted her own daughter, Lucibel, for Gratiana. As atonement Marwood marries Lucibel who has posed in a male disguise as Milliscent. The second plot deals with the courtship of Jane, Justice Landby's daughter, by Lodam, a glutton, and Rawbone, a miser. She, however, loves Haver, a poor young man who serves Rawbone in disguise. A mock duel occurs between Lodam and Haver in his master's clothing. Justice Landby, who has penetrated Haver's disguise, sends him and Jane to be married, in spite of the horrified miser's protests.

From the foregoing outline, it is seen that the main plot is a form of the Ginevra, or slandered innocence story, which occurs in Ariosto and Shakespeare, as well as in the works of many others. Beauford, Marwood, and Gratiana correspond to Shakespeare's Claudio, Don John, and Hero in Much Ado About Nothing. Cardona and Lucibel very roughly parallel the Borachio and Margaret of Shakespeare's play. The mock duel between Lodam and Haver as Rawbone recalls Sir Andrew and Viola as Cesario in Twelfth Night, with a hint of Sir Hugh and Doctor Caius in The Merry Wives of Windsor.

Lodam, Jane's corpulent suitor, is certainly drawn after Falstaff (Henry IV, Parts I, II, The Merry Wives of Windsor). Cf. also Lazarillo in The Woman Hater, and Greedy in A New Way to Pay Old Debts (1625). Rawbone, as a young usurer, is a novelty. Note Hornet in The Constant Maid, with the Niece who is stolen from him, as a conventional Elizabethan money-lender. As immediately suggesting the character, note Overreach in A New Way to Pay Old Debts. Cf. also the Usurer in A Looking-glass for London, Barabas in The Jew of Malta, Shylock in The Merchant of Venice, Jacques in The Case is Altered, Sordido in Every Man out of his Humor, Volpone, etc., in Volpone, the Richer Pennyboy in The Staple of News, Sir Moth Interest in The Magnetic Lady (1633), Lorenzo in May-Day, Mammon in Jack Drum's Entertainment, Quomodo in Michaelmas Term, Lucre, etc., in A Trick to Catch the Old One, Bartervile in If This Be Not a Good Play, the Devil Is in It, Lopez in Women Pleased, Morecraft in The Scornful Lady, Hog in The Hog Hath Lost his Pearl, Earthworm in The Old Couple, Bloodhound in A Match at Midnight, Mendicant in The Court Beggar (1632?), Vermin in The Damoiselle, Quicksands in The English Moor, Littlegood in A Fine Companion. The above list comprises both money-lenders and misers. For both Lodam and Rawbone as foolish suitors, and as poltroons, see under Chap. IV, Sects. 44, and 47. Cf. Lodam and Greedy in A New Way to Pay Old Debts. Cf. Camelion with Scarabeo in The Maid's Revenge, and note Carion in The Supposes,

Launcelot in The Merchant of Venice, Pachieco in The Woman Hater, Penurio in Women Pleased, Lazarillo in Love's Cure. Note that Andelocia, Old Fortunatus, I, 2, says to his starving servant, Shadow, ". . . Here comes another shadow," to which the servant replies, "It should be a chameleon, for he is all in colors." For the disguise of Haver as a servant, cf. Giovanni in The Gentleman of Venice, and note the disguised suitors, as in The Arcadia, The Humorous Courtier, The Bird in a Cage, etc. Cf. especially Mucedorus in Mucedorus, Lacy in The Shoemakers' Holiday, Old Flowerdale in The London Prodigal (not a lover), Friscobaldo in The Honest Whore, Part II (not a lover), Sencer in The Wise Woman of Hogsdon, Gerardine in The Family of Love, Montague in The Honest Man's Fortune, Pisander in The Bondman, Antonio in A Very Woman. For Justice Landby, see Justice Clement in Every Man in his Humor and note Justice Clement in the later Constant Maid. Note Jane as a first sketch of Shirley's clever young woman (see under Chap. IV, Sect. 40).

Act I, Sc. 1. For the discussion of the wedding invitations by Belfare and Isaac, cf. Sir Quintilian and Flash, Satiromastix, p. 188. For the brief characters of Rawbone and Lodam, with that of the former, I, 3, following, see Chap. IV, Sect. 21. Isaac's remark concerning Lodam that he is "something given to the waist, for he lives within no reasonable compass" (p. 368) is from the conversation of Falstaff and Bardolph, Henry IV, Part I, III, 3. Note also the Chief Justice and Falstaff, *ibid.*, Part II, I, 2.

Sc. 2. For Isaac with the wedding invitations, note I, 1, I, 3, and see Romeo and Juliet, I, 2. Gifford notes in this scene references to the practices of the Catholic Church. Cf. The Gentleman of Venice, V, 2, The Grateful Servant, III, 3. For Marwood and Beauford, see I, 4, following.

Sc. 3. For Landby's character of Rawbone, cf. I, 1, and

see Chap. IV, Sect. 21. His proposed test of Jane resembles that of Fernando, The Brothers, III, 1, V, 3. See Chap. IV, Sect. 15, for parallels. For Camelion's lament over his leanness, cf. Scarabeo, The Maid's Revenge, III, 2. Note also Carion, The Supposes, II, 4, and Launcelot, The Merchant of Venice, II, 2.

Sc. 4 continues the latter part of Sc. 2 in which Marwood promises to make an important discovery to Beauford. The communication is to the effect that Marwood has enjoyed Gratiana. Swinburne seems inclined to find the source for this incident and for the actual repudiation in II, 3, in A Woman is a Weathercock, II, 1 (Fortnightly Review, April 1, 1890, p. 465). However, the breaking off of a match because of scandalous reports concerning the bride occurs in Much Ado About Nothing, III, 2, The Triumph of Love, Sc. 2, A Fair Quarrel, V, 1, The Partial Law, II, 2, The Jealous Lovers, II, 2 (1632). Note also The Royal Master, II, 2, III, 1, and The Grateful Servant, V, 1.

Act II, Sc. 1. See under The Cardinal, III, 2, for the preparations for the wedding, and for Cardona's errands, cf. The Taming of the Shrew, IV, 1.

Sc. 2. Beauford's forcing Marwood to fight him is paralleled in A Fair Quarrel, III, 1. Note also in Shirley's later Court Secret, IV, 2, and Example, IV, 3, V, 2.

Sc. 3. See under The Brothers, V, 1, for the waiting of the wedding guests for the bride-groom. For Beauford's repudiation of Gratiana as unchaste, cf. Claudio, Much Ado About Nothing, IV, 1, Chough, A Fair Quarrel, V, 1 (note that Beauford does not break off the match publicly as does Claudio, nor is the scene comic as in the second play cited). Note A Woman is a Weathercock, II, 1 (the marriage has taken place in this city when the bride's alleged impurity is exposed).

Act III, Sc. 1. The reported disappearance of Marwood's body from the place of the duel is paralleled in The
Trial of Chivalry, III, 2, The Deserving Favorite, III, 1
(1629), Love Crowns the End, p. 10 (1632), The Floating
Island, IV, 12 (1636). Koeppel derives Gratiana's return
of his presents to Beauford from Ophelia's return of Hamlet's gifts, Hamlet, III, 1 (Shakespeare's Wirkung, pp. 56–
57). For Landby's attitude toward Beauford and Gratiana, cf. Benedick, Much Ado about Nothing, IV, 1, etc.
Landby is more convincing than Shakespeare's character.

Sc. 2. Rawbone's wooing Jane in legal terminology is
drawn on in Honoria and Mammon, III, 2. For his dating
his document, see the discussion of the date of the play.
Cf. his critical remarks (p. 406) with Catherina's, The
Bird in a Cage, IV, 2. For Jane's jeering him, see Chap.
IV, Sect. 20. See under The Humorous Courtier, II, 2,
IV, 2, V, 3 (Volterre) for Lodam's learning. Cf. also Dog-
berry and Verges, Much Ado About Nothing, III, 3, 5,
IV, 2, V, 1 (as general parallels), and Sebastian and
Launcelot in Monsieur Thomas, I, 2, etc. For his "pocas
palabras" (p. 408), cf. The Spanish Tragedy, III, 14, and
note "pauca verba," The Merry Wives of Windsor, I, 1.

The challenging of Lodam by Rawbone, the former of
whom thinks the other a coward, while the latter intends
his servant to fight for him, is based upon Twelfth Night,
III, 2, 4. There Sir Toby influences Sir Andrew to challenge Viola in disguise as Cesario, by alleging the supposed man to be a coward, and then, after having frightened the last with tales of Sir Andrew's prowess, in turn
tells Sir Andrew of "Cesario's" skill with the sword.
Note also Epicœne, IV, 2, for two cowards who are afraid
of each other.[1] Rawbone's substitution of Haver for him-

[1] The expression "molecatcher" (p. 410) is similarly applied in
The Ball, II, 2.

self has influenced The Witty Fair One, V, 2 (Treedle and
the servants). For the mention of "swordmen" (p. 412),
cf. A King and No King, IV, 3, V, 1, 3, Love's Cure, III, 2,
The Guardian, I, 1. It should be noted that this scene as
far as Lodam and Rawbone are concerned is a possible
source for A New Wonder: A Woman Never Vexed, III, 1
(1631), and The Combat of Love and Friendship, II, 4
(1636).

Sc. 3. Cf. Beauford and Sir John Belfare with Leonato,
Antonio, and Claudio, Much Ado about Nothing, V, 1. In
both the enraged father, whose daughter, deserted on her
wedding-day, is supposed dead, meets the bridegroom and
challenges him. Like the old men in Much Ado, Belfare
harps on his age and insists he is not too old to fight.
For the news of Gratiana's "death," cf. ibid.

Act IV, Sc. 1, which is concerned purely with the ad-
vancing of the action of the play, has apparently no parallels, save for the intercepted letter (see under Love Tricks,
II, 2).

Sc. 2 is concerned with Milliscent's telling Gratiana of
Marwood's part in her unhappiness.

Sc. 3. Lodam's sending Camelion (who is now in his
service) to look for Rawbone recalls Sir Hugh's asking
Simple to keep watch for Caius, The Merry Wives of Windsor, III, 1 (note also II, 3). Cf. Lodam's fright with Sir
Hugh's "melancholies," The Merry Wives, III, 1. Note
also Oliver's awaiting Young Flowerdale, The London
Prodigal, III, 3. The actual meeting of the combatants
seems to come from Twelfth Night, III, 4, IV, 1. Lodam's
surprise (after having been assured of Rawbone's cowardice) at the bravery of Haver in his master's clothes,
and his submission to him are close to Sir Andrew's going
in search of the disguised Viola whom he thinks a coward,
and his meeting instead Sebastian, her double, who, on

being attacked, beats him soundly.   Rawbone's imagining
himself tried and condemned for Lodam's murder (pp.
424–25) is utilized in The Traitor, III, 1.   Other comic
duels occur in Shirley's Contention for Honor and Riches,
Sc. 3, Honoria and Mammon, I, 1, Captain Underwit, IV, 3.
Cf. The Two Angry Women of Abington, IV, 3, The Fair
Maid of the West, Part I, II, 3, The Little French Lawyer,
IV, 4.   For Landby's eavesdropping during the scene, see
Chap. IV, Sect. 30.   Lodam's account to Landby of his
opponent's injuries is based on Bubulcus' story, Love
Tricks, IV, 6.   Cf. his giving up his sword with Device,
Captain Underwit, V, 1.   Both incidents recall Roughman,
The Fair Maid of the West, Part I, II, 3, Daw, Epicœne,
IV, 2, Protaldye, Thierry and Theodoret, II, 2, Bessus, A
King and No King, III, 2.

Sc. 4.   Beauford's melancholy is utilized in the suggestion of Aimwell's previous low spirits, The Witty Fair
One, IV, 1.   His ordering his lodging darkened so that he
may ''dwell in night'' has some affinity with Sir Solitary
Plot's habits in the later Example (I, 1, for instance).   A
parallel to Beauford's new way of living occurs in the
life of Marcellina while mourning her husband, as described in Monsieur D'Olive, I, 1, and represented, ibid.,
II, 1.   The entrance of Milliscent as Marwood's kinsman
and avenger seems related to Aspatia's appearance as her
own avenger in The Maid's Tragedy, V, 4.   Milliscent (or
Lucibel) postpones, however, her duel with Beauford, until
Gratiana shall have been cleared of the charges against
her.   Beauford's lamenting the supposed drowning of
Gratiana after he has learned of her innocence recalls Ger-
trude concerning Ophelia, Hamlet, IV, 7.   Note Cardona's
assertion of Gratiana's chastity, as a variation of The Gentleman of Venice, V, 2.   For the presence of Gratiana in
the chest, cf. The Bird in a Cage, IV, 2, and The Night-

walker, II, 3, as variations.   See also Fortune by Land and
Sea, III, 1, The Family of Love, II, 4, The Knight of the
Burning Pestle, V, 3.   Various instances of a similar use
of a chest occur in the continental prose literature of an
earlier date, generally in a comic manner.   For Gratiana's
resurrection here and that of Marwood, V, 2, following, see
Chap. IV, Sect. 29.

Act V, Sc. 1.   For Belfare's madness, see under Love
Tricks, II, 2, and cf. Leonora in A Very Woman, II, 3, and
Spinola in Imperiale, IV, 2 (1639).   His appearance with
Isaac and the Physician who comment upon his state seems
based upon Lady Macbeth's sleepwalking while the Gentlewoman and the Doctor watch her (Macbeth, V, 1).   Cf.
Belfare's ''To the mind you can Apply no salutary medicine'' with Macbeth's ''Canst thou not minister to a mind
diseas'd?'' *ibid.*, V, 3.

Sc. 2.   Landby's pretended opposition to the marriage
of Jane and Haver is later used in The Gamester, V, 2.
Note the parallels in Pericles, II, 5, and a Fair Quarrel,
V, 1.   If either of these is a source, it is the latter.   For
Beauford's trial, see Chap. IV, Sect. 17.   This scene is
used again in The Constant Maid, V, 3.   Marwood's oppor-
tune discovery of himself is paralleled there.   See also
How a Man May Choose a Good Wife from a Bad, p. 81,
The Blind Beggar of Bednal Green, III, 2 [3, properly],
The Fleire, V, The Coxcomb, V, 3, The Parliament of
Love, V, 1, The Goblins, V, 5 (1638).   Note the same in
The Deserving Favorite, V, 1 (1629), and observe the dis-
covery of the real murderers in The Lovers' Progress, V, 3.

Intercourse with the wrong man or woman, usually on
account of darkness, such as is revealed to have taken place
here, is found also disclosed later in The Arcadia, IV, 3,
and as pretended in The Gamester, III, 4, IV, 1.   Cf. also
Grim, the Collier of Croydon, II, 1, All's Well that Ends

Well, V, 3, Measure for Measure, V, 1, The Fair Maid of the West, Part II, II, 1, A Maidenhead Well Lost, IV (1633), Sophronisba, IV, 1, The Insatiate Countess, III (interrupted), The Hog Hath Lost his Pearl, I, 1, The Witch, IV, 1, V, 3, The Changeling, V, 1, A Game at Chess, V, 2, The Queen of Corinth, V, 4, A Match at Midnight, V, 1, The Parliament of Love, V, 1, Albovine, IV, 1, The Hollander, V, 1 (1635) (attempted), Alphonsus, Emperor of Germany, IV, 1 (1636?), The Amorous War, V, 8 (1639). Note also the appearances in Much Ado about Nothing, III, 3, although matters do not go so far as in the plays cited. For Milliscent as a woman in male disguise, see Chap. IV, Sect. 32. For the use of the title of the play, see Chap. IV, Sect. 31. See Love Tricks for epilogues by comic characters. Epilogues in prose (this to The Wedding is, save for a concluding couplet) occur in Endymion, Campaspe, Sapho and Phao, Gallathea, Midas, Henry IV, Part II, Antonio and Mellida, The Two Angry Women of Abington.

## II. THE WITTY FAIR ONE

There is no single source for The Witty Fair One. Apparently Bartholomew Fair furnished some hints for the plot which deals with Violetta and Aimwell, while Fletcher's comedies of intrigue (such as Monsieur Thomas) seem to have influenced the story of Penelope and Fowler. There are also what may be traces of a recollection of Middleton's comedies of London life (notably Michaelmas Term, and A Chaste Maid in Cheapside) in the play. The Brothers also exerts a strong influence upon the present comedy.[2]

[2] See Swinburne's damnatory remarks concerning The Witty Fair One, The Fortnightly Review, April, 1, 1890, p. 463. For an excellent judgement of Swinburne's appreciation (or depreciation) of

The plot of The Witty Fair One runs thus:

Sir George Richley has arranged a match between his daughter, Violetta, and a wealthy gull, Sir Nicholas Treedle. Violetta and Aimwell, a poor gentleman, fall in love. Sir George is warned of their affection by Brains, a confidential servant who guards Violetta. Her marriage is hurried along. Violetta forms a plot with Sensible, her maid, whom Sir George has dismissed as being privy to the love affair with Aimwell. Violetta goes out to shop, attended by Brains. Aimwell designs to kidnap her, but is forestalled by Treedle's Tutor whom Violetta has encouraged in his suit to her. When the Tutor attacks Brains before Sir George's house, Violetta runs in, and Sensible dressed like her former mistress comes out, and is escorted away by Brains after he has put the Tutor to flight. Brains is arrested for assaulting the Tutor who then takes the supposed Violetta away in triumph. Sir Nicholas sallies out, rescues Sensible, and immediately marries her, thinking her Violetta. In the meantime, Violetta has met Aimwell and they have been married. A rather loosely connected subplot deals with Fowler and Penelope, Sir George's niece. Fowler, who pretends sickness, is visited by Penelope. He tells her that the same remedy has been prescribed for him as the Jewish physicians prescribed for King David. Accordingly, they arrange an assignation. Penelope, however, on Fowler's appearance, attempts at first to put him to shame. Then she pretends to see signs of death in his face. He is treated as dead by his friends, in furtherance of Penelope's plot for his reformation, and goes finally to his own funeral. There, through Penelope's arraignment of him for his vicious life, he becomes penitent and receives her hand in marriage. The two other couples make their

Shirley, see Nason, James Shirley, the Annotated Bibliography thereto affixed.

appearance and Sir George is reconciled to his daughter and Aimwell, and Sir Nicholas to his wife, née Sensible.

From the above outline it will be seen that roughly Shirley's Aimwell = Jonson's Wellborn in Bartholomew Fair; Brains = Waspe; Sir George = Overdo; Treedle = Cokes; Violetta = Grace; and Sensible = Dame Purecraft. Cf. Violetta and her relations with Treedle, with Hilaria and Bubulcus in Love Tricks (see Chap. IV, Sect. 40, for analogues to Violetta, and Penelope as well, as witty young women). Note Blithe and Nehemiah in The New Academy (1628). For Treedle and his Tutor, cf. especially Tim and his Tutor, A Chaste Maid in Cheapside, Onos and his Tutor, The Queen of Corinth, Capritio and Miscellanio, Holland's Leaguer (1632), Asotus and Ballio, The Jealous Lovers (1632) (see also Chap. IV, Sect. 45). See under the discussion of Gorgon in Love Tricks for analogues to Brains. For Fowler as a vicious young gentleman, see Chap. IV, Sect. 38. For Sir George Richley, the overbearing greedy father, see Chap. IV, Sect. 42. Note Winnifride as a maid's name in Michaelmas Term, and Jack Drum's Entertainment. Cf. Sensible, as a feminine clever servant, with Nerissa in The Merchant of Venice.

Shirley uses the young man and woman who play various tricks upon each other, as do Fowler and Penelope, in the later Hyde Park, Example, and Constant Maid. Similar characters occur in The Ball and Captain Underwit, as well. Note also Maria and Petruchio, The Woman's Prize, the Lady and the Elder Loveless, The Scornful Lady, Frank and Jacomo, The Captain, Thomas and Mary, Monsieur Thomas, Dinant, Lamira, etc., The Little French Lawyer, Oriana, Mirabell, etc., The Wild Goose Chase, Clarindore and Bellisant, The Parliament of Love.

Act I, Sc. 1. Cf. Richley's description of Brains (p.

279) with the characterization of Waspe, Bartholomew Fair, I, 1.

Sc. 2. Gifford notes a likeness in the four lines of Aimwell's speech (p. 280) beginning with "Oh, my stars," to Helena's (whom he calls "Helen") " 'Twere all one . . . ," All's Well that Ends Well, I, 1 (Gifford seems to misquote Shakespeare in his citation). For Aimwell's application of Worthy's reference to cards to his own love-affair, cf. The Two Angry Women of Abington, I, 1, A Woman Killed with Kindness, III, 2, The Dumb Knight, IV, 1, The Spanish Curate, III, 4 (chess). Cf. Aimwell's florid description of Violetta's charms together with the same in III, 3, following, with Octavio's praise of Domitilla, The Royal Master, I, 2. Note The Wars of Cyrus, I, The Captain, III, 1, A New Way to Pay Old Debts, III, 1. His description of the effect of her singing upon the birds seems related to the contest of Parthenophill and the nightingale as described in The Lover's Melancholy, I, 1 (1628); probably the latter is the source. Worthy's character of Richley recalls Plenty's description of his mode of living, The City Madam, I, 2. Cf. also the characters, Chap. IV, Sect. 21.

Sec. 3. For the wit combats between Fowler and Penelope, here and in II, 2, see Chap. IV, Sect. 19, and cf. the later Gamester, III, 1. It is a development here from The Wedding, III, 2, apparently. Note also for the lady's part Love Tricks, IV, 1, The Wedding, I, 2, III, 2, as containing the germ of Penelope's wit. The lines beginning "Your hairs are Cupid's nets . . ." (p. 287), are found in two forms in Shirley's Poems (VI, 459 ff.). This is an evident satire upon Davenant. The lines are almost literally quoted from a speech of Florello's in praise of Bertolina, The Siege, IV, 1. Davenant's play under its earlier title, The Colonel, was entered for publication January 1, 1629–30,[3] so that it had been probably in existence for some little time. See under The Young Admiral, IV, 4, for a borrowing from The Siege. Other satire on Davenant occurs in Lady Alimony, I, 3 (1635) (Fleay, Stage, p. 358). Perhaps Habington's reference to poets "blemish'd with the stain Of impure life" (commendatory verses to The Wedding) is directed at Davenant whose features bore evidences of "impure life." It is going too far to say that Shirley hits at Davenant in his criticism of contemporary poetry (see under The Bird in a Cage, IV, 2). For this satirical courtly compliment by Fowler, cf. Angellina, The Sisters, IV, 2, and note Treedle, III, 2, following.

Fowler's views on women are drawn on by Horatio, The Duke's Mistress, II, 1 (see also Love in a Maze, IV, 2, V, 3) and on marriage by Carol, Hyde Park, I, 2. Cf. Frank, The Fair Maid of the Exchange, p. 14 ff. Gifford's "ridiculous pun" upon salad and sallet (p. 289) is paralleled in Henry VI, Part II, IV, 10. Note the reference to horseracing and Hyde Park (p. 290). Swinburne finds the source of Violetta's ambiguous message to Aimwell in The Fawn, III, IV (The Fortnightly Review, April 1, 1890, p. 465). See, however, the list of analogues in Chap. IV, Sect. 28, both for the message and Aimwell's interpretation of it.

Act II, Sc. 1. Cf. Mar-text, as Treedle's chaplain with Sir Oliver Martext, in As You Like It. Cf. Treedle and the Tutor at lessons with the disputation of Sir Boniface and Sencer, The Wise Woman of Hogsdon, IV, 1, and Tim Yellowhammer and his Tutor, A Chaste Maid in Cheapside, IV, 1. Note the reference to the expedition to the

[3] It did not appear, however, until 1673, in the Davenant folio.

Island of Rhé in 1627 (p. 293), and observe the Tutor's satire upon contemporary fashions (p. 294 ff.).[4]  For the latter, cf. the later Lady of Pleasure, IV, 2.

Sc. 2.  Brains' fears of a plot against him as guardian of Violetta are utilized in more detail in The Example, I, 1, etc. (Sir Solitary Plot).  His reference to Penelope as a sick maid that "wants a man to recover" her is employed in The Sisters, IV, 4 ("She is sick of the younger gentleman") and is paralleled in The Sad Shepherd, I, 2 ("She's sick of the young shepherd that bekissed her"). Note in connection with Brains' use of the word "kick-shaw" as a derogatory nickname (p. 299) that it is employed as a proper name in the later Lady of Pleasure (see also The Example, II, 1).  Note the reference to Dametas and Pamela in The Arcadia (p. 300).  An allusion to Sidney as a poet occurs in Love in a Maze, I, 2. For Brains' eavesdropping (at last successful), see Chap. IV, Sect. 30.

For Fowler and Penelope, cf. I, 3, and the later Gamester, III, 1, and see Chap. IV, Sect. 19.  Koeppel calls Clare's dubbing Brains "Old Truepenny" a recollection of Hamlet, I, 5 (Shakespeare's Wirkung, p. 56).  For Aimwell's character of Treedle (p. 306), cf. I, 3, and see Chap. IV, Sect. 21.  The passage is thoroughly in the manner of the character-books.  Koeppel, as cited above, parallels Aimwell's "He speaks words, but no matter" with the Queen's "More matter, with less art," Hamlet, II, 2.  The character is paralleled in Love in a Maze, I, 2.  Treedle's introduction is followed in manner in Love in a Maze, I, 2, and The Constant Maid, II, 1, where foolish suitors make their first appearances as such.

Act III, Sc. 1.  Cf. Brains' stealing Violetta's letter

---

[4] For his remarks on the study of other nations rather than England, cf. Freshwater, The Ball, III, 3.

with Edgworth's stealing the license, Bartholomew Fair, IV, 3. See under Love Tricks, II, 2, for the intercepted letter. For a somewhat similar bed-room scene, note the later Captain Underwit, IV, 5.

Sc. 2. For the reference to a "twelvemonth and a day" (p. 310), cf. Every Man in his Humor, III, 3. Love's Hue and Cry, the poem provided for Treedle by his Tutor, is found in all the collections of Carew's poems. It occurs, however, with some variations among Shirley's own Poems (VI, 410–11), so it may reasonably be called his. Hazlitt and Ebsworth, however, assign the poem to Carew (Carew's Works, p. 128, Carew's Poems, p. 180, respectively). See Vincent (Carew's Poems, p. 259) and Schelling (Mod. Lang. Notes, XI, 273 ff.), who consider the verses Shirley's. Two other poems of Shirley's, it should be noted occur in Carew's works. Cf. Treedle's betraying his not being the author of the poems with Montenegro, The Maid's Revenge, I, 2. Cf. Goosecap, Sir Giles Goosecap, V, 2. Cf. his buying his verses with the Compliment School, Love Tricks, III, 5. For Treedle's original verses, see Chap. IV, Sect. 22, and note Angellina's criticism, The Sisters, IV, 2. Cf. Fowler in I, 3. Treedle does not quote (p. 313) from the prologue to Cynthia's Revels, as Gifford, with his usual unscholarly inaccuracy, says, but from the epilogue. A possible reference to A Match at Midnight is made by Treedle (p. 313).

Sc. 3. For Aimwell on Violetta's charms, see under I, 2. Brains' exchange of the letters from and to Aimwell as revealed here and in Sc. 5, recalls The Widow, I, 1, 2. Cf. the shattering of Aimwell's expectations after his boasts to Clare with Jack Drum's Entertainment, II (Camelia's cold reception of Brabant). Note the laments over the faithlessness of lovers in Love in a Maze, IV, 1, and The Constant Maid, III, 4, IV, 1. Cf. Aimwell's resolution of

going to a tavern with Fairfield in the later Hyde Park,
IV, 1.

Sc. 4. Cf. Fowler's "illness," pretended in order to
work upon Penelope's sympathy, with that of Marc-
Antonio, Love's Pilgrimage, IV, 3. Note also the later
Captain Underwit, III, 1, V, 4, as derived from this scene.
Analogues more or less close occur in Englishmen for My
Money, V, 3, Sir Giles Goosecap, V, 2, The Fair Maid of
the Exchange, p. 49, A Mad World, My Masters, III, 2,
The Woman's Prize, V, 1, The Triumph of Honor, Sc. 1,
Monsieur Thomas, II, 1, II, 5, III, 1, 3, The Wild Goose
Chase, IV, 3, Rule a Wife and Have a Wife, V, 3, Greene's
Tu Quoque, p. 554, The Parliament of Love, IV, 1, 5.
Note Don Quixote, Part II, Chap. 21. Cf. Manly as a
doctor with the Cousin in Shirley's Constant Maid, II, 2,
and Fulbank in Honoria and Mammon, III, 5. Cf. the
similar disguises which occur in The Fair Maid of Bristow,
A Mad World, My Masters, III, 2, Amends for Ladies, V,
2, Match Me in London, V, The Wonder of a Kingdom,
II 1, III, 1, The Duke of Milan, V, 2, Goffe's Orestes, IV,
6, 'Tis Pity She's a Whore, II, 1, The City Wit, II, 2,
etc., V, The Northern Lass, V, 1, The Court Beggar, IV, 3.

For the pretended quickening of Fowler's pulse at Penelope's approach and Manly's diagnosis of his "sickness,"
cf. The Queen's Arcadia, I, 2 (where the agitated person
is neither ill nor pretends to be), and note Plutarch's Lives
(Demetrius), V, 412 ff., Bandello, Novelle, Part II, Novel
41, Painter, The Palace of Pleasure, Part I, Novel 27, Burton, The Anatomy of Melancholy, Part III, Sec. 2, Mem.
4, Subsec. 1. A parallel for Manly's prescription for Fowler's complaint occurs in The Virgin-Martyr, IV, 1. Cf.
also The Bible, Kings, I, I, The Seven Sages of Rome,
Tale VII (Senescalus), The Anatomy of Melancholy, Part
III, Sec. 2, Mem. 5, Subsec. 5. Penelope's questioning

Fowler as to his previous dealings with women is used again in The Ball, III, 4. For Manly's telling Aimwell's fortune, see under Love Tricks, V, 1, and The Maid's Revenge, III, 2. Manly's agreeing to poison Fowler is drawn on in The Constant Maid, II, 2. See also under The Humorous Courtier, V, 2.

Sc. 5. For the discovery of Violetta's letter, see under III, 3. Letters are delivered by characters who believe their contents to differ widely from what they really contain in The Lady of Pleasure, III, 2, and As You Like It, IV, 3. Cf. with Sensible's dismissal that of Felisarda, The Brothers, II, 1. Cf. Violetta plotting with Sensible the former's escape with The Brothers, IV, 3.

Act IV, Sc. 1. Cf. Sensible's revealing the plot for Violetta's flight with Jacinta's letter to Francisco, The Brothers, IV, 1. Note the parallel in Wily Beguiled, p. 295 ff., in which the Nurse tells Lelia of the plans for her escape to Sophos.

Sc. 2. For Violetta and the Tutor, cf. Lelia's encouragement of Churms in order to facilitate her flight to Sophos, Wily Beguiled, p. 298 ff. Note also Holland's Leaguer, V, 2 (1632). For Violetta's pretending love for Treedle in order to deceive her father, see Chap. IV, Sect. 6. Note Treedle's mention of the footmen in connection with Startup, The Constant Maid, II, 1. Cf. Treedle's allusions to the university scholars and their plays with Captain Underwit, I, 1. Note the mention of ''Bartholomew fairings'' (p. 333).

Scs. 3 and 4 represent Fowler's assignation with Penelope. Note his allusion to the Summer Islands, because of their relation to The Tempest, and to Waller's Battle of the Summer Islands. For his being received with music, see under The Grateful Servant, IV, 4, 5. See under The Traitor, V, 2, for parallels to the stipulation of darkness.

For Winnifride's "cold," cf. The Brothers, IV, 3. For the test of Fowler, announced, p. 336, see Chap. IV, Sect. 15. See under The Grateful Servant, III, 4, for Penelope's plot for Fowler's reformation. Fowler's making love to the (supposed) maid when at an assignation with her mistress recalls The Parliament of Love, II, 3. For his railing on the supposed Winnifride, cf. I, 3, and see Chap. IV, Sect. 20. Cf. Penelope's foiling Fowler's designs with Mrs. Wilding's plan, The Gamester, V, 2 (reported), The Little French Lawyer, III, 3, Rule a Wife and Have a Wife, V, 5, The Wonder of a Kingdom, IV, 1, The Captives, III, 3. Note also The Picture, IV, 2 (1629), News from Plymouth, IV (1635). Penelope's attempting to make Fowler believe himself dying has a general resemblance to the rejuvenating of Rufaldo, Love Tricks, I, 1. Closer parallels occur in the doubtful Love's Pilgrimage, IV, 3, Roister Doister, III, 3, Every Man in his Humor, IV, 6, Epicœne, IV, 2, The Woman's Prize, III, 4, The Humorous Lieutenant, III, 5, Rule a Wife and Have a Wife, V, 5. See also the Decameron, Day IX, Novel 3.

Sc. 5. Cf. the attack of the Tutor on Brains by taking advantage of which Violetta escapes with the onslaught of Knockem and Whit on Waspe while Edgworth steals the license, Bartholomew Fair, IV, 3. Note Miscellanio in Holland's Leaguer, V, 4 (1632), as an imitation of the Tutor. The substitution of Sensible for Violetta is based upon The Brothers, IV, 3. Cf. for Violetta's flight, Fair Em, III, 3, George-a-Greene, p. 260, Wily Beguiled, p. 311 ff.

Sc. 6. Cf. Brains's arrest immediately after the escape of his charge with that of Waspe after the loss of the license, Bartholomew Fair, IV, 3.

Act V, Sc. 1. Note Treedle's mention of his marriage license, and cf. Bartholomew Fair, I, 1, etc. For Treedle's

mention of the Prodigal Son in the hangings, cf. The Lady
of Pleasure, I, 2, The Constant Maid, I, 2, II, 1. Note also
A Mad World, My Masters, II, 2, If This Be Not a Good
Play, the Devil Is in It, pp. 325, 348 ff. (a prodigal in hell),
The Hollander, IV, 1 (1635). For the excitement concerning Violetta's escape, cf. A Chaste Maid in Cheapside, IV,
1, 2. Cf. Fowler's experiences while "dead" with Michaelmas Term, V, in which Quomodo prowls about to
see how his supposed death is taken. Cf. Fowler's striking the First Gentleman with Rodamant in the later St.
Patrick for Ireland, IV, 2, V, 1 (see parallels there cited).
For Fowler's characters of those he sees while supposedly
dead, see under Love Tricks, III, 5 (Infortunio in hell),
and see Chap. IV, Sect. 21.

Sc. 2. Treedle's desiring the Footman to kill the Tutor
recalls Rawbone and Haver, The Wedding, III, 2. For
the reference to the High German fencer, see under The
Opportunity, III, 1. For Treedle's stealing away the
wrong woman, see under The Brothers, V, 2.

Sc. 3. The epitaph on Fowler's hearse To The Self-
Loved Narcissus recalls Shirley's poem of Narcissus (VI,
463 ff.).[5] For Fowler's conversion, see under Chap. IV,
Sect. 10. For analogues to Treedle's marrying Sensible
in the belief that she is Violetta, see The Merry Wives of
Windsor, V, 5, A Trick to Catch the Old One, V, 2, Wit
at Several Weapons, V, 1, The Captain, V, 5, The Mad
Lover, V, 4, Rule a Wife and Have a Wife, III, 4, Holland's Leaguer, V, 5 (1635), Wit in a Constable, V, 1
(1639). Note that in The Brothers, V, 2, Estefania's disguise is penetrated before the wedding, as in The Guardian,
IV, 2. This scene is drawn on again by Shirley in Love

[5] Narcissus, the Fountain of Love, was assigned by Mrs. Burre
to John Spencer, July 3, 1630. What this entry in the Stationers'
register refers to is uncertain.

in a Maze, V, 5. See also Captain Underwit, V, 4, and
The Variety, V, 1. Note in regard to Treedle's calling
Sensible "lady-bird," the title given the disguised page in
Love in a Maze. Violetta in the expression, "wit without
Brains," perhaps refers to Wit Without Money.

### III.  LOVE IN A MAZE

It seems from the prologue and epilogue that The
Changes, or Love in a Maze, was written for the King's
Revels Company, who were acting at the time of its li-
censing (January 10, 1631–32), at the Salisbury Court
Theatre. The players were probably desirous of recouping
their fortunes by the presentation of a comedy from one
of the chief dramatists of the day (cf. Murray, Eng. Dram.
Cos., I, 219–20). The certainty of the acting of this play
by other than the Queen's Men in 1631–32 is a strong
point against those who argue that Shirley did not write
The Brothers in 1626 for the King's Company (see under
The Politician and The Brothers).

The plot of Love in a Maze runs thus:

Chrysolina and Aurelia, daughters to Goldsworth, both
love Gerard, a gentleman, who loves both but who cannot choose between them. Their ambitious mother designs
to marry Aurelia to Sir Gervase Simple, a foolish knight.
Thornay, who is privately betrothed to Eugenia, falls in
love with the sisters also. He and Gerard arrange that
no matter which the former shall select, the latter shall
be content with the remaining sister. Thornay pretends
that Chrysolina does not love Gerard but loves him.
Gerard now courts Aurelia. In the meantime, Eugenia is
designed by her uncle, Sir John Woodhamore, to marry
Yongrave, who loves her. She employs Yongrave to beg
Thornay, whom she loves, to return to her. Chrysolina
learns of Thornay's perfidy, and of Yongrave's nobility,

so she dismisses the former and begins to love the latter. Thornay now returns to Eugenia, while Yongrave consoles himself with Chrysolina. Out of love for Chrysolina, Aurelia has rejected Gerard, but learning of her sister's passion for Yongrave, she becomes reconciled with Gerard. Sir Gervase, meantime, having been refused by Aurelia is attracted by a page introduced as "Lady Bird" by Caperwit, a facetious poetaster, who is also a suitor to the sisters, and pays his addresses to "her." By the connivance of Yongrave Thornay is married to Eugenia. Gerard and Yongrave marry Aurelia and Chrysolina, while Sir Gervase who has gone through a ceremony with "Lady Bird" discovers "her" true sex, and is properly confounded.

Love in a Maze, which, as far as the intricate plot and tangled love-threads go, furnished some hints for The Court Secret,[6] shows a strong influence of The Lovesick Court of Brome (1627) upon the love entanglements of Gerard. Shirley has introduced new complications by the reversal of the situation (in Brome's play, a lady cannot choose between two supposed brothers), and by the introduction of new characters. For the foolish Mrs. Goldsworth, with her pressing Sir Gervase as a suitor to Aurelia, Eastward Ho appears to have been drawn upon. There seems in the entanglement of the love-affairs a suggestion of the typical pastoral (a form popular at court about this time). See Chap. III for comments on the fickleness shown by various characters.

For the simple Sir Gervase and his man Thump, the Page as Lady Bird, and Woodhamore as a tyrannical parent, see Chap. IV, Sects. 45, 41, and 42. Cf. Goldsworth with Touchstone in Eastward Ho. Note that he is prej-

6 Glapthorne's Ladies' Privilege (1635) is, in part, founded upon Love in a Maze.

udiced against Sir Gervase as the latter is toward Sir Petronel. Cf. Mrs. Goldsworth with the foolish ambitious citizens' wives, such as Mrs. Touchstone in Eastward Ho. Note also as parallels Fallace in Every Man out of his Humor, Chloe in The Poetaster, Mrs. Yellowhammer in A Chaste Maid in Cheapside, and Lady Frugal in The City Madam. Caperwit is later used by Shirley (with variations) in the Confident Rapture of The Example. Cf. Civet in The London Prodigal, Geron ("a humorous coxcomb and a scholar") in The Lovesick Court, Crazy in The City Wit.

Act I, Sc. 1. For the eavesdropping of Goldsworth and Woodhamore, cf. III, 3, IV, 1, 3, V, 1, and see Chap. IV, Sect. 30. The brief character of Simple (p. 277) is based on that of Treedle, The Witty Fair One, II, 2. See Chap. IV, Sect. 21.

Sc. 2. Note in connection with the dialogue of Simple and Thump, Treedle's "lesson," The Witty Fair One, II, 1. For the mention of the "gingling" of spurs (p. 277) cf. Every Man out of his Humor, II, 1, Monsieur D'Olive, III, 1, The Jealous Lovers, I, 2 (1632). Cf. Simple's introduction with that of Treedle, The Witty Fair One, II, 2. Simple's pun on the mullet in his coat of arms recalls The Merry Wives of Windsor, I, 1 (note Simple is there a servant's name). The little dispute between Goldsworth and his wife concerning Simple suggests Touchstone and Mrs. Touchstone regarding Sir Petronel, Eastward Ho, I, 1. Cf. also The Fair Maid of the Exchange, p. 59. Note for Caperwit's introduction, Haircut, The Lady of Pleasure, I, 2. Note the pun on "corantos" (p. 282), and see under The Gamester, III, 3. For Caperwit's compliments, cf. Fowler's satire, The Witty Fair One, I, 3, and note Confident Rapture in the later Example, I, 1. See also Device, Captain Underwit, II, 2. Koeppel derives Aurelia's playing on his salutation from Boyet's "daughter-beaming eyes," Love's Labor's Lost, V, 2 (Shakespeare's Wirkung, p. 59). For the reference to Sidney (p. 284), cf. The Witty Fair One, II, 2. Note the reference also to Chaucer. For Simple's bashfulness and his requiring his servant's aid in his courting (in II, 2, also), cf. Slender, The Merry Wives of Windsor, I, 1, Bubble, Greene's Tu Quoque, p. 556, Asotus, The Jealous Lovers, I, 8 (1632), Pupillus, The Noble Stranger, III (1638). Note also Belleur, The Wild Goose Chase, II, 3, Holdfast and Shallowit, Wit in a Constable, IV, 1 (1639), and Capritio, Holland's Leaguer, III, 3 (1632). Note that Simple, as before mentioned, is the name of Slender's servant and that Gervase is the Christian name of Bubble's man, both of whom encourage their respective masters in their courtships, as cited above. Cf. the compliments of Caperwit to Simple with those of Hedon and Asotus, Cynthia's Revels, I, 1. Cf. Simple's admiration of Caperwit's oaths with Every Man in his Humor, III, 1, A Fair Quarrel, IV, 1. The mention of Caperwit as a "vainglorious flash" (p. 286) recalls Sir Petronel Flash in Eastward Ho. See Histriomastix, II, 1, for an allusion to him. The situation of Chrysolina and Aurelia in love with the same man is a reversal of The Lovesick Court, I, 2, where Philargus and Philocles, supposed brothers, love the same woman. Gerard's inability to choose between the two is a reversal of Eudina's situation, *ibid.* Parallels are The Lovers' Progress, I, 2, The Two Noble Kinsmen, III, 6, IV, 2, Randolph's Amyntas, I, 1. Note also Antonio's hesitation between the sisters, The Maid's Revenge, I, 2, and Jacinta's pretense of wavering between her suitors, The Example, III, 1. See The Ball, I, 2, and Phillis of Scyros, II, 2.

Act II, Sc. 1. For Thornay's agreeing to bear Eugenia's love-message to his rival, Yongrave, see Chap. IV, Sect. 5.

Sc. 2.  Cf. the discussion by Chrysolina and Aurelia
of their love for Gerard with Philargus and Philocles, The
Lovesick Court, II, 1, where each woos Eudina for the
other.  Note The Ball, I, 2, for a use of this scene.  Cf.
Aurelia's offering to die for her sister (p. 295) with Philo-
cles' preferring death to the loss of Philargus' friendship,
The Lovesick Court, I, 2.  For the attempts of each to
resign Gerard to the other, cf. the later Gamester, IV, 2,
and the doubtful Phillis of Scyros, IV, 3.  See also, Chap.
IV, Sect. 4.  Cf. Gerard's soliloquy with that of Eudina,
The Lovesick Court, I, 2.  Their questioning him as to
which he loves and his answer are used in The Ball, I, 2.
Cf. Eudina's answer to Philargus, The Lovesick Court,
III, 3.  For Simple's courting Aurelia with Thump's encouragement, see under I, 2.  For his verses to her, see
Chap. IV, Sect. 22, and under The Sisters, IV, 2.  See
The Bird in a Cage, IV, 2, for the criticisms of poetry ut-
tered by Goldsworth and Caperwit.  Eckhardt considers
the word "hatch'd" (p. 301) as noted by Gifford, to be
derived from Troilus and Cressida, I, 3 (Archiv., CXVI,
408).

Sc. 3.  For the shifting back and forth of Gerard's affections between Chrysolina and Aurelia, see The Lovesick Court, II, 1, where Eudina accepts first one and then
the other of the supposed brothers.  Cf. also the spurious
Phillis of Scyros, III, 1.  For other occurrences of fickleness like Gerard's and Thornay's elsewhere in the play,
see Chap. III.

Act III, Sc. 1.  For Simple's courtship of Aurelia, see
under The Witty Fair One, IV, 2.  Note the later Con-
stant Maid, II, 3, and cf. Roister Doister, III, 4, Wily
Beguiled, p. 261, Wit at Several Weapons, I, 1, Women
Beware Women, III, 3, The New Academy, II, 1, IV, 1,
'Tis Pity She's a Whore, II, 6, The Ordinary, IV, 3 (1634),

The Lady Mother, III, 2. Koeppel derives Simple's use
of "brief" and "tedious" (p. 309) from either A Midsummer Night's Dream, V, 1 ("A tedious brief scene"),
or All's Well that Ends Well, II, 3 ("that's the tedious
and the brief of it") (Shakespeare's Wirkung, p. 60). For
what Aurelia might require of Simple, see under Love
Tricks, IV, 1, and cf. The Northern Lass, I, 6. For
Aurelia's pretense of affection for Simple (p. 310), cf. V,
1, and see Chap. IV, Sect. 6. Cf. the appearance of "Lady
Bird" with that of Estefania, The Brothers, III, 2. Her
entrance, which is a device of Caperwit's, suggests that of
Mariana (introduced in disguise by Pinac), The Wild
Goose Chase, III, 1. Cf. her opening speech with Meercraft's directions, The Devil is an Ass, II, 1. Note in connection with the "lady's" name and those of her relatives, Mrs. Fitchow and Widgeon, The Northern Lass.

Sc. 2. For Yongrave as Eugenia's emissary to Thornay,
cf. II, 1, and see Chap. IV, Sects. 3 and 5.

Sc. 3. For Chrysolina's eavesdropping, cf. I, 1, IV, 1,
3, V, 1, and see Chap. IV, Sect. 30. Yongrave's exposure
of Thornay to Chrysolina is used in a comic way in The
Example, II, 1. Note also The Opportunity, V, 2. Chrysolina's tolerance of Thornay is a sort of test of him and
Yongrave, for which see Chap. IV, Sect. 15.[7] Note that
by the end of this scene Simple, Caperwit, Thornay, Yongrave, and Gerard have been cast off by their mistresses.

Act IV, Sc. 1. Cf. Eugenia's mourning over the faithlessness of man with Gerard, V, 3, IV, 3, and see under The
Witty Fair One, III, 3. Here as in V, 3, songs are sung
to allay melancholy. For Chrysolina's eavesdropping, cf.
I, 1, III, 3, IV, 3, V, 1, and see Chap. IV, Sect. 30. Yon-

---

[7] Swinburne makes the unusually absurd statement that Shirley
was not a gentleman at heart because of Thornay's slander of
Eugenia (The Fortnightly Review, April 1, 1890, p. 469).

grave in the speech beginning "There's the honor of my service . . ." (pp. 330–31) paraphrases Foscari's soliloquy beginning "Lest my own passion . . . ," The Grateful Servant, III, 3.

Sc. 2. For Gerard's melancholy, see IV, 1, V, 3. Note Thornay's experiences at the university. His being intended for the church recalls Shirley's few years' experience as a clergyman, and causes one to surmise whether there may not be autobiography here. Cf. Gerard's ideal commonwealth with Horatio's railing, The Duke's Mistress, II, 1, or The Witty Fair One, I, 3, and see Chap. IV, Sect. 20. For Caperwit's criticism of masques in plays, see V, 5, following, The Royal Master, II, 1, The Bird in a Cage, IV, 2, The Coronation, IV, 3. Cf. the later Lady Mother, II, 1 (1635). Note in Chap. IV, Sect. 18, how Shirley introduced masques into his own plays.

Sc. 3. For Aurelia's misinterpretation of Chrysolina's previous speeches as revealed, p. 341, see Chap. IV, Sect. 27. See under The Constant Maid, I, 1, for Simple's quotations from The Spanish Tragedy, III, 2, 12. Cf. I, 1, III, 3, IV, 1, V, 1, for the eavesdropping of Caperwit and Yongrave, and see Chap. IV, Sect. 30. Note Caperwit's bombast (p. 343), and cf. Love Tricks, III, 5. For Simple's boasts of the favors he has received from "Lady Bird," see under Love Tricks, V, 3. See Chap. IV, Sect. 1, for Chrysolina's admitting to Yongrave her love for him.

Act V, Sc. 1. Cf. Woodhamore's surprising Eugenia and Thornay with Catalina's surprising Berinthia and Antonio, The Maid's Revenge, II, 2. For Eugenia's pretense of love for Yongrave to deceive her uncle, cf. III, 1, and see Chap. IV, Sect. 6. The trick by which the marriage of Eugenia to Thornay instead of Yongrave is accomplished seems suggested by A New Way to Pay Old Debts, IV, 1, 3.

Sc. 2 is principally concerned with the arranging for Caperwit's masque, V, 5.

Sc. 3. For Gerard's misanthropy, see under IV, 1 (Eugenia), 2, and cf. The Constant Maid, IV, 1. For the allusion to the golden arrow in the song, cf. The Virgin-Martyr, I, 1, as Gifford suggests, and see under Cupid and Death.

Sc. 4. The crossing of the stage by the various couples on their way to be married recalls the flight of Francisco and Jacinta, The Brothers, IV, 4.

Sc. 5. For Caperwit as a conjurer, see under The Maid's Revenge, III, 2. Cf. Mrs. Goldsworth's foolish interruptions with the comments of the Citizen's Wife, The Knight of the Burning Pestle. The *dénouement* of the play comes in Caperwit's masque, for which cf. especially A Woman is a Weathercock, V, 2, and The City Wit, V, in both of which cases of gulling occur. Note also the later Constant Maid, IV, 3, Northern Lass, II, 6, and Lady Mother, V, 2. See also under The Cardinal, III, 2, for the masque as a vehicle for various elements, and note The Hector of Germany, V, 5. For Simple's marriage to the Page as Lady Bird, see under Love Tricks, IV, 1, and for the exposure of his lies concerning his intimacy with "her," see *ibid.*, V, 3. For the evidences of Simple's having purchased his knighthood (p. 364), cf. I, 1, and note Sir Petronel Flash in Eastward Ho, IV, 1, Sir Abraham Ninny in A Woman is a Weathercock, I, 2, Sir Phillip Luckless in The Northern Lass, I, 4. See The Variety, IV, 1, The Fleire, III, 1, The Turk, II, 3 (and Adams' note thereto, p. 86), The Alchemist, II, 1.

## IV. HYDE PARK

Roughly, the difference between Hyde Park and The Witty Fair One is the same as that between The Scornful Lady and Monsieur Thomas. In place of the lady who

strives to escape the snares set for her by a debauchee, we
have the lady who is led by innate perversity to try to
escape marriage with an honest suitor. Note The Taming
of the Shrew (the lady is scornful after marriage, also),
Much Ado About Nothing, Greene's Tu Quoque, A Cure
for a Cuckold, The Little French Lawyer, Rule a Wife
and Have a Wife (here the wife learns to love her husband), The Combat of Love and Friendship (see *dramatis
personæ*) (1636), The Fool Would Be a Favorite (1638),
The Obstinate Lady (1638–39) (two representatives).
The Enoch Arden story which occurs in Hyde Park is
found also with variations in The Shoemakers' Holiday
(where Lacy is a name), What You Will,[8] The Witch, A
Cure for a Cuckold, A Wife for a Month (V, 3). Hyde
Park is one of a small group of plays dating from about
1632 and dealing with some London locality, the name of
which occurs in the title of the play. Cf. Bartholomew
Fair (1614), Covent Garden (1632), Tottenham Court
(1633), The Weeding of the Covent Garden (1632), The
Sparagus Garden (1635).

The plot of Hyde Park runs as follows:

Mrs. Bonavent, whose husband is thought to have been
lost at sea, consents to marry Lacy. Her cousin, Carol, a
witty young woman with three suitors—Fairfield, Venture,
and Rider,—attempts to dissuade her from marrying.
Carol is courted by Fairfield but jeers him, as she does
Venture and Rider. Fairfield resolves to tame Carol, so
he asks her a boon which she grants. This he reveals to
be that she shall neither love him nor ask his company.
On going to the races in Hyde Park, Carol sees Fairfield
with his sister whom she does not know. Becoming jealous,

---

[8] Swinburne (The Fortnightly Review, April 1, 1890, p. 470)
derives the return of Bonavent in the present play from What You
Will.

she sends for him, but rails at him on his appearance. To Carol's consternation, he departs in a passion. After the races, she receives a despondent letter from Venture in which he threatens suicide. She subscribes Fairfield's name to this and then sends for him again. She upbraids him for writing to her so, and then offers to make him amends. He is obdurate for a time, but finally yields and they arrange their marriage. In the meantime, the missing Bonavent has returned in time for his wife's wedding. After revenging himself for a slight put upon him by Lacy, he reveals himself to his wife, and later, in a masque, to the rest of the company. Also the jealous Trier who is betrothed to Julietta, Fairfield's sister, to test her introduces Lord Bonvile to her. Under a mistaken idea as to her position Bonvile makes advances to her which are rejected. He is converted by her defense of her honor. She ends her betrothal with Trier because of his jealousy, and at the close of the play is inclining toward Bonvile.

For Lord Bonvile, cf. the profligates listed in Chap. IV, Sect. 38. He is the first of Shirley's wild young noblemen in realistic comedy, such as Fitzavarice in The Example, and Lord A. in The Lady of Pleasure. For Carol, the sprightly witty young woman, her two foolish suitors, Venture and Rider, and the Page, see Chap. IV, Sects. 40, 44, and 48.

Act I, Sc. 1. The exposure of Carol's trick upon Venture and Rider, regarding their presents to her, with their jeering each other and Trier's merriment at their expense is drawn on in The Ball, III, 2. Note as a possible source, the exposure of the Duchess's suitors, The Humorous Courtier, V, 3. See The Example, II, 1. For Bonvile's crossing the stage, thus furnishing material for a brief characterization of him, see under The Politician, I, 1. Note that Trier uses the phrase "lady of pleasure" (p. 464) which is the title of a later realistic comedy (see also II, 3, following, and The Gamester, I, 1).

Sc. 2. Cf. Carol's sentiments on marriage (pp. 469, 475) with those of Fowler, The Witty Fair One, I, 3. Note also Meletza, What You Will, IV, 1. Carol's opinion of love (p. 470) is drawn on by Jacinta, The Example, II, 1. Cf. her reference to the "tedious tales of Hollingshed" (p. 471) with Miramont's "A dull old tedious ass; thou art ten times worse . . . than dunce Hollingshed," The Elder Brother, II, 1. Note the allusion (p. 471) to Cupid's Whirligig. See Chap. IV, Sect. 19, for the witcombat between Carol and Fairfield. Cf. especially The Scornful Lady, I, 1.

Act II, Scs. 1 and 2. For the appearance of Bonavent and his being forced to join in the wedding festivities of his wife and Lacy, cf. What You Will, III, 1.

Sc. 3. For Trier's test of the virtue and fidelity of Julietta, which begin in this scene, see Chap. IV, Sect. 15. Note, also, especially Fidelio's trial of Faustina, Holland's Leaguer, II, 2 (1632). Bonvile's conduct towards Julietta whom he thinks a prostitute recalls that of Clarindore towards Bellisant, The Parliament of Love, II, 3. Note that in Jack Drum's Entertainment, IV, Brabant Senior introduces Monsieur to his wife whom he has represented as a courtesan. Cf. the courting of Julietta's woman by Bonvile's Page with the addresses of Constantia as a page to Adriana, Ram Alley, I, 1. Note the later Gamester, II, 1, and Example, I, 1.

Sc. 4. For the railing of Carol and Venture and Rider, see Chap. IV, Sect. 20. Note that the ballad of The Devil and the Baker, mentioned, p. 487, is alluded to in The Bird in a Cage, III, 2. Cf. Fairfield's coming to take his leave with the Elder Loveless, The Scornful Lady, I, 1. His attitude of independence is that of Loveless, *ibid.*, IV,

1, V, 1. Note the reference to the brazen head (p. 488) and cf. Friar Bacon and Friar Bungay. A hint for his condition to Carol that she do not love him, etc., is found in The Brothers, III, 2. Cf. also The Lady Errant, II, 2 (1635), Wit in a Constable, III, 1, IV, 1 (1639), The Queen of Arragon, IV, 1 (1640). See under Love Tricks, IV, 1, also for stipulations. Note the mention of the Sparagus Garden (p. 490).[9]

Act III, Sc. 1. For Trier's eavesdropping, cf. III, 2, and see Chap. IV, Sect. 30. For Bonvile's advances to Julietta, cf. V, 1, and note The Parliament of Love, II, 3. Cf. Carol's jealousy of Julietta, whom she sees with Fairfield, with the Lady and Welford introduced by Loveless as his mistress, The Scornful Lady, V, 1. See under The Lady of Pleasure, III, 2, and cf. The Just Italian, II, 1. Note the footrace.

Sc. 2. Cf. Carol's scoffing at Fairfield after having sent for him, and so having discovered that his determination in II, 4, was pretense, with The Scornful Lady, III, 1, The Wild Goose Chase, IV, 1, 2, A Cure for a Cuckold, IV, 2. Cf. her reception of Fairfield with the Sister's of Courtwell, Captain Underwit, II, 2. For Trier's eavesdropping, cf. III, 1, and see Chap. IV, Sect. 30. Cf. the oration put by Carol in Fairfield's mouth with that of Depazzi, The Humorous Courtier, IV, 1. Koeppel derives the camomile comparison (p. 502) from Henry IV, Part I, II, 4, and cites a parallel to the figure in that play in The Miseries of Enforced Marriage, IV, 1 (Shakespeare's Wirkung, p. 70). Cf. The City Nightcap, III, 1, and Honor's Academy, Pt. V, p. 210 (cited by Scott [?], Anc. Eng. Dram., III, 335, note). Eckhardt draws the euphemism concerning the garter (p. 503) from Falstaff's reference to pitch, Henry

[9] For the reference to Spring Garden (p. 490), see under The Ball, IV, 3.

IV, Part I, II, 4 (Archiv., CXVI, 408). For Carol's geographical description of Fairfield, see The Comedy of Errors, III, 2, The City Wit, IV, 1, Holland's Leaguer, V, 4, and note The Anatomy of Melancholy, Part III, Sec. 2, Mem. 5, Subsec. 3 (cf. Eckhardt, as cited above). See under Chap. IV, Sect. 20, for the railing in this scene. Cf. Carol's remorse here and in V, 1, at her treatment of Fairfield with that of Lady Frampul, The New Inn, IV, 3, V, 1.

Act IV, Sc. 1. For the suggestive and appropriate cry of the cuckoo, here and in IV, 3, cf. A Cure for a Cuckold, V, 2. Note also Randolph's Amyntas, II, 5 (III, 3, 4, for other birds' cries). Fairfield proposes to elevate his spirits with sack (p. 509) as Aimwell does in The Witty Fair One, III, 3.

Sc. 2 consists of a soliloquy by Bonavent.

Sc. 3. This scene is memorable in being, according to tradition, the first in which horses were introduced on the stage (after the Restoration). Hence, Hyde Park is the ancestor of Ben Hur, The Whip, etc. Note that Kickshaw's ''horsemanship in Hyde Park'' is mentioned, The Lady of Pleasure, I, 1. The races are alluded to in The City Match, V, 2 (1639), and in Wit in a Constable, II, 1 (1639). Rider quotes Margery Eyre's ''But let that pass'' (p. 510), from The Shoemaker's Holiday (observe that Dekker's play contains an Enoch Arden story). For the cuckoo's cry, see under IV, 1. Venture's racing song may have been supplied or suggested by Shirley's patron, the then Earl of Newcastle. For the reference to the cup at Newmarket (p. 513), see under Captain Underwit, III, 3. Cf. Carol's commendations of the song and Venture's reception of them with Volterre, The Humorous Courtier, III, 1. Note the facetiousness of the Page (p. 515) as a sort of attempt at courtliness. Bonvile's description of the race (p. 519) which has taken place off-stage is related to the various narrations by a character on the stage to the audience of actions which could not be actually represented. Cf. Rudens, I, 2 (shipwreck), Soliman and Perseda, I, 3 (tournament), The Silver Age, III (death of the Nemean lion), The Brazen Age, p. 190 (hunt of the Caledonian boar), Fortune by Land and Sea, IV, 1 (sighting a sail), The Captives, I, 3 (shipwreck), Julius Cæsar, V, 3 (battle), King Lear, IV, 6 (Dover cliff), Bonduca, III, 5 (battle), The Double Marriage, II, 1 (sighting a sail), II, 4 (escape of a boat), The Sea Voyage, I, 2 (shipwreck), The Hector of Germany, IV, 6 (approach of a ship), The Prisoners, V, 2 (1637) (shipwreck). Note also Dick of Devonshire, I, 3 (approach of a hostile fleet). For the lines (apparently quoted) with which Bonvile greets the triumphant Jockey, there is no source. Note the lost play of Titus and Vespasian (Henslowe's Diary, p. 14) and various poems on the same subject at various times (Dekker's Canaan's Calamity, for instance). Note that Bonavent, like Freevil in The Dutch Courtesan, V, 1, makes his return known first to his wife but desires to remain incognito until he can work out certain plans. For his resurrection here (cf. V, 2), see Chap. IV, Sect. 29. Note especially also What You Will, V, 1, The Witch, V, 3, A Cure for a Cuckold, II, 3. For Carol's trick with Venture's letter, cf. the Duchess and the letter she causes to be forged as from Andrugio, More Dissemblers besides Women, III, 2.

Act V, Sc. 1. For Carol's change of heart towards Fairfield and her lamenting to Julietta her previous cruelty towards him, see under III, 2, and cf. Much Ado about Nothing, III, 1, The Dumb Knight, II, 1. The mention of the amended letter and Carol's despatching Trier in search of Fairfield as its author parallel the Duchess' actions,

More Dissemblers besides Women, III, 2, IV, 1, 2.   For
Julietta's defense of her virtue against Lord Bonvile in
the following dialogue, see Chap. IV, Sect. 9, and under
Love's Cruelty, IV, 2.   See under The Royal Master, III,
3, for Julietta's remarks on true nobility (pp. 529–30).
For Bonvile's conversion, see Chap. IV, Sect. 10.   Carol's
advances toward a reconciliation with Fairfield and his
cautious reception of them during most of the scene suggests the Lady and Loveless, The Scornful Lady, V, 1, 2.
For his raillery, cf. III, 2, and see Chap. IV, Sect. 20.   Her
production of the letter and his ignorance of it recall the
Duchess and Andrugio, More Dissemblers Besides Women,
IV, 2.   The text of the letter itself suggests Orlando Furio-
so's speech, Love Tricks, III, 5.   For the reconciliation of
Fairfield and Carol, note especially Benedick and Beatrice,
Much Ado about Nothing, V, 4, Aspero and Florimel, Hu-
mor out of Breath, III, 4, the Lady and Loveless, The
Scornful Lady, V, 2, Lessingham and Clare, A Cure for
a Cuckold, V, 2, Lovel and Lady Frampul, The New Inn,
V, 1.   Note also for the manner of their making their
match, Tissefue and Crispinella, The Dutch Courtesan,
IV, I.

Sc. 2.   Cf. Julietta's casting off Trier on account of his
constant jealousy with The Humorous Lieutenant, IV, 8
(not an exact parallel), The Bondman, V, 1, The Picture,
3, and note The Fool Would Be a Favorite, V (1638) (similar in the matter of rejection).   For the masque (such
as it is), see Chap. IV, Sect. 18.   Willow garlands are
worn by masquers in The Northern Lass, II, 6.   Cf. Sir
Giles Goosecap, V, 2, The Wild Goose Chase, IV, 1, The
Hollander, V, 1.   Cf. What You Will, V, 1, and The Shoemaker's Holiday, V, 2, for Bonavent's disclosure of his
identity.   See IV, 3, and Chap. IV, Sect. 29, for his resurrection.

## V. THE GAMESTER

According to Sir Henry Herbert (Officebook, as quoted by Malone, Shakespeare Variorum, III, 236), The Gamester is founded on a plot suggested by King Charles to the poet. Whether the King is responsible for the story of Beaumont and Violante or that of Wilding and Hazard is, of course, not certain. The latter has always been considered his, but there is no positive evidence of the fact.

Langbaine gives the source of the intrigue of Wilding, Penelope, etc. (III, 1, 4, IV, 1, V, 1, 2), as a story in the Ducente Novelle of Malespini (Part II, Novel XCVI), and also notes the occurrence of the tale as Novel VIII of the Heptameron of Marguerite of Navarre (Dramatic Poets, p. 479). The fact that a French Queen and French manners influenced the court of Charles I, and that the Heptameron furnished partial sources for Love's Cruelty and The Traitor makes it probable that we have in Queen Marguerite's novel the source for a part of The Gamester. There can, however, be no certainty as to the version of the story used, for, besides the form found in Les Cent Nouvelles Nouvelles (Novel IX), and the Decameron (Day VIII, Novel 4), there are many occurrences of it in Italian, French, and Latin (both in prose and verse).[10] For the various versions of the story see the Bibliophilists' Society edition of the Heptameron, II, 217–18 (Appendix A).

The plot of Shirley's play is as follows:

Wilding makes love to his ward, Penelope, who is related to his wife. She promises to yield upon the condition that he secure his wife's consent. Wilding asks his wife to urge his suit to Penelope, and she pretends to do

---

[10] Miss Ott grants that judging from the play, Shirley could have used the Heptameron, as well as the Ducente Novelle (Die Italienische Novelle im Englischen Drama, p. 118).

so, but, finding the girl obdurate, desires her aid in a plot for Wilding's reformation. Penelope then pretends to consent to her guardian's propositions and an assignation is arranged. Wilding, however, is gaming when the time to meet her arrives and, being unwilling to leave the dice, sends Hazard in his place, with the idea that the substitution would not be discovered owing to the darkness and silence stipulated by Penelope. The next day, Hazard boasts to Wilding of the pleasant evening he has spent, and then Mrs. Wilding upbraids her husband for his design upon Penelope and tells him that she had supplied her relative's place. In despair Wilding arranges a match between Hazard and Penelope, hoping that he may thus keep his predicament a secret. At last, he accuses his wife of infidelity, whereupon he learns that the two ladies had planned to receive him with lights and to attempt his conversion, but that on Hazard's appearance they had won him to take part in making Wilding think himself a cuckold. In the almost totally disconnected secondary plot, Beaumont is supposed to have slain his friend Delamore. Sir Richard Hurry, father of Leonora to whom Delamore is betrothed, proposes to obtain Beaumont's pardon if he will marry Leonora. He refuses to do this, although Violante, his mistress, offers to give him up in order to save his life. Delamore is announced then to be alive, and Hurry's proposition but a test. A farcical third story deals with the acquiring by Young Barnacle of a reputation for bravery, and the cooling of his "courage."

In Queen Margaret's tale (the version of the story which will be followed in this discussion) Sandras = Shirley's Hazard; Bornet = Wilding; a servant-girl = Penelope; and Bornet's wife = Mrs. Wilding. Shirley follows the story as told in the Heptameron fairly closely, where he uses it.

The situation of Beaumont seems modeled upon that of Beauford in The Wedding. There are also some touches from The Grateful Servant, apparently, both in the character of Violante, and in the relations of Wilding and his wife. Cf. Wilding as a dissolute husband with Lodwick in The Grateful Servant, and note Chap. IV, Sect. 38. For Hazard, "the Gamester," see the character so-called, in Essays and Characters (Bk. I, Character 15), by John Stephens, the Younger. Cf. Young Barnacle and his Uncle with Onos and his Uncle in The Queen of Corinth. See also Chap. IV, Sect. 45, for Young Barnacle and Dwindle. Note that Young Barnacle is Shirley's only genuine city-gull of the type of Brome's Toby in The City Wit, for instance. As has been noted (Chap. III), Old Barnacle is one of Shirley's few essays at a character definitely connected with business. For the Page, and for Penelope as a "witty fair one," see Chap. IV, Sects. 40 and 48. The injured and neglected Mrs. Wilding recalls Astella in The Grateful Servant.

Act. I, Sc. 1. The conversation of Wilding and Penelope may be drawn from the persecution of the servant-girl by her master in the Heptameron tale. There seems a recollection of Lodwick's pretended courtship of Astella (in earnest here), The Grateful Servant, II, 1. See also the courtship of Luciana by Antipholus of Syracuse, The Comedy of Errors, III, 2. Note Wilding's reference to subsidies (p. 188) as an allusion to a subject much before the public at the time of the play's presentation. For the eavesdropping of Mrs. Wilding, cf. IV, 2, and see Chap. IV, Sect. 30. Note that Astella eavesdrops in The Grateful Servant, as cited above. For the conversation of Mrs. Wilding and her husband, see under *ibid*. Wilding's asking his wife to procure Penelope for him recalls Lorenzo and Sciarrha, The Traitor, II, 1, and the parallels noted under that scene. Note also Fitzavarice and Lady Plot in the later Example, II, 1, Hippolito and Livia, Women Beware Women, II, 1, and cf. Mrs. Wilding's patience with that of Mrs. Arthur, How a Man May Choose a Good Wife from a Bad. Wilding's characterization of himself as a "coxcomb" (p. 192) may refer to the play of that name which bears some slight resemblance to The Gamester.

Note the pacific speeches of Wilding and Hazard (p. 193 ff.), as perhaps written in for the King's benefit. Cf. The Custom of the Country, II, 1, The Little French Lawyer, I, 1, and The New Inn, IV, 3. Note Old Barnacle on "blades" (p. 199) (for which see Chap. IV, Sect. 21).[11] For the uses of the term "lady of pleasure," cf. Hyde Park, I, 1. For the epithet to which Hazard takes exception (p. 195), cf. the Colonel and Ager, A Fair Quarrel, I, 1. Old Barnacle's reference to his cudgel-playing in his youth recalls Shallow's reminiscences, Henry IV, Part II, III, 2. Cf. Young Barnacle (described as a modest youth from the university) with Frederick in the later Lady of Pleasure, Tim in A Chaste Maid in Cheapside, Charles in The Elder Brother, Capritio in Holland's Leaguer, Holdfast in Wit in a Constable (1639). For Old Barnacle's plan to secure a reputation for bravery for his nephew, see under The Young Admiral, III, 1, and cf. The Imposture, II, 2 The particular source here is probably Bawdber's hiring De Vitry to submit to an insult from Protaldye, Thierry and Theodoret, III, 1.

Act II, Sc. 1. For Mrs. Wilding and the Page, cf. Hyde Park, II, 3. What she learns of her husband's habits agrees with the account of Bornet's infidelity in The Heptameron. Mrs. Wilding's laying her husband's suit before Penelope is ostensibly a courtship by proxy, but is really

[11] See also under The Ball, IV, 1.

a test (see Chap. IV, Sect. 15). Her asking Penelope to pretend to agree to Wilding's propositions is paralleled in The Heptameron. See under The Grateful Servant, III, 4, for the plot which Mrs. Wilding here sets under way for her husband's reformation. For Wilding's offer to kick his wife, see under Love Tricks, I, 1.

Sc. 2. See Chap. IV, Sect. 26, for drinking scenes. For the fiddler's entrance, see under Love's Cruelty, III, 1, and note the throwing of wine in Sueno's face by Haraldus, The Politician, III, 3. For the use of the word "scolopendra" (p. 213) see The Duke's Mistress, where a character bears that name. For the mention of "Erra Pater," cf. The Scornful Lady, IV, 1, The Elder Brother, I, 2, The Loyal Subject, III, 4, The Chances, IV, 3 (Erra Mater), The Queen, I. The quarrel between Young Barnacle and Hazard seems based upon Thierry and Theodoret, III, 1, where Protaldye, being affronted by De Vitry, strikes him according to previous agreement (see under I, 1). See The Young Admiral, IV, 1, The Doubtful Heir, V, 3, and The Imposture, V, 1, and note also The Fair Maid of the West, Part I, III, 2, Amends for Ladies, III, 4, Davenant's Siege, IV, 1.

Sc. 3 is occupied with Sir Richard Hurry's pretense at forcing Leonora to marry Beaumont.

Act III, Sc. 1. For the plans for the assignation of Wilding with Penelope, see under The Traitor, V, 2. The arrangements correspond with those in the Heptameron. Especially close analogues occur in All's Well that Ends Well, III, 7, IV, 2, Measure for Measure, IV, 1, and The Parliament of Love, III, 3. Mrs. Wilding's announcing to Penelope that she will meet Wilding in her place is paralleled in the Heptameron. For the witty passage between Penelope and Hazard, see Chap. IV, Sect. 19, and note The Witty Fair One, I, 3, II, 2.

Sc. 2. Old Barnacle's remarks on widows (p. 229) seem suggested by An Hundred Merry Tales, VIII, IX. Cf. Honoria and Mammon, III, 3. Koeppel, however, conjectures a recollection of The Wife of Bath's Prologue (Ben Jonson's Wirkung, p. 115, note). For the allusion to the Donzel del Phebo, see under The Maid's Revenge, I, 2. Note that Young Barnacle never appears actively engaged in wooing Leonora.

Sc. 3. For the crossing of the stage by characters who are commented on for the benefit of the audience, see under The Politician, I, 1. Here formal characters are given, for which see Chap. IV, Sect. 21. The description of the Lord is borrowed from in The Example, I, 1, and The Lady of Pleasure, I, 1. For his dancing while walking, cf. Sir Toby's advice to Sir Andrew, Twelfth Night, I, 3.[12]

The Coranto, which Young Barnacle reads as he enters, is mentioned in Love in a Maze, I, 2, The Ball, IV, 3, The Staple of News, I, 2, The Noble Soldier, IV, 2, The Late Lancashire Witches, prologue (1633), The Ordinary, IV, 1 (1634), The Lady's Trial, I, 1 (1638). See also "Corantos or Weekly News," Character XII, in Lupton's Country Carbonadoed and Quartered into Characters (1632), Jonson's Execration upon Vulcan, and A Young Man Courting an Old Widow, in Musarum Deliciae. A satirical comedy by Brathwaite called Mercurius Britannicus was printed in 1641. For the "news . . . from Terra Incognita," see The Ball, V, 1, The Example, IV, 1, V, 1, The Variety, I, 1, Law Tricks, IV, 2, Wit Without Money, II, 4, The Chances, III, 1, A Wife for a Month, II, 1, The Staple of News, I, 2, III, 1, News from Plymouth, IV (1635), The Ladies' Privilege (1635), I, 1 (Frangipan's news), Wit in a Constable, V, 1 (1639), The London

---

[12] See under The Ball, II, 2, for the jest upon his head of hair (page. 234).

Chanticleers, Sc. 6 (1637), The Obstinate Lady, II, 1 (1638–39). Note the satire on newspapers in Love Tricks, I, 1, and see The Example, IV, 1.

Sc. 4. For the various gamblers coming from play and discussing their fortune, cf. The Wise Woman of Hogsdon, I, 1. Gaming is represented on the stage also in The Nice Wanton, p. 465 ff., Michaelmas Term, II, 1, Your Five Gallants, II, 3, A Christian Turned Turk, I, 1, Valentinian, II, 1, A New Wonder: A Woman Never Vexed, II, 1, and is described in The Lady of Pleasure, V, 1. Wilding's sending Hazard to meet Penelope in his place differs from the Heptameron novel in that there the husband meets the supposed servant and then sends his friend in to her.

Act IV, Sc. 1. For the blustering Young Barnacle's being cowed by Wilding's Page in a false beard, see, as a source, The Queen of Corinth, IV, 1, where Neanthes' Page roars Onos into abject submission. Cf. also The Fair Maid of the West, Part I, II, 3, Bonduca, IV, 2, The Little French Lawyer, IV, 5, The Maid of Honor, II, 1. Note also V, 1, following, Love Tricks, II, 1, The Imposture, III, 2, etc., All's Well That Ends Well, III, 6, IV, 1, 3, A Fair Quarrel, IV, 4, Thierry and Theodoret, III, 1. Pistol in the Falstaffian plays of Shakespeare is alluded to in the dubbing of the Page Ancient Petarre (p. 246). The Page's disguise doubtless suggested Ascanio as a Swiss, The Opportunity, III, 1. For Dwindle's typographical figure applied to the Page (p. 247), see under Love Tricks, I, 1.

Mrs. Wilding's upbraiding Wilding for his profligacy and her informing him that she had taken her cousin's place on the preceding night are paralleled in the Heptameron as also her sprightliness, as noticed by Wilding (p. 249). For the last, see also under The Grateful Servant, V, 1. Shirley introduced no ring, however, as does Queen Marguerite. For the apparent intercourse by mistake, see

under The Wedding, V, 2. See under The Gentleman of
Venice, V, 2, for Wilding's conviction that he is a cuckold.

Sc. 2. For the prison setting, see Chap. IV, Sect. 14.
Cf. Hurry's attempt to persuade Beaumont to wed Leonora,
whose betrothed he has supposedly slain, with the Colonel
and his Sister, concerning Ager, who has wounded the
former, A Fair Quarrel, IV, 2. See also under The Maid's
Revenge, V, and The Court Secret, V, 2. For Violante's
eavesdropping, and her subsequent offer to release Beaumont in order to save his life, see Chap. IV, Sects. 30 and
4. Note also the later Court Secret, V, 2.

Act V, Sc. 1. In Wilding's suggesting to Hazard that
he marry Penelope as a reparation to her, there is a slight
suggestion of Beauford and Marwood, The Wedding, II,
2, but cf. Russell and Fitzallen, A Fair Quarrel, V, 1.
Note also the King and Montalto, The Royal Master, IV, 1.
According to Gifford, Hazard and Wilding refer (pp. 262–
63) to the same story as does Timon, Timon of Athens,
V, 1. Cf. The Gentleman of Venice, V, 4. Hazard's re-
ducing Young Barnacle to submission may be founded
either on Thierry and Theodoret, III, 1, where De Vitry
strikes Protaldye, on the ground that blows with the hand
were not in his contract, or on The Little French Lawyer,
IV, 5.[13] See under IV, 1, and cf. Every Man in his Humor, IV, 5, and Every Man out of his Humor, V, 5.

Act V, Sc. 2. For the pretended test of Penelope by
Hazard, cf. II, 1, later in this scene, and see Chap. IV,
Sect. 15. The "trial" of Beaumont before Hurry suggests
that of Beauford, The Wedding, V, 2. See also Chap. IV,
Sect. 17. Cf. The Wedding, V, 2, for Hurry's seeming
objections to Beaumont. For Hurry's giving Violante to

13 See under The Ball, I, 1, for the terming of Young Barnacle
a "shotten herring" (p. 266); and see ibid., IV, 1, for "let it go
round" (p. 267).

Beaumont, see *ibid.*, and cf. A Fair Quarrel, V, 1. Delamore's resurrection, as reported here seems based upon
that of Marwood, The Wedding, V, 2. See also Chap. IV,
Sect. 29. For Hurry's test of Beaumont and Violante (p.
276), see the beginning of the scene, II, 1, and Chap. IV,
Sect. 15. Cf. Wilding's accusing his wife of unchastity
with Mayberry, Northward Ho, I, 3. Cf. Hazard's account
of the reception prepared for Wilding at his rendezvous
with Penelope with that accorded Fowler, The Witty Fair
One, IV, 3, 4. For Hazard's assertion of the virtue of
Mrs. Wilding, see under The Gentleman of Venice, V, 2.
See Chap. IV, Sect. 10, for parallels to Wilding's conversion. The title of the play is used in the text, as well as
in the *dramatis personæ* for which, see Chap. IV, Sect. 31.

## VI. THE EXAMPLE

The Example, according to Stiefel, is based upon a Spanish original (Romanische Forschungen, V, p. 196, note).
However, as in all of Shirley's plays from foreign originals, incidents and characters from the native drama have
been drawn on.

The plot of the comedy follows:

Lady Peregrine, whose husband, Sir Walter, is with the
army abroad, is courted by Lord Fitzavarice. He offers
to cancel all of Sir Walter's debts which he has bought up,
and, in time, to pay the others, if she will gratify his desires. She refuses indignantly, and, on his offering violence, faints. Fitzavarice is now converted, and gives her
her husband's mortgage. On returning to England, Peregrine is informed by his wife that his debts are settled.
When he learns by whom, transported with jealousy, he
goes in search of Fitzavarice. He challenges the latter,
but, before they can meet in the field, is arrested for debt
through the machinations of Confident Rapture, Fitz-

avarice's parasite. On learning of Peregrine's imprisonment, Fitzavarice pays the debt for which he was arrested.
Now convinced of his wife's innocence, Sir Walter attempts
a reconciliation with his benefactor, but Fitzavarice, on
a point of honor, insists on the duel. Both are wounded,
honor is satisfied, and they become friends. Fitzavarice,
who has fallen in love with Jacinta, Lady Peregrine's sister, is betrothed to her. Jacinta has been courted by Vainman and Pumicestone, two foolish fortune-hunters, with
whom she makes sport during the play, while Confident
has wooed her with the intention of prostituting her to
Fitzavarice, if his suit had been successful. The humors
of Sir Solitary Plot, uncle to Jacinta and Lady Peregrine,
who suspects a plot in everything furnishes some of the
comic scenes of the play. He is cured of his suspicious-
ness by a plot of Jacinta's in which she employs Vainman
and Pumicestone.

Sir Solitary Plot is a Jonsonian humorist, pure and simple, founded, it would seem, upon Sir Politic Would-be in
Volpone. Like the typical Jonsonian character, his name
is descriptive of his humor. Mendoza in the later Court
Secret with his monomania is a personage of the same general type. Note Sir Solemn Trifle and Sir Furious Inland
in News from Plymouth (1635) as humorists who are
nearly contemporary. Lady Plot is a sort of first draft
of Lady Bornwell in The Lady of Pleasure. Cf. Levi-
dulche in The Atheist's Tragedy, and Corisca in The Bondman. For the dissolute Fitzavarice, the foolish lovers,
Vainman and Pumicestone, and the witty Jacinta, see Chap.
IV, Sects. 38, 44, and 40. Rapture is a combination of the
ancient parasite (note Scentlove, etc., in the later Lady
of Pleasure) and the wit (cf. Caperwit, Love in a Maze).
Cf. also Balbus, Proculus, Chilax, and Licinius in Valentinian, Timon, Charinthus, and Menippus in The Humor-

ous Lieutenant, Castruccio in The Double Marriage, Sorano in A Wife for a Month, Liladam in The Fatal Dowry.

For the use of the title of the play in the prologue, note III, 1, V, 3, and the epilogue and see Chap. IV, Sect. 31. Collier surmises that the four lines beginning "Nay, he that in the parish" are based on Heminge and Condell's preface "To the Great Variety of Readers" prefixed to Shakespeare's Comedies, Histories, and Tragedies (1623) (Hist. Eng. Dram. Poet., III, 347, note).

Act I, Sc. 1. For the opening of the play, cf. Match Me in London, I (opening). For Sir Solitary's manner of living, cf. Marcellina, Monsieur D'Olive, I, 1 (described), II, 1 (represented), Epicœne, II, 1, 3, III, 2 (note Morose cries "A plot! a plot!"). Note The Wedding, IV, 4. For Sir Solitary's "plots," note Brains, The Witty Fair One, II, 2, Fulbank and Maslin, Honoria and Mammon, I, 1, Asinus Lupus, The Poetaster, IV, 2, Sir Politic Would-be, Volpone, II, 1, IV, 1 (in each of these scenes a character named Peregrine is introduced), the Intelligencers in The Woman Hater, III, 2. Gifford asserts that Dormant alludes (p. 286) to Endymion in Endymion; note The Gentleman of Venice, V, 3. See under The Gamester, III, 3, for Dormant's little character of Fitzavarice (p. 287). Cf. The Lady of Pleasure, I, 1, Captain Underwit, I, 1, and note Chap. IV, Sect. 21. See under The Politician, I, 1, for Lady Plot's crossing the stage with Confident while her husband watches them and comments on their conversation. Cf. his eavesdropping with V, 3, and see Chap. IV, Sect. 30. The Page's conversation with Lady Peregrine recalls Hyde Park, II, 3, and The Gamester, II, 1. For Confident's wooing Lady Peregrine as Fitzavarice's proxy, see under Chap. IV, Sect. 3. See Chap. IV, Sect. 21, for his character of Fitzavarice (although it is not typical, but rather individual). Cf. Hippolito, Love's Cruelty, IV, 2, for Confident's making love to the lady on his own account, and cf. Maria on tasters in the later Lady of Pleasure, II, 2. See under The Humorous Courtier, I, 1, II, 2, etc., for Jacinta's encouragement of him. For the attempt of Fitz- · avarice to use Peregrine's debts as a means of gaining a hold on his wife, see under The Duke's Mistress, IV, 1.

Act II, Sc. 1. For the bargain of Vainman and Pumice-stone as to their courting of Jacinta, cf. as a source Ubaldo and Ricardo, The Picture, III, 6. Note later Topsail and Cable, News from Plymouth, II (1635), Orco and Androlio, The Distresses, I, 1 (1639?). For the use of "kick-shaw" (p. 297), cf. The Witty Fair One, II, 2, and note Kickshaw in The Lady of Pleasure. Note the attitude of Lady Plot towards Fitzavarice as repeated with Lady Born-well and Lord A., The Lady of Pleasure. Lady Plot's assisting Fitzavarice in his pursuit of Lady Peregrine recalls Livia in Women Beware Women, II, 1. Note Mrs. Wilding's pretense of aiding her husband with Penelope, The Gamester, I, 1.[14] For the alchemical terminology addressed to Jacinta (p. 304), cf. The Alchemist, II, 1, as Gifford suggests. For her witty passages with Fitzavarice, see Chap. IV, Sect. 19. See under Hyde Park, I, 2, for her sentiments on marriage (pp. 304–05). The attempts of Pumicestone and Vainman in turn each to injure the other in Jacinta's opinion are drawn from The Ball, III, 3. For similar incidents, see The Lady of Pleasure, II, 1, The Constant Maid, I, 2. Gifford notes under the former, The Picture, IV, 2, as a source. It is the source probably for the entire group in Shirley, although cf. Wit at Several Weapons, I, 1. Note Cartwright's Siege, IV, 1 (1637). For her playing off the two suitors against each other, see under Hyde Park, I, 1. Jacinta refers (p. 309) to a speech of Falstaff's, Henry IV, Part I, II, 4. Cf. The

14 For the siege figure (p. 302), see under The Ball, II, 2.

Shakespeare Allusion Book, I, 391, 283, 223, and Koeppel, Shakespeare's Wirkung, p. 77. See also The Humorous Lieutenant, IV, 2.

Sc. 2. Cf. II, 1, for Lady Plot's assisting Fitzavarice in his designs upon her niece.

Act III, Sc. 1. For Fitzavarice's advances to Lady Peregrine and her defense of her chastity, see Chap. IV, Sect. 9, and under Love's Cruelty, IV, 2. Note the use of the title in the text (p. 313), and cf. the prologue, V, 3, and the epilogue (see Chap. IV, Sect. 31). For Fitzavarice's use of the dagger, cf. Greene's Tu Quoque, p. 569, and see under The Traitor, III, 3. See under St. Patrick for Ireland, III, 2, for his attempt at rape. For his pretense of having been testing Lady Peregrine, see Chap. IV, Sect. 16, and cf. IV, 2. Ward mentions Lady Peregrine's dream (p. 315) in connection with The White Devil, I, 2 (Hist. Eng. Dram. Lit., III, 111, note). For the conversion of Lord Fitzavarice, see Chap. IV, Sect. 10. See under Love in a Maze, I, 2, for Jacinta's pretended inability to choose between Vainman and Pumicestone, and observe that she proposes a test for them. Cf. Peregrine's jealousy on learning of Fitzavarice's gifts to Lady Peregrine with that of Othello, Othello, IV, 1, etc., Orleans, The Honest Man's Fortune, I, 2, Gomera, The Knight of Malta, III, 2, Foreste, The Cruel Brother, IV, 1 (possibly a source). See under The Gentleman of Venice, V, 2, for Peregrine's thinking himself a cuckold. Gifford notes the allusion to Tilly (p. 328).

Act IV, Sc. 1. For the Page's use of "soldad," see under The Humorous Courtier, II, 2. Cf. III, 1, IV, 2, for Fitzavarice's test of Confident, and see Chap. IV, Sect. 15. Note the King's test of Montalto, The Royal Master, IV, 1. Confident's expression of his willingness, should he win her, to prostitute Jacinta to Fitzavarice recalls Allwit

in A Chaste Maid in Cheapside, and Knavesby in Anything
for a Quiet Life.   See also under The Gentleman of Venice,
IV, 3.   For Confident's plotting the arrest of Peregrine
to prevent the duel with Fitzavarice, cf. If You Know Not
Me, You Know Nobody, Part II, p. 273 ff.   For the reference to Gallobelgicus (p. 335), cf. The Poetaster, V, 3, The
Heir, I, The Fair Maid of the Inn, IV, 2, The Hollander,
III, 1 (1635), Wit in a Constable, I, 1 (1639), note Howell's
Familiar Letters, I, 231, and see under Love Tricks, I, 1,
and The Gamester, III, 3.   An allusion to Wallenstein (p.
335) is noted by Gifford.   See under The Bird in a Cage,
IV, 1, for extended allusions to contemporary events.   The
arrest of Peregrine seems to be based upon that of Proudly,
who is arrested by prearrangement (but without the com-
plicity of his adversary) as he is about to fight a duel,
Amends for Ladies, IV, 3.   Cf. also The Roaring Girl,
III, 3, A Fair Quarrel, I, 1.

   Sc. 2.   For the comic test of Vainman and Pumicestone
set under way in this scene by Jacinta,,cf. III, 1, IV, 1, and
see Chap. IV, Sect. 15.   The source of her requiring dumb-
ness of Vainman is, as the reference to that play (p. 337)
suggests, The Dumb Knight, II, 1 (silence is there required
of Phylocles, not Pyrocles, as Gifford's note states).   Cf.
for a comic test, Cartwright's Siege, IV, 6 (1637), and for
the imposition of silence partial or entire, A Shoemaker a
Gentleman, I, 3, III, 1, and The Combat of Love and
Friendship, II, 4 (1636).   Cleora in The Bondman, II, 1,
vows not to speak until her lover's return.   Note also The
Queen, II, and The Fool Would Be a Favourite, IV (1638).
An ultimate source in English is perhaps The Cruelty of a
Widow, etc., Fenton's Tragical Discourses, Discourse XI.
Shirley has comic conditions in Love Tricks, IV, I, The
Witty Fair One, III, 4, Hyde Park, II, 4, The Ball, III, 4.
For Confident's informing Fitzavarice (p. 341) of Pere-

grine's arrest, note Amends for Ladies, IV, 3 (the reception of the informants in the two plays differs).

Sc. 3. For the prison-setting (an under-sheriff's house), see Chap. IV, Sect. 14. Cf. Peregrine's release through the efforts of Fitzavarice with that of Mountford in A Woman Killed with Kindness, IV, 2, and of Charlemont, The Atheist's Tragedy, III, 3. With V, 2, cf. the persuading of Peregrine to a duel with Fitzavarice with A Fair Quarrel, II, 1, III, 1, A Cure for a Cuckold, III, 1, A Very Woman, I, 1. Note also The Wedding, II, 2, and The Court Secret, IV, 2.

Act V, Sc. 1. For Vainman as an "ambassador from Dumbland," cf. Mute and Morose, Epicœne, II, 1. The attempt at curing Sir Solitary of his mania is derived possibly from Peregrine's trick upon Sir Politic, Volpone, V, 2. The trick upon Sir Solemn, News from Plymouth, V (1635), is based on this scene. For masquerading before a monomaniac, see under Love Tricks, III, 5.

Sc. 2. Note that, as in The Maid's Revenge, IV, 3, the duellists (Peregrine and Fitzavarice) are related through the affection of the latter for Jacinta. Like Proudly, Amends for Ladies, IV, 3, Fitzavarice has no second. See under IV, 3, for the persuading of Peregrine to fight.

Sc. 3. For the eavesdropping, cf. I, 1, and see Chap. IV, Sect. 30. Cf. the prologue and III, 1, for the occurrence of the title in the text here and in the epilogue, and see Chap. IV, Sect. 31. For the reconciliation of Sir Solitary and Lady Plot, see the later Lady of Pleasure, V, 1.

## VII. THE LADY OF PLEASURE

The Lady of Pleasure reverses The Grateful Servant and The Gamester, in which a husband is reformed by his wife's plot. In this comedy it is the wife who is brought to repentance by the contrivances of her husband. The

play seems influenced most by The Noble Gentleman and
The Just Italian. The parallels will be shown in the
course of the discussion.

The plot of the play follows:

Lady Bornwell, who has persuaded her husband, Sir
Thomas, to reside in London, plunges into the pleasures
and dissipations of city life with such eagerness, that he
warns her his estate will not bear her extravagances. She
refuses to limit her expenses, whereupon Sir Thomas resolves to cure her of her extravagance by pretending to
become dissipated also. To arouse his wife's jealousy he
pays court to Celestina, a rich young widow who is attracting attention by her reckless expenditures. Unknown
to Lady Bornwell, Decoy, a bawd, tries to arrange a meeting between the former and her kinsman, Lord A. He
sends a letter to Lady Bornwell in which he warns her
against Decoy. However, Lady Bornwell uses Decoy to
arrange a meeting for her with Kickshaw, a worthless gallant. The assignation is kept but without Kickshaw's
learning who it is that has favored him. Instead of keeping silent about his mysterious mistress as he had promised,
Kickshaw boasts of his amour. This, together with some
twinges of conscience, some jealousy of Celestina, and the
announcement by Sir Thomas that their estate will be exhausted in a month, causes Lady Bornwell to become penitent for her past way of living. In the meantime, Lord A.
has visited Celestina, whose beauty he has heard praised,
and has been attracted to her. She tests him and finds
him disloyal for the time being to his dead love, Bella-
Maria. He makes dishonorable advances to Celestina
which she repulses in such a way as to convert him.

For Lord A., cf. Bonvile in Hyde Park, and Fitzavarice
in The Example, and see Chap. IV, Sect. 38. His clients,
Scentlove, Kickshaw, and Littleworth belong to the same

class as Venture and Rider in Hyde Park, for whom see
Chap. IV, Sect. 44. Littleworth, it should be noted, is the
name of the disguised Meanwell in The Ordinary (1634).
The relations of Lady Bornwell (who has been mentioned
in connection with Lady Plot in The Example) and Littleworth may have been developed from those of Marine's
Wife and the Gentleman in The Noble Gentleman or of
Alteza and Sciolto in The Just Italian. Her extravagance,
and that of Celestina, recalls the profusion of Timon,
Timon of Athens, and of Torrenti, The Wonder of a Kingdom (see under I, 1, of Shirley's play).

In Haircut, the barber, who masquerades as a courtier
is an early example of what was afterwards a familiar
figure—the menial as a gentleman (this does not consider
exchanged identity, as in Supposes, The Taming of the
Shrew, etc.). Barbers occur in Midas, The Dutch Courtesan, Epicœne, The Staple of News, Monsieur Thomas, The
Knight of the Burning Pestle, The Fatal Dowry, The Lovesick Court, The Fancies Chaste and Noble (1635). Note
that Haircut is neither a poltroon, nor a gull. Decoy, the
procuress, is, unless we include the Maquerelle in The Triumph of Peace, the only person of her profession introduced in Shirley's plays. Cf. Splay in How a Man May
Choose a Good Wife from a Bad, Mrs. Drury in A Warning for Fair Women, the Abbess in The Death of Robert,
Earl of Huntington, Maquerelle in The Malcontent, Faugh
in The Dutch Courtesan, Cataplasma in The Atheist's
Tragedy, Mrs. Overdone in Measure for Measure, the Bawd
in Pericles, Birdlime in Westward Ho, Mrs. Horseleech in
The Honest Whore, Part II, the Old Lady in Match Me
in London, Mother Gruel in Michaelmas Term, the Courtesan in A Mad World, My Masters, Collaquintida in The
Dumb Knight, Sweatman in Greene's Tu Quoque, Madam
Gulman in The Poor Man's Comfort, Ardelia and Phorba

in Valentinian, the Bawd in The Chances, Sulpitia in The
Custom of the Country, Leucippe in The Humorous Lieu-
tenant, Cassandra in A Wife for a Month, the Bawd in
The Royal King and Loyal Subject, Mildew (a male bawd)
in The Captives, Scapha in The English Traveller, Malaena
in All's Lost by Lust, Secret in The City Madam, the
Bawd in The Unnatural Combat, Calipso in The Guardian,
Mrs. Coote in A Match at Midnight, Timpanina in The
City Nightcap, the Bawd in Holland's Leaguer, Shaparoon
in The Queen, Olympia in The Princess (1637), Veneria in
Messallina (1637).

Act I, Sc. 1. For the allusion to "Sellenger's Round,"
cf. The Fair Maid of the West, Part II, II, 1, The Late
Lancashire Witches, III, 1, The Court Beggar, V, 2, and
see p. 79, The World's Olio of Margaret Duchess of New-
castle (quoted by Firth, Life of the same, p. 157, note).
See The Noble Gentleman, I, 1, II, 1, and The Just Italian,
I, 1, as sources for the Steward's and Bornwell's expostu-
lations on Lady Bornwell's lavishness. Cf. also Timon of
Athens, II, 2, The Scornful Lady, I, 2, Wit without Money,
I, 1, The Elder Brother, I, 1, The Parliament of Love, I, 4,
The English Traveller, I, 2. The incident is used again in
Captain Underwit, I, 1. See also I, 2, following. For
the extravagance of Lady Bornwell as described by her
husband, cf. The Constant Maid, I, 2, Anything for a Quiet
Life, I, 1, IV, 1 (pretended), and The Wonder of a Kingdom, III. Note the references to The Ball and The Family
of Love (p. 9), and cf. Captain Underwit, I, 1. For Decoy
and Lady Bornwell, cf. III, 2, and note Calipso and Iölante,
The Guardian, I, 2. See under The Example, I, 1, for the
little descriptions of Kickshaw and Littleworth by the
Steward and cf. II, 2, III, 2. See for characters, Chap. IV,
Sect. 21. Kickshaw, Littleworth and Lady Bornwell concerning Celestina (p. 14) recalls Lucio, etc., regarding

Mariana, Measure for Measure, V, 1. Bornwell's announcing that he will outdo his wife in revelry and her reception of the news seem based upon Altamont and Alteza, The Just Italian, I, 1. Cf. also Clerimont's changing his manner of living, The Noble Gentleman, III, 1.

Sc. 2. For the expostulations of Celestina's Steward concerning his mistress' extravagance, see under I, 1. Celestina's ordering new appointments for her coach suggests Maria, The Woman's Prize, III, 2. Gifford notes in connection with the gold-shod running-horse (p. 19), the mention of "Toby with his golden shoes," Hyde Park, IV, 3. For the allusion (p. 19) to the Prodigal Son in needle-work, cf. that to Joseph (p. 17), and see under The Witty Fair One, V, 1. Haircut's introduction of himself as a wooer recalls Caperwit, Love in a Maze, I, 2.

Act II, Sc. 1. Bornwell's soliloquy in which he announces that he will attempt to cure his wife's extravagance recalls The Grateful Servant, III, 2, and the plans for reclamations of persons there listed. For the arrival of Frederick from the university, cf. A Chaste Maid in Cheapside, III, 2, The Elder Brother, I, 2, The Muse's Looking-glass, IV, 2. Note Young Barnacle, The Gamester, I, 1 (reported return from the university). See under The Humorous Courtier, IV, 1, for the reference to the foreign artist (p. 25). Note in connection with Lady Bornwell's opinion of Frederick, Old Barnacle concerning his nephew, The Gamester, I, 1. Cf. also Sebastian's opinion of Thomas, Monsieur Thomas, I, 2.

Sc. 2. For the characters of Scentlove and Haircut by Celestina, cf. I, 1, III, 2, and see Chap. IV, Sect. 21. Note Confident, The Example, I, 1, for Maria's remark concerning tasters (p. 295). See under The Example, II, 1, for the attempts of Haircut and Scentlove to discredit each other before the ladies. Gifford suggests that Celestina borrows from Sophia in The Picture, IV, 2. Gifford's "allusion" to Henry IV, Part I, II, 2, is not well founded. The "fretting" of "gummed velvet" is frequently alluded to in Elizabethan plays. Cf. The Ball, IV, 1, Henry IV, Part I, II, 2, The Malcontent, I, 1, The Woman Hater, IV, 2.[15]   For the repartee between Bornwell and Celestina, see Chap. IV, Sect. 19.

Act III, Sc. 1.   For Lord A. at his toilet, cf. The Humorous Courtier, V, 2, A Woman is a Weathercock, I, 2, The Fatal Dowry, IV, 1, The Bashful Lover, V, 1, The Staple of News, I, 1.   For the use of the title of the play in the text, see Chap. IV, Sect. 31, and note Hyde Park, I, 1, II, 3, The Gamester, I, 1.   See under The Opportunity, IV, 1, for the dictated letter.   Lord A.'s remaining faithful to the memory of Bella-Maria is utilized in The Royal Master, V, 2.   Note as a source, The Great Duke of Florence, I, 2.   The speech beginning "Bid her appear in all the ornaments . . ." (p. 49) is based on Tamburlaine, Part I, V, 2 ("If all the pens . . .").   Cf. The Iron Age, Part II, V, 1.

Sc. 2.   For Decoy's delivering a letter the contents of which differ much from what she thinks, cf. The Witty Fair One, III, 5.   Bornwell's attempting to make his wife jealous by introducing Celestina is based apparently upon The Just Italian, II, 1.   Alteza in that play does not become jealous, and like Lady Bornwell she resorts to a lover.   Cf. Hyde Park, III, 1.   For the characters of the wits (p. 52), cf. I, 1, II, 2, and see Chap. IV, Sect. 21. Probably a contemporary application.   For the plot against Celestina, see The Ball, III, 2.   The conversation in French between Lady Bornwell and Celestina is paralleled in Henry V, III, 4, IV, 4, V, 2, and The Hollander, II, 1 (1635) (not in substance).   Frederick's answering Celes-

---

[15] See Parrott, Chapman's Comedies, p. 879.

tina in Latin when she speaks to him in French parallels
Tim's wooing the Welshwoman in Latin, A Chaste Maid in
Cheapside, IV, 1. Cf. Kataplectus, The Muse's Looking-
glass, IV, 2, and note that in all three plays the hearers are
horrified by the display of learning. For Frederick's
parody of a passage in The Spanish Tragedy, II, 1, note
V, 1, and see under The Constant Maid, I, 1. The jeering
of Celestina by Kickshaw and Littleworth, and Bornwell's
defense of her are based on The Ball, III, 4. For the
jeering and the eavesdropping of Bornwell, see Chap. IV,
Sects. 20 and 30.

Act IV, Sc. 1, is based directly upon The Grateful Servant, IV, 4, 5. For Kickshaw's entering blindfolded, see
under The Gentleman of Venice, III, 3. See under The
Traitor, V, 2, for the assignation in darkness. Decoy disguised as an old woman recalls Flavia, The Young
Admiral, IV, 1. Her pretended relations with devils or
succubae are related to Belinda's disguise, The Grateful
Servant, IV, 5. Note also Erectho, Sophronisba, IV, 1,
and the Succubus, A Mad World, My Masters, IV, 1. For
Kickshaw's description of Decoy (pp. 64–65), cf. Horatio,
The Duke's Mistress, III, 2, IV, 1. Note that in the first
scene cited the expression "good madam Kickshaw" occurs. Decoy's assurance that she will change in appearance suggests the "Loathly Lady" story (cf. the ballad
of The Marriage of Sir Gawaine, and Women Pleased.
Note Erectho, Sophronisba, IV, 1). For her expatiation
on the delights of love, cf. The Grateful Servant, IV, 5,
and for the allusion to Venus and Adonis, see under The
Doubtful Heir, IV, 2. (All points of resemblance to The
Grateful Servant, IV, 4, 5, have not been noted).

Sc. 2. Cf. Littleworth on dress and fashions with
The Witty Fair One, II, 1. For the satire on pandering
and preferment at court, see under Love's Cruelty, I, 2,

and note, for instance, The Fancies Chaste and Noble, I, 1, 3 (1635). Koeppel says that the Steward's allusion to "Sir Pandarus" (p. 69) refers to Troilus and Cressida (the play) (Shakespeare's Wirkung, p. 61). However, it may as properly be to Chaucer's poem of the same name (note the reference to Chaucer, Love in a Maze, I, 2). For the reference to the "Bear at the bridge-foot" (p. 72), cf. V, 1, following, No Wit, No Help Like a Woman's, V, 1, The Puritan, I, 4, The Northern Lass, I, 5, A Mad Couple well Matched, II, 1 (1636).

Sc. 3.   For Celestina's trial of Lord A., see Chap. IV, Sect. 15.   Note that she pretends to make love to him (see Chap. IV, Sect. 2).   Lord A.'s "If you durst be the example, etc." (p. 80), recalls Fitzavarice, The Example, V, 3, "Let me salute the example of chaste honor."   Note Shirley's tribute to the King and Queen (p. 81).

Act V, Sc. 1.   For the description of gaming (pp. 81–82), cf. The Gamester, III, 4.   A slight hint for Bornwell's announcement of his future extravagance occurs in The Just Italian, I, 1, in which Altamont mentions the luxuries with which he will surround Alteza.   Note Marine's disposing of his land, The Noble Gentleman, I, 1.[16]   For the allusion to the "poor knight of Windsor" (p. 85), cf. Eastward Ho, IV, 1, and note The Constant Maid, III, 2. Littleworth's falling into the Thames, as described, p. 86, recalls Sir Moth Interest's falling into the well, The Magnetic Lady, V, 6.   Frederick's courting of his aunt (p. 87) suggests the attentions of Asotus to his stepmother, Corisca, The Bondman, II, 2.   Frederick parodies a line from The Spanish Tragedy, III, 14 (cf. III, 2, and see under The Constant Maid, I, 1).   For the interchange of "sweet gentleman" and "sweet gentlewoman" (p. 88),

[16] For the mention of "regalias" (p. 83), see under The Ball, III, 3; and for the allusion to the Stillyard (p. 84), cf. ibid., IV, 1.

note The Sisters, IV, 2, and see The Scornful Lady, IV, 1. Cf. Kickshaw's telling of his assignation with the "fiend," contrary to his instructions, with the medieval tales of the fairy mistress group, as the Lai of Sir Launfal. For the mention of Lachrymæ (p. 93), cf. The Knight of the Burning Pestle, II, 5, The Fair Maid of the Inn, IV, 2, The Maid of Honor, I, 1, The Picture, V, 3, The Partial Law, III, 3, Microcosmus, III (Anc. Brit. Dram., II, 526, note). For Celestina's defense of her virtue and Lord A.'s conversion, see Chap. IV, Sect. 9 (note also later in the scene). Cf. the reference to Platonic love with The Duke's Mistress, III, 2. See under Love's Cruelty, II, 2, for Lord A.'s invitation to love. Cf. Celestina's parody with that of the Sister, Captain Underwit, II, 2. Cf. Scentlove as a coward with Bubulcus, Love Tricks, II, 1, and note The Wedding, IV, 3. The conversion of Lady Bornwell parallels that of Alteza, The Just Italian, V, 1. Cf. The Grateful Servant, V, 2, The Witty Fair One, V, 3, The Gamester, V, 2, and for the penitence of both her and Kickshaw, see Chap. IV, Sect. 10.

## VIII. Look to the Lady

Look to the Lady, from the title apparently a comedy of manners, was entered in the Stationers' Register, March 11, 1639–40. It may have been withdrawn from publication on Shirley's return from Ireland. No trace of it has ever been found either as having been acted or printed. Possibly it may be identified with Captain Underwit (see Chap. X). This, however, is scarcely more than a conjecture.

## IX. The Constant Maid

Fleay dates The Constant Maid in 1634, because of the quotations in it from The Spanish Tragedy (reprinted

1633), and because the titlepage of the edition of 1661 states it to have been acted by the Queen's Men at the Cockpit (from which they moved to Salisbury Court during the stay of Shirley in Ireland).  He attaches, too, some significance to an allusion to Warbeck (III, 2) and calls attention to the production of Perkin Warbeck in 1633 (Anglia, VIII, 407).  These three points are valueless separately or taken together as far as determining the date of The Constant Maid.  Shirley quotes or parodies lines from The Spanish Tragedy in eight other plays, while in at least twenty-five plays, by other authors from before 1600 to 1641 Kyd's tragedy is alluded to, quoted from or parodied (cf. Koeppel's Marlowe, Kyd . . . im Spiegel des Dramas, pp. 20–42).  These various allusions are scattered along through forty-five years without regard to the appearance of editions of The Spanish Tragedy.  The evidence of the titlepage of the 1661 edition of The Constant Maid is absolutely worthless, for there the play is called Love Will Find Out a Way and the author is given as "T. B."  Obviously no reliance can be placed upon any portion of the titlepage save that referring to the printer, date, etc.  Furthermore, the allusion to Perkin Warbeck may be to that personage as a pretender, and not as a character in a play.  Indeed, the reference is explained better as such.  In short, because of the absence of any record of its having been licensed in England, and because of the lack of a statement on the titlepage of the edition of 1640 as to its having been acted in England, it seems most advisable to fix the production of The Constant Maid between 1636 and 1640 and to place its presentation in the Dublin theatre.  That the comedy was not played in London is nearly proved by the presence of the mock-court scenes.

As Schelling says, The Constant Maid resembles to a

certain extent The Lady Mother (1635) (Eliz. Dram., II, 279, note, 295, note). Ward notices a likeness in some respects to The Noble Gentleman (Hist. Eng. Dram. Lit., III, 115, note). Some hints also may have been drawn from Wit at Several Weapons, while there is also a general influence of Brome's comedies visible.

The plot of The Constant Maid runs as follows:

Hartwell, a gentleman, whose failing fortunes force him to turn away his servants and shut up his house, loves Bellamy's daughter, Frances. In order to test Hartwell, Bellamy reveals to him a pretended passion for him. Hartwell is advised by his friend, Playfair, to meet the mother's advances. Frances' Nurse who overhears their conversation places Frances and Startup, her boorish suitor who is favored by the Nurse, where they can hear Hartwell's dialogue with Bellamy. The Nurse then plots with Close, a former servant of Hartwell's, who is in Startup's service, to admit his master to Frances' room in the night. Close reveals the plan to Hartwell, who disguises himself as Startup and who is taken by the Nurse to her mistress' chamber. Frances recognizes him, but to test him pretends to think him Startup and simulates love for him. Her mother approaches and Hartwell leaves, thinking Frances in love with Startup. Bellamy then tests Frances by requiring her to give up Hartwell to her. Close has frightened Startup from the house by pretending that Hartwell is in pursuit of him, and they are taken up by the watch. Hartwell is arrested on a charge of making away with his rival. At his hearing before the justice he pleads guilty in desperation, but is released when Startup appears. His relations with Frances then are straightened out. A subplot deals with the Niece of Hornet, a usurer, whom Playfair loves. She pretends madness, and is treated by Playfair's Cousin as a doctor. A pretended pursuivant appears with a command for Hornet to appear at court. While he is being entertained by a mock-king, his Niece is stolen away and married to Playfair. When he discovers her flight, he offers to cancel the Cousin's bond for her restoration, but is gulled again, as she appears as Playfair's wife.

"Love will find out the way," which occurs as title to the edition of 1661, is found, seemingly as a quotation from a "ballet," in The Sparagus Garden, I, 2. The various characters, furthermore, suggest Brome strongly. They correspond roughly thus: Shirley's Startup = Brome's Nehemiah in The New Academy, Nonsense and Widgeon in The Northern Lass, Clotpoll in The Weeding of the Covent Garden, Swayne in The Court Beggar (1632–40), the brothers Hoyden in The Sparagus Garden, Sir Amphilus in The Damoiselle (1637–38) ; Hornet, his Niece, and the Cousin = Mendicant, Clarissa, and Frederick (paralleled by Playfair more nearly), in The Court Beggar, and Vermin, Alice, Dryground, etc., in The Damoiselle ; the Nurse, Close, and Bellamy = the Nurse, Wat, and Bellamy in A Mad Couple Well Matched (1636). Besides these the Niece = Flavia in The Novella, and Close = Jeremy in The City Wit and Pate in The Northern Lass. The influence of Brome on Shirley's plot will be taken up later.

See under The Wedding (and note Chap. IV, Sect. 42) for Hornet, the usurer, under Love Tricks for Close, the clever servant, and see Chap. IV, Sect. 44, for Startup, the foolish boorish wooer. Hornet may have been intended as a Jew (see IV, 3, V, 2, 3) ; in that case, cf. Barabas, The Jew of Malta, and Shylock, The Merchant of Venice. For the Nurse, note Decoy in The Lady of Pleasure (there is a Nurse in the *dramatis personæ* of The Maid's Revenge, but none in the play), and cf. the Nurses in The Night-

walker, Roister Doister, The Supposes, Dido, Queen of
Carthage, Titus Andronicus (hardly analogous), Romeo
and Juliet, Wily Beguiled, The Golden Age (a disguise),
The Silver Age, A Shoemaker a Gentleman, a Cure for a
Cuckold, Appius and Virginia, The Little French Lawyer,
The Wonder of a Kingdom, Goffe's Orestes, The Rebellion
(1639).

Act I, Sc. 1. Hartwell's dismissing his servants and
Close's refusing to leave him recall Timon, his servants,
and Flavius, Timon of Athens, IV, 2. Of the quotations
by the Servants (p. 451) the first is from a speech of the
Duke of Castile's, The Spanish Tragedy, III, 4, the second
and fifth are from Hieronimo's speeches, *ibid.*, II, 4, while
the third is from an unidentified source, and the fourth
is misquoted from Mucedorus, IV, 3. Gifford's note, therefore, which derives all five from ''the outcries of poor old
Jeronymo in The Spanish Tragedy'' is incorrect. Shirley quotes, paraphrases, and parodies lines from The
Spanish Tragedy in The Politician, III, 2, St. Patrick for
Ireland, III, 2, The Bird in a Cage, III, 4, The Opportunity,
I, 1, The Sisters, IV, 1, The Wedding, III, 2, Love in a
Maze, IV, 3, The Lady of Pleasure, III, 2, V, 1, and again
in V, 3, of the present play. For a fairly complete list of
references of one kind and another to The Spanish Tragedy,
see Koeppel, as cited above.

Sc. 2. Cf. Hornet's suit to Bellamy with Dotario and
Æmilia, A Fine Companion, II, 4, and Sir Geoffrey and
the Lady, The Lady Mother, III, 1. Cf. his desire to keep
his niece single in order to possess her dowry with Falso's
intention, The Phœnix, I, 6. See under The Example, II,
1, for his attempt at discrediting Hartwell. Cf. Hartwell's description of Hornet with that of Dotario by
Æmilia, A Fine Companion, II, 4, and of Lovell by Grimes,
The Lady Mother, I, 1. See Chap. IV, Sect. 21. For the

luxuries of Bellamy's house as listed by Hornet, cf. The
Lady of Pleasure, I, 1, 2. Cf. Earthworm and Theodore,
The Old Couple, II. See under The Witty Fair One, V,
1, for the Prodigal Son in hangings. For Hornet's "pre-
cepts" and his revelation of his own character, cf. More-
craft, The Scornful Lady, II, 3, and Overreach, A New
Way to Pay Old Debts, IV, 1. See under The Bird in a
Cage, II, 1, for the comparison of Hornet to a "monster,"
and note that Crackby is similarly designated in The Lady
Mother, I, 3 (note Moroso, The Woman's Prize, II, 6).
Hartwell's ordering Close to work into the Nurse's confidence is borrowed from Antonio and Diego, The Maid's
Revenge, II, 2. For Bellamy's avowal to Hartwell of her
love for him (pretended), see Chap. IV, Sect. 2. A source
may be the Lady's courtship of Bonvile, The Lady Mother,
III, 1 (note *ibid.*, III, 2).

Act II, Sc. 1. An allusion (p. 462) occurs, apparently
to Verges in Much Ado about Nothing. For the eavesdropping here and in II, 3, see Chap. IV, Sect. 30. See
under The Duke's Mistress, III, 2, IV, 1, for Playfair's
description of Bellamy (cf. Chap. IV, Sect. 20). Gifford's
identification of the "harlot's story" in the hangings with
that of the Prodigal Son is too absurd for comment. See
under The Witty Fair One, II, 2, for the introduction of
Startup. Cf. Startup's use of "sweet lady" and "sweet
gentleman" with Josselin, Edward IV, Part I ("and so
forth"), Mrs. Eyre, The Shoemaker's Holiday ("but let
that pass"), Hobson, If You Know Not Me, You Know
Nobody, Part II ("bones a me"), Sir John, The Merry
Devil of Edmonton ("grass and hay; we are all mortal"),
the Host, *ibid.* ("I serve the good Duke of Norfolk"),
Simson, The Return From Parnassus, Part I ("as they
say"), Flower, The Fair Maid of the Exchange ("it is a
good conceit"), Goosecap, Sir Giles Goosecap ("tickle the

vanity on't," and "because we are all mortal"), Touchstone, Eastward Ho ("we are all mortal"), Brewer, A
New Wonder: A Woman Never Vexed ("mother o' pearl").
Note in connection with Close's reference to Startup as a
"widgeon" that Widgeon is a foolish character in The
Northern Lass. For Startup's desire to buy wit and his
mention of a "hundred pieces," cf. Tim Hoyden and his
hundred pounds for making him a gentleman, The Sparagus
Garden, II, 3; Pupillus' intention of becoming a wit and of
paying for it, The Noble Stranger, I (1638); and Gudgeon's
coming to court to buy a favorite's position, The Fool Would
Be a Favorite (1638). Note Sogliardo, Every Man out of
his Humor, I, 1, who wishes to be a gentleman at any cost.
For Startup's account of his ancestry (p. 467), cf. Treedle
on his university career, The Witty Fair One, IV, 2. For
Startup's attitude towards his rival Hartwell, cf. Simple
and Caperwit, Love in a Maze, I, 2, and then Bubulcus and
Antonio, Love Tricks, II, 1. Note also The Lady Mother,
III, 2.

Sc. 2. For Playfair's Cousin as a doctor, cf. The Witty
Fair One, III, 4. The source of the use of this disguise
as used here is perhaps Pate's gaining admission to the de-
ranged Constance as a doctor and his part in the subsequent
stealing of her away by Luckless, The Northern Lass, V, 1,
2, 3. Cf. also A Fine Companion, V, 2. Here Aurelio, as a
physician, steals away Valeria, daughter to Littlegood, a
usurer, under the pretext of taking her to his house for
treatment when she pretends madness. Cf. Lope de Vega,
El Acero de Madrid, I, 4, II, 2, 3, 4. Note Fidelio as a
scrivener gaining access to his mistress, Falso's Niece, The
Phœnix, III, 1. For the simulated madness of the Niece,
see under The Cardinal, V, 3. See under The Witty Fair
One, III, 4, for Hornet's hint to the mock-doctor concerning his niece's death. The allusion of the Cousin to the

great man who poisoned his countess is seemingly contemporary (perhaps, however, to Leicester).

The summoning of Hornet to court and the pretended
honors bestowed on him in a mock-court are derived by
Ward from The Noble Gentleman (Hist. Eng. Dram. Lit.,
III, 115, note). Cf. also Crazy's plot against Sarpego in
which a bogus court-messenger appears, The City Wit, III,
2. Disguises similar to that of the Servant as a pursuivant
are found in Every Man in his Humor, IV, 9, A Tale of
a Tub, II, 1, The Roaring Girl, IV, 2, News from Plymouth,
V.

Sc. 3. For Startup's courtship of Frances, see under
Love in a Maze, III, 1, and cf. The Lady Mother, III, 2.
For his informing her of a love-affair between her mother
and Hartwell, cf. Sir Gregory, Wit at Several Weapons,
I, 1. Hartwell's making love to the mother to forward his
affair with the daughter is derived from The Arcadia,
II, 1, III, 3, perhaps, but cf. Wit at Several Weapons,
I, 1. For the apparent rivalry of mother and daughter,
cf. also The Turk, III, 4, The Devil's Law-case, III, 3, and
The Lady Mother. See Chap. IV, Sect. 30, and cf. II, 1,
for the eavesdropping.

Act III, Sc. 1. For the reference to "keeping the door,"
see under St. Patrick for Ireland, II, 2.

Sc. 2. For the Cousin as King, see under The Imposture,
II, 3. For his state, note The Noble Gentleman, IV, 4.[17]
Note the allusion to Perkin Warbeck (p. 484) (the play?).
See under The Humorous Courtier, III, 1, for "rotten in
my head." Cf. the cozening of Hornet by a mock call to
court with Sneakup and Sarpego, The City Wit, III, 4.
Cf. "Sir Giles Hornet" with Sir Giles Overreach, A New
Way to Pay Old Debts, and the historical Sir Giles Mom-

[17] For the statesman's toothpick (p. 483), cf. The Grateful
Servant, III, 1, and see under The Ball, I, 1.

pesson. For Hornet's honors, see The Noble Gentleman,
II, 1. For the diverting of his attention from home affairs,
cf. The Spanish Curate, IV, 3, 5. Cf. the flight of his
niece which takes place in his absence to that of Alice, The
Damoiselle, I, 1 (1637–38), which occurs when her father
is lured away from home. "Poor knights of Windsor"
(p. 486) are alluded to in The Lady of Pleasure, V, 1.
Note the references to contemporary events (p. 488). For
other references to monopolies, cf. The Cruel Brother, I, 1,
Love and Honor, II, 1, The Noble Stranger, III (1638).

Sc. 3. Cf. the pretended pursuit of Startup by Hartwell with that of Sir Solitary by Peregrine, The Example,
III, 1 (in earnest). Note The Picture, IV, 2 (the predicament of Ubaldo and Ricardo). There Ubaldo's clothes are
worn by Hilario, as Startup's are by Hartwell. Note
Brainworm's theft of Formal's clothes, Every Man in his
Humor, IV, 6, in connection with Close's device for securing Startup's garments (see III, 1, also).

Sc. 4. For Hartwell's being in disguise, but recognized
and teased by Frances, cf. Love's Labor's Lost, V, 2, and
Much Ado about Nothing, II, 1. Note that her pretending
to believe him Startup and expressing love to him resembles
closely the Niece's punishment of Cunningham for his
addresses to the Guardianess, Wit at several Weapons, II,
2, and see also her actions toward Cunningham as Sir
Gregory, ibid., III, 1. See The Opportunity, II, 3, for
confusion of personages. Note also A Fine Companion,
V, 1, in which Careless and Dotario are confused. For
Hartwell's despondency, see IV, I, and cf. Aurelio, A
Fine Companion, IV, 2, on being shown Valeria's ring
by Spruse. See under The Witty Fair One, III, 3. For
the test of love, cf. IV, 2, and see Chap. IV, Sect. 15. Cf.
The Maid's Revenge, II, 2, for Frances' pretense of love
for Startup, and see Chap. IV, Sect. 6. The trial which

terminates unfortunately is found in Hyde Park, V, 1, and The Queen, IV.  Note The Variety, IV, 1.

Act IV, Sc. 1.  For the setting (the fields), cf. The Two Angry Women of Abington, IV, V.  For Startup's lack of clothing and his complaints as to the cold, cf. The Nightwalker, IV, 5, V, 1, Blurt, Master-Constable, IV, 3, The Little French Lawyer, IV, 4, 5.  See for similar scenes in the dark, The Nightwalker, The Merry Devil of Edmonton, IV, The Two Angry Women of Abington, IV, V, Englishmen for My Money, IV, 1, If You Know Not Me, You Know Nobody, Part II, p. 302 (a fog), Thierry and Theodoret, V, 1, The Queen's Exchange, V, 1, Cartwright's Siege, V, 5, 6, 7 (1637), The Distresses, II, 1 (1639), Wit in a Constable, V, 1 (1639).  For Hartwell's entrance with a lanthorn and Close's intercession with him for Startup, cf Wildbrain and Heartlove, and Maria's later appearance, The Nightwalker, III, 1.  For Hartwell's lamenting the inconstancy of Frances, see under III, 4, and cf. Love in a Maze, V, 3.  For the Constable and Watch and their arrest of Close and Startup, cf. Much Ado about Nothing, III, 3, Blurt, Master-Constable, IV, 3, The Coxcomb, I, 6, The Heir, IV, A Tale of a Tub, The Lady Mother, V, 1, Wit in a Constable, V, 1 (1639).  Note the arrests of the clever servants in The Witty Fair One, IV, 6, and Bartholomew Fair, IV, 3.

Sc. 2.  For the Countryman in search of Startup, cf. Michaelmas Term, II, 2.  Note that Crackby asperses the Lady, The Lady Mother, V, 2.  For Bellamy's test of her daughter, see what is perhaps the source, *ibid.*, III, 1, in which the Lady tests Bonvill.  See also Chap. IV, Sect. 15.  Frances' offer to renounce Hartwell seems based on The Lady Mother, IV, 1.  Here the Lady discloses her passion for Thurston to Clariana who gives him up to her, and consents to act as an intermediary.  Note that

Timoclea asks Amada, her daughter, to give up Muleasses to her, The Turk, IV, 1. For renunciations, see Chap. IV, Sect. 4. Cf. Frances' lines concerning her death with those of Amidea, The Traitor, IV, 2.

Sc. 3. For Playfair's description of his lady, see under The Royal Master, I, 2. Cf. the induction to The Taming of the Shrew for Hornet's thinking himself dreaming (p. 505). Note The Arabian Nights' Entertainments. For Hornet's keeping the door at the masque and his troubles with the crowd, cf. The Triumph of Peace, p. 280 ff., The Maid's Tragedy, I, 2, A King and No King, II, 2, The Humorous Lieutenant, I, 1, A Wife for a Month, II, 6, Henry VIII, V, 4, etc. For the masque, see Chap. IV, Sect. 18. Cf. for the introduction of Cupid, The Royal Master, II, 1, and The Coronation, IV, 3. For "Venus' dandiprat" (p. 511), see under The Royal Master, II, 1. The masque and the Niece's part in it is derived, perhaps, from The Northern Lass, II, 6, in which a runaway lady appears before her uncle as a masquer, but cf. Wit at Several Weapons, V, 2. Cf. Love in a Maze, V, 5, for the revelation of a marriage in a masque, and note especially The Lady Mother, V, 2.

Act V, Sc. 1. Cf. the arrest of Hartwell for the murder of Startup with that of Bubulcus, Love Tricks, IV, 6. His false confession of having killed Startup recalls The Duke's Mistress, V, 2, 3. Cf. The Lady Mother, V, 1, The Goblins, V, 5 (1638), Brennoralt, V, 3 (1639).

Sc. 2. Cf. Hornet's discovery of his niece's flight and his lamentations with Shylock, The Merchant of Venice, II, 8 (reported), III, 1 (source perhaps). For the Cousin's reference to the knighting of Hornet (p. 514), cf. The Noble Gentleman, II, 1 (on the tumult at court over the honors of Marine). For the bargain between the Cousin and Hornet which involves the cancellation of a debt for the return of the Niece, cf. Epicœne, V, 1, The Roaring Girl, V, 2, The Antiquary, V, 1, The City Match, V, 4 (1639). Note The Bird in a Cage, V, 1, and its analogues.

Sc. 3. For the trial scene, see Chap. IV, Sect. 17. Note, for Hartwell's reaffirmation of his guilt, The Lady Mother, V, 2, in which the Lady repeats her confession. Note also Thorowgood's attempt to take her guilt upon himself, *ibid.* For the settlement of the difficulties of Hartwell and Frances, cf. Beauford and Gratiana, The Wedding, V, 2. See under *ibid.*, for the opportune appearance of Startup. Note the resurrections of Thorowgood, Bonvill and Belisia, The Lady Mother, V, 2, and see Chap. IV, Sect. 29. See under I, 1, for the quotation from The Spanish Tragedy, II, 4. For Startup and the Countryman's daughter, cf. Michaelmas Term, V, 3. The last line of Startup's last speech (p. 521) recalls Dogberry, Much Ado about Nothing, IV, 2. Gifford notes (p. 522) a mention of the "herb to open locks" in The Sad Shepherd, II, 2 (unfinished, and unprinted until 1641). For the final baffling of Hornet, cf. The Merchant of Venice, IV, 1, Michaelmas Term, V, 3, The Family of Love, V, 3, Wit at Several Weapons, V, 2, etc. Cf. also Love Tricks, V, 3, and The Wedding, V, 2.

# CHAPTER X

## ENTERTAINMENTS, ETC., COLLABORATED, AND DOUBTFUL PLAYS

### A. ENTERTAINMENTS, ETC.

### *I. A Contention for Honor and Riches*

According to Fleay (Biog. Chron., II, 238) A Contention for Honor and Riches was never meant to be acted, nor was it. There is no evidence of the piece's not having been played save the absence of any reference to a presentation on the titlepage of the old edition of 1633. The Contention is asserted by Fleay to have been composed in June, 1631. On what grounds, that critic fails to state. A more probable date is 1630, a year in which Shirley seems to have had no plays licensed.

Fleay's theory that in Sc. 1 Shirley ridiculed the Lord Mayor's pageants which Heywood wrote between 1631 and 1639, and so began a paper warfare between the two, is absolutely without foundation. In the first place, if the Contention was written in June, 1631, we have Shirley performing the feat of satirising a series of shows the first of which was produced some five months later. But setting aside considerations of dates, we find all the evidence against Fleay's theory. First, if Ingenuity is Shirley, as Fleay thinks (and it seems probable), it would be he who would ridicule the shows, and not Clod, the sordid bumpkin; and secondly all likelihood of any malicious satire on the pageants of Heywood or anyone else is removed by the fact that in Sc. 3 Ingenuity, whether Shirley or not, rebukes Clod for having ridiculed "The noble citizens, and traduc'd Their yearly Triumph," to which Gettings responds, " 'Twas his ignorance." Later, in the discussion of The Triumph of Beauty, the "quarrel" between Shirley and Heywood will be disposed of.

Fleay's statement that the source of the Contention is the eighth novel of the fifth day of the Decameron is one of the most extraordinary assertions ever made. There is absolutely no resemblance between the plots of the novel and the morality.

The basic idea of the Contention was utilized by Shirley in the masque in The Coronation, IV, 3, where Polidora presents to her recreant lover, Arcadius (or Demetrius), an allegory representing Love's being won away from Honor by Fortune.

A Contention for Honor and Riches, which, as it stands, is a moral masque in three scenes, was worked over at his leisure by its author, and in the form of a full-fledged morality in five acts with added action and characters was published in 1659 under the title Honoria and Mammon. In view of this fact and since the expanded version was never acted, only those points which occur in the Contention will be noted here, while immediately Honoria and Mammon will be discussed, in its relationships, etc., to the Contention and to the drama in general.

Sc. 1.   For Clod's mention of "pancake bells," see Deloney's Pleasant History of the Gentle Craft, Part I, Chap. XV (p. 132).

Sc. 3.   Dyce suggests an allusion by Lady Riches to the failure of the Dutch and English fleets to capture the Spanish plate fleet in 1625.

## II.  *Honoria and Mammon*

This morality, according to Shirley's preface, seems to have been many years growing out of A Contention for Honor and Riches before its publication in 1659.  This fact, together with those cited under the previous section, is the excuse for discussing Honoria and Mammon in this place although it was its author's last work in dramatic form to appear in print.

The morality and the allegorical play were by no means extinct dramatic types in England after 1600.  We have, to name only a few, the following productions which frankly belong to these classes or which verge very closely upon them:  Cynthia's Revels, The Staple of News, The Magnetic Lady, Lingua, The Whore of Babylon, The Sun's Darling, Two Wise Men and All the Rest Fools, A Game at Chess, Pathomachia, Microcosmus, The Floating Island, The Muse's Looking-glass.  Hence, Honoria and Mammon is by no means a novelty in form even in the last years of the Elizabethan drama.

Although founded on A Contention for Honor and Riches, Honoria and Mammon by reason of its greater length and expanded plot differs in certain respects from the former considerably.  The characters are renamed in Honoria and Mammon and those which in the Contention have no names are christened.  The Soldier of the Contention = Conquest of Honoria and Mammon; Ingenuity = Alworth; the Courtier = Alamode; Gettings = Fulbank; Maslin = Clod; Lady Honor = Honoria; Lady Riches = Aurelia Mammon.  Also various named and unnamed characters have been added.  The name of Phantasm, the Vice of Honoria and Mammon, is derived from an epithet applied by the Soldier to the Courtier.  Some of the more concrete figures of the latter piece resemble characters in

other dramas; for instance there are likenesses between
Conquest and Winfield in The Ball, and Alamode and Sir
Ambrose Lamount in the same play. The "courtier a la
mode" and the "madame a la mode" are mentioned in
The Variety, II, 1, and III, 1, respectively. Cf. Captain
Underwit, I, 1, V, 1, The Variety, V, 1, The New Academy,
V, 1, for the use of the term. The name of Traverse sug-
gests Sir Marmaduke Travers in The Ball, and that of
Aurelia Mammon, Aurelia Clara Pecunia in The Staple
of News.

Honoria and Mammon may thus be summarized:

Conquest, a soldier, Alworth, a scholar, and Alamode,
a courtier, are suitors for the hand of Lady Honoria, while
the citizen Fulbank and the countryman, Maslin, are
suitors to Lady Mammon. Alworth is introduced to Mammon by Honoria, but she disdains him. Fulbank and Maslin quarrel over Mammon, but their common cowardice
prevents their fighting. Alamode and Conquest fight over
Honoria and the latter is victorious. Phantasm, a demon,
who is Mammon's gentleman usher, leads Fulbank on in
his pursuit of his mistress who accepts him. Phantasm
then tempts Traverse, a lawyer, to win Mammon from
Fulbank. He does so and bears her away in triumph, and
in turn, Alamode who has been unsuccessful with Honoria,
wins her from Traverse, and carries her to his country
seat. There Maslin becomes her favored lover, but is forsaken by her for Conquest, who seems her final choice. In
the meantime, Honoria has chosen Alworth in preference
to Conquest and Alamode. She tests Alworth, and finds
him worthy of her, but he becomes ill as the result of the
strain of the trial. Traverse, who is a suitor to Honoria
as well as to Mammon, is introduced as a doctor for Alworth. He gives out that Alworth is dead, and carries
off Honoria to the country. Conquest, with a band of

soldiers, goes there in search of Honoria, and frees her. Alworth appears in disguise, and as he discovers himself to Honoria is recognized and made prisoner by Conquest. Conquest, however, yields up Honoria to his rival who has previously proposed to renounce his own pretensions to Honoria. Then Conquest turns to Mammon, and Honoria and Alworth are united, while the offending characters, Fulbank, and the others, are pardoned.

At the opening of A Contention for Honor and Riches, Ingenuity is repulsed by Riches, and the two quarrel. Clod and Gettings, her suitors, enter, and after a war of words the former challenges Gettings. Next the Courtier and Soldier are shown courting Honor with Ingenuity present. Honor and the last leave the stage, after which the Courtier and Soldier quarrel. As they approach the point of fighting, Honesty and No-Pay appear and frighten them away. Clod and Gettings are now shown as about to engage in a duel. Foul-Weather-in-Harvest and Long Vacation enter, and the opponents are reconciled because of their fear of these spectres. Riches appears and accepts Gettings but gives a reversion of his husbandhood to Clod. The Soldier and the Courtier appear in search of Honor, but turn their attention to Riches. Then Honor and Ingenuity enter as just married. After a moment's surprise a general reconciliation takes place.

Act I, Sc. 1. Gifford sees an allusion (p. 7) to the rapacity of the patrons of benefices under the Long Parliament. The passage is founded, however, on Sc. 1, A Contention (p. 293). Fulbank on Apollo and the Muses (pp. 8–9) is based on *ibid.* (p. 295) and Maslin (p. 10) on city pageants is condensed from Clod on the same (pp. 296–97). For the discussion of learning (p. 7), cf. The Royal Master, II, 1. Fulbank's arraignment of Maslin is drawn from A Contention, p. 298. Maslin's and Ful-

bank's apprehension of a plot (p. 11) recalls Sir Solitary
Plot's humor in The Example. As poltroons trying to es-
cape fighting, the same pair seem founded on Lodam and
Rawbone, The Wedding, IV, 3. Their device of cutting
each other and then pretending to have fought is based on
Henry IV, Part I, II, 4. Cf. also Love Tricks, IV, 6.

Sc. 2. Conquest's speech to Honoria (p. 14) is based
on that of the Soldier to Honor, A Contention, Sc. 2 (p.
300). Cf. As You Like It, II, 7, Jaques on the soldier
in his seven ages speech. For Honoria's test of Mammon,
cf. II, 2, and see Chap. IV, Sect. 15. Alamode regarding
Conquest (p. 15 ff.) and Conquest on Alamode (p. 17 ff.)
are based respectively on A Contention, Sc. 2 (pp. 302 ff.,
304 ff.). For the use of "leveret" (p. 16), cf. Captain
Underwit, II, 1. The mention of the battle of Amboyna
(p. 18) should be noted.

Act II, Sc. 1. Phantasm's leading on of Fulbank here
together with III, 1, 2 (with Traverse and Alamode respectively) seems based on Giotto and the Duchess' suitors
in The Humorous Courtier. Cf. also the ladies and their
suitors in The Ball. For Fulbank's day-dreams (p. 20),
together with those of Maslin, IV, 2, see under The Royal
Master, III, 3. For Fulbank's mention of The Mirror
of Knighthood, see Koeppel, Reflexe der Ritter Romane
im Drama, p. 212, note. The expression "I confess"—
"And be hang'd" (p. 24) is said by Gifford to be pro-
verbial.

Sc. 2. For the characters of the wise courtier and good
soldier (pp. 27–28) see Chap. IV, Sect. 21. Alworth's
speech (p. 29) with some variations is the same as To L.
for a Wreath of Bays Sent, Shirley's Poems (VI, 413).
For Honoria's test, cf. I, 2, and see Chap. IV, Sect. 15.

Act III, Sc. 1. Cf. Traverse and his books, pp. 32, 36,
with the parallels noted in Chap. IV, Sect. 23. Gifford's

note (p. 32) on the ''Writs'' from the context is obviously
wrong. They are apparently persons dressed in parchment who act as Traverse's demons (see p. 39). For
Phantasm's suggestion that Traverse himself court Mammon, cf. I, 2, III, 2. Gifford notes Phantasm's use of the
common pun on ''angels,'' p. 34. For Maslin's eavesdropping, p. 37, together with the instances at p. 39, and
in IV, 3, V, 1, 2, see Chap. IV, Sect. 30. Cf. Traverse's
courtship in legal terms (p. 38) with that of Rawbone,
The Wedding, III, 2. For the mention of Cuckold's
Haven, p. 40, see Eastward Ho, IV, 1, and Northward Ho,
III, 2.

Sc. 2 is concerned with Phantasm's attracting Alamode
to the pursuit of Mammon. Cf. II, 1, III, 1.

Sc. 3. For the hints of Traverse to the Doctor concerning the death of Alworth (p. 44), cf. The Humorous Courtier, V, 2, and the analogues there cited. Traverse refers
(p. 45) to A Hundred Merry Tales, IX. Cf. The Gamester, III, 2.

Sc. 4 shows Alamode starting with Mammon for the
country.

Sc. 5. Cf. Traverse as a doctor with Manly, The Witty
Fair One, III, 4. Cf. the entering and reentering of
characters from Alworth's bedside with tidings of his condition and finally of his death with The Brothers, IV, 1.

Act IV, Sc. 1. The name ''Squanderbag,'' applied to
a character in this scene and later, is derived from Scanderbeg, for whom see The Gentleman of Venice, III, 1.
There may be in the generosity of the Citizens, p. 53 ff.,
some reference to conditions after the death of Oliver.
Certainly some contemporary application is probable.

Sc. 2 is chiefly concerned with Maslin's visions for which
see under II, 1.

Sc. 3. ''Thou messenger of horror, what's the matter?''

(p. 63) is one of Shirley's few verbal anticlimaxes. For Fulbank's martial experiences (p. 64), cf. The Knight of the Burning Pestle, V, 2, 3. For Alworth's resurrection (p. 66) see Chap. IV, Sect. 29.

Act V, Sc. 1. See for the drinking scene Chap. IV, Sect. 26. An allusion to Dulcinea del Toboso from Don Quixote occurs at p. 69. The vanishing of Phantasm (p. 73) should be compared with that of Archimagus, St. Patrick for Ireland, V, 3.

Sc. 2. For the laying of the scene in a prison, see Chap. IV, Sect. 14. For Alworth's and Conquest's renunciations of Honoria, see Chap. IV, Sect. 4, and see the same (Sect. 10) for the repentance of Traverse (p. 79). Cf. the account of Maslin's robbery (p. 83) with The Sisters, I, 1, and note the analogues listed there.

### III.  The Triumph of Peace

Shirley's Triumph of Peace, the most magnificent and elaborate of English masques, was presented by the four Inns of Court before the King and Queen at Whitehall, February 3, 1633–34, as a testimonial of their loyalty, and as a sort of counterbalance to the barrister Prynne's Histriomastix. Its cost is said to have been about twenty-one thousand pounds. The masque so pleased the King and Queen that within a week after the first presentation it was repeated at their command.

Koeppel (Ben Jonson's Wirkung, pp. 186–87) relates The Triumph of Peace to Jonson's Vision of Delight, which was presented at Court at Christmas, 1617. There are some resemblances in the scenes, and in the antimasques, while Peace and Phant'sy are characters in Jonson's masque. We have Hours represented in each, and both end with the approach of morning (Aurora in Jonson

and Amphiluche in Shirley). However, The Vision of
Delight was not printed until 1640, so we must suppose
that if Shirley did utilize it, he based his borrowings upon
some account of the masque, verbal or otherwise (there is
not much probability that he had seen it).

Among the interesting points in connection with The
Triumph of Peace should be noted the seven scenes, the
gorgeous sets, and the elaborate machinery. Koeppel derives the antimasque of projectors from The Devil is an
Ass (as in II, 1), in which persons of that type play a
considerable part (Ben Jonson's Wirkung, p. 178). Cf.
also Engine, the projector, in Captain Underwit (II, 3,
especially). See The Emperor of the East, I, 2, The Court
Beggar, I, 1, The Antipodes, IV, 9. The author has un-
wittingly played the prophet in presenting several of the
participants in this antimasque (p. 269 ff.). The Coun-
try-fellow unmistakably is concerning himself with a thresh-
ing machine, the Fourth Projector has invented a diver's
suit, and the Sixth is certainly the discoverer of the steam-
boat, and the modern caisson foundations for buildings.
For the mention of Rabelais (p. 270), cf. Koeppel, Rabelais
Anspielungen im Drama. Cf. the Thieves (p. 272) with
The Sisters, I, 1, etc. For the Satyrs and Nymphs who
enter after the Thieves, see The Grateful Servant, IV, 4.
These are followed by Don Quixote and Sancho Panza
who tilt at a Windmill (see Don Quixote, Part I, Chap.
VIII) and then assault a Country-Gentleman and his
Servant who beat them off. For the member of the
"Black Guard" (p. 280), see The White Devil, I, 2, and
The Queen, I. Near the end of the masque (p. 282) we
have an astonishing lapse. The new moon is visible just
before sunrise. For the "feather-footed Hours" (p. 283),
see under The Triumph of Beauty.

## *IV.   The Triumph of Beauty*

The Triumph of Beauty, which was printed with Shirley's Poems in 1646, is said by Fleay (Biog. Chron. II, 244) to have been presented privately about May, 1640. As usual, no evidence is advanced by Fleay for the date he has set, and there seems to be none for any particular date between 1625 and 1646.

Already, in connection with The Contention for Honor and Riches, the "quarrel" between Heywood and Shirley which Fleay "discovered" has been mentioned.   Fleay further advances the theory (Biog. Chron. II, 244) that in his Love's Mistress Heywood retaliated upon Shirley for his "ridicule" of the older author's pageants by exhibiting his opponent as Corydon, the Clown, and as the "ignorant ass" introduced in I, 1 (cf. Biog. Chron. I, 299).   He likewise finds many allusions to Shirley's Arcadia in Love's Mistress.   As a matter of fact, the only allusions to any Arcadia at all are due to Heywood's confusing of Thessaly and Arcadia.   Too, Fleay identifies the clowns of Love's Mistress thus: Midas = Christopher Beeston, Corydon = William Beeston, and says that Midas prefers the song to Pan, the Arcadian god (Shirley's Arcadia), to Heywood's song to Apollo (perhaps an intended revival of Apollo and Daphne) (Biog. Chron. I, 299).   How Corydon could simultaneously be Shirley and Beeston with any appropriateness or probability Fleay has not deigned to explain.   Nor has he informed us how he identified the "ignorant ass" among five other asses in Heywood's play as Shirley.

In Anglia, VIII, 409–10, Fleay states that Shirley replied to Heywood's attack in Love's Mistress by representing him as Bottle in The Triumph of Beauty.   He speaks in another place (Biog. Chron. I, 244–45) of Shirley's having "succeeded" Heywood as dramatist for the King's Men in 1640, and seems to believe that this had something to do with the feud between the two. Fleay, himself, however, shows that Heywood between 1625 and 1642 had one play produced by the King's Men,[1] so this "fact" can have had little influence on the relations between the two (Stage, pp. 341, 362).

As a matter of fact, the feud between Shirley and Heywood rests on as flimsy foundations as the celebrated jealousy of Jonson toward Shakespeare which Gifford demolished a century ago. Fleay has contradicted himself so badly, and has trumped up a chronology so obviously to suit his theories that "allusions" much less veiled than those which he has pointed out are necessary to establish any case whatsoever.

As Langbaine noted two hundred and twenty-five years ago (Dramatic Poets, p. 485), The Triumph of Beauty, as far as the comic portion is concerned, is based on A Midsummer Night's Dream, I, 2, III, 1, in which the Athenian artisans prepare to play Pyramus and Thisbe. The latter part of The Triumph is founded on the old story of the judgment of Paris. Although there seems no indebtedness, The Arraignment of Paris, II, 1, should be compared with the masque from p. 329 ff. The entrance of the Hours (p. 340) and the mention of Eunomia, Diche, and Irene (p. 34) suggest The Triumph of Peace. In that masque (p. 283) also occurs the expression "feather-footed Hours" which is found in The Triumph of Beauty (p. 341), as well as in Captain Underwit, V, 1 (p. 395).

## V.   Cupid and Death

The masque of Cupid and Death was presented March 26

[1] As a matter of fact, Heywood seems some years earlier practically to have ceased writing for the stage.

(New Year's Day), 1653, before the Portuguese Ambassador by "Mr. Luke Channen, etc." The masque is based upon the story of the exchange of the arrows of Cupid and Death in the course of their stay over night at an inn. The source is probably that suggested by Langbaine (Dramatic Poets, p. 478)—John Ogilby's Æsop's Fables, I, Fable 39. This book was published in 1651 with commendatory verses by Shirley (Poems, VI, 513–14). Versions of the fable occur in L'Estrange's Fables and Stories Moralized (Fable CXXX), and in Select Fables of Esop and Other Fabulists, Bk. II, Fable 51. Boswell in the Shakespeare Variorum (XX, 67, note) cites several references to the story, among others, in Venus and Adonis, ll. 947–48, and The Virgin-Martyr, I, 1.[2]

The Chamberlain's terming Cupid the "Prince D'Amour" (p. 347) recalls Davenant's masque with that title. On the next page a contemporary allusion is found in the Chamberlain's mention of the past "rantings" of the gentry. For the characters of Folly and Madness, pp. 349–50, see Chap. IV, Sect. 21. Cf. Despair with a halter (p. 351) and the Chamberlain (p. 362) with Rodamant, St. Patrick for Ireland, V, 1. Shirley refers (p. 352) to Hobbes' Leviathan, which had appeared two years earlier. The Chamberlain's being struck by Death with Cupid's arrow and his consequent falling in love with his Apes (pp. 361–62) seems to contain a reminiscence of Titania and Bottom, A Midsummer Night's Dream, III, 1.

### VI. The Contention of Ajax and Ulysses for the Armor of Achilles

The Contention of Ajax and Ulysses, which was published with Honoria and Mammon in 1659, according to

[2] The allusion to Cupid's arrow here seems, however, to be to another story; cf. Love in a Maze, V, 3.

the titlepage was privately presented as an entertainment. Fleay dates the piece about 1640 (Biog. Chron. II, 247), but there seems no authority for this statement. More probably it was presented at a time nearer that of its publication. It is unlikely that Shirley would have kept The Contention by him for nineteen years, especially since we find him publishing Cupid and Death in the year of its presentation.

As Dyce says, The Contention of Ajax and Ulysses is founded on the first section of the thirteenth book of Ovid's Metamorphoses (see also The Iron Age, Part I, V, 1). Shirley's rendering of the strife between the heroes is close to Ovid's version. A considerable portion has been sacrificed and some rearrangements have been made. The long speeches of Ajax and Ulysses which we find in the Latin are broken into by their auditors in the English version. The first part of Sc. 1 of The Contention up to p. 376 is Shirley's, and in Sc. 2, only the suicide of Ajax is from Ovid. The pages are Shirley's, as is the braggart and poltroon, Polybrontes, who appears in Sc. 2 (cf. these characters with the analogous ones cited in Chap. IV, Sects. 48 and 47). Cf. the madness of Ajax (Sc. 2) with the analogues under Love Tricks, II, 2. For the eavesdropping (p. 393), see Chap. IV, Sect. 30, and for the prophecy of Calchas (p. 395), see under St. Patrick for Ireland, I, 1.

## B. Collaborated and Doubtful Plays

Langbaine's statement that Shirley left behind him several plays in MS. at his death (Dramatic Poets, p. 475), Malone's statement in regard to Love's Pilgrimage (Shakespeare Variorum, III, 226), and Hitchcock's assertion that Shirley completed several plays of Fletcher's (An Historical View of the Irish Stage, p. 12, quoted by Ward, D. N. B., LII, 130), together with the natural de-

sire of scholars to find an author for anonymous plays, are
responsible for the attribution to Shirley in entirety, or
in part, of fourteen plays (exclusive of The Ball, The
Nightwalker, and Chabot). These include A Yorkshire
Tragedy, The Faithful Friends, The Laws of Candy, The
Nice Valor, The Noble Gentleman, Dick of Devonshire,
Phillis of Scyros, The Lovers' Progress, Captain Under-
wit, Love's Pilgrimage, The General, No Wit, No Help
Like a Woman's, Andromana, Double Falsehood. To these
may be added conjecturally at least, The Variety, and The
Humorous Lovers of the Duke of Newcastle.

There seems to be no need of discussing in detail Shirley's "share" in A Yorkshire Tragedy, The Faithful
Friends, The Laws of Candy, The Nice Valor, The Noble
Gentleman, Phillis of Scyros, The Lovers' Progress, Love's
Pilgrimage, The General, No Wit, No Help Like a Woman's, and Andromana. The consensus of critical opinion
is that in most of these plays Shirley had no part. As to
the others the judgment of the best authorities is that he
had nothing to do with them. Since there is no apparent
reason for disagreeing with the earlier critics, the above
plays are passed over in the present consideration of the
doubtful and collaborated plays. In the appended notes
brief bibliographies to the discussions of the authorship of
these plays are given.

## BIBLIOGRAPHICAL NOTES

A Yorkshire Tragedy; Biographia Dramatica, III, 427; Quarterly Review, VII, 290; Brooke, Shakespeare Apocrypha, Introduction, xxxiii. ff.

The Faithful Friends; Boyle, Englische Studien, VII, 75, *ibid.*,
XVIII, 294; Oliphant, *ibid.*, XV, 331, note.

The Laws of Candy; Boyle, Englische Studien, VII, 75, *ibid.*,
XVIII, 294; Oliphant, *ibid.*, XV, 331, note; Chambers, Beaumont
and Fletcher Variorum, III, 468.

The Noble Gentleman; Dyce, Works of Beaumont and Fletcher, I, lxxvi; Boyle, Englische Studien, VII, 75, *ibid.,* XVIII, 294; Fleay, *ibid.,* IX, 27; Oliphant, *ibid.,* XV, 331, note.

The Nice Valor; Prölss, Das neuere Drama der Engländer, p. 189.

Phillis of Scyros; Greg, Past. Poet. and Past. Dram., p. 247 ff.

The Lovers' Progress; Weber, Works of Beaumont and Fletcher, XIII, 427; Dyce, Works of Beaumont and Fletcher, I, lxxix, XI, 3; Boyle, Englische Studien, IX, 25-26.

Love's Pilgrimage; Malone, Shakespeare Variorum, III, 226; Weber, Works of Beaumont and Fletcher, XIII, p. 295; Dyce, Works of Beaumont and Fletcher, I, lxxx, XI, 217; Boyle, Englische Studien, VIII, 53; Oliphant, *ibid.,* XV, 346 ff.

The General; Halliwell[-Phillipps], Dict. of O. E. Plays, p. 106; Fleay, Anglia, VIII, 414; Schipper, James Shirley, p. 241.

No Wit, No Help like a Woman's; Bullen, Works of Middleton, I, xl.

Andromana; Genest, Stage, IV, 113; Greg, Past. Poet. and Past. Dram., 330-31.

The above bibliographical notes may be supplemented by Ward, Hist. Eng. Dram. Lit., Fleay, Biog. Chron., Schelling, Eliz. Dram. See also Bullen (John Fletcher), D. N. B., XIX, 303 ff., and Ward (James Shirley), *ibid.,* LII, 126 ff.

## I.  Dick of Devonshire

Dick of Devonshire, an anonymous tragicomedy, was published from Egerton MS. 1994, British Museum, by Bullen in 1883 in Vol. II of his first series of Old Plays. In his introduction, Bullen attributed the play tentatively to Heywood, while in a subjoined note Fleay is quoted as believing Davenport the author. In Anglia, VIII, 405-6, Fleay repudiated his earlier attribution, denied Heywood's authorship, and assigned the play positively to Shirley. Dick of Devonshire, he asserted, was in reality the play licensed November 4, 1626, as The Brothers, while the play later printed under that name was licensed in 1641 as The

Politic Father (see under The Politician, Chap. VI, for a
disproval of the identification of The Brothers and The
Politic Father).

As nearly as can be judged, Fleay's reasons for assigning Dick of Devonshire to Shirley are these: Dick of
Devonshire contains an allusion to "the stories of Two
Brothers" (V, 1); it contains no political allusions and it
is certainly Shirley's (Anglia as cited and p. 411; Biog.
Chron., II, 237). These are no reasons at all. "Dick of
Devonshire" is mentioned three times in the course of the
play (II, 1, 4, III, 3), so Bullen's title may be the original
one; and the internal evidence is all opposed to Shirley's
authorship. The play, which is founded on a contemporary pamphlet,[3] is purely popular in tone, and therefore
in both particulars unlike any other play of Shirley's.
It is partly a glorification of an English common soldier,
which is not a Shirleian theme. Contrary to Shirley's
usual practice, there are two practically entirely dissoci-
ated plots. That dramatist, it must be remembered, was
a Catholic, and but a comparatively recent convert in
1626. However, the author of Dick of Devonshire makes a
character allude to the "yoke of Rome," and causes his
hero, Dick, since he is a good Protestant, to refuse to confess to two priests. There is an anti-Spanish sentiment
evident in the play. Nowhere does Shirley show any anti-
Spanish tendencies. On the contrary, he seems to have
gone to Spanish literature for the sources of several plays.
The villainy of Henrico, which is the theme of the more
romantic plot, is unconvincing and bungling, quite unlike
the machinations of Shirley's Lorenzo or his Flaviano, to
compare a less notable example. In short, while Bullen's
assignment of the play to Heywood may reasonably be

[3] Three to One (Arber's English Garner, I, 621 ff.).

questioned, there can be no doubt that Shirley had no hand
in it whatsoever.[4]

## II.  The Ball

The Ball was licensed November 16, 1632, as by Shirley
alone.  In a note to the entry in his Officebook, Herbert
says that certain courtiers were represented in the play so
naturally that he would have forbidden it, had not Beeston,
the manager of the Queen's Men, promised that the comedy
would be altered (Shakespeare Variorum, III, 231–32).
In 1639 The Ball was printed as by Chapman and Shirley.

In regard to this apparent dual authorship various opin-
ions have been voiced, both as to the manner of collaboration and the amount of it.  Gifford asserted the larger
portion of the play to be Chapman's, while Dyce thought it
almost entirely Shirley's.  Parrott, Ward, Neilson, Koeppel, Swinburne, Schelling, Boas, Lehman, and Fleay agree
with Dyce in believing The Ball, as it stands, to be almost
altogether, if not entirely, the work of Shirley.  The opinion of earlier students of the drama was that the two
authors actually wrote together on the play (cf. Gifford).
Fleay first declared The Ball to be clearly an old play of
Chapman's revised by Shirley (Anglia, VIII, 406).  Later,
he decided that the play was originally Shirley's, and that,
having been objected to by Herbert, on account of person-
alities contained in it, the obnoxious passages were expunged and their places supplied by bits of Chapman's
composition (Biog. Chron., II, 238–39).  Lehman's theory
(Chabot, pp. 26–27) that no part of the play is Chapman's
seems unfounded in view of the fact that five years after
the death of Chapman in obscurity and poverty, there

[4] Cf. Nason, James Shirley, Chap. II.

could have been no reason for coupling his name with Shirley's on the titlepage of a play.[5]

Fleay's revised theory, as stated above, gives what seems to the writer the most probable solution of the problem of the manner in which Shirley and Chapman "collaborated" on The Ball. It is very reasonable, in view of the facts in the case, to believe that since Shirley's play was objectionable to Herbert, as he states, Beeston, in order to secure its licensing, agreed to have it revised. Perhaps Shirley, offended at the strictures of the Master of the Revels, refused to alter it; at any rate, Chapman seems likely then to have been called from his retirement to change it so as to meet with official approval. These changes were probably the writing in of inoffensive passages in place of those stricken out, and the changing of the name of certain characters. In two places (IV, 3, V, 1) we have in the old edition proper names other than

[5] After the above discussion of the authorship of The Ball was prepared, Parrott's edition of Chapman's Comedies has appeared. In his Introduction to the play (p. 869 ff.) Parrott advances the theory that the entire play is Shirley's, and that misled by the fact that Chabot, which was entered in the Stationers' Register at the same time as The Ball, was by Shirley and Chapman, the publishers ascribed the present comedy on the titlepage to the two writers. The inconsistency between the names of certain characters in IV, 3, and V, 1, he holds to be due to a hasty revision by Shirley himself. Parrott's case is a good one but hardly entirely convincing. The many analogues which he cites in action and language may indicate no more than that Shirley had at least the chief part in the composition of the play. That the assignment of The Ball to Shirley and Chapman was the result of such a mistake as Parrott believes to have occurred is at best only a probability.

It should be observed that in the following discussion of The Ball the material drawn from Parrott's excellent introduction and notes to the play is given in the footnotes, and that elsewhere the present author has, except where noted, utilized the results of his own independent study of the comedy.

those of the *dramatis personæ*, namely, Stephen for Lamount, Lionel for Travers, and Loveall for Rainbow.
These not improbably are Shirley's names, and perhaps
in them part of his offense lay, for he may have used the
Christian names of certain courtiers as designations for
his gulls.  On account of these discrepancies in nomencla-
ture, Fleay assumes that the scenes in which they occur
are Chapman's.  Certainly V, 1, has reminiscences of
Chapman about it, but IV, 3, cannot be so easily judged.
After all, even if Fleay's theory is correct, it may be that
the latter of these scenes, if not the former, is entirely
Shirley's and that the use of the new (or old) names is
an oversight on Chapman's part (see Nason, James Shirley, Chaps. IV and IX).

Whatever was the method of collaboration pursued, it is
plain that the conception and plot of The Ball are Shirley's and most of the dialogue besides.  The Ball is a representative of The Scornful Lady type of play to which
Hyde Park is perhaps Shirley's finest contribution (see
under Hyde Park for analogues).  At the same time, the
comedy is complicated by the introduction of the theme of
The Humorous Courtier (the leading on of vain, foolish
suitors to declarations of love and subsequent confusion).
An echo of Love in a Maze is found in Lord Rainbow's
seeming inability to decide whether he loves the Lady
Rosamond or Lady Honoria the better (I, 2).  They and
Lady Lucina are Shirley's typical clever young ladies (see
Chap. IV, Sect. 40).  Schipper is reminded by the last
and her maid, Scutilla, of Portia and Nerissa in The Merchant of Venice (James Shirley, p. 104).  Bostock is the
ordinary bragging poltroon, and the three (in all, five)
suitors are typical foolish gentlemen (see Chap. IV, Sects.
47 and 44).  Ward suggests that Coryat, who is mentioned in II, 1, furnished some hints for Freshwater, the

"traveller" (Hist. Eng. Dram. Lit., III, 107). Gifford
derives him from Puntarvolo in Every Man out of his
Humor. Volterre in The Humorous Courtier is a related
character. For Frisk, the French dancing-master, see
Eckhardt, Ausländertypen (Materialien, XXXII), p.
94 ff. (a discussion of French characters in Elizabethan
drama). Note also *ibid.*, p. 81 ff., and see under Love
Tricks.

The plot of The Ball runs thus:

A rich young widow, the Lady Lucina, has as suitors
Sir Ambrose Lamount, Sir Marmaduke Travers, Bostock,
and Colonel Winfield. She has the first three call at her
house, while Winfield eavesdrops, and pretends to favor
each in turn, and leads him to disclose his folly. She
then jeers Winfield who vows to conquer her. The three
suitors meet as they are on their way to procure their
licenses, and discover they have been tricked. Urged on
by Winfield who meets them, they go to Lucina's house
and rail on her. Winfield now takes her part and beats
Bostock. Lucina regards Winfield more favorably, but
tests him by vowing she will not marry him unless he will
swear he has "been honest of his body." This he will
not do. She then tests him again by announcing that she
is really poor. Suspecting a trick, he asserts that her
poverty makes no difference. She then accepts him because of his honesty. To prove that The Ball is not immoral, Lucina takes Winfield to one at Lord Rainbow's,
and the play ends with the ball and a masque. The un-
masking of Bostock, the coward, of Barker, the pretended
cynic, of Freshwater, the traveller, and further tricks upon
Travers and Lamount by Rosamond and Honoria, together
with the revenge of the latter upon Lord Rainbow for his
indiscreet remarks concerning their love for him, are rather
episodic additional incidents in the play.

Act I, Sc. 1. For the reference to the Lady of the Lake, see under The Royal Master, IV, 1. Cf. Bostock's threats against Lamount and his change of tone on the latter's entrance with Tucca and Horace (Koeppel, Ben Jonson's Wirkung, p. 110). For the allusion to the Knight of the Sun (p. 7) see under The Maid's Revenge, I, 2.⁶ Cf. for the reference to Bethlem Gabor (p. 13) The Bird in a Cage, under IV, 1.

Sc. 2. For the quarrel of Rosamond and Honoria over Lord Rainbow, cf. A Midsummer Night's Dream, III, 2, and see also Chap. IV, Sect. 20. Rainbow's inability to choose between the ladies is drawn from Gerard's similar predicament in Love in a Maze, I, 2, II, 3. For the eavesdropping in this scene, and in II, 3, V, 1, see Chap. IV, Sect. 30.

Act II, Sc. 1.⁷ A reference to Coryat, the traveller, occurs, p. 22. He was a common butt for Elizabethan dramatists (cf. The Queen of Corinth, IV, 1, as noted by Ward, Cam. Hist. Eng. Lit., V, 389, note).

Sc. 2 consists of four short speeches.

Sc. 3. Cf. the dancing-lessons here and in III, 1, with Hippolito's fencing-lesson, Love's Cruelty, II, 1. See The Variety, III, 1.⁸ The projects ascribed to Travers by Lucina (pp. 27–28) suggest those of Engine, The Devil is

---

⁶ For the reference to "five to one" (p. 9), cf. Every Man in his Humor, II, 1, The Tempest, III, 3. See The Gamester, V, 1, Henry IV, Part I, II, 4, for the terming Freshwater a "shotten herring" (p. 9). See for the mention of the toothpick (p. 10) The Grateful Servant, III, 1, The Constant Maid, III, 2, Volpone, II, 1 (Parrott, as cited, p. 877). The term "a complete gentleman" (p. 12) does not occur in Love in a Maze, I, 1, as Parrott says it does (ibid., p. 878).

⁷ For the ballad-woman and the "singing in her head" (p. 22), cf. All Fools, V, 1 (ibid.).

⁸ "Molecatcher" (p. 25) is applied to Rawbone in The Wedding, III, 2 (ibid.).

an Ass, II, 1. Cf. also the projects in The Triumph of
Peace, and Captain Underwit, II, 3.[9] For Winfield's
eavesdropping, note I, 2, V, 1, and see Chap. IV, Sect. 30.
Winfield's comparison of his courtship of Lucina to a siege
(p. 35) suggests Suckling's lines 'Tis now since I sat down
(published 1646).[10]

Act III, Sc. 1. See for the dancing-lesson under the
preceding scene.

Sc. 2.[11] The comparing of notes by rivals for a lady's
hand and the discovery that she had been tricking them
and their subsequent actions are drawn from Hyde Park,
I, 1.

Sc. 3. For Freshwater's satire on the foreign painters
in London (pp. 45–46), see under The Humorous Courtier,
IV, 1.[12] What painter the dramatist refers to here is unknown. He seems to have had a wife of doubtful virtue
who was intimate with a butcher. For Barker's attempt
at injuring Rainbow in the estimation of the ladies, see
under The Example, II, 1.

Sc. 4. The suitors' railing on Lucina is drawn from
Hyde Park, II, 4. The incident occurs again in The Lady
of Pleasure, III, 4. There, Bornwell, like Winfield, hears
the wits' jeering and defends the lady against them. In
Hyde Park, Fairfield enters as Rider and Venture leave.

[9] The mention of Lamount's "head of hair" (p. 31) is paralleled in
The Gamester, III, 3. For the allusion to the "Knights of the post"
(p. 33), cf. Love Tricks, I, 1. See King John, I, 1, All Fools, III,
1, and Steevens' note to the first play for Bostock's coming in at the
"wicket" (ibid.).

[10] Cf. The Example, II, 1 (ibid., pp. 878-79).

[11] For "your nose is wiped," cf. All Fools, V, 1, The City Wit,
V (ibid., p. 879).

[12] Cf. Freshwater on the "dejecting" of Englishmen (p. 45) with
the Tutor, The Witty Fair One, II, 1. For the allusion to "regalios"
(p. 46), see The Lady of Pleasure, V, 1 (ibid.).

Cf. also Montague and the suitors, The Honest Man's Fortune, V, 3. Fleay's statement that Winfield's "This is a tale of a tub, lady" (p. 54), is a reference to Jonson's play (which had not yet appeared) (Biog. Chron., II, 239) is plainly incorrect. A "tale of a tub" is an untruth told to divert the auditor from some action or opinion which the speaker does not desire done, or formed. Winfield's "Is't possible to be honest at these years?" (p. 54) seems a reminiscence of Evadne's "A maidenhead, Amintor, At my years?" The Maid's Tragedy, II, 1, or Manto's "A virgin, madam, at my years?" The Renegado, III, 1. For the test of Winfield, cf. IV, 3, and see Chap. IV, Sect. 15.

Act IV, Sc. 1. Cf. Bostock's account of his quarrel with Winfield and of his own conduct with Bubulcus' story of his duel, Love Tricks, IV, 6. For the allusion to "gumm'd taffeta" (p. 56), see under The Lady of Pleasure, II, 2.[13] Koeppel thinks Bostock's "This talking will undo me" (p. 60) was suggested by Parolles' remarks on his tongue, All's Well that Ends Well, IV, 1 (Shakespeare's Wirkung, p. 60). Koeppel compares Barker and Parolles. For analogues to Lord Rainbow's lines on true nobility, pp. 62–63, see under The Royal Master, III, 3.[14]

Sc. 2. Cf. the ladies' trick upon Lamount and Travers with Lillia-Bianca and Pinac, The Wild Goose Chase, IV, 1, 2.[15]

[13] "Running o' the ticket" (p. 56) is mentioned in The Bird in a Cage, I, 1, II, 1; note Sir Giles Goosecap, IV, 2 (ibid.). "Let it go around" (p. 57) occurs in the same connection as above in The Gamester, V, 1 (ibid. p. 880).

[14] For the mention of the Stilyard (p. 62), cf. The Lady of Pleasure, V, 1, and see Parrott, as cited. For the allusion to the "blades" (p. 63) see The Gamester, I, 1 (ibid.).

[15] Parrott notes "figaries" (p. 67) and IV, 3 (p. 73) as occurring in Love Tricks, II, 5 (sic; there are but two scenes in the act), The Bird in a Cage, III, 2, 3 (ibid.).

Sc. 3. For the allusion to Venus and Adonis (p. 72) see under The Doubtful Heir, IV, 2. Cf. Koeppel, Reflexe der Ritter Romane im Drama, p. 202, note, for the references to Guy of Warwick and Bevis of Hampton (p. 72). Hyde Park and Spring Garden are alluded to as places of resort (p. 74).[16] For the allusion to "corantos" (p. 74), see under The Gamester, III, 3. Lucina's pretense of poverty in order to test Winfield (p. 76) is based seemingly on Lady Heartwell's conduct toward Valentine, Wit without Money, V, 4. For the test itself, cf. III, 4, and see Chap. IV, Sect. 15.

Act V, Sc. 1. See under Captain Underwit, III, 2, for an analogue to Freshwater's "travels," and note the burlesque news, The Gamester, III, 3. For Rainbow's eavesdropping, see Chap. IV, Sect. 30. Fleay finds a reference (p. 79) to Bartholomew Fair (Biog. Chron., II, 239). The title of the play, as Freshwater gives it, is Martheme. No play is known, however, with a title resembling that mentioned by Freshwater. Following is a reference to the actresses who appeared in London in 1629. The Queen may be alluded to among "some ladies, inns o' court gentlemen, and others" who desired actresses on the English stage. Shirley, himself, might be included in the second class. For the masque, see Chap. IV, Sect. 18, and note also under The Coronation, IV, 3, Cupid in Shirley's masques.

## III.  The Nightwalker

The Nightwalker, or the Little Thief, was licensed May 11, 1633, as by Fletcher and corrected by Shirley.[17] In 1640, it was published as by Fletcher alone, having been

---

[16] Cf. Hyde Park, II, 4 (ibid., p. 881).

[17] For the source, see Miss Ott, Die Italienische Novelle im Englischen Drama, p. 74 ff.

entered in the Stationers' Register for Master Crooke and William Cooke, April 25, 1639, as The Nightwalters [sic], together with three other plays of Shirley's, and Fletcher's Wit without Money.

The date of the earlier version of The Nightwalker is a point concerning which scholars disagree. Thorndike places the play in 1612 (The Influence of Beaumont and Fletcher on Shakespeare, p. 92) ; Fleay dates it about 1614 (Biog. Chron., I, 197) ; while Oliphant advances a date before 1610 or after 1613 as the time of its first presentation (Englische Studien, XV, 350).

As to the amount of "correcting" which Shirley did there is a greater difference of opinion. Most scholars find extensive alterations by him. Boyle considers the play entirely Fletcher's to the end of III, 2. Of the remainder, III, 5, 6, IV, 3, 4, 5, V, 1, 2, down to "enter Heartlove," and from "enter Nurse, Maria, etc.," to the end of the play is Fletcher's, while the rest is Shirley's (Englische Studien, VIII, 53). Oliphant gives to Fletcher I, 1 (from Heartlove's entrance to the end of the act), II, 1, 2, 3, and the last nine speeches of 4, III, 1, 2, 3 (from Lurcher's entrance), 5, IV, 1, 3, 4. To Fletcher and Shirley he gives I, 1 (to Heartlove's entrance), II, 4 (from Lurcher's entrance), III, 3 (to Lurcher's entrance), 4, 6, IV, 5, V, 1, 2 (from "Maria goes to Alathe" to the end). Shirley alone he thinks the author of II, 4 (to Lurcher's entrance), IV, 2, 6, V, 2 (to "Maria goes to Alathe") (Englische Studien, XV, 350). Fleay asserts that the unaltered Fletcherian portions are I, 2, 4, 5, 6, 7, 8, II, 1, 2. The scenes altered by Shirley are III, 1, and V, 2, while I, 3, III, 3, IV, 1, 3, 4, V, 1, were rewritten by Shirley (Biog. Chron., I, 197). In Englische Studien, IX, 21, Fleay says Shirley's part may be traced by the names Wildbrain and Nicholas, Fletcher's by Wildgoose and

Toby.   Were this the case, I, 2, 6, would be the only scenes untouched by Shirley.

It seems rather unlikely that The Nightwalker should have been subjected in 1633 to any such extensive revision as the scholars above quoted seem to believe to be the case. It will be noticed that their results are not at all the same. They even do not agree upon the ascription of III, 3, 4, to Shirley whose hand is certainly evident in the allusions to Histriomastix.   Further, why should Fletcher's work have been practically rewritten? He had by no means gone out of fashion in the eight years since his death: witness how his plays held the stage, how they influenced contemporary drama, and how they were alluded to by writers of the time.   Had Shirley rewritten The Nightwalker in any such way as Boyle, Oliphant, and Fleay indicate, it would probably have been entered as his, and certainly his name would have been at least on the titlepage of the 1640 edition.

What seems most probably to have occurred in the case of this play is that Shirley made some slight changes in it, such as the changing of the names of the original Wildgoose and Nicholas, and the introduction of the references to Histriomastix already noted.   That his revision was a hasty and rather perfunctory one seems indicated by the fact that both the names "Wildgoose" and "Wildbrain" are found in I, 4, and "Nick" and "Toby" in II, 1, and III, 1.   The unmorality of the play seems certainly Fletcher's.   There seems to be no reason why Fletcher's dialogue should have been rewritten to a considerable extent by Shirley.   The case is like that of The Ball, probably: a hasty alteration of a play by changing the *dramatis personæ* (accounting thus for the discrepancies in name) and the introduction of some speeches, with perhaps an alteration of others (cf. Dyce, Works of Beaumont and

Fletcher, XI, 121. He thinks the greater part of the play Fletcher's).

## IV. Chabot

The Tragedy of Chabot, Admiral of France, was licensed April 29, 1635. It was entered in the Stationers' Register for Master Crooke and William Cooke, October 24, 1638, as by Shirley and was published in 1639 as by Chapman and Shirley.

Scholars have been nearly unanimous in attributing the greater part of Chabot to Chapman. Gifford, Dyce, the Quarterly Review critic (XLIX, 29, note), Nason, Boas, Ward, Swinburne, Schipper, Lehman, and Neilson, agree in assigning the larger portion, or even all the play, to Chapman. Only Genest, Parrott and Fleay give Shirley any considerable share in it. Genest (IX, 553) assigns the first two acts to Chapman, and the last three to Shirley. To Chapman's share in Genest's division of the play, Fleay adds the prose speeches in III, 1 (sic; 2, in fact), and V, 2 (Biog. Chron., II, 241). Parrott finds a careful revision of the play by Shirley, with occasionally a completely rewritten scene (Chapman's Tragedies, p. 633).

Parrott's investigation, as being careful and searching, merits discussion. According to him, Chabot was composed by Chapman in 1612 or 1613, the source being the 1611 edition of Estienne Pasquier's Recherches de la France, Bk. V, Chap. XII. The play, when completed, was turned over to the Queen's Revels Company and so descended to Queen Henrietta's Men. At Chapman's death the play was resurrected, furbished up by Shirley, and reproduced. Shirley has cut down long epic speeches, expunged sententious moralization, filled in with lively dialogue, and has strengthened the figures of the wife and Queen for a feminine interest. Following in a condensed

form are Parrott's judgments as to the authorship of the
various scenes of Chabot as expressed in his notes to that
tragedy (Chapman's Tragedies, p. 639 ff.) : I, 1—almost
pure Chapman; 2—Shirley at the beginning and elsewhere, but in bulk Chapman's; II, 1—wholly Shirley's in
metre, diction and ease of dialogue; 2—essentially Chapman's; revision by Shirley visible; 3—essentially Chapman's; possibly cut at l. 134; III, 1—almost wholly Shirley's; simplicity, clearness of diction; jealousy and change
of heart of the Queen Shirley's; 2—almost wholly Chapman's; elaborate prose speeches more in his style than
Shirley's; Shirley has touched up the scene and seems to
have imitated it in The Traitor, III, 1; hence he must
have known the play in MS. (!); IV, 1—Shirley and
Chapman blended; first 120 lines mainly Shirley's, and
latter part of the scene revised by him; V, 1—originally by
Chapman, and revised by Shirley; evidences of double
authorship evident; 2—mainly, if not wholly, Chapman's;
prose speeches certainly his and the greater part of the
verse, although Shirley may have added and revised some
lines; 3—a substratum of Chapman, heavily overlaid with
Shirley.

It appears hardly probable that such an extended and
careful revision of Chabot was made by Shirley. What
may with a reasonable degree of certainty be said is that
the scenes involving the Queen and the Wife (III, I, IV, 1)
owe more or less to Shirley. In addition to this, Ward's
theory that the prose speeches in III, 2, and V, 2, are
Shirley's (Hist. Eng. Dram. Lit., II, 446) seems very well
founded. The fact of the matter is, it would seem, that
Chabot, like Chapman's other tragedies, having been devoid of any comic element at all when it came into Shirley's hands, he supplied the deficiency by paraphrasing,
perhaps, the Advocate's speech in the original play and by

emphasizing his change of sides. The mention by the Proctor-general (or Advocate) of a scarcity of fish as inducing mortal sin by preventing fasting on the proper days (III, 2) may perhaps be taken as pointing toward a Catholic author, such as Shirley was. Parrott's conjecture that Shirley borrowed for Rogero's speech, III, 1, The Traitor, from these scenes is undoubtedly without foundation. The true situation seems to be that Shirley here borrowed from the comic element of his own earlier play.[18]

It is perhaps worth noting that the Proctor-general of III, 2, is called the ''Advocate'' in IV, 1, and V, 2. This inconsistency points to a hasty alteration of the play which is indicated also by the fact that only five characters are named in the tragedy. Shirley practically always provided names for his characters.

## V.  Captain Underwit

In 1883, Bullen published in his second volume of Old Plays (first series) a comedy from Harleian MS. 7650 which, after Halliwell (Dict. O. E. Plays, p. 42), he called Captain Underwit. In the introduction to his reprint of the play, Bullen attributed it positively to Shirley, and there and in his notes pointed out a number of resemblances to the undoubted plays of Shirley. Captain Underwit is, however, no other than the Duke of Newcastle's Country Captain, which was printed in 1649 with The Variety.[19] The MS. from which Bullen printed the play differs but slightly from the printed version of 1649.

But there is a strong probability, indeed almost a cer-

[18] Schipper suggests that Shirley wrote Chabot's conversation with Allegre, V, 3, his Wife's speech in III, 1, and the Queen's, IV, 1, and elsewhere (James Shirley, p. 182).

[19] The expression "captain for your country" occurs in III, 3, (p. 366).

tainty, that Bullen's attribution of Captain Underwit (or The Country Captain) to Shirley is partially correct. Wood states that Shirley assisted Newcastle in the "composure of certain plays which the Duke afterwards published" (Ath. Oxon., III, 739). To Newcastle Shirley dedicated The Traitor, and to him he addressed the lines found on VI, 435, of the Gifford-Dyce edition. Also, according to Wood, on the breaking out of the Civil War, Shirley entered the royal service under the Duke where he served until the flight of the latter to France (Ath. Oxon., III, 737). In the Plays of the King's Men (Malone Society, Collections, I, 368–69) it may be significant that The Country Captain follows immediately Shirley's Imposture. Here we see ample grounds for conjecturing that Shirley collaborated with his patron on Captain Underwit, at least.

Bullen based his theory of Shirley's authorship on the general style of the play and on a number of resemblances in more minute particulars to passages in various of the undoubted plays of Shirley. In the following discussion some additional points which Bullen overlooked or omitted for want of space or time will be brought forward. The ascription of Captain Underwit, or of any part of it, apparently, to Shirley has met both with approval and with opposition. Firth says that it "seems clear that much of the work is Shirley's. Some of the verses interspersed are Newcastle's. He wrote many passages and doubtless conceived the plan of the play, but to fit it for the stage he had to call in the aid of an expert dramatist and owed more to his assistant than he owned" (Life of William, Duke of Newcastle, Editor's Preface, p. xviii).[20]   Koeppel

[20] The fact that Margaret Lucas was married to the Duke of Newcastle about December, 1645, three years after the closing of the theatres, and over a year after the Duke had left England, helps

thinks the comedy largely Shirley's (Shakespeare's Wirk-ung, p. 64; cf. Ben Jonson's Wirkung, p. 178, where he calls it doubtlessly Shirley's). Swinburne considers it "mainly if not altogether the work of Shirley" (Fort-nightly Review, June 1, 1890, p. 476). On the other hand, Ward does not accord a ready assent to Bullen's ascription of Captain Underwit to Shirley (Hist. Eng. Dram. Lit., III, 120). Fleay, animated by personal pique seemingly, at-tacks Bullen and asperses the soundness of his critical judgment in calling the comedy Shirley's (Biog. Chron., I, 48–49). Dyce says, "The style of his Grace's dramas would certainly have induced me to suspect the truth of this statement [Wood's], if I had not discovered, that a drinking-song which is inserted in the Duke's comedy called The Country Captain is printed among our author's Poems" (I, xliii).

The date of Captain Underwit has been set between 1639 and 1642. The list of the Plays of the King's Men, already cited, shows that the comedy had been acted by August 7, 1641, the date of the document. The earlier date has been set because of the mention of the Pacification of Berwick (I, 1, p. 321) which was concluded in June, 1639. There is also a reference to the great ship (III, 3, p. 369) which was built in 1637. The allusion to the cup at Newmarket, according to historians of the turf, would date the play after 1640 when, they say, racing at New-market began, but there is a reference to Newmarket races in Hyde Park, V, 1 (produced 1632; printed 1637). In I, 2, there is a mention of the "Proclamation commanding the gentry to keep their residence in at their mansions in the Country and forbidding them to make their habitations in London and places adjoining," which was made June 20,

to account for the fact that nowhere in her Life of her husband does she mention Shirley.

1632. This would seem to indicate an earlier date for the play than any heretofore offered, since it seems unlikely that a proclamation at least seven years earlier would be alluded to among other strictly contemporary references.

This allusion, together with certain other points, makes it not absolutely impossible to identify Captain Underwit with what has been considered a lost play of Shirley's— Look to the Lady.[21] This play which would seem to have been a comedy was entered in the Stationers' Register, March 10, 1639–40, but was seemingly never printed. It was the last of the plays entered by John Williams and Francis Egglesfeild. The date of the entry was about the time of Shirley's return from Ireland. It is certainly not impossible, nor is it especially improbable that these publishers, Williams and Egglesfeild had obtained a MS. of Captain Underwit, which they renamed, and were preparing to publish as Shirley's, when that author returning to England discovered their intention and put a stop to the publication of the play, or it may have been that the then Earl of Newcastle halted its printing. The fact that The Arcadia was published by these men under the date of 1640 need not stand in the way, as that may have appeared shortly after the beginning of the year (old style) and before Shirley's arrival in England. Furthermore, Look to the Lady was not licensed for performance in England as far as we know. The only play of Shirley's presented in Ireland and printed during his stay there is The Royal Master which was licensed in England. Look to the Lady, if a rechristened play of Newcastle's and Shirley's, would nearly certainly not have been licensed under the latter's name and hence would not appear in Malone's extracts from Herbert's Officebook. Then no reason has

[21] Nissen says of Look to the Lady "höchst wahrscheinlich nicht von ihm [Shirley] verfasst" (James Shirley, p. 21).

ever been advanced for the withdrawal of this play from
publication and for its never having been published, even
during Shirley's later years when he seems to have put
into print everything available. The title of the supposedly lost play would fit Captain Underwit admirably;
for if ever a woman needed looking to, it is Lady Huntlove
in that play. Then if we are to identify Captain Underwit with Look to the Lady we must place its date before
1636. The preceding year, 1635, would seem approximately appropriate, in view of the fact that we know from
the dedication of The Traitor in that year that the Earl
and the playwright were then more or less acquainted.
Pepys, who saw The Country Captain, October 26, 1661,
calls the performance "the first time it hath been acted
this twenty-five years" (Diary, II, 118). This would
throw the date of performance back to 1636. Pepys' statement, however, cannot be accepted as conclusive. The
early date would account for the otherwise slightly anti-
quated allusion to the royal proclamation. The references
to events after 1635 or '36, may be explained by the supposition that Newcastle, or perhaps Shirley, had revised the
play.

What part of Captain Underwit is Shirley's is extremely
difficult to decide. Firth's opinion, as given above, is hard
to accept. It seems much more probable from the nature
of the plot of the comedy that both Newcastle and Shirley
worked on it together, and that they contributed to the
dialogue together. The allusions to the militia and to the
lord lieutenant in I, 1, seem to indicate Newcastle's hand
(Newcastle, when still Viscount Mansfield, was Lord Lieutenant of Nottinghamshire), as do those to racing and to
horses in Sc. 2, of that act. The numerous literary allusions in the play also are not in Shirley's manner. But
Shirley shows some knowledge of racing in Hyde Park, so

that he may have been responsible for the reference here (see under Hyde Park, IV, 3). It may be asserted fairly safely, however, that the parallels in incident and language noted later indicate the hand of Shirley, for his inveterate repetition of himself has been very plainly shown in the foregoing chapters.

The plot of Captain Underwit is a combination of themes from three of Shirley's plays. The intrigue of Sir Francis and Lady Huntlove is based on Lady Bornwell and her followers in The Lady of Pleasure; Courtwell's winning of the Sister is derived from the courtship of Carol by Fairfield in Hyde Park; and the gulling of Underwit by Dorothy is founded on the trick played on Sir Nicholas by Sensible in The Witty Fair One. As to characters, in Huntlove we have a repetition of Bornwell in The Lady of Pleasure. Lady Huntlove is of the same type as Lady Bornwell in the same play and Lady Plot in The Example. Device is related to Kickshaw and Littleworth in The Lady of Pleasure, while nearly a repetition of Caperwit in Love in a Maze. Underwit and Thomas are examples of the foolish gentleman and servant, already dealt with in Chap. IV, Sect. 45. Engine, the projector, as Koeppel says, may be derived from Engine and Meercraft in The Devil is an Ass (Ben Jonson's Wirkung, p. 178). Cf. also the projectors in The Triumph of Peace, The Antipodes, and The Court Beggar. The Sister belongs to the witty young woman type, for which see Chap. IV, Sect. 40. Dorothy, the witty maid, has for prototype Sensible in The Witty Fair One; she is a sort of female Gorgon (see Love Tricks), or Brainworm.

An outline of Captain Underwit follows:

Sir Richard Huntlove, who is advanced in years, grows jealous of his young gay wife and goes down from London

to his estate in the country.  With the pair go Sir Francis
Courtwell who loves Lady Huntlove, her Sister, and Courtwell, a nephew of Sir Francis who is in love with her,
Device, a fantastical gallant, Engine, a projector, Captain
Underwit, Huntlove's stepson by his first wife, who has
just received his commission in the trained bands, Captain
Sackbury, a drunken old soldier and his mentor, and Dorothy, Lady Huntlove's maid who has designs on Underwit.
Sir Francis prevails upon Lady Huntlove to grant him an
assignation.  He pretends illness, and remains at home
while Huntlove goes hunting.  Suddenly returning, the
latter surprises them together, but his wife pretends to be
sleep-walking and she and her lover come off safely.  They
then arrange another meeting.  Lady Huntlove pretends
to have a toothache.  She rises from her bed to pace the
floor, and Dorothy slips into her place, while her mistress
goes to Sir Francis' room.  However, he has fallen asleep,
so she leaves a note by him and returns to her room.  A
third assignation is arranged.  Sir Richard and Sir Francis
leave for London.  The latter is to fall from his horse and
simulate injury so as to be forced to return to Sir Richard's.  He does fall in reality, is seriously hurt, and, taking his misadventures as a warning, is converted to penitence.  His nephew, who has been jeered by the Sister, re-
pays her in her own coin and leaves her.  Device then steals
Courtwell's sword, but is pursued by him.  He then
demonstrates Device's cowardice before his mistress.  She
is attracted by Courtwell's coldness toward her, confesses
her love to him, and the two are married.  Dorothy has a
footman come to Sir Richard with a letter which states
that she is the runaway daughter of a wealthy knight.
Underwit learns of the letter, and, thinking her of good
birth, marries her after which the imposition is revealed.

Engine furnishes some comic passages by pretending madness as a device for escaping from the consequences of some of his projects.

Act I, Sc. 1. The allusions to the trained bands, and to the Lord Lieutenant would indicate Newcastle's hand as noted. For the reference to Bardolph's definition of "accommodated," see Henry IV, Part II, III, 2 (cf. II, 2, for another allusion to Shakespeare). For the business with the list (p. 321), cf. The Opportunity, IV, 1. For the character of Captain Sackbury (pp. 322–23), see Chap. IV, Sect. 21. Sir Richard's desire to return to the country is based on The Lady of Pleasure, I, 1 (cf. also The Noble Gentleman, II, 1). For the use of the expression "a la mode" (p. 329) see under V, 1, and cf. Honoria and Mammon, and The Variety, II, 1, III, 1, V, 1. Cf. the mention of a ball (p. 330) with The Ball and The Lady of Pleasure, I, 1. Bullen notes (p. 330) a parallel between Device's reference to the "new play," and The Witty Fair One, IV, 2. Sir Francis' speech to the Sister (p. 334) beginning "Sweet lady, I beseech you muzzle your beagle . . ." is utilized in The Variety, II, 1, by Newman to Simpleton in the lines beginning "Dismiss your beagles. . . ."

Act II (Sc. 1). For "Bu'oy" for "good-bye" (p. 338), cf. The Constant Maid, I, 1, and note "God bu'y," Henry VI, Part I, III, 2, Hamlet, II, 2, IV, 5. Bullen suggests that "Agamemnon in the play" (p. 339) refers to Troilus and Cressida; Koeppel in Shakespeare's Wirkung, p. 65, considers the allusion to be to Shirley's Contention of Ajax and Ulysses. Other plays in which Agamemnon figures are The Iron Age, Parts I, II (printed 1632), and Goffe's Orestes (1623; printed 1633). An allusion to The Alchemist occurs, p. 339. For the use of "leveret" (p. 340) Bullen cites Honoria and Mammon, I, 2.

Sc. 2. References to taverns occur, p. 341. Cf. The

Lady of Pleasure, IV, 2, The Wedding, II, 1, Wit without
Money, II, 4.  For the mention of Shakespeare's Plays
(p. 342), see under I, 1.  Device and the Sister (p. 344 ff.)
suggest Caperwit's courtship, Love in a Maze, I, 2, II, 2.
The Sister and Courtwell (p. 348 ff.) seem based on Carol
and Fairfield, Hyde Park, I, 2.  Koeppel points out a
parody by the Sister (p. 349) of Hamlet, I, 4, 5, (Shakespeare's Wirkung, p. 65).  Cf. the use of "sweet sir"
(p. 349) with Startup's use of the same in The Constant
Maid.  The ballad of The Lady's Downfall is referred to
(p. 350).  Bullen refers for Courtwell's ornate speech to
the Sister and her parody in reply (p. 350) to The Lady
of Pleasure, V, 1.  The law-French (p. 351) suggests Shirley's hand.

Sc. 3.  Bullen finds a close parallel in The Duke's Mistress, IV, 1, for "To chain him with the cordage of his
hair . . ." (p. 353).  Koeppel finds a plagiarism (p. 354)
in Engine's projected monopoly of periwigs from The
Court Beggar, I, 1 (Ben Jonson's Wirkung, p. 179).
There is certainly some relationship between the two passages.  For projectors, see under The Triumph of Peace.

Act III, Sc. 1.  The arrangements of Sir Thomas and
Lady Huntlove in this scene and in V, 4, for securing a
meeting suggest Fowler's pretended illness, The Witty
Fair One, III, 4.  Note, as a parallel to her dream, Kate's
"sleep-walking," Northward Ho, III, 2.  For the lady's
excuses to her husband, cf. The Lovers' Progress, III, 3.

Sc. 2.  For Device's verses, see Chap. IV, Sect. 22.  Cf.
his "travels," as set down in the verses, with The Ball,
V, 1, and Bobadill's various adventures as recounted in
Every Man in his Humor, and note The Antipodes.

Sc. 3.  "Rotten," as meaning "to have by heart," conjectured "rooted" by Bullen (p. 366), occurs in The
Humorous Courtier, III, 1, The Constant Maid, III, 2.

For the pretended madness of Engine (p. 368 ff.), see under The Cardinal, V, 3 (cf. also Love Tricks, II, 2). As a source, see The Devil is an Ass, V, 3, 5. Cf. the mention of the cup at Newmarket (p. 368) with Hyde Park, IV, 3 (not Sc. 1, as Bullen cites it).

Act IV, Sc. 1. For the drinking scene (according to Bullen occurring at the end of the MS.), see Chap. IV, Sect. 26. The Catch printed among Shirley's Poems (VI, 439) was inserted at the opening of this scene. A reference to The White Devil occurs, p. 375.

Sc. 2. "The receipt of cosenage" (p. 379) seems an allusion possibly to such plays as The Parson's Wedding. Engine's vomiting projects (p. 380) is based on Crispinus and his vocabulary, The Poetaster, V, 1, but cf. The Devil is an Ass, V, 5.

Sc. 3. For Courtwell's railing on the Sister, see Chap. IV, Sect. 20, and especially Hyde Park, II, 4, V, 1. Bullen refers (p. 384) to The Duke's Mistress, IV, 1. Cf. Courtwell's speech, "I shall be very loath . . ." (p. 383) with Fowler's, The Witty Fair One, I, 3 (p. 287). "Sister's thread" (p. 384) Bullen finds employed in Hyde Park, V, 1, The Honest Whore, Part I, IV, 3, The Lady's Trial. Fletcher's Woman Hater is referred to, p. 387 (cf. The Humorous Courtier, II, 2). Cf. the trick by which Device gets Courtwell's sword with Fulbank's artifice in Honoria and Mammon, I, 1.

Sc. 4 consists of a soliloquy by Sir Francis.

Sc. 5. The pretended toothache of the lady suggests that of Calista, The Lovers' Progress, III, 3. For somewhat similar scenes, cf. The Witty Fair One, III, 1, The City Nightcap, II, 1. A reference to Dametas and the bear, Sidney's Arcadia, pp. 70–71, occurs, p. 392.

Sc. 6. An analogue for this scene occurs, perhaps, in

some collection of stories (a lady comes to her lover's room, finds him asleep, and goes away, leaving him a note).

Act V, Sc. 1. "Your Alamode" (p. 395) (see I, 1) suggests Alamode in Honoria and Mammon. For the expression "feather'd footed servant," see under The Triumph of Beauty. See Chap. IV, Sect. 1, for the Sister's confession of her love to Courtwell, and for their reconciliation, cf. Carol and Fairfield, Hyde Park, V, 1. For "myself in this small volume Against your bulk in folio" (p. 399), cf. Love Tricks, I, 1. The reference to the city pageants (p. 399) should be compared with A Contention for Honor and Riches, Sc. 1, and Honoria and Mammon, I, 1. For Courtwell's eavesdropping, see Chap. IV, Sect. 30. Device's cowardice recalls Bubulcus, Love Tricks, II, 1.

Sc. 2. Sir Francis plans to counterfeit a fall from his horse.

Sc. 3. Bullen quotes a line which occurs in The Bird in a Cage, IV, 1.

Sc. 4. Dorothy's gulling Underwit seems based on Sensible and Treedle, The Witty Fair One, V, 3. For the conversion of Sir Francis, see Chap. IV, Sect. 10.

### VI, VII.   Other Plays of the Duke of Newcastle

Besides Captain Underwit, or The Country Captain, the Duke of Newcastle seems to have been sole or part author of The Variety (published 1649), The Humorous Lovers (published 1677), The Triumphant Widow, and a translation of Molière's L'Etourdi (adapted by Dryden as Sir Martin Mar-all). He also contributed five scenes to the Duchess of Newcastle's Lady Contemplation (Firth's edition of The Life of William, Duke of Newcastle, p. 109, note). "A book containing songs and sketches of plays

in the handwriting of the Duke is preserved at Welbeck''
(*ibid.*).  Only Captain Underwit and The Variety, according to Schelling (Eliz. Dram., II, 283), were produced before the Civil War.  The Variety shows to a certain degree the influence of Shirley (cf. Schelling, *ibid.*), but
there is little to lead one to believe that he had anything
to do with its composition.  It is a dull and labored comedy
with little wit and less characterization.  The Academy,
III, 1, is strongly reminiscent of the Compliment School
of Love Tricks, III, 5.  Among the characters, Galliard,
the French dancing-master, and Simpleton, the gull, with
his servant, James, recall respectively Le Frisk in The
Ball, and the foolish masters and men listed in Chap. IV,
Sect. 45.[22]

Some considerable part of The Triumphant Widow was
incorporated in Shadwell's Bury Fair, thereby leading
Firth (Life of William, Duke of Newcastle, Editor's Preface, p. xix) to conjecture very reasonably that Shadwell,
having aided the Duke in composing the play, was merely
taking back his own work.

The Humorous Lovers, which was seen by Pepys, March
30, 1667 (Diary, VI, 233, mentioned 254), is, in spite of
that gentleman's censure (almost a certain sign of a play's
worth), an amusing piece of work.  In plot it shows such
a strong influence of Shirley as to suggest a deliberate
drawing upon that writer's work, and in style it resembles
Shirley's plays also, as it has passages of very lively and
entertaining dialogue.  It contains reminiscences of The
Ball, Hyde Park, Love in a Maze, and Love Tricks.  The
strong probability of its being probably only the result of
a study of Shirley or, at most, the working up of a rough

---

[22] The Variety was made into a droll and published as The French
Dancing Master in The Wits (1672) (Life of the Duke of Newcastle,
p. 109, note by Firth).

draft of a comedy, prevents a more detailed consideration in this place. There is no evidence of its having been acted before the Civil War.

### VIII. Double Falsehood

On December 13, 1727, Double Falsehood, or The Distressed Lovers, was presented at Drury Lane, as a play "written originally by W. Shakespeare; and now revised and adapted to the stage by Mr. Theobald, the author of Shakespeare Restored" (see Genest, III, 203–4). The play seems to have been not unfavorably received, having been acted twelve nights (Biog. Dram., II, 173). Double Falsehood was revived at Covent Garden, April 24, 1767, as Gibson's benefit (Genest, V, 136), and was played as Hull's benefit on May 6 of the same year (*ibid.*). Other performances were at Bath on May 19, 1781 (with Mrs. Siddons as Leonora), and on May 23, 1793 (*ibid.*, VI, 210, VII, 117, respectively). It was played at Covent Garden "for the first time in twenty-six years," June 6, 1781, as Wild's benefit (*ibid.*, VII, 34). First printed in 1728, the play went into a second edition in the same year. It was also issued in Dublin. Later editions are those of 1740, and 1767 (Jaggard, Shakespeare Bibliography, p. 304).

The source of Double Falsehood is the History of Cardenio, as related in Don Quixote, Part I, Chaps. XXIV, XXVII, XXVIII, XXIX, XXXVI, of which it is a fairly close dramatization. Adventures on The Black Mountains, a tale published in London in 1729, which has been given as the source of the play (Jaggard, Shakespeare Bibliography, p. 3) cannot be its original unless, of course, Double Falsehood is a forgery, and the story had already gone through one edition, but neither of these suppositions is likely. Schevill's article (Mod. Phil., IX, 269 ff.) in which he attempts to prove that Theobald, as sole author of the play, founded it upon the novel is a jumble of conjecture, assumption and prejudice which proves or disproves nothing.

In his dedication of the printed play to Dodington, in his preface, and on the titlepage, Theobald attributes Double Falsehood to Shakespeare. From his preface we learn that Theobald had three MSS. of the play in his possession, all of which, we may infer, were more or less defective in sense. One copy, which was over sixty years of age, was in the handwriting of Downes, the prompter, and had been ''early in the possession of the celebrated Mr. Betterton, and by him designed to have been ushered into the world.'' With this MS., Theobald informs us, there was connected a story that Shakespeare had composed the play during his retirement from the stage and had given it as a ''present of value to a natural daughter of his, for whose sake he wrote it.''

More as a result of animosity toward Theobald than of any exercise of judgment, he was accused by some critics of forging the play. Others, as we learn from the preface, attributed it to Fletcher. The first opinion, we may dismiss, for there is no reason to believe that Theobald did not have the MSS. which he claimed to possess.[23] As to the Shakespearian authorship, no one has agreed with Theobald from his own day to the present save Gamaliel Bradford, Jr. (The Nation, New York, LXXXVIII, 328). Bradford identifies the play with the lost History of Cardenio by Shakespeare and Fletcher (cf. also Mod. Lang. Notes, XXV, 51 ff.). Halliwell-Phillipps, Oliphant, Schelling, Lee, and Ward reject Theobald's theory. Lounsbury

[23] Double Falsehood is listed among Theobald's works in Biog. Dram., I, 706. Reed is said to have considered it Theobald's, by Jaggard who agrees with him (Shakespeare Bibliography, p. 304). It is not given in Halliwell's Dict. O. E. Plays.

thinks the play not Theobald's, and sees in it many marks of an Elizabethan origin, although it may be a forgery (The Text of Shakespeare, p. 148 ff.).

Various other authors for the original play have been suggested. Malone is quoted as believing it to have been written by Massinger (Biog. Dram., II, 173). Farmer in his Essay on the Learning of Shakespeare, p. 37, attributes Double Falsehood to Shirley, basing his attribution on the style and Langbaine's statement regarding the plays which Shirley left in MS. Dyce agrees with Farmer (see the former's Works of Shirley, I, lix) and asserts that had he possessed one of Theobald's MSS. he would have included the play in Gifford's and his edition of Shirley. Genest also adopts Farmer's view as does a writer (Gifford?) in the Quarterly Review, VII, 290).

However, we cannot reasonably attempt to determine the authorship of Double Falsehood, while the extent of Theobald's alterations is a matter of doubt. If, as Farmer says, only one passage is Theobald's, it would be an easy matter to apply various verse-tests and thereby arrive at something like the truth about the authorship of the old play. However, there are what seem unmistakable signs of Theobald's hand throughout the play,[24] and doubtless he contributed passages which can hardly be recognized, for he was by no means an unskilled writer of blank verse, and besides was thoroughly steeped in the drama of the Elizabethan period.

Collins' judgment on the play seems most just. He is "all but certain that it [Double Falsehood] was founded on some old play, . . . but that it is for the most part from Theobald's own pen" (D. N. B., LVI, 120). On account of Theobald's skill with his pen, which is mentioned above, it would be safer, perhaps, to say a "considerable part" is Theobald's.

[24] Cf. Ward, Hist. Eng. Dram. Lit., III, 120.

# BIBLIOGRAPHY [1]

## A

## BIOGRAPHICAL, CRITICAL, AND NON-DRAMATIC IL-LUSTRATIVE MATERIAL

Anonymous, Art. I. The Dramatic Works and Poems of James
Shirley. The Quarterly Review, XLIX, 1 ff. (April, 1833).
Baker, David E., Reed, I., Jones, S., Biographia Dramatica.
Three vols. London, 1812. (Biog. Dram.).
Baskerville, C. R., The Source of the Main Plot of Shirley's Love
Tricks. Modern Language Notes, XXIV, 100-101. (April,
1909). (Mod. Lang. Notes).
Bradford, Gamaliel, Jr., The History of Cardenio by Mr. Fletcher
and Shakespeare. The Nation (New York), LXXXVIII,
328 (April 1, 1909). Mod. Lang. Notes, XXV, 51 ff. (Feb-
ruary, 1910).
Bullen, A. H. (Editor), Introduction. Captain Underwit. A
Collection of Old English Plays, II, London, 1883. (Bullen,
Old Plays). John Fletcher, Dictionary of National Biography, XIX, 303 ff. (D. N. B.).

[1] The following bibliography does not include all the works of
Shirley, their various editions, etc., nor does it contain the titles of
all the books in which reference is made to Shirley. It is merely a
list of the most important books and articles used in the preparation
of the foregoing study. To avoid the repetition of titles, certain
works which have been referred to in the text or notes are omitted
here. See Nason, James Shirley, for an excellent annotated bibliography of Shirley's works and of books, articles, etc., dealing with
that writer.

The abbreviations for each title which is used in a shortened form
in the text are placed in the bibliography after the titles to which
they refer.

Burton, Robert, The Anatomy of Melancholy. . . . Two vols. Philadelphia, 1836.

Cervantes Saavedra, Miguel de., Don Quixote. Translated by Thomas Shelton. Four vols. London, Philadelphia, 1895. Translated by Doctor Smollett. Five vols. London, 1800.

Chambers, E. K. (Editor), Plays of the Kings' Men in 1641. Collections, I. Malone Society. Oxford, 1911.

Chetwood, William Rufus, A Select Collection of Old Plays. . . . With an account of the authors by the Editor, W. R. C. Dublin, 1750.

Clarendon, Edward Hyde, Earl of, History of the Rebellion and Civil Wars in England. Eight vols. Oxford, 1826. (Clarendon, Hist.).

Collier, J. Payne, The History of English Dramatic Poetry. Three vols. London, 1831. (Hist. Eng. Dram. Poet.).

Dessoff, Albert, Über englische, italienische, und spanische Dramen in den Spielverzeichnissen deutscher Wandertruppen. Studien zur vergleichenden Literaturgeschichte, I, 420 ff. (1901).

Downes, John, Roscius Anglicanus, 1708 (reprinted, London, 1886).

Eckhardt, E., E. Koeppel, Studien über Shakespeare's Wirkung . . . (review). Archiv für das Studium der neueren Sprachen und Literaturen, CXVI, 406 ff. (1906). (Archiv).

Dyce, The Rev. A. (Editor), Introductions, etc. The Works of Beaumont and Fletcher, Eleven vols. London, 1843. (Editor with W. Gifford). The Dramatic Works and Poems of James Shirley. Introduction, Vol. I, notes, etc., VI, 121 ff. Six vols. London, 1833.

Farmer, R., An Essay on The Learning of Shakespeare. London, 1821.

Fleay, F. G., Annals of the Careers of James and Henry Shirley, Anglia, VIII, 405 ff (1885). A Biographical Chronicle of the English Drama, 1559-1642. Two vols. London, 1891. (Biog. Chron.). A Chronicle History of the London Stage, 1559-1642. London, 1890. (Stage). On the Chronology

of the Plays of Fletcher and Massinger. Englische Studien,
IX, 12 ff. (1885-86).

Genest, John, Some Account of the English Stage. Ten vols.
Bath, London, 1832. (Genest, Stage).

Gifford, William, (see under Dyce).

Greg, W. W., A List of English Plays Written before 1643 and
Printed before 1700. Bibliographical Society. London,
1900. Pastoral Poetry and Pastoral Drama. London, 1906.
(Past. Poet. and Past. Dram.).

Halliwell (-Phillipps), J. O., Books of Characters (including Essays and Characters by John Stephens the Younger [1615];
London and the Country Carbonadoed and Quartered by D.
Lupton [1632]). London, 1857. A Dictionary of Old English Plays, London, 1860. (Dict. O. E. Plays). Outlines of
the Life of Shakespeare. London, 1882.

Howell, James, Familiar Letters. Edited by J. Jacobs. Two
vols. London, 1892.

Kerr, Mina, Influence of Ben Jonson on English Comedy, 1598-
1642. New York, 1912.

Koeppel, Emil, Ben Jonson's Wirkung auf zeitgenössische Dramatiker und andere Studien . . . Anglistische Forschungen.
Heft 20. Heidelburg, 1906. (Ben Jonson's Wirkung).
Quellen Studien zu den Dramen George Chapman's . . .
Quellen und Forschungen . . . , LXXXII. (1897). (Quellen Studien). Studien über Shakespeare's Wirkung auf
zeitgenössische Dramatiker. Materialien zur Kunde des älteren Englischen Dramas, IX. Louvain, 1905. (Shakespeare's Wirkung).

Langbaine, Gerard, An Account of the Dramatic Poets. . . .
[London, 1691]. (Dram. Poet.).

Lee, Sir Sidney, Lady Mary Wroth. D. N. B., LXIII, 161-62.
A Life of William Shakespeare. New York, 1909.

Lehman, Ezra (Editor), Introduction, The Tragedy of Chabot,
Admiral of France. Philadelphia, 1906.

Malone, Edmund, etc., The Plays and Poems of William Shakespeare. . . . Twenty-one vols. London, 1821. (Shakespeare
Variorum).

Marguerite, Queen of Navarre, L'Heptameron. Paris, 1863. Heptameron. Edited by E. A. Vizetelly. Five vols. London, 1894.

Mennis, Sir John, Smith, James, Facetiæ (Musarum Deliciæ, etc.). Two vols. London, 187—.

Munro, John (Editor), The Shakespeare Allusion Book. Two vols. New York, London, 1909.

Murray, J. F., English Dramatic Companies, 1558-1642. Two vols. London, 1910. (Eng. Dram. Cos.).

Napier, H. E., Florentine History. Vol. V. London, 1857.

Nason, A. H., James Shirley, Dramatist. New York.

Neilson, W. A., Ford and Shirley. Cambridge History of English Literature, VI, 221 ff. New York, Cambridge, 1910. (Cam. Hist. Eng. Lit.).

Newcastle, Margaret Cavendish, Duchess of, Life of William, Duke of Newcastle. Edited by C. H. Firth. London, New York, n. d.

Nissen, P., James Shirley. Hamburg, 1901.

Oldham, John, Works. London, 1703.

Ott, Adèle, Die Italienische Novelle im Englischen Drama. Zürich, 1904.

Overbury, Sir Thomas, Miscellaneous Works. Edited by E. F. Rimbault. London, 1890.

Parrott, T. M. (Editor), The Plays and Poems of George Chapman. Vols. I, II. London, New York, n. d.

Pepys, Samuel, Diary. Edited by H. B. Wheatley. Nine vols. London, 1893.

Plutarch, Lives. . . . Shakespeare's Plutarch. The Shakespeare Library. Edited by C. F. Tucker Brooke. Two vols. London, New York, 1909, *ibid.*, translated by Sir Thomas North. Tudor Translations. Six vols. London, 1896.

Potter, Alfred C., "Slick-free" or "stick-free." Mod. Lang. Notes, XXVII, 199. (1912.)

Prölss, Robert, Geschichte des neueren Dramas. Band II, Hälfe 2. Leipzig, 1882.

Reynolds, John, Triumph of God's Revenge against . . . Murder. Edited by Samuel Pordage. London, 1679.

Riche, Barnabe, Riche, his Farewell to Military Profession. Publications of the [Old] Shakespeare Society. Vol. XXXIII. London, 1846.

Ristine, F. H., English Tragicomedy. New York, 1910.

Schelling, F. E., Elizabethan Drama, 1558-1642. Two vols. Boston, New York, 1908. (Eliz. Dram.). Poems of Shirley Attributed to Carew and Goffe. Mod. Lang. Notes, XI, 273 ff. (1896).

Schevill, R., Theobald's Double Falsehood. Modern Philology, IX, 269 ff. (1911-12).

Schipper, J., James Shirley, Sein Leben und Seine Werke. Wien, Leipzig, 1911. (James Shirley).

Segni, Bernardo, Istorie Fiorentine. Pubblicate per cura di G. Gargani. Firenze, 1857.

Sidney, Sir Phillip, The Countess of Pembroke's Arcadia. London, 1627.

Stephen, Sir Leslie, and Lee, Sir Sidney (Editors), The Dictionary of National Biography. Sixty-three vols. London, 1885-1900. (D. N. B.).

Stiefel, A. L., Die Nachahmung spanischer Komödien in England unter den ersten Stuarts. I. Romanische Forschungen, V, 193 ff. (1890). III. Archiv. CXIX, 309 ff. (1907).

Swinburne, A. C., James Shirley. The Fortnightly Review, CCLXXX, 461 ff. (April 1, 1890).

Thorndike, A. H., The Influence of Beaumont and Fletcher on Shakespeare. Worcester, 1901. (Editor), Introduction. The Maid's Tragedy and Philaster. Belles Lettres Series. Boston, New York, 1906. Tragedy. The Types of English Literature. Boston, New York, 1908.

Traill, H. D. (Editor), Social England. Vols. III, IV. New York, London, 1895.

Varchi, Benedetto, Storia Fiorentina. Vol. V. Milano, 1804.

Various Authors ("the greatest Wits of the Age," viz., the Duke of Buckingham, the Earl of Rochester, etc.), Poems on Affairs of State. Three vols. London, 1703.

Ward, Sir A. W., A History of English Dramatic Literature. . . .

Three vols. London, 1899. (Hist. Eng. Dram. Lit.). James
Shirley. D. N. B., LII, 126 ff.

Wood, Anthony, Athenae Oxonenses. Edited by Phillip Bliss.
Five vols. London, 1813.

Von Wurtzbach, Wolfgang, Lope de Vega und seine Komödien.
Leipzig, 1899.

# B

## DRAMATIC TEXTS

### I. Collections of Plays

Ancient British Drama, The. Edited by Sir Walter Scott. Three vols. London, 1810. (Anc. Brit. Dram.).

Collection of Old English Plays, A. Edited by A. H. Bullen. Four vols. London, 1882-85. (Bullen, Old Plays).

Materialien zur Kunde des älteren Englischen Dramas. Hrsgn. von W. Bang. I-XLI. Louvain, 1902-13. (Materialien).

Nero and Other Plays. Various Editors. Mermaid Series. London, New York, n. d. (Nero, etc.).

Old English Drama. Edited by T. White. Four vols. London, 1830. (O. E. Dram.).

Old English Plays. Edited by C. W. Dilke. Six vols. London, 1814-15. (O. E. Plays).

School of Shakespeare, The. Edited by R. Simpson. Two vols. New York, 1878. (Sch. of Shakes.).

Select Collection of Old Plays, A. Edited by R. Dodsley. Twelve vols. London, 1744. (Dodsley 1). *ibid.* Reëdited by W. C. Hazlitt. Fifteen vols. London, 1874. (Dodsley 4).

Shakespeare, Apocrypha, The. Edited by C. F. Tucker Brooke. Oxford, 1908. (Shakes. Apoc.).

Specimens of the Pre-Shakespearian Drama. Edited by J. M. Manly. Two vols. Boston, etc., 1897. (Manly, Specimens).

### II. Dramatic Works and Separate Plays

Anonymous, The Costly Whore. Bullen, Old Plays, IV. London, 1885. The Distracted Emperor. *ibid.,* III, London, 1884. Every Woman in her Humor. *ibid.,* IV. The Fair

Maid of Bristow. Edited by A. H. Quinn. Philadelphia, 1902. Grim, the Collier of Croydon. Anc. Brit. Dram., III. Lady Alimony, Dodsley, 4, XIV. The Life and Death of Captain Thomas Stukeley. Sch. of Shakes., I. The Life and Death of Jack Straw. Dodsley 4, V. The London Chanticleers. Dodsley 4, XII. Nero. Edited by H. P. Horne. Nero, etc. Nobody and Somebody. Sch. of Shakes., I. The Partial Law. Edited by B. Dobell. London, 1908. Pathomachia. Collectanea Adamantaea, XXII. Edinburgh, 1887. The Pilgrimage to Parnassus with the Two Parts of The Return from Parnassus. Edited by W. D. Macray. Oxford, 1886. (George Chapman?). Sir Giles Goosecap. Bullen, Old Plays, III. The Trial of Chivalry. *ibid.* The Wars of Cyrus. Edited by W. Keller. Shakespeare Jahrbuch, XXXVII. Berlin, 1901. Wily Beguiled. Dodsley 4, IX. The Wisdom of Doctor Dodypoll. Bullen, Old Plays, III.

Barnes, Barnaby, The Devil's Charter. Edited by R. B. McKerrow. Materialien, VI. Louvain, 1904.

Barry, Lo[rding], Ram Alley. Anc. Brit. Dram., II.

Beaumont, Francis, and Fletcher, John, Works. Edited by George Darley. London, 1839.

Behn, Aphra. The Plays, Histories, and Novels. Six vols. London, 1871.

Berkeley, Sir William, The Lost Lady, Dodsley 1, X.

Brandon, Samuel, The Virtuous Octavia. Edited by R. B. McKerrow. Malone Society. Oxford, 1909.

Brewer Anthony, Lingua. Anc. Brit. Dram., II. The Lovesick King. Edited by A. E. H. Swaen. Materialien, XVIII. Louvain, 1907.

Brome, Richard, Dramatic Works. Three vols. London, 1873.

Calderon Barca, Pedro de la, Dramas. Translated by D. F. M'-Carthy. Two vols. London, 1853.

Carlell, Lodowick, The Deserving Favorite. Edited by C. H. Gray. Lodowick Carlell, etc. Chicago, 1905. The Fool Would Be a Favorite. London, 1657. Osmond, the Great Turk. London, 1657.

Cartwright, William, Comedies, Tragicomedies with Other Poems. London, 1651. The Ordinary. Anc. Brit. Dram., III.

Chapman, George, Plays. Edited by R. H. Shepherd. London, 1874. Comedies. Ed. by T. M. Parrott. London, New York, 1914.

Chettle, Henry, Hoffman. Hrsgn. von R. Ackermann. Bamburg, 1894.

Cokain, Sir Aston, Dramatic Works. Edited by J. Maidment and W. H. Logan. Edinburgh, London, 1874.

Colman, George, the Younger, The Mountaineers. London, 1805.

Cooke, J., Greene's Tu Quoque. Anc. Brit. Dram., II.

Cowley, Abraham, Love's Riddle. Works. London, 1687.

D. T. (Davenport, R., Dekker, T?), The Bloody Banquet. London, 1639.

Daborne, Robert, Plays. Edited by A. E. H. Swaen. Anglia, XX, XXI. (1897-99).

Daniel, Samuel, Complete Works. Edited by the Rev. A. B. Grosart. Four vols. n. p., 1885.

Davenant, Sir William, Dramatic Works. Edited by J. Maidment and W. H. Logan. Five vols. Edinburgh, London, 1872.

Davenport, Robert, The City Nightcap. Anc. Brit. Dram., III.

Day, John, Works. Edited by A. H. Bullen. London, 1881. Humour out of Breath. Edited by A. Symons. Nero, etc. The Maid's Metamorphosis (conjecturally Day's). Bullen, Old Plays, I. The Parliament of Bees. Edited by A. Symons. Nero, etc.

Dekker, Thomas, Dramatic Works. London, 1873. Best Plays. Edited by E. Rhys. Mermaid Series. London, New York, n. d.

Dibdin, Thomas, The Cabinet. London, 1805.

Dryden, John, Comedies, Tragedies and Operas. Two vols. in one. London, 1701.

Edwardes, Richard, Damon and Pythias. Anc. Brit. Dram., I.

Field, Nathaniel, Amends for Ladies. Edited by A. W. Verity. Nero, etc. A Woman is a Weathercock. *ibid.*

Fisher, Jasper, Fuimus Troes. Dodsley 4, XII.

Fletcher, John, See under Beaumont, Francis. Sir John Van Olden Barnavelt (with Massinger). Bullen, Old Plays, II.

Fletcher, Phineas, Sicelides. Edited by the Rev. A. B. Grosart. Poems, III. n. p., 1869.

Ford, John. See under Massinger, Phillip. The Queen (conjecturally). Edited by W. Bang. Materialien, XIII.

Freeman, Sir Ralph. Imperiale. London, 1655.

Garrick, David, The Gamesters. London, 1778.

Gascoigne, George, and Kinwelmersh, F., Supposes and Jocasta. Edited by J. W. Cunliffe. Belles Lettres Series. Boston, London, 1906.

Glapthorne, Henry, Plays and Poems. Two vols. London, 1874. The Lady Mother. Bullen, Old Plays, II.

Goffe, Thomas, The Courageous Turk. London, 1656. The Raging Turk, and Orestes. London, 1656. The Second Maiden's Tragedy (conjecturally). Edited by W. W. Greg. Malone Society. Oxford, 1909.

Gould, Robert, The Rival Sisters. London, 1696.

Greene, Robert, and Peele, George, Dramatic and Poetical Works. Edited by the Rev. A. Dyce. London, New York, 1861. Selimus. Edited by W. Bang. Malone Society. Oxford, 1908.

Guarini, Battista, Il Pastor Fido. Trans. by Sir Richard Fanshawe. London, 1676.

Habington, William, The Queen of Arragon. Dodsley 1, X.

Haughton, William, Englishmen for My Money. Dodsley 4, X.

Heywood, Thomas, Dramatic Works. Six vols. London, 1874. Best Plays. Edited by A. W. Verity. Mermaid Series. London, New York, n. d. The Captives. Bullen, Old Plays, IV. The Four Prentices of London. Anc. Brit. Dram., III. How a Man May Choose a Good Wife from a Bad (conjecturally). Edited by A. E. H. Swaen. Materialien, XXXV. Louvain, 1912. The Royal King and Loyal Subject. O. E. Plays, VI.

Holman, J. G., Abroad and at Home. London, 1796.

Hughes, T., etc., The Misfortunes of Arthur. Dodsley 4, IV.

Jonson, Ben, Works. Reëdited by F. Cunningham from W. Gifford's edition. Three vols. London, n. d.

Johnson, Charles, The Wife's Relief. London, 1712.

Killigrew, Henry, The Conspiracy. London, 1638.

Killigrew, Thomas, Comedies and Tragedies. London, 1664. The Parson's Wedding. Anc. Brit. Dram., III.

Kirke, John, The Seven Champions of Christendom. O. E. Dram., III.

Kyd, Thomas, Works. Edited by F. S. Boas. Oxford, 1901. The First Part of Jeronimo (doubtful). Anc. Brit. Dram., I. The Spanish Tragedy. Manly, Specimens, II.

Lee, Sophia, Almeyda, Queen of Granada. London, 1796.

Lodge, Thomas, The Wounds of Civil War. Edited by J. D. Wilson. Malone Society. Oxford, 1910.

Lyly, John, Dramatic Works. Edited by F. W. Fairholt. Two vols. London, 1892.

Machin, Lewis, The Dumb Knight. Anc. Brit. Dram., II.

Marlowe, Christopher, Works. Edited by F. Cunningham. London, n. d. Lust's Dominion (doubtful). Dodsley 4, XIV.

Marmion, Shackerley, Dramatic Works. Edited by J. Maidment and W. H. Logan. Edinburgh, London, 1875. The Antiquary. Anc. Brit. Dram., III.

Marston, John, Works. Edited by J. O. Halliwell [-Phillipps]. Three vols. London, 1856. Histriomastix. Sch. of Shakes., II. Jack Drum's Entertainment (doubtful). *ibid.*

Mason, John, The Turk. Ed. by J. Q. Adams, Jr. Materialien, XXXVII.

Massinger, Phillip, and Ford, John, Dramatic Works. Edited by Hartley Coleridge. London, 1840. Best Plays of Phillip Massinger. Edited by A. Symons. Mermaid Series. Two vols. London, 1889.

May, Thomas, Two Tragedies. London, 1654. Antigone. London, 1631. The Heir. Anc. Brit. Dram., I. The Old Couple. *ibid.*, III.

Mayne, Jasper, The Amorous War. London, 1648. The City Match. Anc. Brit. Dram., II.

Mead, Robert, The Combat of Love and Friendship. London, 1654.

Middleton, Thomas, Works. Edited by A. H. Bullen. Eight vols. Boston, New York, 1885.

Milton, John, Comus. Edited by D. Masson. Poetical Works (Globe). London, 1909.

Munday, Anthony (and Chettle, Henry), The Downfall of Robert, Earl of Huntington, Dodsley 4, VIII. The Death of Robert, Earl of Huntington, *ibid.*

Nabbes, Thomas, Covent Garden. London, 1638. Hannibal and Scipio. London, 1637. Microcosmus. Anc. Brit. Dram., II. Tottenham Court, London, 1638.

Nash, Thomas, Summer's Last Will and Testament. Dodsley 4, VIII.

Newcastle, William Cavendish, Duke of. See under Shirley, James.

Oulton, W. C. Frightened to Death. London, 1817.

Peele, George. See under Greene, Robert.

Plautus, T. Maccius, Comœdiæ. Publiée sous la direction de M. D. Nisard. Théatre Complet des Latins. Paris, 1851.

Porter, Henry, The Two Angry Women of Abington (Part I). Edited by H. Ellis. Nero, etc.

Powell, George, Alphonso, King of Naples [London], 1691. (MS. titlepage). A Very Good Wife. London, 1693.

Preston, Thomas, Cambyses. Manly, Specimens, II.

Quarles, Francis, The Virgin Widow. Edited by the Rev. A. B. Grosart. Complete Works, III. n. p., 1881.

R., T., The Nice Wanton. Manly, Specimens, I.

Randolph, Thomas, Poetical and Dramatic Works. Edited by W. C. Hazlitt. Two vols. London, 1875. The Muse's Looking-glass. Anc. Brit. Dram., II.

Rawlins, Thomas, The Rebellion. *ibid.*, III.

Richards, Nathaniel, Messallina. Edited by A. R. Skemp. Materialien, XXX. Louvain, 1910.

Rowley, Samuel (and Dekker, Thomas?), The Noble Soldier. Bullen, Old Plays, I.

Rowley, William, All's Lost by Lust. Edited by E. C. Morris. Belles Lettres Series. Boston, London, 1908. A Match at Midnight. Anc. Brit. Dram., II. A New Wonder; A Woman Never Vexed. Dodsley 4, XII. A Shoemaker a Gentleman. Edited by C. W. Stork. Philadelphia, 1910.

Rutter, Joseph, The Shepherd's Holiday. Dodsley 1, VII.

Shakespeare, William, Complete Dramatic and Poetic Works. Edited by W. A. Neilson. Boston, New York, n. d.

Sharpe, Lewis, The Noble Stranger. London, 1640.

Sharpham, Edward, The Fleire. Hrsgn. von H. Nibbe. Materialien, XXXVI. Louvain, 1912.

Shirley, James, Dramatic Works and Poems. Edited by W. Gifford and the Rev. A. Dyce. Six vols. London, 1833. Best Plays. Edited by E. Gosse. Mermaid Series. London, New York, n. d. Andromana (not Shirley's). Anc. Brit. Dram., III. Captain Underwit (or The Country Captain) (with the Duke of Newcastle). Bullen, Old Plays, II. *ibid.* The Hague, 1649. The Variety. London, 1649. Dick of Devonshire (not Shirley's). Bullen, Old Plays, II. Double Falsehood (doubtful). London, 1728. Filli di Sciro, or Phillis of Scyros (not Shirley's). London, 1655. The Humorous Lovers (with the Duke of Newcastle?). London, 1677. The Traitor. A Tragedy: with Alterations, etc. (prompter's book, probably). London, 1692.

Shirley, Henry, The Martyred Soldier. Bullen, Old Plays, I.

Smith, Wentworth, The Hector of Germany. Edited by L. W. Payne, Jr. Philadelphia, 1906.

Stevenson, W., Gammer Gurton's Needle. Manly, Specimens, III.

Strode, William, The Floating Island. Edited by B. Dobell. Poetical Works. London, 1907.

Suckling, Sir John, Works. Edited by A. H. Thompson. London, New York, etc., 1910.

Toilor, Robert, The Hog hath Lost his Pearl. Anc. Brit. Dram., III.

Tatham, John, Dramatic Works. Edited by J. Maidment and W. H. Logan. Edinburgh, London, 1879.

"Tirso de Molina," (Gabriel Tellez), El Castigo del Penséque. Biblioteca de Autores Españoles, V. Madrid, 1850.

Tasso, Torquato, Aminta. Trans. by J. Dancer. London, 1660.

Tompkins, J., Albumazar. Anc. Brit. Dram., II.

Tourneur, Cyril. See under Webster, John.

Udall, Nicholas, Roister Doister. Manly's Specimens, II.

Wadeson, A., Look about You. Dodsley 4, VII.

Webster, John, Dramatic Works. Edited by W. Hazlitt. Four vols. London, 1897. Best Plays of John Webster and Cyril Tourneur. Edited by J. A. Symonds. Mermaid Series. London, New York, 1893.

Wilkins, George, The Miseries of Enforced Marriage. Anc. Brit. Dram., II.

Wilmot, R., etc., Tancred and Gismunda. Dodsley 4, VII.

Wilson, Arthur, The Swisser. Publié . . . par A. Feuillerat. Paris, 1904. The Inconstant Lady. Oxford, 1814 (summarized by Genest, Stage, VIII, 445-46).

Yarington, Robert, Two Tragedies in One. Bullen, Old Plays, IV.

# INDEX

# INDEX

## A

### General

Action off stage described, 355.

Adams, J. Q., Jr., 122, 349.

Allusions; to "keeping the door," 225-26; to monsters, 291; to contemporary events, 294, 402; to the "High German," 302.

Anatomy of Melancholy, 195, note, 201, 237, 268, 338, 354.

Arber, E., 41, note, 305, note, 406, note.

Ariosto, Ludovico, 323.

Aristophanes, 126.

Barbers, 373.

Barry, Lo[rding], 92.

Bandello, Matteo, 338.

Baskerville, C. R., 118, note, 135.

Bawds, 373-74.

Beaumont and Fletcher (see Beaumont, Francis, and Fletcher, John).

Beaumont, Francis (see Fletcher, John), 6, 10, 12, 22, 25, 28, 46, 92, 94, 176, 285, 305.

Bede, 151.

Beeston, Christopher, 176, 255, 279, 400, 407, 408.

Beeston, William, 400.

Behn, Aphra, 37, 40, 59.

Berkeley, Sir William, 12.

Bibliographical figures, 121-22.

Biographia Dramatica, 40, 404, 432, note.

Boas, F. S., 407, 417.

Boasting, 133.

Bonarelli, Guido, 16.

Books, used; seriously, 84-85; comically, 85.

Boswell, A., 402.

Boyle, R., 10, note, 404, 405, 415, 416.

Bradford, G., Jr., 432.

Brathwaite, R., 362.

Brewer, A., 92, 94.

Brome, A., 30.

Brome, R., 7, 11, 12, 19, 30, 35, 93, 117, note, 202; characteristics of his plays, 15; influence on Shirley, 199 ff., 343 ff., 381 ff.

Brother and sister in love, 251, 311.

Brown, T. Allston, 33, 35, 39.

Bullen, A. H., 282, 302, 405, 406, 419, 420, 421, 426, 427, 428, 429.

# B

## Plays and Masques

Abroad and at Home, 37.

Acero de Madrid, El, 385.

Aglaura, 12, 184, 186, 188, 203, 205, 214, 277.

Agrippina, 179, 262.

Albertus Wallenstein, 15, 71, 72, 177, 178, 180, 208, 211, 319.

Albovine, 12, 59, 66, 85, 87, 88, 97, 99, 100, 123, 163, 177, 182, 201, 204, 216, 239, 243, 331.

Albumazar, 86, 91, 105, 111, 119, 123, 135, 211, 245, 316, 318.

Alchemist, The, 1, 83, 86, 107, 123, 139, 169, 194, 196, 236, 283, 291, 294, 318, 349, 368, 426.

All Fools, 83, 114, 235, 283, 411, note, 412, note.

All Mistaken, 34.

All's Lost by Lust, 67, 70, 81, 83, 103, 112, 160, 180, 204, 217, 227, 229, 374.

All's Well that End's Well, 65, 71, 76, 90, 109, 113, 163, 167, 197, 233, 237, 259, 264, 265, 275, 330-31, 334, 347, 361, 363, 413.

Almeyda, Queen of Granada, 33.

Alphonso, King of Naples, 33.

Alphonsus, Emperor of Germany, 73, 80, 97, 163, 184, 188, 331.

Alphonsus, King of Arragon, 90, 127, 224, 225, 295.

Amends for Ladies, 69, 70, 72, 81, 87, 88, 96, 104, 130, 133, 141, 196, 202, 266, 267, 319, 338, 361, 370, 371.

Aminta, 16, 131.

Amor con Amor se Paga, 293.

Amorous War, The, 77, 80, 273, 331.

Amphitruo, 227.

Amyntas (Randolph's), 67, 112, 114, 141, 224, 345, 354.

Andromana, 46, 98, 100, 177, 271, note, 404, 405.

Antigone, 224, 227.

Antipodes, The, 79, 80, 85, 87, 88, 187, 239, 240, 268, 399, 424, 427.

Antiquary, The, 69, 123, 218, 219, 235, 283, 301, 390.

Antonio and Mellida, 79, 90, 95, 103, 104, 107, 113, 114, 180, 243, 288, 289, 296, 331.

Antonio's Revenge, 74, 78, 79, 84, 179, 188, 189, 212.

Antony and Cleopatra, 84, 86, 88, 90, 98, 102, 109, 143, 224, 250.

Anything for a Quiet Life, 69, 83, 90, 96, 132, 179, 218, 237, 238, 239, 370, 374.